Bhakat Prasad Mazumdar Commemoration Volume

IMAGING THE PAST

Indian History from Harappan Times to the Present Age

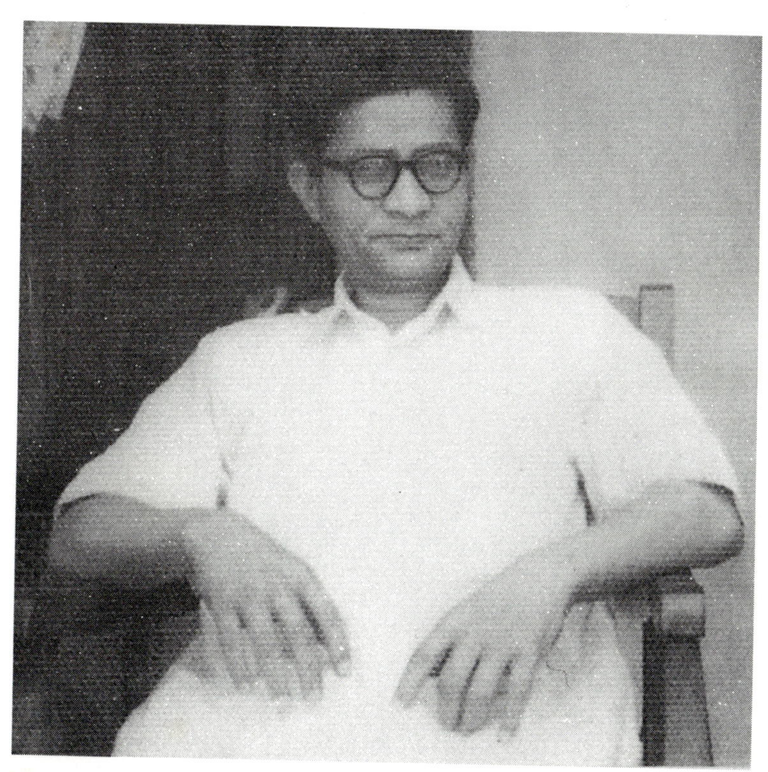

Bhakat Prasad Mazumdar
b. March 1, 1924 *d.* December 18, 1989

Bhakat Prasad Mazumdar
Commemoration Volume

IMAGING THE PAST

Indian History from Harappan Times to the Present Age

Edited by
Samarendra Narayan Arya

IMAGING THE PAST: Indian History from Harappan Times to the Present Age
Edited by Samarendra Narayan Arya

First Published, 2013

ISBN 978-93-5002-246-7

Published by
AAKAR BOOKS
28 E Pocket IV, Mayur Vihar Phase I, Delhi 110 091
Phone : 011 2279 5505 Telefax : 011 2279 5641
info@aakarbooks.com; www.aakarbooks.com

Printed at
Mudrak, 30 A, Patparganj, Delhi 110 091

Contents

Editor's Page

It is a matter of great satisfaction that the present volume, a small token of homage to a great soul and motivator is finally out. The chief credit for the work goes to the contributors who responded with great interest and took very little time to send in their contributions. They all deserve our sincere thanks. However, the likes of Professor R.N. Nandi, Professor Sumanta Niyogi, Professor Chittabrata Palit and Dr. Vivekanand Jha deserve special thanks for covering an extra mile to facilitate this publication. In a work of this nature it is not always possible to maintain uniformity in the system of annotations and transliteration marks. Since, however, the readers are already familiar with different formats, these are unlikely to affect the readability of the book. Mr. K.K. Saxena of Aakar Books deserves special thanks for going all the way to bring out the volume in double quick time.

Karttika Poornima
Patna, 2013

S.N. Arya

What is Inside

The present book *Imaging the Past* is divided into two segments, the first segment relates to reminiscences concerning the life and achievements of a great scholar of History and noble soul late Bhakat Prasad Mazumdar. The other segment provides incisive studies on different aspects of Indian History from Harappan times to the present age. For evoking interest of the readers both specialists and non-specialists a brief idea of the contents of these contributions may be in order here.

R.C. Thakran in his presentation underlines that human settlements are not confined to water courses alone rather these are located in greater number in areas away from the rivers. People survive in these areas with the help of surface water available in the locality as well as man-made depressions. R.N. Nandi in his study states that the term 'pur' occurring more than a hundred times in the *Ṛgveda* always represented a fort, a rampart or a strong hold. He holds the view that the Vedic Aryans in their pur-encounters always intended to capture the forts with surrounding agricultural land and water-bodies and not destroy them as is commonly believed.

S.C. Mishra in his article throws light on the origin, evolution and different aspects of the cult of Rama Hvastra as described in the *Zend Avesta.* The problem of identification of the river Saraswati has been discussed at length by R.K. Sharma in his paper. He sides with H.C. Raychaudhuri that ancient *Saraswati* may be identified with the present Sarasuti-Ghaggar, He contends that the river Ghaggar was evidently the lower part of Sarasuti. P.C. Venkatasubbaiah shows in his article that the socio-cultural and economic groups of agro-pastoral and pastoral cum agriculturists can be identified on the basis of diverse eco-system in which these originated and flourished. This is followed by Suvira Jaiswal's study in which she examines the interaction of gender, class and caste in agricultural production on the basis of early north Indian sources. Annapurna Chattopadhyaya in her paper underlines the ethno-cultural relations of Bihar and Bengal in ancient period. She contends that in cultural and ethnic settings all these people were quite allied during later Vedic and post Vedic times.

The importance of cross road-cults has been examined by P. Gupta with special reference to stupa architecture of the Buddhists. The paper offers interesting ideas for closer investigation by interested scholars. Shailendra Mohan Jha in his paper argues in favour of a new methodology in relation to the study of punch marked coins. Vivekanand Jha throws fresh light of Aśoka's Dhamma on the basis of meticulous study of the emperor's edicts. The article provides a new dimension to the study of Aśoka's Dhamma. The study of G.P. Singh is based on a thorough examination of the travel accounts of two travellers—Apollonius, a Greek and his companion Damis, an Assyrian who visited North West India in the first century AD. These two travel accounts have so far not been studied at length.

On the basis of literary and epigraphic sources S.N. Arya in his paper examines various terms denoting the resting places of different brāhmaṇical deities in early India. The study of Radha Madhav Bharadwaj bears out the importance of oral tradition in brāhmaṇical circles for preserving and transmitting ancient scriptures. Shanta Rani Sharma in her paper emphasizes the significance of wide-spread monetary exchange during the Pratihara rule. Karabi Mitra elaborates different stages in the evolution of river Saraswati from the position of a mighty river during early Vedic times to the status of a full fledged divinity during the early medieval period.

Making a thorough study of the *Kośalānanda Kāvyam* and other related sources, Shishir Kumar Panda examines the claim of Rajput origin by Chauhan kings of South Kośala. Further, he argues that they played a significant role in the growth of history and culture of western Orissa. Conflicts between left hand and right hand castes of south India during the 17th and 18th centuries are brought to bear upon her study by Radhika Sheshan.

Sumanta Niyogi in his study points out the similarities and differences between the European and Indian renaissance. He argues that despite certain basic differences the intellectual events of 19th century Bengal can be legitimately described as renaissance tradition. Susnata Das in his interesting article argues that despite regional diversities and contradictory interests, there was a common national motivation behind the upsurge of 1857. The study of Binodini Das examines the interplay of social and environmental compulsions behind the origin and development of various social and religious celebrations in Orissa, particularly among the tribal communities.

In his presentation Chittabrat Palit argues that Gandhi was a prophet of environment friendly sustainable growth as opposed to material cum greed motivated process of development. Lipi Ghosh in her paper draws attention to the gradual formulation of India's look east policy aiming at developing greater understanding and co-operation vis-à-vis South East Asian Countries. G.J. Sudhakar, in his article probes into socio-economic survey of the functions of Madras Provincial Co-operative Society during the period 1935-45.

It is hoped that the volume will be able to cater to the tastes and interests of readers and motivate further investigation in the concerned research areas.

1

Dada: As I Knew Him

Bhagaban Prasad Majumdar

I am happy to recollect the fond memories of my eldest brother, Bhakat Prasad Mazumdar, a giant among intellectuals and a saint among friends and admirers. Sincerity was the hallmark of his personality whether the job at hand was administrative or academic or personal relationship. His profound respect for parents was a model for the younger ones and his affection for those junior to him was always honest and straightforward. His attachment to close friends including schoolmates was extraordinary and he maintained this rapport till the end of his life. Not used to expressing these emotions openly, he was basically soft and amiable. Even in adverse circumstances he stood his ground with remarkable dignity and composure. This happened right through his life despite tremendous physical infirmity.

Stricken with anchylosing spondylitis at the early age of 26 at a time when treatment of the disease was not very developed in our country and merely a year after his marriage, his was a battle for nearly forty long years. All forms of treatment were tried; expert medical advice sought from abroad but there was not much relief. The body wilted but the spirit grew stronger. He bore his ailment with uncommon poise and composure. He hated self-pity as much as he detested giving in meekly. Dr. B. Mukhopadhyay, the doyen of orthopedic surgeons in the country and abroad, once remarked that Professor Mazumdar with his indomitable will-power could be the model for all orthopedic patients. Even in times of personal adversity he displayed equanimity.

Domestic stress or official problems had little impact on his normally placid temperament. I remember how when he was the Head of the Department of History, Patna University, a big group of postgraduate students one morning assembled at our residence to pressurise him into getting some grievances redressed. I was not present in the house when they arrived but on my return I found them all sitting on dharna on the floor. And in their midst was the guru on a chair, unruffled but clearly hurt. He was profoundly religious at heart; of all the brothers and sisters he was the one who truly shared our father's Vaishnava faith. His stoicism perhaps came from his religious temperament.

The fact that he managed to ignore his physical suffering and devote most of his time to research made him achieve what normally many able-bodied academicians fail to do. Scholars have their own favourite hours of work that are productive, some start work at dawn, some in the afternoon and some, like students, follow the regular routine. My brother loved working late at night. When others slept he kept himself deeply engrossed in study with the ashtray on the table and unmindful of impaired vision.

Always keen to attend to academic and social engagements, he looked neither for an excuse nor for cover when not making one. Vagaries of weather could not normally deter him, time or distance failed to dampen his enthusiasm. I often lagged behind as I failed to turn up at a function we were both supposed to attend while he was unfailingly present on time.

In Jitan and Ramkishan he had two extremely dutiful rickshaw-pullers of our neighbourhood who were always prepared to take him to any place at any hour. They used to wait ungrudgingly for a couple of hours when he visited Professor S.H. Askari or Professor R.S. Sharma or Professor Qeyamuddin Ahmed–all residing quite a long distance from our residence.

Amiable and quiet by nature there was in him a childlike simplicity. The little ones in the family had a special relationship with him. Basking in the sun on winter mornings he descended to their level and indulged in warm-hearted conversations. He was extremely fond of tea. When offered tea irrespective of the time he would never turn down the offer. On certain days he returned around 9 or 9.30 at night, dinner time close at hand, but would be pleading for a mere half cup of tea. Cigarettes were no less a passion. When he developed congestion of the lungs some five years before his death, the physician coaxed him into giving up smoking. Like an obedient schoolboy he nodded in agreement. A couple of days later he was apprehended smoking in the bathroom.

He was used to maintaining daily accounts of expenditure. Every little detail would be entered. Anybody sent by him to fetch something from the market would be required to submit the account. Undoubtedly this would be meticulously audited. No trickery, no cover-up, no double-dealing. Even delay in submitting accounts would be treated as misappropriation. He often openly expressed his righteous indignation at his wife's habit of not giving the details of accounts after shopping. She in turn would give vent to her anger for his impatience.

I am not competent to say anything about my brother's scholarship nor am I in a position to make an objective assessment of the man. I have only tried to look back at the past to capture moments of pleasure and pain. He was not granted a life that can be described as full but he certainly had in him qualities that helped the lives of many become vibrant and purposeful.

2

Professor Bhakat Prasad Mazumdar: A Jewel in the Crown of Patna University

C.P.N. Sinha

I was a first year student in Patna College in 1953. The session started on 13th July which was a Monday. Coming from a rural background, I was excited being a student of the premier college of the state. Kalimuddin Ahmad was the Principal of the college and Dr. K.K. Datta was the Head of the Department of History. There were many eminent scholars in the college.

On this day at about 4 p.m. I saw Professor Bhakat Prasad Mazumdar near the Patna College main gate. Probably he was waiting to catch a rickshaw. He was in the company of Professor Ram Sharan Sharma and Professor Yogendra Mishra. It was just a coincidence that I happened to be there, I greeted them with folded hands. Professor Mishra knew me previously and he introduced me to Professor Sharma and Professor Mazumdar. Professor Mishra spoke about my native village and my performance at the Matriculation examination. Professor Mazumdar listened to Professor Mishra with interest and he instantly congratulated me. In the meantime, the rickshaw-puller arrived and Professor Mazumdar left for his residence. This was my first interaction with Professor Mazumdar which continued till the cruel hands of destiny snatched him from our midst.

In the course of time, I learnt many things about Professor Mazumdar. He was the eldest son of Dr. Biman Bihari Mazumdar, a well-known teacher of History and later Political Science. Mazumdar Sahab's younger brother Bhagaban Prasad Majumdar was a friend of mine, who later taught English at Patna University.

In September 1961 the BPSC under the chairmanship of Shri K.S.V. Raman, ICS recommended my name for appointment as a lecturer in History at TNB College, Bhagalpur. The University at Bhagalpur had been established in 1960 and posts were advertised. After the interview I went to Patna College in the afternoon. I met Professor Mazumdar and Dr. D.N. Verma there. Dr. Verma took me to the library and informed me about my selection. Dr. Verma was the owner of a brand new Fiat car and he requested Mazumdar sahib and me to get into his car. We readily did so. Dr. Verma dropped Professor Mazumdar at his Dariyapur Gola residence and we proceeded towards Gandhi Maidan. Dr. Verma entertained me at the Palace Hotel and again expressed his happiness over my selection. Later on I was asked by my seniors to apply against PU vacancies, but I had a bitter memory that my appointment in 1960 could not materialise, and hence I decided to keep away from the PU appointments, and I have no regrets.

As a student of History, I have seen many aspects of Professor Mazumdar's personality. He was an excellent person, soft spoken but tough and above all a humanist. In 1954 the Patna University Honours' teaching was centralised. Arts and Commerce classes were conducted at Patna College and Science Honours classes were conducted in Science College. In the History Department Prof. Mazumdar of B.N.College and Prof. Mala Bose (later Ghosh) of Magadh Mahila College were known as popular teachers in the Patna College campus. In the course of time, I became close to them. Professor Mazumdar was very kind to me and always extended his helping hand. At times he lent me books which were not readily available in the library and advised me to study hard. In many ways he was the fountainhead of inspiration to students and researchers. It is an established fact that Professor Mazumdar was physically handicapped but he continued to have effective control over his students on account of good behaviour and sound scholarship. He was a gentleman and scholar with considerable command over his students. He had the goodwill and good wishes of countless admirers. He had goodwill for everybody and malice for none. This trait of his character endeared him to one and all.

Dr. K.K. Datta was a regular morning and evening walker. After his usual rounds he used to meet people in his bungalow situated on the campus. At one such 'mini durbar', Professor Mazumdar was also present. Later on I reliably learnt that Professor Mazumdar used some complimentary words about me and that went a long way to help me and raised my image in the eyes of Kali Babu (as he was affectionately called).

I was at Bhagalpur, but my contact with Professor Mazumdar continued. As a student I used to visit his house with my classmate Som Nath Roy, who retired from Burdwan University. As a teacher I used to visit him alone and always found him extremely hospitable.

Professor Mazumdar was an example of plain living and high thinking. He was a devout family man and inspiring teacher and supervisor, a noble soul and above all a "great-pragmatist". Times have changed and now it is extremely difficult to get teachers of the calibre of Professor Bhakat Prasad Mazumdar. Despite serious health hazards he helped everybody who came into contact with him.

He assumed the shape of a gigantic humanist, an inspiring saint and a man of proven honesty and integrity. Professor Mazumdar is not in our midst but his inspiring words still ring in my ears. I am extremely thankful to Professor S.N. Arya who reminded me to pay my respectful homage to my late guru Professor Bhakat Prasad Mazumdar. Professor Mazumdar is no more but he will stay in the hearts of his students and close associates.

3

Bhakat Prasad Mazumdar: A Life of Struggle and Dignity

Rajendra Ram

I was very close to the late Bhakat Prasad Mazumdar on account of my subject of Ph.D. research (*A History of Buddhism in Nepal: A.D. 705-1396*) registered under Dr. Yogendra Mishra, a familiar name among historians of his time. When I joined the post of Library Assistant in the Department of History, Patna University in September 1964, Dr. Mazumdar was the Head of the Department of History in B.N. College. He also used to engage classes in the Postgraduate Department located in Darbhanga House where I was fortunate in having his frequent presence in connection with his search of books relating to early medieval Indian history.

In those days the Postgraduate Department of History under the stewardship of the late Professor R.S. Sharma was a meeting point for intellectual luminaries from all over the country. Some of the stalwarts were A.L. Basham, K.A. Nilkant Shastri, Nihar Ranjan Ray, D.D. Kosambi, D.C. Sircar, Biman Bihari Mazumdar, Ramdhari Singh Dinkar and Anantha Sayanam Ayangar. The names speak for themselves as well as the prestige of the department in the eyes of contemporary intellectuals. The visits were mainly in connection with the annual meetings of the Historical Society of the department besides extra mural lectures and periodic seminars.

The late senior Mazumdar became a permanent member of the department for some time following the assignment of a Senior Research Fellowship by the UGC. His affection flowed to all who were engaged in serious historical investigations and I was no exception to this. One day my joy knew no bounds when the senior Mazumdar offered reprints of two articles (H.P. Sastri, "Notes on the Sunyata Philosophy of Northern Buddhists," *JBTRS,* Vol. II, No. 3, 1984 and "Bengali Buddhist Literature," *The Calcutta Review,* 1917) to me. He also lent me a useful book entitled, *The Decline of Buddhism in India,* by R.C. Mitra.

Coming back to the junior Mazumdar, the worthy son of a worthy father, I learnt from my friends and senior colleagues that during his early days Dr. B.P. Mazumdar was a very handsome personality with an attractive and fair look. Later he suffered a paralytic attack leading to extreme physical debility. He had to engage a permanent rickshaw-puller who virtually used to lift him in the course of his trips from home to different places at Patna. But once coming down to the surface he managed successfully with the help of a stick. However, this physical disability never caused any disparage and discomfort to the main currents of his intellectual activity. He commanded the unstinted respect and regard of students by dint of his learned lectures in classrooms. He was a sharp and clear-headed speaker at fortnightly seminars leading to lively discussions among the scholars present on the occasion. In that way his knowledge about original sources pertaining to early medieval Indian history was highly appreciated by scholars. Above all, he was well-versed in literary and epigraphic sources particularly those related to the Pala dynasty of Bihar and Bengal. I owe him many valuable pieces of information connected with my research. He was very close to my supervisor, Dr. Yogendra Mishra to whom he paid regular visits and I was fortunate to listen to their interactions and always tried to make good these inputs. The Vaishali Bhavan (Tikia Toli, Mahendru), the home of Dr. Mishra was his favourite point and in almost every trip to it he mentioned coming over there via Mukunda Dham, the residence of Dr. R.N. Nandi. Dr. Mishra used to enjoy the statement of Dr. Mazumdar's passing touching remark—"O! Nandi is also a lovely member of our literary society, an expert swimmer, dipping into the ocean of literary sources." As a matter of fact these moments now enable me to mention that some unknown force was active by dint of providence to help those people in transforming their physical and emotional sufferings to health and so long as they were alive they did not miss the moments of being together, face to face.

I shall not forget the blessings in the course of Dr. Mazumdar's visits to my humble rented house (Dayal Bhavan, Mahendru) on the Ashok Rajpath. He was fond of talking in Bangladeshi Bengali with my wife. I sat like a stranger before them as my wife narrated her migratory reminiscences to the late Mazumdar. The reminiscences related to Lalbagh Kalibari of Dhaka, dedicated to the famous deity Dhakeshvari Devi, and a famous proverb—*"Bala, Buddhi Aar Taka Taar Naam Dhaka"*(strength, learning and wealth, thy name is Dhaka).

Dr. Mishra and Dr. Mazumdar, both suffered extremely from their ailments, one passed through the trials and travails of bronchial asthma and the other through his paralytic aftermath. A mutual sharing of experiences led them to a mystic awareness, courage and genuine zest for knowledge. Endowed with a never say die spirit they never gave way to their dependence on others. So long as they lived, they never failed to share their companionship, sitting together, sipping tea and discussing endlessly matters of intellectual interest much of which was incomprehensible to me during my early research years.

I am tempted to recall here an agonising moment in the academic career of the late Dr. Mazumdar when he rightfully staked claims to the post of Professor at Patna University. I should not go into a detailed account of the event as nobody is present to certify the points of credibility. At one point, Dr. Mishra who too had applied for the post of Professor of History at Patna University asked me to accompany Dr. Mazumdar who had to put his points of merit, capability and relevant issues for being university professor before an authority entitled to take a decision. As Dr. Mazumdar went inside to meet this authority, I stood outside near his favourite rickshaw-puller. After half an hour, Dr. Mazumdar came out and we rushed back to the Vaishali Bhavan where Dr. Mishra was waiting with eagerness. In the course of conversation I heard a note. The said authority had retorted to Dr. Mazumdar: "You should know your limitations!". With characteristic dignity and composure Dr. Mishra shot back, "Mazumdar sahib, we have lost one battle, but the war is not yet over!" The ordeal ended on a happy note on May 26, 1973 when Dr. Mazumdar became university professor along with Dr. Mishra.

Thirty-eight years of teaching service at Patna University in various capacities full of love, respectability and intellectual achievements marked an illustrious period of life worth emulating. Even after superannuation from Patna University, Dr. Mazumdar continued his activities as if nothing had gone round after retirement. His family life was peaceful, dedicated to Vaishnavism. His father, his younger brother, his sons (one of them an I.A.S. officer) all maintained the ideals of a joint family beneath one roof. In memory of his father, Dr. B.B. Mazumdar he spared a suitable amount for extramural lectures on the pulpit of the Asiatic Society of Bengal, 1 Park Street, Kolkata. In his private life he cultivated an august standard with austerity but he was compassionate towards the poor and the needy. I am witness to his occasional donative spirit which frequently prompted to spare suitable amounts of money to many people-peons of Darbhanga House, floating beggars extending their palms before him. He attained Nirvana (Death) on December 18, 1989 leaving us to survive with struggle, study and dignity. A life of sixty-five years with laurels of victory, achievements and utter humility surely carves out a niche in history.

4

Professor B.P. Mazumdar: A Guardian Teacher

S.N. Arya

Professor B.P. Mazumdar taught us early medieval Indian history in the M.A. during the late 1970s. I cannot recall a day when Professor Mazumdar missed his class. His punctuality was superb despite his physical problem. Whichever topic he discussed in the class, he based on the source material and hence he had to go into depth. He did not switch over to other topics till he finished all aspects of the previous one. I remember very well that Professor Mazumdar covered the history of Kanauj and the life of Harṣavardhana at great length and took several weeks in the process. Often, he told us in the class, 'When you borrow books from the library, make best use of them, because these have to be returned to the library within the stipulated time and there will be difficulties if you needed the book again'.

Though Professor Mazumdar was soft, kind and affectionate to all students, he permitted me to come to his residence with answer notes in the evening, but the date and time had to be fixed beforehand. One evening when I reached his place, I found him sitting in the chair and ready to go somewhere else and the rickshaw-puller was awaiting him outside his residence, and he was waiting for me. When I met him with all regards, he immediately said that I was two minutes late. At that moment I took his comments lightly, but gradually I realised that the man was truly devoted to punctuality which might be the secret of success in his life.

The late Mazumdar very carefully corrected the answer scripts, changed several sentences and in the end suggested some more useful readings. His deep interest in giving a better shape to answer scripts is a lesson for all teachers and students. Professor Mazumdar was a source of inspiration to students. He wanted that students should not be limited to only course study but also attend seminars and lectures. It was early 1980, he once called me to the department and wrote on my notebook, 'Professor D.C. Sircar will deliver a lecture at 5 pm in the K.P. Jaiswal Research Institute. Must listen to him'. I attended Dr. Sircar's lecture on the Cultural History of Bihar and was profoundly benefited. This was the way he encouraged students particularly the more serious ones.

The late Mazumdar was a perfect guardian teacher, a quality which earned him a great reputation. Professor Mazumdar believed a teacher should rise above the textbook level of teaching and show concern for the career and conduct of the students. His inner self was so fascinating that it left a permanent impression on all those who came into his contact. But at the first appearance no one could believe behind a soft and kind hearted man there was a strict administrator. Probably no one knows this better than myself. Once I had unfortunately lost a book borrowed from the departmental library and as such I was asked to deposit the fine of rupees twenty-five at the time of filling up the examination form for the M.A. Thirty years ago rupees twenty-five was a princely sum particularly for a student coming from a lower middle class background. But in spite of my pleadings, Professor Mazumdar did not relent and I had paid the fine.

When the M.A. final year results were out, I met Professor Mazumdar and informed him that with his blessing I was able to secure a first class first in the merit list. On hearing this, Professor Mazumdar became visibly emotional. After a while he took out rupees twenty-five from his pocket and wanted to give it to me. It took me great pains to convince him that what he had given me in the form of guidance and good wishes could never be paid back and it would make me look very small if I took the money from him. Then he wrote some lines on a small piece of paper and told me to ask Chet Narayan Jha to type it. It was my character certificate which I still hold dear to my heart.

His affection for me has been a lifetime treasure and even after his retirement, I regularly kept in touch with him to seek his blessings and guidance. His cherished memory continues to haunt all of us who were close to him in some way or other. I am thankful to the Almighty for the opportunity to pay my homage to the departed soul.

5

Bhakat Prasad Mazumdar: A Face in the Crowd

R.N. Nandi

The eldest son of a legendary scholar Biman Bihari Mazumdar, Bhakat Prasad was born with an indomitable never-say-die spirit. This was first evidenced when in the prime of his youth he was struck with a deadly attack of rheumatoid arthritis which made as many twists and turns of his body as it was capable of. But with a divine glow inside, an undying humour and a toddler's smile on his lips, Bhakat Prasad stood tall and towering in the midst of all types of affliction. On certain occasions he would jocularly remark, 'look how bounteous god has been to me in showering ailments and disabilities on me'.

Extremely amiable in nature, Bhakat Prasad would not miss a single occasion to be at your place whether you were celebrating or mourning, whether you were in a marriage pandal or in a nursing home recovering from certain ailments. His sociable nature prompted him to socialise with friends and colleagues whenever he had free time, these particularly happening during the evenings. For short distances he commuted on rickshaws with the rickshaw-puller virtually lifting him on to the seat and from it to the doorsteps of his friends and colleagues. But for colleagues who lived far away from his Dariyapur Gola residence, he would first travel to the Gandhi Maidan auto stand where the rickshaw puller would lift him from the rickshaw and make him comfortable on the side seat of the auto driver holding a rod behind with his right hand and the stick in his left hand, the front seat by the side of the driver because he was unable to get in and out of the normal passengers' seats. This strenuous journey was undertaken by Professor Mazumdar particularly in relation to the late Professor Qeyamuddin Ahmad who lived nearly ten kilometres away from the late Mazumdar's residence. The auto driver would drop him on the Ashok Rajpath near the Khajekala Sabji market from where he would limpingly walk some distance to reach Professor Ahmad's residence. On his way back Professor Ahmad or his son Imtiyaz would accompany him and help him to cross the Ashok Rajpath and sit him well once again by the side of the auto driver and see him off.

Bhakat Prasad was an extraordinary teacher who always wanted the best from his pupils. Whether he was lecturing in a classroom or evaluating preparatory answer scripts, he wanted his students to rise above the level of textbook knowledge and go in for deeper studies towards a holistic understanding of the subjects concerned. Those who could fall in line got the best out of the late Mazumdar's intellectual abilities with easy access to his personal collection of books. His main purpose was to motivate his students to access the original sources as far as they could. I can recall a day from my M.A previous year classes when Professor R.S. Sharma stepped in to address the class in place of Professor Mazumdar who was absent on that day. Around that time, Professor Mazumdar was discussing the history of the Pala dynasty. When Professor Sharma learnt this, he asked the students to tell him something about the Pala kings of Bengal and Bihar. When no response was forthcoming, a boy from the middle benches stood up to defend his friends and started describing a scene from the huge gathering of kings and feudatories who had turned up at the army camp of a Pala king on the banks of river Ganga to pay their customary homage. On this occasion, the boy continued, "the horses had raised so much dust from their hooves that the sky became invisible and the incoming boats which embanked the river front at Mudgagiri (Munger)sometimes looked like a mountain range shadowing the bright sun and sometimes like the dark and deep clouds of the rainy season." Professor Sharma was delighted to hear a fifth year student of history quoting verbatim from the Prasasti of Kings appearing in Pala copper plate grants and wanted to know the source of this information. From Professor Mazumdar's lectures, pat came the reply.

A meticulous evaluator of answer scripts and hard taskmaster, the late Professor Mazumdar would not even mind his own physical discomfort while reading through the pages of such scripts. The present writer has fond memories of how the senior Mazumdar, while passing from one room to another would take a side glance at the script being examined by his son and affectionately caution him saying 'Bhakto, take care, the letters are too small'. But the taskmaster remained engrossed in the script like he was doing up one of his own research papers. I can also recollect how Professor Mazumdar was on the miserly side in terms of awarding grades to the answer scripts prepared by his students. But this, he knew pretty well would immensely benefit the students. Once I approached him with a script on the Metternich System. As Professor Mazumdar was busy with some routine work he asked a junior colleague to go through it till he finished his work. Always amiable and friendly with students, the junior colleague the late Tara Prasad Lal Das read through the material and awarded a near distinction grade. After Professor Mazumdar had finished his work, he took the script and started correcting it. Soon the whole material became colourful with deletions, additions and critical marginal notes providing insights and information always unlikely in the prescribed readings. He then took out an exclusive study on the Metternich System from the library and handed it over to me with the advice to redo the whole thing.

A reminiscences page is not the right space to evaluate the face of a creative man in the public domain particularly for one who has observed him from very close quarters. But if opinions in the public domain matter, the late Mazumdar was a man with a difference which any probing mind would find difficult to miss out. The three dimensions of his public life related to his teaching skills, his intellectual output and his performance as a dour administrator. For a start, Mazumdar was the only teacher in the department of twenty-five faculty members who did not carry one-time prepared notes or exercise books to the classroom and dictate to the students from these materials. He believed, teaching meant motivating students for higher level readings with curiosity to reach out to basic source materials. He always raised his bar above the level of textbooks and reached out to the primary sources for the content of his absorbing lectures. If he was teaching the history of Kashmir he would quote verbation from the *Rājatarangiṇī* of Kalhana. If it was the history of Kanauj, he would take the students straight into the *Harṣacharita* of Bāṇabhaṭṭa. And if it was the history of the Pala dynasty he would speak from the *praśasti* (eulogy) of Pala inscriptions and the *Rāmacharita* of Sandhyakar Nandin. In the course of lecturing, his powerful voice packed with occasional punches resonated in the classroom with a spellbound effect on students.

At the exit level of university education it was refreshing to learn about two subaltern movements not far removed from one another in point of time. One was the Damara rebellion of Kashmir and the other the Kaivarta uprising of Bengal. It was also interesting to learn about a Hindu king of Kashmir (12th century) who appointed a high officer for uprooting the metal images from temples (*Devopāṭana mahanyaka*) and melt them to help the cash-starved royal exchequer. This was in sharp contrast with what the Maurya kings did for the same purpose of enriching the treasury by ordering fashioning of idols which were pushed into the markets to generate revenue. All this demolished the perception (misperception) of unchaining and everlasting Sanatana Hindu society of ancient India

Readers of this volume who can spare some time to go through the writings of the late Mazumdar appended at the end of the book would be surprised to notice not only the sheer mass of creative output but also the diversity of themes and the depth of investigation, the last one only after going through some of the writings. Clearly, his intellectual interests varied from the Ram Cult in early medieval India to forms of land measurements in northern India, Nagas in the Pre-Buddhistic Age, rise and decline of *Tirthas* in the Mathura Region, iron industry in Northern India on the eve of the Turko-Afghan Period, the perturbed individual and *Vedanta*, divine love in Indian Sufism and Vaishnavism, *Tirthas* in Bihar, Madhya Yuger Yuddha O Bharatiya Samaj (war of the medieval ages and Indian society), political geography of Bihar, common man in the political philosophy and Gandhian reorientation, Panchayat Raj administration in Bihar besides useful contributions on Jimutvahan Sen and Ram Manohar Lohia to the *Dictionary of National Biography*.

Despite a frail physique the late Mazumdar was endowed with rock-bottom honesty and a stubbornness of purpose. This saw him through a brief spell of rough weather when he took over the reigns of the department in April 1980. Besides being a hard taskmaster in managing the affairs of the department he also took a keen interest to promote intellectual output of the colleagues in the form of seminars and lectures, both in-house and extra-mural with the departmental library as an essential appendage. After taking over the reins of the department his attention was drawn to the fact that there was a huge backlog of unpaid bills against the departmental library. During the four years of his tenure, Dr. Mazumdar scrupulously cleared these pending bills year after year. When Dr. Mazumdar left the department, there were hardly any unpaid bills in the name of the library although this constrained the usual flow of the new acquisitions.

6

Rivers and Protohistoric Settlements: Negotiating Contrasting Perceptions in the Light of Recent Explorations in Rajasthan

R.C. Thakran

Right from the very inception of human life on this planet a host of forces have remained in operation in some form or the other to shape the process of development. These very forces have caught the attention of students and scholars of history, archaeology and a number of allied disciplines, and several attempts have been made either to identify the prime moving forces or to delineate the relative importance of the forces in constant operation. This debate has naturally never been linear and the multiplicity of views on the theme underlines either one or the other or the group of factors as being the crucial one in this context. However, the contrasting views on the theme have sharpened the ongoing debate as well as refined enquiry continually over the years. A substantial space has been enjoyed by the natural forces and among them watercourses certainly occupied still greater space. These, of course, have constantly occupied the centre stage through human history. Is it because of their being so integral to human existence? Or is it a mere cultural construct conditioned by our own concerns? These are some points among others posed by the settlement data recovered during the last four seasons (2003-06) of archaeological investigations in north-western parts of Rajasthan (in the Shri Ganganagar and Hanumangarh districts) traversed by the seasonal Ghaggar river, being equated with the ancient Saraswati which I would like to assess in the following lines along with whether the river water was always really a precondition for the very existence of human life in the past.

Process of Archaeological Research

The areas under review caught the imagination of none other than the late. A. Ghosh, the then Director General of the Archaeological Survey of India, in the early second half of the preceding century, after a few years of the partition of the country and transfer of the then known and almost all the known Harappan settlements to Pakistan.[1] Ghosh surveyed the areas, mainly along the banks of the Ghaggar river for being contiguous to the known Harappan zone in Pakistan. With the result several Harappan and PGW sites were discovered in this part; this was, of course, a welcome development not only to fill up the cultural vacuum created by the partition but also to give a fillip to the prospects of archaeological research in this part of the union of India. [2] Unfortunately this hope was belied in the subsequent years for absence of any productive attempt and addition to what was produced by Ghosh, particularly in this part. Obviously precise reasons for such a miss are not explicit enough but this impending gap certainly offered an excellent opportunity and tremendous scope for intensive archaeological as well as geological and hydrological investigations. Keeping in view the potential and promise held out by the region, the present probing of this area was undertaken four years ago by me and as a result of this intensive combing several settlements belonging to different cultural stages were discovered in addition to collecting information on geological formations, hydrological conditions and ethnographic practices of survival.

The fieldwork during the last four seasons was based on a village-to-village basis and first covered almost all the villages along both the banks of the Ghaggar. Secondly the villages away from the river banks were encompassed.[3] During the course of the exercise a survey of wells and bore wells was undertaken in addition to the ancient settlement remains for assessing the quality, quantity and depth of the ground water, and nature of the water-bearing sediments. As a result of this exercise about 111 new sites were discovered and several sites reported earlier by Ghosh were also revisited in the process.[4] I also happened to visit some of the sites such as Bhirdana[5] in Haryana, Baroor[6], Chak-86 and Tarkhanwala Dera[7] in Rajasthan which were being excavated by different Circle Officers of the Archaeological Survey of India(ASI) around that time. Besides the famous urban site of Kalibanga was also visited for fresh insights.[9] The combined body of the archaeological data discovered hitherto presented the following cultural sequence.

Emerging Cultural Sequence

The history of human activities begins primarily with the early Harappan period.[9] In stark contrast to the cultural history of the Bahawalpur area in the west and that of the Trans-Indus areas situated further west[10], though some shreds of Hakra ware are said to have been discovered from Baroor[11], where the early Harappan phase is represented by fourteen settlements.[12] This is followed by the mature Harappan phase with nice settlements. The late Harappan phase largely remains unrepresented for want of such evidences, though a faint late Harappan evidence from Baroor and a few OCP sites such as Bhukarka Theh, Lal Khan wali Dani ka theh and Sardarpura ka theh-II are worth mentioning. If the quality of the ware from these sites is any indication the antiquity of the OCP seems to parallel the Harappan phase and thus tends to cover a time span from early to late Harappan levels. The general perception of cultural interregnum after the Harappan was broken by the presence of PGW remains from eleven locales in this area. Interestingly, nine of the explored sites broke new grounds, whereas the other two were preceded by the mature Harappan remains. This was succeeded by the early historical period that is broadly represented by forty-nine settlements with cultural remains of the Rangmahal and Kushan period. The large number of settlements is in conformity with the general pattern of development marked already in this period in the adjoining area of Haryana. We do have remains of the different phases of the medieval period from 24 settlements that speak of the presence of human activities during this succeeding period. These are in fact the remains of the deserted settlements only and we do not know how many of the settlements of this period are under the habitations of the modern village settlements. The number of modern villages is of course very high (3886) compared to the combined strength of all the past known settlements. The exponential increase in the number of modern village settlements in the Ghaggar bed is the outcome of the official incentive offered by Maharaja Ganga Singh of Bikaner State in the pre-independence period and by the Chief Minister of Punjab, Pratap Singh Kairon, which resulted in the teeming of the entire area with human activities.[13] In the context of the ancient settlements data, there is a strong possibility of getting more settlements with the progress of the field enquiry.[14]

Locational Analysis

The locational analysis is very crucial in archaeological studies and it covers a rage of parameters but in the present context I would deal primarily with the locational relationship of the settlements to the water course of the Ghaggar river through different stages of the cultural developments. This certainly calls for a thorough analysis of the location of the settlements and the role of the forces that went into the making of these settlements. This would trace the relationship between the settlements and the natural forces including the Ghaggar river on the one hand and naturally also attempt to explore the relative influence of the natural as well as social forces in the making of the settlements on the other. Our endeavour would also be to identify the prime variable or variables involved in shaping the pattern of settlements. Hence this analysis demands a comprehensive review of the possible role played by these variables at different stages of the development of settlements in this area. In this context we could begin with the first phase of human history, i.e. the early Harappan phase.

We have fourteen sites to represent the early Harappan phase and six of these (Kalibanga, Baroor, Tarkhanwala Dera, Chak-78, etc.) are found situated either along the bank of the Ghaggar watercourse or close to it in the Ganganagar and Hanumangarh districts of Rajasthan. Though the number of sites is less than half of the known early Harappan settlements in this part, this is nevertheless a substantial number in the district sense of the numerical strength and thus may also be interpreted to suggest an overwhelming role played by the river to influence the very choice of making a settlement. However, we have to take note of the remaining 8 settlements, which constitute more than fifty per cent of its total known numerical strength. These are located in areas as far away as seventy kilometres from the river. The areas of the location of these settlements are obviously not as conducive as those of the river zone. Rather, the fact of the matter is that these areas apparently appear very hostile for any presence of human beings and more so in summer for the ground water supply. There is no evidence of any watercourse whatsoever in these areas yet they attracted and induced people to make their settlements at certain specific locales where their very survival was perceived to be possible under these conditions. In order to understand this phenomenon, we need to take note of all the factors at micro level while dealing with choice of people to make their settlements at particular places. The location of a settlement is not a simple archaeological evidence in space for it is always an embodiment of human activities and fraught with a range of possibilities, which, of course, can only be properly understood, explained and situated in their rightful contexts by taking into account all the possible factors that were in operation. However, if one or the other of these possibilities unduly influences our mind the result would also not be in tune with the outcome of a scientific enquiry.

The mature Harappan phase is represented by nine settlements. Six of the nine settlements (Kalibanga, Baroor, Tarkhanewala Dera, Chak-23, Chak-43 and Chak-67) are located close to the river within a radius of zero to six from the lateral margins of the Ghaggar flood plain. Seven of them are preceded by the early Harappan remains while in the case of two settlements a fresh round was broken. As such there is need to explore the interiors of this zone on an extensive as well as intensive basis to bring out the relative role of both the riverine and dry areas. As of now three of the settlements are away from the river zone and these are situated in the zones largely considered to be unfit for any human habitation due to the absence of any water course, perennial or otherwise. These sites call for an explanation as to why the people selected these areas and how they survived in the absence of any tangible sources of surface water supply and the ground water being deep seated as well as brackish.

We do not have any substantial evidence of habitation during the succeeding late Harappan levels from this area. One of them (Baroor) represents faint late Harappan remains, whereas the three others seem to belong to the OCP group, which are contemporary to the Harappan period broadly in this zone. All these sites are away from the Ghaggar river zone and located in the interiors where there is no sign of any water surface or sub surface. The absence of late Harappan remains and the presence need further examination.

During the succeeding period of PGW eleven sites have been discovered from these areas.[16] Nine of these were fresh settlements and the remaining two continuations of the mature Harappan remains. These locations are different from the locations of the Harappan sites to a great extent. The locational analysis of these sites offers some very interesting insights: one, six of the eleven sites are in proximity to the water course (Kuddewala, Pir-ka-Thed, Joginder-ka-Thed, Chak-67, Chak-72 and Chak-86); one of these six sites is very close to the margins(Kuddewala, Pir-ka-Thed, Chak-86), and fourth, two of the sites are about six kilometres away from the river bed (Chak-67-III and Chak-72-II). Over fifty per cent of the known sites are thus in association with the river. But this numerical superiority cannot overshadow the substantial presence of human activities in the form of the five settlements of this group in the areas away from the river zone. These five settlements (GB Chak-48A, Silwani-ka-Thed, Karmali-ki-Dani-ka-Thed) and their locations are equally important to assess the relative impact of the operative (natural and social) variables on the choice of site selection of the people during this period. Cognisance of all such data should, in fact, form the basis of any rational approach to the study of settlements.

This cultural period was followed by a particular type of ceramic tradition popularly known as Rangmahal in archaeological parlance[17], which is also combined with cultural remains of Kushana levels. During this period a spurt in the size of population is noticeable on one hand, the number of settlements is always bigger than the average size of earlier ones.[18] The cultural assemblage is also far richer than any of the preceding period.[19] Twenty-nine of these settlements were made afresh and eight were preceded by the PGW remains. This shows that more areas were brought under human activities during this period, which were perhaps uninhabitable earlier. Still more interesting is the fact that slightly over fifty per cent of the explored sites (25) are located in the river environment. Almost one-third of these sites are located in the flood plain of the river, six are on the banks of the river and the remaining 12 sites are located within a radius of 1.5 to 6 kilometres from the outer limits of the river flood plain. This shows that the process of making human settlements in the riverbed began in the PGW phase for the first time while only one site was strengthened in the Rangmahal period. This trend was further consolidated in the succeeding medieval times. Was it because of any change, positive or negative, in the realm of climatic conditions or in the character of the river? Or was it because of the changing working capability of the people over the period? We shall, however, make an attempt to understand and seek their scientific interpretations in the following lines.

Factors Governing Site Selection

The foregoing shows that the river was not the only factor in the making and sustaining of the majority of the settlements in this area. Nor are the settlements located in a linear manner along the river course. Moreover the water and other benefits of a watercourse were/are not available beyond the limits of its flood plain. There was hardly any device with the people to divert the river water to distant places as it is being done in recent times through the canals. We are also aware of the emerging fact that the ever-increasing human activities during the past constantly embraced more and more pristine areas both in and outside the flood plain. Interestingly, however, concentrations of these very activities constantly grew only in areas away from the river at a faster pace. This means the presence or absence of a river remained immaterial for the substantial number of people with regard to the exercise of their choice of site selection for making their residential settlements.

However, the concentration of human activities in non-riverine zones is not new to these areas for such a scenario has also been observed in Punjab[20], Haryana[21] and Bahawalpur areas in southern parts of west Punjab in Pakistan[22]. All these areas support a very heavy concentration of past settlements in non-riverine areas where the conditions of ground and surface water availability are the same. Rainfall is no different in any respect. There is, of course, a change in soil types, especially in areas away from the Ghaggar flood plain. Contrary to the soils of Haryana and Punjab, these soils are composed primarily of Aeolian sand. The landscape is also more uneven and dotted with sand dunes of diverse denominations with interspersed sandy loam flats(tals). Thus the emerging settlement scenario from the areas under discussion is in perfect conformity to what has been underlined in the contiguous areas of Punjab (both west and east) and Haryana. Here, however, arises a question as to how did the people manage water to sustain themselves as well as their animals in this dry and hostile landscape in the absence of rivers, favourable rains and ground water? We can make an attempt to seek a rational explanation of this query in the following lines.

We have already observed that the nature of the rainfall is of regional character and it varies a great deal from season to season and place to place at local as well as regional levels. A glaring example of this feature was noticed in the year 2005 when the lives of people were made miserable by sudden intensive and flash floods in the driest districts of Badmer and Jaisalmer of Rajasthan.[24] The evidence of the behaviour of rains in this part of the land should serve as a reminder to us about such possibilities of variations in rainfall behaviour in the past as well. Under the given situation of erratic rains, absence of rivers from the vast tracts of land, non-availability of potable ground water and matching capabilities to harness it, a sense of awareness seems to have dawned upon them to harvest rain water in some form or the other. This is not impossible either in view of an average presence of one to three natural depressions in close proximity of the ancient settlements. These very depressions seem to have formed the rain water repositories for the incoming rain water in the form of surface run off from the man made village ponds has been the order of the day not only in this part of Rajasthan but also in Punjab and Haryana.[25] In all these areas, village wells were and are situated on or along these very village ponds. This limited ground water reserve is generated through constant leaching of fresh pond water in the subsoil profile over the period and in this process the extant salt content from the impacted subsoil is washed down in deeper aquifers. This reserve of transformed ground water has been tapped through these wells by the villagers to stave off tough summer seasons. In addition people used to dig wells in their houses, which are known as *tankas, tankis* and *kundas* in Rajasthan[26] and by some other names in Gujarat.[27] In historical times these were both kuchcha and pucca, lined with or without burnt bricks. The size of the wells varied according to the demand and economic capacity of the respective household. These are still in vogue in parts of Gujarat (as I have noticed around Cambay). The inner walls of the kuchcha wells were plastered with a fine clay or clay mixed with lime or with lime alone as conditioned by the circumstances; this was a double-pronged strategy to provide the walls of the wells with a protective cover from being damaged by water and to arrest loss of water through seepage. Rainwater thus stored in these wells was used for their daily chores, especially during the summer season when there is a serious scarcity of rainwater. If ethno archaeology is useful in some form to understand the life of past societies, we can draw some inference regarding the application of this device for harvesting rain water at least on a low scale, which could have helped them to withstand the pressures of irregular water supply from the village ponds. This mechanism demanded labour investment and therefore was feasible for being very cost effective.

Besides we have marked during our field survey that in some of the villages, there has been a stark shortage of surface as well as subsurface potable water. Nevertheless these villages could not only survive but also acquired a reasonably large size if we compare their size with that of the ancient settlements. The people in these villages have devised a unique method to make an arrangement of potable water, for their daily consumption, naturally not at their village levels but from as distant places as twenty-five kilometres. There are large-sized natural depressions in such villages where potable ground water is available in the wells in higher quantities in tune with their respective denominations. Water from these distant places is filled in earthen pitchers and transported on camel back. Particular types of fire clay (storage jars) containers and rope saddles were prepared to hang the jars on both sides of the camel hump and were used for this purpose. But huge quantities of water could not be transported on camel back from such distant places and accordingly the supply fell short of the daily requirement. To make up the shortfall, they mixed the potable water with the locally available brackish or saline water in such proportions that the taste of the potable water was not affected. The potable water thus made available was reserved for cooking and drinking purposes, the rest of the requirement being met by the locally available unpotable water. Since, the camel is known to the people in this part right from the Harappan times, there is every likelihood of it being put to similar use during the Harappan and post-Harrapan times. In case this strategy did not work beyond a point during a very long spell of dry season, people generally migrated to a different site. In archaeology, the practice is known as transhumance.

Still more interesting was the total dependence on the brackish water in a number of villages. Obviously the quality of this water is not as bad as we encounter in this area on an average, the salt content being slightly less than what it contains normally. This water is used for all household purposes except irrigation. This offers further insight into the possible variations in the soil water quality and the range of its being put to diverse usages for survival. The size of such villages is also very big and one of these villages is Makkasar, only five to six kilometres south of Hanumangarh, on the Hanumangarh to Surtgarh highway, the tahsil and district headquarters of the same district. The late Sheopat Singh of this village, the famous leader of the downtrodden and working people, was very helpful in providing me with very useful details and insights about the pragmatic approaches adopted by the people in an environment of technological and natural resource constraints. Such a phenomenon is also noticed in Haryana, in Malwa region of Punjab and western parts of Delhi. The presence of a number of villages surviving with the brackish soil water surely offers a new dimension to evaluate the factors that influenced not only selection of sites but also contributed in some way to sustain them over the period. While dealing with the ancient societies we need to take into account all possible micro as well macro variables which contributed to their making.

Conclusion

Keeping in view the foregoing discussion, we can draw some inferences. Rivers were/are not present everywhere but human activities are there on an average in some form or the other since early Harappan levels in these areas. Nor were people capable of channelising river water to areas beyond their flood plains in any manner. Clearly, the human settlements were/are not confined to water courses alone rather these are located in greater number in areas away form the rivers, where access to river water is impossible and the ground water is usually not potable. In these areas people survived with the help of surface water available in the local, natural as well as man made depressions and ponds. Rain water was harvested in them and people used that in normal conditions. Availability of some potable water in the shallow acquifiers was generated through the leaching of pond water in the subsoil which washed down salt from the soil to a substantial level and thus the water was made potable. In the summer season when water became further scarce people seem to have trapped the transformed ground water through kuccha/pucca wells made in and around these ponds. In still very long dry spells people either brought supply of water from distant places for consumption purposes or resorted to seasonal migration. Finally it appears that in acute situations they survived on locally available potable brackish water only, which means fresh water was also not always a precondition for human survival and making their settlements in particular areas.

NOTES AND REFERENCES

1. All the known major as well as urban settlements went to Pakistan after Partition in 1947 except one settlement of *Koala Nihang Khan* in Ambala district of Haryana, previously in Punjab. This was a Harappan village settlement and its presence was very promising to get more sites during the archaeological exploration. And this expectation was fulfilled with the

discovery of a number of sites in archaeological forays. *Anuual Report of the Archaeological Survey of India* 1929-30, New Delhi, 1935, pp.131-2.

2. A Ghosh 'The Rajputana Desert- Its Archaeological Aspects' in the *Bulletin of the National Institute of Sciences of India,* 1, 1952, pp. 37-42.
3. It is very important to make it distinctly clear that my fieldwork was circumscribed by the geographical and resources constraints. With the result that this survey was confined to primarily those villages which were either connected by roads or were easily accessible. Extensive work needs to be done to make it further broad based and all encompassing, which would follow in the seasons to come. Once it is accomplished the picture would be clearer.
4. It is very pertinent to make it clear that details about all the sites explored by A.Ghosh are not accessible and therefore it is difficult to give details of each settlement. But wherever it is possible we have done what is necessary. I hope full details of these sites will soon be available.
5. The site of Bhirdana was being excavated by the personnel from the Excavation Branch, Nagpur, under the leadership of Mr. Rao, Mr. Sameer Dewan and Mr. Prabhash Sahu who were kind enough to provide us necessary inputs about the findings.
6. This site of Baroor in Rajasthan was being excavated by the Patna Circle of ASI, under the leadership of Dr. (Mrs.) Pramila Sant. The work was being supervised by Mr. Sinha and Mr. Sujit Nain of the same circle. Mr. Arun Kumar Khanna was the leader of the trainees of the Institute of Archaeology, New Delhi. They were also very helpful in providing relevant information on the nature of the exposed cultural assemblage.
7. These sites were also being excavated by the personnel of the Patna Circle of the ASI. And they took us around to show the progress of excavation and enlightened us on varied aspects of the settlements.
8. The site is situated just on the left bank of the Ghaggar and a good site Museum was being constructed a little away from the site alongside the road from Pilibanga.to Kalibanga.
9. The term 'early Harappan' is being used nere to denote a stage of the Harappa civilisation that precedes it in chrono-cultural terms.
10. We know that a good deal of archaeological fieldwork has been done by Rafiq Mughal in the 1970s of the preceding century in the Bawalpur area of Pakistan. During his explorations, Mughal identified 99 sites representing a cultural phase termed by him *Hakra culture,* which is earlier than the early Harappan phase. And thus the history of the human race in this part is earlier than the early Harappan of the areas under discussion; this is very important evidence to understand the very process of beginning and chronological sequence of expansion of the activites in different areas of the Harappan zone. M.R. Mughal, 'Recent Archaeological Researches in Cholistan' in G.L. Possehl ed. *Harappan Civilisation,* New Delhi, 1982,pp. 85-6; Idem 'New Archaeological Evidence from Bahawalpur' in *ME,* XIII, Pune, 1989, pp. 93-8; Idem 'Archaeological Field Research Since Independence' in the *Sindoligical Studies,* Summer-Winter, 1990, pp. 31-8.
11. Personal communication with Sinha and Nain.

12. I could not verify how many of these sites were discovered by A.Ghosh. This is very crucial and will try to do what is necessary if the list of sites explored by Ghosh is available with full details.
13. *Ganga Nagar District Census Handbook,* Series 18, A Village Directory, Ganga Nagar 1981.
14. Several villages in the interior are still to be visited and there is a strong possibility of getting some more sites during this prospective fieldwork. But the interiors are also full of mobile sand dunes which may preclude full details of past settlements, though we could discover some of the settlements submerged under the ever intruding Aeolian sand.
15. There are two important excavated settlements, Banawali (Haryana) and Kalibanga (Rajasthan), the latter does not have any late Harappan evidence. It is suggested that people in late Harappan levels did not find these areas convenient enough on account of deteriorating climatic conditions. But these very areas have produced OCP settlements contemporary of the late Harappan phase. And thus there is a strong need to probe this point further.
16. The PGW sites reported by Ghosh could not be compared due to non-availability of information about them.
17. This type of ceramic ware was identified for the first time at the site of *Rangmahal* village in Suratgarh tahsil of district Hanumangarh, Rajasthan in the 1960s of the last century. The site was also excavated in a limited manner and is now under the protection of the ASI.
18. The average size of the settlements consists of several acres. On an average each settlement of this group is substantially bigger than the bigger Harappan settlement of Baroor in this area.
19. These sites enjoy very thick cultural deposits with very high frequency and a variety of cultural objects, which speak of great productive activities.
20. R.C. Thakran, 'The Myth of Saraswati River: A Locational Analysis of Harappan Sites' in Kesavan Veluthat and P.P. Sudhakaran (eds.) *Advances in History,* Calicut, 2003, pp.22-43; idem 'Punjab-Its Prothohistoric Past: Problems and Issues' *Presidential Address (Ancient Section)* at *The Punjab History Conference,* Punjabi University, Patiala, March, 2002, pp.12-26; Idem 'Assessment of the Role of Rivers in Promoting Protohistoric Settlement Patterns In Punjab' in the proceedings of *The Punjab History Conference,* Patiala, 2001, pp. 29-43.
21. R.C. Thakran, 'Protohistoric Settlement Patterns in Haryana' in K.M. Shrimali ed. *Reason and Archaeology,* Delhi, 1999, pp.43-67; Idem, *Kya Harappa Sabhyata Saraswat Thi* (Hindi), Joshi Adhikari Institute, New Delhi, 2002.
22. Mughal, op.cit.
23. It has already been stated that there is a heavy concentration of ancient settlements in areas where river water is out of the question.
24. *Sahara Times,* New Delhi, September 9, 2006, p. 22; Sunday *Times of India,* New Delhi, August 27, 2006, p. 7; *Sahara Samaya* (Hindi), New Delhi, September 9, 2003, p. 10-11.
25. This has been commonly marked during my fieldwork in these areas, R.C. Thakran *Settlement Archaeology (Haryana),* Gyan Publishing House, New Delhi, 2000.

26. In most of the houses in western Rajasthan people construct pucca wells, especially in the courtyards, with wooden or concrete covered tops. I was informed by Chaudhary Sudesh Kumar Binda, an educated and highly enlightened resident of village 24 GB in Anupgarh tahsil of Hanumangarh district, that earlier these wells were lined with lime plaster in order to protect their inner walls from being eroded by water as well as to arrest loss of water through seepage. Such wells are also constructed at times in the fields. These wells are used to harvest rainwater in them and thus the harvested rainwater is used for drinking purposes. While we were excavating the early Harappan settlement of Dabadi, tahsil Bhadra, district Hanumangarh from March to June 2007, we also used water from such a well during our stay. This well was constructed by Ch. Hari Singh, resident of Dabadi village, close to this field in the Gaon Samalat land reserved as pastures.
27. The practice of making wells, especially inside the houses, was also witnessed in the Cambay town of Gujarat during my visit in 2005-6 for collection of information on carnelian bead manufacturing household industries. These wells are also pucca wells and with covered tops. There is, of course, a small adjustable opening provided to draw water from the well. Primarily people survive on this water, at least, for drinking purposes as the ground water is highly brackish for being located on the Arabian Sea shore.

7

Aryans and the Walled Cities

R.N. Nandi

In the *Ṛgveda*, the term Arya (Aryan) represents five or more divergent groups of Vedic speakers who together constituted one of the several ethno-linguistic segments of the Harappan population and appear to have been stakeholders in the rise and fall of Harappan cities, first as collaborators and later as competitors. The frequency of episodes relating to the control of walled habitations seems to fall in line. Out of more than two dozen vocables representing habitational structures of varying dimension, at least three, namely *pur*, *durga* and *vrjana* clearly stand out as walled habitations of differential size and strength, from mud-walled to mud-brick-walled, red brick-walled and stone-walled, each serving as the hub of social, political and economic activity proportionate to their size.

Introduction

Any reconstruction of urban space in the hymns of the *Ṛgveda* cannot be meaningful without a comprehensive reappraisal of a large mass of information relating to fortified settlements which are variously identified by terms like *pur*, *durga*, *vrtra* and *vrjana*. However, such reconstructions may always elude the investigator who begins the study of *Ṛgveda* hymns with the idea, long dated by now that the Vedic Aryans were nomadic cattle keepers who had nothing to do with urban places, marine navigation and commercial exchanges. Such a perception is surprising in view of the absolute consensus among the scholars that the term *pur*, which occurs more than a hundred times in the *Ṛgveda* always represented a fort, a rampart or a stronghold. Where would the Vedic Aryans come across strongholds or forts except in the greater Indus Valley during the Bronze Age?

In the greater Indus Valley, some form of fortified settlements, which served as the centre of political power and resource accumulation and were made of mud, mud brick or stone would be a common place between 2600 BC and 1500 BC. In this context, an idea has gone round that since Vedic Aryans had nothing to do with urban places, they tried to destroy these whenever they came across any such structures. The 'destruction' of massive stone or brick ramparts is easier said than done and can never be the intent of a people who viewed these settlements as a source of wealth, power and security and fervently aspired to possess as many of these as they could. The conflicts relating to the capture and occupation of fortified resource centres would perfectly fit a situation in which availability of resources became scarce, triggering conditions of small scale but widespread political disturbances and social unrest. The significance attached to strongly built, large masonry structures and the amount of space devoted to descriptions relating to the splendour, massiveness, structural strength, safety of life and property and plentiful resources of the fortified places which automatically made these places a bone of contention and hence the conflicts relating to their capture and occupation by all sections of people, Vedic speakers as well as non-Vedic speakers is too manifest to be glossed over or sidelined.

However, this is precisely what several Vedicists appear to be doing in their writings and that too by handpicking single stanzas and disregarding a large body of information which seems to be at odds with the preconceived notions of these scholars. For instance, the term *tripur*, is used to generalise that all fortified settlements were concentric in plan (Rau, 1976, 6). Similarly, the term *śāradīḥ* which occurs in three stanzas is used to generalise that all fortified settlements were 'autumnal' and therefore temporary in nature (Rau, 1976, 6). The term *armak* which means 'ruins' or 'ruined settlements' is considered to suggest that all fortified spaces were no more than ruins (Falk, 1981).

Taking these observations one by one, one would notice that the term *tripur* does not appear in the *RV* or any other Vedic *Saṃhitas.* The term is mentioned for the first time in certain *Brahamana* texts, but that is another time and another space far removed from the compositions of the *Ṛgveda.* It is however surprising that the *Sanskrit English Dictionary* of Monier-Williams, otherwise quite a dependable lexicon does not mention any of the Vedic texts under *tripur.* One wonders what prompted Rau to make such a sweeping generalisation. As for the term *śāradīḥ*, it may or may not mean autumnal but autumnal surely does not mean 'temporary'. In all likelihood, these relate to mud ramparts or forts situated in some turbulent flood plains and needed major repairs or reconstruction during the month of October as the rains subsided and the floods receded. Potential enemies nearby may have targeted these structures just about the time they were to be repaired or reconstructed.

Similarly, the term *armaka* (ruins) occurs in two stanzas of a hymn in the first book and on both occasions it is used as a qualifier for the expression *vailasthāna*, meaning place of the dead. Ruined and dilapidated structures without any resources and inhabitants would be all around on the Harappan mainland during the post 2000 BC period following the desertion and dilapidation of almost all urban places. Though this may superficially justify Witzel's contention that the *Ṛgveda* is a bronze age composition post dating the Harappan civilisation, maximally between 1900 BC and 1250 BC (Witzel, 1999), the *RV* narrative on *pur* is not about ruined or dilapidated structures but about potential masonry building centring resources and political power. Burial grounds would be around even during the mature phase of Harappan urbanisation (2600-2300 BC) but there would be no ruined structures during this period. Ruined structures would not also be around during the decaying stages of Harappan cities (2300-2000 BC), at least during the earlier half. But one must remember that political conflicts which occupy so much space in the *Ṛgveda* were not for the capture of ruins or burial grounds but for large masonry constructions providing adequate resources and full security to the political chief, his entourage, his assets and his subjects. During the mature phase of Harappan urbanisation (2600-2300 BC), the scope for such conflicts would be minimal. But these would be quite relevant during the decaying stages of Harappan cities on the mainland, which archaeologists date between 2300 BC and 2000 BC when recourses became scarce on account of persistent geo-climatic disorders and when conflicts for greater access to recourses and recourse centres became the order of the day.

From a contrived position such as this, it is not at all difficult to argue that the *RV* does not know of large cities such as that of the Indus civilisation but only of 'ruins' (Falk 1981) and of 'small forts' (Rau 1976). Additionally for Whilehm Rau (Rau, 1973:1), the *pur* represented a 'hastily erected temporary structure' with stone or mud ramparts. However, judging by the resources and time consumed by the construction of a large masonry structure like a fort or citadel, which was intended to ensure security of life or property for a long period of time, these could hardly be characterised as 'hastily erected' or 'temporary'. As for the idea of a 'small fort', Rau does not mention any word which means 'small'. Contrary to this, there are words like '*pṛthvī*' (broad), '*urvī*' (large), '*bahulā*' (numerous), and '*mahī*' (massive), *aśmamayī* (stone-built), *āyasī* (strong as metal), *shasrasthūṇa* (many-pillared), *śatadura*' (with many gates), and *śatabhuji* (full of resources) used to highlight the imposing architecture of fortified settlements (*pur*).

It is curious that Rau did not even look up the writings of his predecessors, many of whom seem to have dug up almost the whole range of information on *pur* rather than handpicking particular stanzas which Rau believed could buttress his misinformed perception about Vedic Aryans and their social milieu in the *RV.* For instance, Macdonell and Keith cite nearly a score of stanzas providing information on *pur* (Macdonell and Keith, 1912), the total number of appearances being one hundred and ten. In these twenty odd passages, the two authors furnish most of the valuable information which leaves no doubt about the large area and massiveness of masonry constructions characterising these walled settlements. It is another matter that they found the information unbelievable and accordingly rejected the observation made by Pischel and Geldner to the effect that the *pur* represented towns with wooden walls and ditches which too is not correct since the *RV* never mentions a *pur* or fort with wooden walls. The predicament, though incongruous with their other informed observation that the Vedic Aryans were quite familiar with marine navigation and overseas trade which would be unlikely in the absence of some form of urban places, is understandable in view of the times they lived and the ideas that circulated in those days. The fortified Harappan cities, which could furnish a reasonable context to Rgvedic *pur,* were yet to be excavated. However, given their expertise it is odd that they translated the word *śatabhuji* as 'hundred walls', whereas the term with its suffix *bhuji,* and adjective of *bhuj,* meaning enjoyment, should be translated as 'furnished with a hundred pleasures of life'.

A recent study, which proposes to 'reinvestigate' the discourse relating to the Rgvedic *pur* clears up much of the mix-up resulting from the writings of Wilhelm Rau and his supporters though it stops just short of actual ground reality prevailing during the Harappan early and middle bronze ages and involving all segments of the Harappan population, Vedic speakers and non-Vedic speakers. (Sthuhrmann, 2008, 1-2). This is primarily because of a fix which affects almost all Western Vedicists and many of their credulous South Asian followers which relates to the characterisation of Vedic Aryans as 'semi-nomadic pastoralists' who could not have any thing to do with urban places. Sthuhrmann dismisses Rau's interpretation of the Rgvedic *pur* as 'unconvincing' and states that 'the kavis are not chroniclers, authors of tracts on siege methods, nor critics of architecture' and as such there is no reason 'Why should they make a big deal about streets at right angles, if discernable at all, and great baths?'. Sthuhrmann is almost at home when he states that 'the items that actually can be excerpted from the verses fit the cities of the Indus civilisation quite well; at any rate, nothing speaks against it. To my mind, this scenario is not excluded even for the end of the mature Harappan phase and the beginning of the late Harappan phase around 1900 BC' (Sthuhrmann, 2008, pp. 1-2). Apart from pushing the upper limit of the *Ṛgveda* compositions to the end of the 'mature Harappan phase' or 2300 BC (1900 BC for Sthuhrmann) when urban places on the Harappan mainland began to degenerate, the observation underlines the profundity of historical depth in general and of urban space in particular in the *RV*. This clearly is a mismatch for Sthuhrmann's other observation that 'as semi-nomadic pastoralists, they were interested in the *pur* only because of their designs or bounty, but they did not reside there'. The confusion would have cleared if the scholar had looked deeper into the material and noticed that Vedic speakers not only fervently aspired to inhabit walled settlements but even placed this defensive architecture on a par with the highest of their gods. Not much effort is needed to expose the ridiculous nature of Sthuhrmann's 'plunder and run' theory. Sample the passages in which the Aryan raiders 'demolished' 99 forts of a non-Aryan detractor and retained the 100th citadel for habitation (*niveśane śatatamā aviveṣa*—7.19.5; *śatatamaṃ veśyam*–1.26.3). Add up to this frequent prayer for inhabiting forts or citadels and enjoy many pleasures of life and security from marauders (1.58.8; 1.189.2; 7.95.1; 7.15.14; 7.3.7). Sthuhrmann's 'plunder and run' theory runs into further difficulty in view of the stanzas in which the capture of forts is bracketed with the subjugation of its inhabitants and the capture of surrounding land and water bodies (1.131.4; 1.174.2; 3.45.2; 3.51.2; 10.89.7). The last two required the so-called raiders to stay put to make good use of the cultivable land and drainage resources lying outside the captured fort. Also, make no mistake that the Aryans got possession of forts only by capturing and occupying these from their non-Vedic speaking Dāsa enemies as erroneously argued by most scholars for so long. On the contrary, they built their citadels (*dṛṃhitāni puraḥ*) too and fought among themselves for dispossessing one another from their strongholds like Sudāsa did in relation to Anu and Puru (*anavasya gayaṃ tṛtsave*, 7.18.13).

Vedic Gods and Walled Settlements

For an understanding of the urban space in the *RV*, a full view of the association of different Vedic gods with walled settlements or forts which the Vedic poets describe as *pur* and which contained all the aspects of urban life conceivable during the bronze age in north-western South Asia seems imperative. Scholars who seem to write for a gullible target audience are either unable or unwilling to get into the thick of the matter and re-examine the discourse relating to *pur* or fort leave no stone unturned to sideline anything that might highlight the importance attached to fortified urban spaces in the compositions of *Ṛgveda* poets. However, some familiarity with the evidence may situate the discourse on an entirely different empirical platform and provide fresh perspectives on the problem. For a start, the investigator must allow for the hyperbolic statements made by Vedic poets relating to the 'destruction or demolition' of a fort or citadel which was neither possible nor desirable. Why should a people destroy something which they aspired for and which they considered as praiseworthy as the highest of their gods. If anything, these expressions were intended to overdo the actions of political chiefs (or their patron gods, Indra and Agni in most cases) attacking a particular stronghold. Surely the hyperbolic eulogy of the raiding chief was not without reasons since a poet or eulogist flourished in this manner. The whole emphasis was to capture and occupy the citadel, subjugate its chief and his subjects, take possession of the resources inside the fort and exercise control over surrounding countryside from this new seat of authority. Browsing through the stanzas which provide *pur*-related information, one hundred and ten in all, one would notice that there is not a single pejorative characterising a fort or citadel though the inmates including the defending chiefs and subjects are variously denounced as non-sacrificing (*ayajyum,* 1.131.4) and foul-mouthed or ill-spoken (*mṝdhravāchaḥ* 1.174.2).

Any careful investigator would notice that the forts or citadels occupied a pride of place in the narrative of *Ṛgveda* poets who frequently associate these structures with most important Vedic gods. Anything associated with the gods and their actions is always praiseworthy and desirable rather than avoided and deprecated. Indra, Agni and Soma, who among themselves account for as many as six hundred of one thousand odd hymns (Sukta) recorded in the text, Indra with 250 hymns, Agni with 200 hymns and Soma with 150 hymns are clearly the most important of gods praised by the Vedic-speaking people of the *RV.* In several stanzas, these gods are ceremoniously associated with forts or citadels as protectors and procurers of these walled settlements. In one stanza, the poet states that Indra is to be praised like one praises the fort (*dhṛṣṇu puraṃ na archata* 8.69.8). The ruling chief controlling a fort is frequently likened to the fire god Agni and Soma, the god of sacrifices. Compare the statement 'soma settles down in the vessel like the king resides in his citadel' (*chambo viśat janaḥ puri na* 9.107.10) and 'People worship the fire god like a king in the fort' (*adha hi vikṣu īdachaḥ asi puri iva jūryaḥ raṇvaḥ*-6.2.7). In the first passage, *janaḥ* means a man but the use of nominative singular clearly distinguishes one man, the lordship from other inhabitants of the castle. This is appropriate too since soma is frequently regarded as the king who rules the sacrifice. In the other passage, the fire worshipped by people is stated to be like a desirable guest, a charming lordship in the citadel and adorable like a son. The river Saraswatī which is described as the best of the goddesses and greatest of the rivers has, among all the rivers mentioned in the *RV* the largest number of stanzas dedicated to it, is set to protect inhabitants of its banks with metal-like-strong citadels (*āyasīḥ* pūḥ-7.95.1) meaning that people on the banks of this river lived in fortified settlements and were therefore quite secure and happy. Elsewhere, the collective storm gods Maruts are implored to enrich the devotees with forts containing a 'hundred' or many pleasures of life (*śatabhuijibhiḥ pūrbhiḥ*, 1.166.8) so that the devotees can nourish their progeny (*tanayasya puṣṭiṣu*) and get rid of the evil, probably caused by non-believing detractors outside the fort. Sometimes, the *pur* or fort becomes a synonym of righteousness like in a stanza of the first book (1.58.8) which implores the fire god Agni to protect the chants man (*gṛṇantam*) from all deadly scenes (*aṃhasaḥ uruṣya*) just as he protects them with metal hard strongholds (*Āysībhiḥ pūrbhiḥ*). The passage may also mean that Vedic speakers who inhabited fortified settlements ostensibly also remained unaffected by all types of sinful acts. The sanctity of life in fortified settlements, whether made of stone, brick or mud is roundly emphasised in the text. For instance, it is stated that even in mud forts (*āmāsu pūrṣu*-2.35.6), people who do not flinch from righteousness (*apramṛṣyam*), are never destroyed by non-sacrificers (*arātayaḥ*) or non-believers (*anṛtāni*). At one place, the fire god is urged to provide sprawling agricultural land, many spacious forts for the happiness and welfare of people and their posterity (*naḥ pṛthvī cha puḥ bahulā urvī bhava* 1.189.2).

Harappan Citadels and the *Ṛgveda*

For further insights into to the discourse, a classification of the entire textual material relating to fortified places and possible correlates from the Harappan bronze age sights might be in order here. The nominal stem *pur* occurs in over hundred stanzas together with its declensions and compounds. Add up to this the number of stanzas which relate to episodes involving the remaining three terms *vṛtra, bṛjana* and *durga.* In every case, the composers conjure up the image of large and strongly built masonry structures made of mud, mud-bricks, red-bricks and stone, each building with several gates and many pillars.

Defensive Architecture

The defensive nature of fortified settlements is fairly well underlined by terms *dṛḷhā* (6.20.7; 6.32.3; 5.19.2), *driṃhitāni* (7.18.13), *dṛṃhitā* (1.51.11; 7.99.5) all of which mean strongly built. The expression occurs more than half a dozen times in the text and relates to forts ruled by Ārya chiefs (7.18.13) as well as Non-Ārya chiefs (1.51.11). The other expression that signifies the defensive nature of fortification is *āyasī* meaning strong like metal and frequently used in the instrumental case *Āyasībiḥ Pūrbhiḥ*. The passages which mention this expression invariably relate to important Vedic gods, who are said to either 'destroy' (read capture) metal like forts of enemies (2.20.8) or protect the Arya people by putting them inside these forts (7.15.14; 1.58.8; 7.3.7).

The term *Āyasī* is an adjective of *Ayas*, which during the early bronze age could mean iron as well as bronze or copper. Though the iron age is said to begin around 1200-1100 BC, small scale use of unprocessed iron objects from excavated sites of the third millennium BC in Sind and Afghanistan may suffice to suggest that the knowledge of iron technology was already around but not perfected. The three decorative objects of bronze discovered from the early bronze age site of Mundigak are found associated with iron balls or buttons made from unprocessed nodules. There is no dearth of hematite, magnetite and lollingite nodules in certain early bronze age sites of the Greater Indus Valley, the first two types reported from southern Afghanistan (Shaffer: 1984) and the last one from Mohenjo-daro (Marshall: 1931). Of the two 'parallel piped' indistinct objects found at Mundigak, one measures 7x4x3 cms and weighs 1 kg and the other 11x7x3.2 cms and weighs 3 kg. At Said Qala, the indistinct objects number 28 of which, 18 weighs between 500 grams and 3000 grams, nine between 300 grams and 500 grams and one 171 grams. The single indistinct iron object found at Deh Morasi Ghundai (Dupree: 1963) is a used magnetite nodule.

All this might suggest the familiarity of certain early bronze age communities of Afghanistan and Sind with iron ores, which can be easily obtained through open mining rather than, any specialised knowledge of iron ore processing. It is quite likely that certain early bronze age communities of the Greater Indus Valley collected hematite nodules for pigments and the leftovers were put to sundry uses, like hurling missiles at the enemies from inside the defensive walls. The latter practice seems to simulate the hurling of metallic bolts (*āyasaṃ vajram* 10.48.3) by Indra in the *Ṛgveda.* The iron balls weighing between three hundred and three thousand grams could surely do fairly well as deadly missiles hurled with great force from inside or outside fortified settlements and, accordingly may represent the bolt or *bajra* of Indra.

Since both iron and copper (more appropriately bronze) were high density metals which ensure both strength and durability, the use of the term *āyasī* meaning metal like in relation to strongly built defensive architecture like forts or citadels seems quite appropriate. The Vedic-speaking Aryans or any people for that matter could not have praised the structural strength of these buildings unless they were themselves familiar with these walled habitations as residents and rulers. The Vedic poets leave no room for speculation in this respect when they associate the highest of their gods with the citadels, first as captors and procurers and then as protectors and presiders of these walled settlements. Inside the forts, the priests offered their oblations to gods and kept the sacrificial fire burning with chants men on their job. Fervent desires to settle down in the forts, which provided all enjoyments of life and security are frequently heard in the text and, to this effect, whoever ruled a citadel was an enemy whether Ārya or Non-Ārya (7.18.13).

Construction Material

The descriptions of walled settlements appearing in the *Ṛgveda* bear characteristic similarity to walled habitations and citadels found throughout the Greater Indus Valley and belonging to different stages of Harappan urbanisation. There were mud brick ramparts, like at Amri, where the wall was made of sun-dried bricks (Kenyor, 1998, 44) and stone built citadels like at Kotdigi. Many of these settlements, particularly the mega cities ranged between 100 and 250 hectares which matches fairly well with bardic description of forts as broad and large. The mud or mud-brick rampart is simulated in the expression *āmāsu pūrṣu* (2.35.6) meaning raw or unbaked structures while the stone rampart is characterised as *aśmamayī* (4.30.20; 2.35.6) or built of stone. In certain areas, the bards may have come across structures in which limestone was the principal construction material or structures with a thick shining coat of lime on the outer walls to motivate the simile 'forts like crystal' or 'crystalline forts' (*Puraḥ Na Śubhrāḥ* 5.41.12). Despite usual mix-up with unrelated water myths, this part of the stanza surely relates to fortified settlements at certain sites like Dholavira, Rohri and Surkotda where limestone was liberally used as a construction material. Depending on availability, limestone was also used at other sites, liberally or sparingly. The excavator of Dholavira informs us that during the earliest three stages limestone was used on a large scale with certain prominent parts of structures getting a lustrous polish (R.S. Bisht, personal communication). At its prime, the whole structure certainly gave the appearance of a huge bright mansion.

Greed Plan

A good artist's view of the greed plan inside a fortification with roads and lanes criss-crossing with houses in between can be seen Fig.3.19 (Kenoyer, 1998, p. 52 :: Kenoyer, Jonathan Mark, *Ancient Cities of the Indus Valley Civilisation,* American Institute of Pakistan Studies, Oxford University Press, Bangalore and Islamabad, 1988). Such a view of the inside of a fort can be visible to anyone standing on top of a high wall. This may have inspired some of the *RV* poets to compare the inside of a walled city with a spider's net (*aurṇa vābha*). The expression *vṛtraṃ aurṇvābham*, meaning the coverer spinning a net like structure as the spider does in relation to the cobweb capturing resources (insects) for consumption appears in two passages (2.11.18, 8.32.6). Like the spider, the walled settlements also capture and control valuable resources preventing outside access to these social goods. Commenting on one of the passages (2.11.18), Sayan states that *aurṇvabh* may be a corrupt form of *aurṇnābaham* but omits the other passages (8.32.26) from a similar consideration. *Urṇnābh* is fibre navelled and the adjective *aurṇnbaham* something relating to the spider, clearly the spider's net. The overall layout of Indus cities and villages is distinguished by the orientation of streets and buildings according to the cardinal directions—east and west, north and south. The resulting grid pattern of the cities is much like the plan of the compartmented houses of Neolithic Mehargarh or the geometric seals from the early Chalcolithic period (Kenoyer, 1998).

Many Pillars

Given the fact that the Vedic speakers constituted an important segment of a multi-linguistic Harappan population during the bronze age and, perhaps even earlier, the bardic descriptions of Harappan cities during the mature and post-mature phases need careful examination. Since the Harappan settlements, large cities, needling towns and villages, were all covered habitational sides, stone-walled, brick-walled or mud-walled pillars of different dimensions would be an integral member of architecture particularly in relation to heavily built large buildings. Since all bardic descriptions have some kind of relation with major divinities, the descriptions of large pillared houses also relate to the most powerful of Vedic gods, the lords of the cosmos, Mitra and Varuṇa. At one place the two divinities are said to reside in their thousand-pillared mansion (*sahasrasthūṇe dhruve sadasi*, 2.41.5) and at another place their worshippers are said to inhabit similar thousand-pillared mansions by the grace of the two gods (*suktaṃ kṣtraṃ sahasrathūṇam*-5.62.6).

At Mohenjo-daro, the west mound revealed a series of walls, pillars, wells, drains, and the like which obviously indicate structures of some formal importance. Of these, there is one known to the excavators as the Assembly Hall. Badly preserved, it is nonetheless one of the most striking monuments at Mohenjo-daro. It consisted of a broad pillared hall opening principally to the north, i.e. towards the highest part of the site. Twenty rectangular pillars approximately five feet by three feet in size supported the roof. The pillars were arranged in rows of four with five pillars in each row (Fairservis, 1971). At Dholavira, in the fortified middle town at the northern gate has two side rooms that may have had large wooden pillars set on heavy ring stone bases. The discovery of these ring stones *in situ* helps to explain the numerous ring stones found out of context in the streets and dumps of Mohenjo-daro and Harappa (Kenoyer, 1998, p. 53).

Numerous Gateways

Compared to the pillars, gates and gateways are much more prominently visible from outside the fort. In a heavily built fort with walls measuring five metres in thickness and eleven metres in height (Kenoyer, 1998), there was no scope for either breaking the walls or scaling these by the enemies. As such, the most vulnerable points would be the gates of the fort in case of attacks by the enemies. Of the numerous episodes of *pur* encounter, the poets never mention the breaking or scaling of the walls, but there is no dearth of instances in which the raiders broke open the gates to facilitate their entry into the forts. Incidentally, this may also suggest that attacks came about the time when the gates had been closed for the day. Since the gates were made of wood, pressure exerted by a large number of attackers may have loosened the doors and finally broken. In relation to *pur* encounters, frequent reference is made to flaming missiles (*Aśani*) hurled by defenders from inside the fort as well as the attackers from outside the fort. The flaming missiles may have targeted the wooden doors, which, if taken by the fire could be quickly burnt down giving the raiders entry into the fort. Perhaps this may be the significance of the fire god Agni burning down the forts (6.16.39). Turning to the textual evidence, the stanzas refer to Indra or the raiding chief flinging open the doors of a fort (*puraṃ na vidarṣasi* –8.32.5; *asya puraḥ vi ṛṇoḥ viśvāḥ duraḥ*—6.18.5). Another stanza refers to the members of the attacking party entering the fort from all sides, evidently using the gates on all sides of a walled city (*dṛḷhāṃ puraṃ ā viviśu*-5.19.2). Since the Vedic speakers themselves inhabited fortified settlements (7.18.13) provided with a large number of doors (*te vṛhantaṃ mānaṃ sahasradvāraṃ gṛhaṃ jagām*-7.88.5), they were aware of the strong and weak points of a defensive structure like forts or citadels and could work out the strategy of the raids accordingly. This is also how they took possession of wealth accumulated in forts with hundred or numerous doors (*anarvā śatadurasya yat vedaḥ varpasā abhibhkta*-10.99.3).

At Dholavira, three nested rectangular city walls enclose the habitation areas, with the highest area located to the south, on top of a low hill. The outer wall covers an area approximately 771m X 616.8 m and is constructed entirely of mud brick, with large square bastions and two major gateways located at the centre of the northern and southern walls. The fortified middle town has four gateways, one in the centre of each wall. The acropolis sits approximately 13 metres above the lower town and has one gateway in the centre of each of its four walls. Dholavira has a single walled mound internally subdivided into three or four walled sectors (Kenoyer Fig. 3.6) the highest being in the southern portion and not in the west as at Mohenjo-daro and Harappa.

At Harappa, each major mound was surrounded by a massive mud-brick wall with brick gateways and bastions located at intervals along each face. At the gateway itself, the mud-brick city wall is over 9 metres wide and may have had additional bastions making it up to 11 metres wide. The gate itself is made from baked brick with one-metre thick walls firmly bonded to the mud-brick city wall. A small projection on the inner eastern edge of the brick gate may indicate stairs leading to the top of the wall. The opening in the gate is only 2.8 metres wide, just large enough to allow one ox cart at a time to pass into or out of the city. The top of the gate was probably covered and may have had rooms or lookout posts, which are commonly depicted in gateways of the historical cities.

Fort as a Resource Centre

The centrality of a fortified settlement, the nucleus of a politically administered territory in the hegemonic conflicts of the Harappan middle bronze age can hardly be over emphasised. The degeneration of interactive and interdependent urban places, triggered by persistent geo climatic disorders like low precipitation and inadequate fluvial recharge which gave rise to widespread resource crunch in all sectors of production and distribution disrupted the homogeneous and harmonious nature of urban life and created conditions in which every political chief preyed on the resources of another political chief (Nandi, 2009).

The resources controlled by the fort were of two types. One that related to accumulation inside the fort and the other immovable assets outside of it. The goods that found their way into the safe precincts of a walled city comprised grain stores, livestock, precious metal like gold and bronze, ornaments fashioned from gemstones, liquid money like *nick* gold coins, carriages of different types, textiles of diverse nature besides markets and workshops. Most of the time, the goods accumulated inside the fort are summarily described, as wealth (*saubhagā* 3.15.14; *vedanam* 4.30.13; *bhojanāni* 7.5.3; *vājasanim* 3.51.2; *rayim* 1.8.1; *–vasu* 6.47.22,; *rdhas*- 6.47.22; *dhnni* 1.130.7). The details of what this wealth consisted of is also not wanting. A good view of commodities which exchanged hands in the form of gifts offered by the kings or goods purchased in the market is provided by *Dānastuti* passages in different portions of the text. Gifts of gold, gold like objects and gold bars (*hiraṇya piṇdan*) figure in the composition of a Bhārdvāja bard who, in addition to these items, also received from the king Devodāsa, ten horses (*daśa aśvān*), ten treasure troves (*daśa koṣān*), ten costly garments (*daśa vastrā*) and plenty of eatables (a*dhibhozanam*, 6.47.23). In another instance, the poet records the gifts of a hundred gold coins (*sata niṣkān*), forty red horses and ten decorated chariots made by a Sindhian ruler (1.126.2-5). Little wonder, the poets frequently describe the forts as replenished with a hundred enjoyments of life. At one place prayers are offered to Maruts for providing forts with a hundred pleasures of life so that the progeny of Vedic speakers may prosper in the safe abode of these forts (1.166.8). At another place, the bard equates the fire god Agni with a large metal strong fort provided with a hundred pleasures of life so that 'all our people may be well protected and prosperous' (*naḥ śatabhujiḥ mahī āyasī puḥ bhava*-7.15.14).

The assets outside the fort were, however, much more important since these generated whatever was stored inside the fort. The immovable assets were fertile agricultural land, drainage resources, pastures, forests and depending on topography of the territory also hills and coastal colonies. Besides, trade routes traversed by caravaneers with different types of merchandise also constituted an important source of the fort's accumulation. Scholars adept at ignoring information which is at odds with their notional ideas can hardly observe that in most cases of *pur* encounter, the fort is captured together with its surrounding land and drainage-related water bodies. In other words the capture of a fort meant the capture of political territory controlled by it. Depending on the bardic diction particularly metrical arrangement of the stanzas, different terms are used in different portions to denote land and drainage resources. In one instance (1.131.4), the raiding chief subdued (*śāsaḥ*) the non-sacrificing (*ayajyum*) master of the fort and snatched away (*amuṣāḥ*) from him or took possession of vast stretches of land (*mahī pṛthvī*) and water courses (*imāḥ apaḥ*). Another stanza (1.189.2), which is a prayer to the fire god Agni expresses a fervent desire for widespread territory and multiple forts blessed with happiness and to be enjoyed for generations together. The term *pṛthvī* means a political territory and the fort the nucleus of political authority in that region.

REFERENCES

1. Dupree: 1963:: Dupree, Louis, "Deh Morasi Ghundai: a Chalcolithic site in south-central Afghanistan", *Anthropological Papers of the American Museum of Natural History* 50: 59-135.
2. Fairservis, 1971::Fairservis, Walter, *The Roots of Ancient India, The Archaeology of Early Indian Civilisation,* The Macmillan Company, Toronto, Onatario, 1971.
3. Kenoyer,1998:: Kenoyer, Jonathan Mark, *Ancient Cities of the Indus Valley Civilisation,* American Institute of Pakistan Studies, Oxford University Press, Bangalore and Islamabad, 1988.
4. Marshall, 1931:: Marshall, Sir John, *Mohenjo-daro and the Indus Civilisation,* London: Arthur Probsthain.
5. Macdonell and Keith, 1912:: Macdonell A.A. and Keith, A.B., *The Vedic Index of Names and Subjects,* First Edition, London, 1912, Reprint, Motilal

Banarsidass Publishers, Delhi, 1958, 1967, 1982.

6. Nandi, 2001:: Nandi, R.N., *Aryans Revisited,* Munshiram Manoharlal, New Delhi, 2001, p. 54.
7. Nandi, 2009:: Nandi, R.N., *Ideology and Environment: Situating the Origin of Vedic Culture,* Aakar, Delhi, 2009.
8. Parpolla:: Parpola, Asko, "The Coming of the Aryans to Iran and India..." in *International Journal of Dravidian Linguistics,* Vol. XVII, No. 2, p. 112.
9. Rau, 1973:: Rau, Whilhelm, "The Meaning of *pur* in Vedic Literature" (*Abundlungen der Marburger Gelehrten Gesellchaft Jg.* 1973:1) Munchen, 1976. For a summary of Rau's arguments see Asko Parpola, "The Coming of the Aryans to Iran and India..." in *International Journal of Dravidian Linguistics,* Vol. XVII, No. 2, p. 112.
10. Rau, 1976, 6:: Rau, Whilhelm, "The Meaning of *Pur* in Vedic Literature"*Abhandlungen der Marburger Gelehrten Gesellschaft*, III/1 Muenchen : W. Finck 1976; Witzel, 2001, 53:: Witzel, Michel, "Autochthonous Aryans? The Evidence from Old Indian and Iranian Texts", *Electronic Journal of Vedic Studies,* Vol. 7, Issue 3 (May 25), 2001, pp. 1-105.
11. Shaffer, 1984:: Shaffer, Jim G., "Bronze Age Iron from Afghanistan: Its Implications for South Asian Protohistory" in *Studies in the Archaeology and Palaeoanthropology of South Asia,* Kenneth A.R. Kennedy and Gregory L. Possehl (eds.), Oxford and IBH Publishing Co., New Delhi, Bombay, Calcutta, American Institute of Indian Studies, 1984.
12. Sthuhrmann,2008, 1-2:: Sthuhrmann, Rainer, 'Revedisch Pur' *Electronic Journal Vedic Studies,* Vol. 15, Issue 1, 2008, pp. 1-42
13. Witzel, 1999, 96:: Witzel, Michel, "Substrate Languages in Old Indo-Aryan", *Electronic Journal of Vedic Studies,* Vol. 5, Issue 1, September, 1995.

8

The Rise, Development and Ramifications of the Rama Hvastra Cult in the *Zend-Avesta*

S.C. Mishra

The present paper is a small attempt in the direction of analysis and determination of the origin, development and ramifications of the Rama Hvastra cult gleaned from the study of thirty-four references to this deity and its variants, interspersed in the *Zend-Avesta**, 'The Commentary on Law'. These references are found strewn over different sections of the book in the form of invocations, recitations of prayers, offer of sacrifices and performance of various rituals practised over a period of time by the votaries of the deity, beginning from the period of the first compositions of hymns in 1500 BC to the period of final redaction in the 4th century.

1. From Reference to the Context

Of these variants, the name of deity Rama Hvastra occurs fourteen times. Rama Hvastra is invoked fourteen times, whereas Rama is invoked only once. There are two captions of prayers in the name of 'Ram' and 'Ram Yast'. In addition to these, there occurs another name, constituted by the name of this deity, i.e. Bahram, with 'Bah' prefixed before Ram. The name 'Bahram' also forms the title of some invocations occurring at three places, two in the chapter called Sirozah and one in a Yast, called 'Bahram Yast'.[1]

As regards the section-wise provenance of the name, or its variants in the book, it may be enumerated as follows. There are, in all, six prayers invoking Rama Hvastra in Sirozah I and II (each day's prayers of 30 days in a month), two under each captions— Murdad, Mihir and Ram. The same deity, i.e. Rama Hvastra, is envoked in eight Yasts (worships), one in Bahman Yast.33, covered under the Ormazd Yast[2], two in Haptan Yast.4 and 9[3], two in Mihir Yast.X and XXXV.144[4], one in Ram Yast.XI.58[5] and one in Afrin Paighambar Zaratust Yast.7[6]. There are in all nine references in invocations, offering sacrificial worship to Rama Hvastra in different

Yasnas. Of these, mention can be made of Yasna numbers I.3[7], II.3[8], III.5[9], VI.2[10], VII.5[11], XVI.4[12], XXII.20[13], XXV.4[14] and LXVIII.15[15], all chanting sacrificial worship to Raman Hvastra. Raman Hvastra is invoked with ceremonial prayers twice in the Visparads (collection of litanies for sacrifice), once in Visparad (in prayers to the Lord of Rituals)I.7[16] and again in the Visparad II.9.[17] The same deity Raman Hvastara occurs thrice in different Gahs (prayers in different 5 divisions of the day). He is worshipped three times in the Gah Havani (prayers offered between 6 to 10 am), the first in Gah Havani I.2[18], the second, in I.7[19] and the third in I.8.[20]

There is only one instance of prayer offered to the deity Rama proper in Yasna No. XLIX.4 of the Gatha Spenta Mainyu (Reserves and Hopes. Honour to Frashaostra and Other Chiefs).[21] Prayers to Rama Havastra have also been recited twice in the 21st caption of 'Ram' covered under Sirozah I and II.[22] Similarly, prayers and sacrifices offered to Verethraghna are recorded at two places under the captions of Bahram' in Sirozah I and II.[23] At another place in Yasna XLVIII (Anticipated Struggles and Prayers for Champions and Defenders) the employment of the word 'Ramam' in the sense of 'quiet is found. In this invocation, the deity Armaiti is called upon to provide home and pastures to the men cultivating meadows. In the next breath a question is raised in the hymn as to who shall give them 'quiet' from the cruel men of evil life and faith[24]. In this regard the remarks of S. Insler are noteworthy, who says that the form *Ramam* has penetrated into this passage under the influence of another Yasna (29.10b). He further observes that the same mistake is repeated in Yasna No. 49.4a, where the last word of the phrase '*ramemca*', also falsely stands in place of orig. *remem*[25]. Notwithstanding this differentiation, it appears a little odd and embarrassing to accept the reading and meaning of the word, which is not in the MSS., unless it is supported by variable readings and cogent meanings.

2. Objectives and Methods

However, in order to discern and trace the beginning, growth, spread and ramifications of the Rama Hvastra cult, it becomes imperative to analyse threadbare the gradual transitions in respect of up or downward movements not only of the central deity under discussion but also of those deities providing some clues to pinpoint their malevolence, benevolence, popularity and course of development. Hence, viewed from these perspectives there are three deities that surround the centre stage in the evolvment of our focal deity and fall under the ambit. Among them, the names of four prominent deities—Rama Hvastra with all his manifestations and variants, Mithra, Vayu and Verethraghna are remarkable for playing important roles in discerning the rise and development of the cult and revealing the directions, fall out benchmarks of their trails.

3. The Genesis and Development of the Rama Hvastra Cult

If one takes a full view of various references to this deity and its variants, one notices various stages in the origin and development of the Rama Hvastra cult and /or its variants. The first stage noticed in the text, comes out from the very title 'Ram', used both in Sirozah I and II, wherein Rama Hvastara is invoked and offered sacrifices.[26] Similar invocations to 'Rama Hvastra' is made under the title of 'Murdad', both in Sirozah I and II.[27]

3.I. Presiding Deity of a Day in a Month

The word 'Sirozah' means 'thirty days' of a month, or which the same numbers of prayers are composed for address to several gods, who preside over each day of a month.

3.II. Semitic and Assyrian Origin of the Practice

It is held that the attribution of each day of the thirty days of a month to certain gods seems to be borrowed from the Semites. The tablets found in the library of Assurbanipal contain an Assyrian Sirozah, that is, a complete list of the Assyrian gods that preside over the thirty days of the month.[28] The continuation of the practice of addressing prayers of each day to a particular deity in the *Avesta* may be a result of the cultural contacts and extension of the boundaries of the people in the Assyrian region.

3.III. Growth in Stature as an Associate of Mithra, the Lord of Wide Pastures

It is clear from the analysis of the prayers dedicated to Rama Hvastra that this deity is invoked in the company of Mithra, who is consistently given the epithet, 'Lord of the Wide Pastures' almost in all prayers. Besides the invocations made in 'Murdad' in Sirozah I and II[29] and also in Haptan Yast.4 and 9[30] recite prayers not only Mithra, the 'Lord of the Wide Pastures', but also to fatness and flocks, plentifulness of corns, and the white Haoma made by Mazda.

3.IV. Pastoral-cum-Agricultural Growth

An analysis, of these identical invocations made elsewhere also in the text[31], shows that the priest is invoking these deities to ensure continuous supply of flocks (of cattle), agrarian corns, drinks and other articles of daily needs deemed essential in his life. The pastoral origin of the deity is also testified by his epithet Hvastra, which means originally 'the god of the resting-place with good pastures[32] or Lord of good pastures'.[33] Keeping in view the meaning of the word, Hvastra as the 'Lord of the pastures', attached to Rama, seeing the association of Mithra, the Lord of pastures, with Rama Hvastra and the recurrence of repeated invocations of priests in hymns for ensuring pastoral and agrarian supply of articles of needs to the deities, the pastoral-cum-agrarian origins of this deity hold good.

4. Growth and Course of Rama Hvastra's Journey under the Shadow of Mithra

The association between Hvastra and Mithra seems to have continued unabated until the hey day and alter the decline of the latter. Mithra, starting from being a deity of pasture land rose to acquire independent position of being a *Yajata,* receiving prayers in his own name and became popular as a deity of a thousand ears and ten thousand eyes. There are at least ten places[34] where the three formulaic epithets of great consequence are used for Mithra in the prayers. The three epithets when read together mean: To Mithra, the Lord of Wide Pastures, who has a thousand ears and ten thousand eyes, a god invoked by his own name; to Rama Hvastra.[35] It is clear from the extract of the above hymn and the others from the different references that the deity of the pastures, Mithra attains a status of independent worship as *yajata* and extends his command over and extensive area where he operates through numerous spies.[36] In course of time, he seems to have surpassed others and reached the pinnacle of glory.

4.I. Mithra at the Meridian of Glory as Sun (Mihir) in the Company of Rama Hvastra

The god, sitting pretty in his house at the summit of Mt. Hraberezaiti, traversed through various stages. At one stage, known to be 'heavenly light', he is acclaimed highly for his numerous attainments in the Mihir Yast. Being a chief in the assemblies, a recipient of sacrifices from the chiefs of nations, the breaker of the skulls of Daevas, he, later surveyed the whole material world by many, he is laden with armours and weapons of various descriptions and the climax of his glory became god of the sun, known in Persian as 'Mihir'.[37]

4.I.A. Towering of Rama Hvastra and Eclipse of Mithra, the Sun (Mihir) by Vayu

That the deity Mithra seems to have been relegated in the background and supplanted later by another most powerful deity in the company of Rama Hvastra, may be noted from the lines of the prayers, which recited the hymns both in the honour of Mithra and Vayu. There is a remarkable decrease in the praise of Mithra. The transitions may be noted in the gradual weakening and drifting away of Mithra from the company of Rama Hvastra in Yasna nos. XVI.4[38] and XXV.4[39]. Yasna no. XXII.20[40] makes the transition explicit, when Rama Hvastra is praised both with Mithra and Vayu, but more predominance and attention is given to the praise of Vayu.

4.II. Rama Hvastra Associate of Ferocious and Destructive Deity 'Vayu'

A formulaic invocation to this deity reads: To Rama Hvastra, to Vayu, who works highly and is more powerful to destroy than all other creatures.[41] In this invocation, which was repeated by a large number of verses, the deity appears to be lofty but ferocious. The destructive and awesome ferocity of the deity does not corrupt Rama Hvasta at all, but surely this association must have given him a frightful aura. Hence, this stage of his association with Vayu should shed off ferociousness and induction of benevolence in him (Vayu), when he is described as bountiful.[42] The eclipse of the sun, Mithra was brought about by Vayu.

4.III. Vayu at its Zenith with Rama Hvastra in Ram Yast

The climax of his power, authority, association with Rama Hvastra, and popularity may be gauged in the Yast dedicated to Rama, as 'Ram Yast',[43] which consists of invocations offered by such celebrities as Ahura Mazda, Haoshyangha, Takhma, Urupa, Yim, Azi Dahaka, Thraetaona, Keresaspa, Aurvasava, Hutaosa and Iranian maids.[44] Vayu, the greatest of the great, blesses the sacrifice and makes invocation unto the strength and vigour of Rama Hvastra.[45] As he pushed back Mithra in the background and took control of the two worlds, he very rightly seems to have called himself, an 'over taker'.[46] He is said to have found out the glory (*hvareno*).[47] His other name, as claimed by him, is Burning.[48] There are certain hymns where Rama Hvastra is without the company of Vayu.[49] By and large, Vayu seems to have remained ferocious except in the 'Ram Yast', where there occurs tremendous changes in its profile. When pleased, he grants boons to such celebrities as Ahur Mazda to conquer all Devas, men, Yatus and Pairikas; and to Yima (yama) by fulfilling his prayer to make men and animals without death waters and plants never dying and the food supply never falling short. But he flatly refused Azi Dahaka the grant of a boon. Viewed from the point of time, Mithra worship in the *Avesta* existed before the Gathic period, i.e. prior to the first composition of the text and fell into neglect during the Gathic period.[50]

5. Other Stages in the Development of Rama Hvastra Cult

So far we have seen that the deity Rama Hvastra has passed through five stages of his development. (1) Starting from his Semitic and Assyrian origins, where he was worshipped as a presiding deity of the day (2) He continued to remain a presiding deity of a day in the *Zend-Avesta* (3) With his association with Mithra, he became a pastoral deity and acted in unison with him as a subordinate deity (4) With the pastoral growth of Mithra's power, he becomes pastoral-cum-agricultural deity (5) Must have obtained frightful aura of ferocity in association with and emerging deity, Vayu. Besides these, he seems to have travelled through five more stages of his developments, which may be enumerated as under: (6) Kept on acquiring independent ascending ritual status among the three and thirty-three deities of the ritual order[51] (7) In the company of Wrath, the demon of Rapine, he sheds the title 'Hvastra' to remain Ramaq and is bracketed in the company of Daevas. Indeed, a very crucial stage in the development of the cult.[52] (8) A change towards benevolence- becomes a deity known for his fullness of welfare[53] (9) Turns into the granter of boons and blessings[54] (perhaps bolstered by Vayu) (10) Becomes provider of abodes and houses to the priests and Mazdayasnian villages[55] (11) Later, he emerges as a-deity, who provides provinces, good health and healing.[56]

NOTES AND REFERENCES

* The three volumes of the *Zend-Avesta* published under *The Sacred Books of the East Series,* ed. F. Max Mueller have been used for texts and translations. *The Zend-Avesta,* part I, *The Vendidad,* translated by James Darmesteter, reprint Delhi, 2005; part II (*The Seriozah, Yasta and Nyayis*), translated by James Darmesteter, reprint Delhi, 207; Part III, *The Yasna, Visparad, Afrinagan, Gahs and Miscellaneous Fragments,* translated by L.H. Mills, reprint Delhi, 2000.

1. The deity Bahram called the genius of victory and equated with Verethraghna, probably a recalcitrant and departed son of Indra and his wife Shachi (Indrani), known also as Vrsakapi in the *Rgveda,* who in many ways challenged and surpassed his parents, leading ultimately to the unfurling of the standards of revolt and hoisting his supremacy as one of the greatest deities in the lands of the *Zend-Avesta.* As a sequel the expulsion of his parents, especially Indra from the very lands and religious folds of Ahur Mazda gave a further fillip to Verethraghna. In the invocation recited in his name, he obliquely dubs his own brought out by the *Rgveda* also. But Verethraghna's ten incarnations—those of a wind, a bull, a horse, a camel, a boar, a youth, a raven, a ram, a buck and at last as a man, in which he appeared to Ahur Mazda, exalt him as the forerunner and harbinger of providing the seeds and a platform of furtherance of the 'ten incarnations (*dasavatar*) theory in India.
2. F. Max Mueller, *The Zend-Avesta,* part II (The Sirozahs, Yasts and Nyayis), translated by Series Editor, reprint, Delhi, 2007, p. 34.
3. Ibid., pp. 37-8.
4. Ibid., pp. 19, 157-8.
5. Ibid., pp. 262-3.
6. Ibid., p. 327.
7. *The Zend-Avesta,* Part III (The Yasna, Visparad, Afrinagan, Gahi and Miscellaneous Fragments), translated by L.H.Hills, published under *The Sacred Books of the East Series,* Editor: F. Max Mueller, Reprint, Delhi, 2007, p. 196.

8. Ibid., p. 204.
9. Ibid., p. 209.
10. Ibid., p. 219.
11. Ibid., p. 223.
12. Ibid., p. 256.
13. Ibid., p. 271.
14. Ibid., p. 276.
15. Ibid., p. 323.
16. Ibid., p. 337.
17. Ibid.
18. Ibid., p. 380.
19. Ibid., p. 380.
20. Ibid., pp. 380-1.
21. *The Zend-Avesta,* Part-III, pp. 163-4. S. Insler says that the MSS. has *ramemca,* yet he translates the line in the passage thus: 'Those who, with ill will have increased fury and cruelty (for the cow)...' Final *ramemeca* should be amended to *ramemca.* cited in *The Gathas of Zarathustra* by S. Insler, published under *Acta Inranica* Tropisieme Series, Textes Et Memoires, Volume 1, Bibliotheque Pahlavi Tehfan-Liege, 1975, Yasna 49.4, p. 298.
22. *The Zend-Avesta,* Part II, pp. 10, 18.
23. Ibid., pp. 10, 17.
24. Ibid., Part-III, p.159. See also f.n. 3, where it is mentioned that "the Pahlavi sees in ramam enforced quiet not 'from' but 'to' the wicked, who shall deal the finishing blow to the wicked."
25. *The Gathas of Zarathustra,* vol. I by S. Insler, published under *Acta Iranica's* Troisieme Series Textes Et Memoires Biblotheque Phalavi, Tehfran-Liege, 1975, pp. 291-2.
26. *The Zend-Avesta,* Part II, pp.10 and 18, at Sl. Nos. 21.
27. Ibid.
28. Ibid., p. 3.
29. Ibid., pp. 5-4.
30. Ibid., pp. 36-8.
31. "We sacrifice unto Ameretat, the Amesha-Spenta: we sacrifice unto fatness and flocks; we sacrifice unto the plenty of corn; we sacrifice unto the powerful Gaokerna, made by Mazda" (From 7. Murdad, Sirozah II, Pt.II, p. 14.).
32. *The Zend-Avesta,* Part-I (*The Vendidad*), translated by James Darmesteter, reprint, Delhi, 2005, p. lxiv, introd. iv.
33. The *Zend-Avesta,* Part II, p. 88.
34. 16.Mihir; Sirozah I (p. 9; Part ii); 16.Mihir; Sirozah II (p.17; Pt. II); Mihir Yast. X (Ibid., p. 119); Mihir Yast.xxxv.144 (Ibid. p. 158); Yasna I. 3 (Part III, p. 196); Yasna II.3 (Pt III, p.204); Yasna III. 5(Part III, p. 209); Yasna VI.2 (Part III, p. 219); Yasna VII. 5(Part III, p. 223); Gah Havan I (Part III, p. 379).
35. *The Zend-Avesta,* Pt. II, 16. Mihir, Sirozah I, p. 9.
36. Ibid., pp. 125-6, 130-1, 134.
37. *The Zend-Avesta,* Part I, *The Vedidad,* translated by James Darmesteter, published under *The Sacred Books of the East* Series, Introduction, IV (f.n.

1, p. 1xi. For his extensive authority, nature and praise, see the details in 'Mihir Yast', part II.).

38. Part III, p. 256.
39. Ibid., p. 276.
40. Ibid.
41. From 21. Ram, Sirozah I and II, pp. 10 and 18 of Part II.
42. *The Zend-Avesta,* XVI.4.
43. *The Zend-Avesta,* Part II, pp. 249-63.
44. Ibid.
45. Ibid., p. 262.
46. Ibid., p. 259.
47. Ibid.
48. Ibid., p. 260.
49. Ibid. Yast. XXIII. Afrin Paighambar Zarathust, Part III, p. 327; Yasna. LXVIII.15, Part-III, p. 323.
50. *The Zend-Avesta,* Part III, p. XXX.
51. In Sirozah 1st Rama Havastra is placed at 16th place in the ritual order of the 33 deities, in Yasna 1.3 at 15th place in Yasna II at seventh, in Yasna III.5 at sixth, in Yasna VI at seventh, in Yasna 7.5 at 5, in Yasna XVI.4 at 113th with bounteous wind, in Yasna XXII.20 at 3rd, in Yasna LXVIII.15 at 1st, in Gah Havan I at eighth place, in Gah Havan.8 at 3rd place and so on.
52. (Yasna XLIX.4) from the Gatha spenta Mainu, Part III, pp. 163-4. Where the deity is called Rama and is in the company of wrath, the demon of Rapine and is bracketed with Daevas.
53. In Yast no. XXIII. Afrin Paighambar Zarathust Yast, Part II, p. 327, Zarathustra spake unto King Vistasp Mayest thou have fullness of welfare like Rama Hvastra. Here the deity is in complete isolation of both Mithra and Vayu.
54. Visparad II.9, Part III, p. 340.
55. The *Zaotar* seeks benediction for a safe abode for a joyful and a long abode for dwellers in his village for every Mazda Yasnian village and succour, see f.n. 56 below.
56. Raman Hvastra prayed for the Province and for healthfulness and healing by the *Zaotar.* See Yasna LXVIII.15, Part III, p. 323.

9

Rgvedic Saraswati: The Problem of Identification

R.K. Sharma

The *Rgveda* makes reference to a number of rivers but it is Saraswati to which greatest attention has been paid in the work. As many as three entire hymns of the *Ṛgveda*[1] in addition to several of scattered passages have been devoted to the river. The river is said to be first born and foremost among the rivers[2], rich in wealth[3] and mighty (*Maho arnah*), she shines on earth as if by her holy deeds.[4] By her might the river breaks the hills and fells trees even though they stand far away from her banks (*Paravataghni*).[5] She is mother of all other rivers (*Sindhumata*)[6], auspicious[7], and beauteous.[8] She is dear protection[9] and an impregnable defence for people, for, she is regarded as a fort of iron (*ayasi puh*).[10]

In the *Mahabharata*, the river Saraswati is said to have originated from the roots of the mythical *Plakṣa* tree (*Plakṣaja*)[11]. She split herself into seven streams, viz. Suprabha, Kancanaksi, Visala, Manasahrada (or Manohara or Manorama), Oghavati, Suvenu and Vimaloda. H.C. Ray Chaudhuri suggests the identification of these rivers as follows[12]:

"The Suprabha flows from Pushkara near Ajmer (It is the name of modern Luni or Salt river on its upper course which, with its numerous feeders has its course in the springs of Aravalli), the Kāñcanākṣī in Naimisa to the north-west of Lucknow; the Visala in the Gaya region; the Manorama in the Uttara Kosala; Oghavati in Kurukshetra near Thaneshwar, the Suvenu (or Surenu)near Gangadvara or Haridwar and Vimaloda on the Himalayas."

In the *Mahābhārata* (3.80.118-119), it is said that after the disappearance of Vinasana, Saraswati appears at three places, viz. Camasobheda, Sivobheda and Nagodbheda. A bath in the Saraswati at Camasodbheda is said to bring fruits of the Agniṣṭoma, that in Sovodbheda equals the donation of one thousand cows and that in the Nagodbheda carries one to Nagaloks. The *Mahabharata* also relates the story of the final disappearance of the Saraswati.

Many scholars have advanced theories regarding the identification of river Saraswati. The different theories may be grouped into two categories, viz. 1. Those who believe that Saraswati and Sindhu are identical and 2. Those who advocate that Saraswati was an independent river.

The first view is held by scholars like Roth[13] Grassmann[14], Zimmer[15], Ludwig[16], Waber[17], Oldenberg[18], Hillebrandt[19], Kaegi[20], Z.A. Ragozin[21], Hopkins[22], K.C. Chattopadhyaya.[23] They base their argument on the phonetic similarity between the Iranian river Harahvati or Haraquaiti (modern Helmend) and Saraswati. They argue that Saraswati is the original name of Sindhu. Ragozin thinks that when the Aryans advanced eastward from eastern Iran, settled along the course of the Indus, the memory of Harahvati, where they had stayed long, was fresh and so they gave Indus the same name, i.e. Saraswati (=Harahvati) in perpetuation of the memory of what had been their long home. Hopkins believe that it was really the river Harahvati and not Indus which was lauded as Saraswati. It is only a 'historical transference' that the Aryans started calling Sindhu as Saraswati later.

A very simple objection to this theory is that why was the Sindhu in this case named as Saraswati and not Harahvati itself? The phonetic similarity between *Sa* and *Ha* does not help much in this case. In the entire Vedic literature, the name Harahvati never appears. Moreover, the river Sindhu is separately sung in the Vedic and post-Vedic literature as the supreme river among all the rivers (*AV.* 14.1.43.). She is leader of all the rivers (RV. 10.75.2.). Into her flowed many other rivers (*RV.* 10.75.4.). In *RV*(10.64.9. and 10.75.5.) Sindhu and Saraswati are mentioned separately. Further, *RV* (10.75.5) enumerates the Vedic rivers in their due order, east to west and Saraswati comes after the Ganga and Yamuna and before Sutudri. The theory of Aryan migration has now been seriously questioned on scientific grounds.

The other scholars who believe that the Saraswati has always been an independent river include Max Mueller[24], Macdonell[25] and Keith.[26] A third group of scholars would like to place the origin of the river in the north-eastern part of India. According to Siva Prasad Das Gupta the Saraswati was a very holy river in the hoary past[27], and it originated in the eastern Himalayas in Assam. He refers to the views of two eminent geologists, viz. Pilgrim and Pascoe who termed the Saraswati as the 'Sivalik River' and the 'Indo-Brahma River' respectively.

According to them the Indo-Brahma river flowed from Assam towards the west to the Punjab and in the gulf of the Arabian Sea. In their opinion the present rivers Yamuna, Ganga, and Gandak were then the tributaries of the Indo-Brahma. Das Gupta identified this Indo-Brahma river with Saraswati of Ancient India. Due to the geological river capture process that occurred twice, the Saraswati system collapsed and was cut into pieces and Ganga, Yamuna, Gandak, etc. became independent rivers. Later, Yamuna cut the waters of Saraswati into her own bed, and she herself confluenced with the Ganga at Allahabad, where even today it is believed that Prayag is the confluence of three rivers, Ganga, Yamuna and Saraswati.

Pargiter[28] and Griswold[29] identify ancient Saraswati with the modern Sursuti which flows to the west of Thaneswar between the Yamuna and Sutlej and is joined by a more westerly stream Ghaggar. H.C. Raychaudhuri[30] also agrees with identification of the ancient Saraswati with the present Sarsuti-Ghaggar. According to him the little stream Sarsuti "rises in a depression at the foot of the Siwaliks which fringes the outer Himalayas, and enters the Ambala and Karnal districts of eastern Punjab. It flows past the sacred sites of Kurukshetra including Sthanu *tirtha* (Thaneswar), and Prithudaka (Pehoa) near which it receives a small affluent called Aruna. It is joined by a number of hills like the Linda and the Markand, enters the Patiala territory and unites with a larger stream, the Ghaggar which likewise rises in the Siwaliks." The river loses itself in the northern part of the desert of Rajasthan at some distance from Sirsa. She disappears for a time in the sand near the village Chalaur and reappears at Bhavanipur. At Balchapur she again disappears, but appears again at Bara Khera. At Urninear Pehoa, she is joined by the river Markand and the united stream still bears the name of Saraswati. Ultimately the Saravati joins the Ghaggar which earlier was evidently the lower part of the it.

REFERENCES

1. *Ṛgveda* 6.61; 7.95, 96.
2. Ibid., *7.95.2*
3. Ibid., *1.3.10; 7.96.3.*
4. Ibid., *1.3.12*
5. Ibid., *6.61.2.*
6. Ibid., *7.36.6.*
7. Ibid., *7.96.3.*
8. Ibid., *7.96.2.*
9. Ibid., *7.95.5.*
10. Ibid., *7.95.1.*
11. *Mbh. 3.82.5-6; Vaman P., 23.13; 34.18.*
12. *Science and Culture,* Vol. 8, No. 12, p. 469.
13. *Petersburg Worterbuch* s.v. Saraswaṭi
14. *Worterbuch zum Ṛgveda,* s.v. Saraswati
15. *Altindisch Leben,* 8-10.
16. *Die Mantra Litterature und das alte Indien,* 201-202.

17. *History of Indian Literature,* tr. by J. Mann and T. Zachariae, 1961, 44n.
18. *Ṛgveda, Textkritische and exegetsche Noten,* II, 63.
19. *Vedische Mythologie,* I, 92f.
20. *Der. Rgvedic,* tr. by R. Arrowsmith, 11.
21. *Vedic India,* 2nd ed. 1961, p. 268.
22. *The Religions of India,* 2nd ed., 1970, p. 31.
23. *Jour., Dept. of Letters,* Calcutta University, Vol. XV, 1927, pp. 1-63.
24. *Vedic Hymns, SBE,* Vol. XXXII, pt. I, p. 60.
25. *Vedic Mythology,* p. 87; *History of Sanskrit Literature,* p. 142.
26. *Vedic Index, s.v. Saraswati.*
27. *PAIOC,* XVIII, p. 535-8.
28. Mark, P., tr 57, n. 16.
29. Griswold, H.D., *The Religion of the Ṛgveda,* p. 300.
30. *SC.,* VIII (12), pp. 468-74.

10

Neolithic Culture in the Upper and Central Pennar Basins of Andhra Pradesh: A Regional Analysis

P.C. Venkatasubbaiah

Introduction

Man-land relationship forms an important topic of discussion among social scientists since the second half of the 20th century, especially in the fields of Geography, Anthropology, History and more specifically in Archaeology, as the latter being one of the interdisciplinary subjects in which more emphasis is laid in the reconstruction of past human cultures that measure and explicit different activities performed in a spatio-temporal context. As such, man-nature analysis could be identified into several conceptual phenomena such as geographical determinism, environmental possibilism, cultural determinism, cultural system components (the interleaf of cultural products and environment), etc. In view of the above said conceptual representation of human culture it has been basically viewed that human beings are treated as creatures of environment and their behaviour could be judged in the realm of environmental context. Their growth and development could be traced by the usage of several approaches in studying various activities (socio-economic, religious, etc.) performed in the web of nature in view of understanding the cultural items in a given time period, if possible (for better understanding), through ethnographic analogy. It exemplifies that man could sometimes modify the environment around him. Hence, it is felt, that environmental features alone were not the causative factors for cultural change and man's cultural behaviour is the deciding factor occupying a physiographic unit of a region in view of the development process either at the biological level or cultural level. However, these have been broadly treated as setting limits for the development of cultural phenomena. But explanation for the nonoccurrence of certain cultural items/features/entities, in a particular time period in a specific environment may not necessarily provide adequate information as it formed a part of the cultural system. So, the social scientists have put more stress on investigating the combination of natural and cultural features in order to reconstruct the total history of human cultures as an integrated study of geographical and historical phenomena (Clark 1985).

However, the concept of cultural ecology emerged as a major trend in archaeology enquiry through the adoption of various methodological frames of research from related fields, especially anthropology (Steward 1955; Leslie White 1959; Butzer 1964, 1975, 1982; Evans 1978; Roberts 1987; Anderson 1973), sociology, geography, etc. which ultimately made the archaeologists study the archaeological record (interrelationship of systemic context and archaeological context) through adaptive strategies that reflected in the material culture of past human societies. Another, but very important, concept useful for the archaeological studies being the concept of economic perspectives of human behaviour (Clark 152, 1953, 1974, 1989b; Boserup 1965; Higgs 1972; Brooks 1987), an outcome that influences the beginnings of New Archaeology, in which the archaeological record (the interrelationship of human settlements in a geographical area) is studied through several methods of biological and other related sciences useful in the reconstruction of a complete picture of the life history of extinct human societies and communities (Binford 1972; Bintliff and Gaffeny 1986 and Blintliff and others 1988; Dimbleby 1978; Ucko and Dimbleby 1969; Ucko and others 1972).

Geographically, a region is a unit of landform with all physiographic features possessing the fauna, flora and other modes of life including human beings who are benefited in a tangible way in the process of symbiosis. Human culture, as one of its prime strategies, endeavour for the survival through economic pursuits mostly depended formerly on hunting, gathering and fishing, as the main mode of acquiring food. The stages of Prehistoric cultures with distinctive typo-technology according to their mental ability and necessity either environmentally determined or culturally determined that continued as a subsidiary one in the next stage of revolution according to development of human life hitherto known as the New Stone Age. An inception of new lifestyle through incipient agriculture, pastoralism which include all possible processes of taming animals intends to use the natural resources available within the understanding the regional environment is a prerequisite which may include several factors, i.e. climate, vegetation, soils and other geomorphic agencies. As such a resource area contains certain substantial important natural resources exploited by human groups with a particular technology by balancing all natural factors that determine the mode of life. It is here that the settlement pattern surveyed in the archaeological research created a demand for both new theory and analytical methodology applicable according to data derived from the field work in which the first emphasis has been considered as a decision-making factor which emphasises first the spatial behaviour; second emphasis on the review of a model dealing with the spatial interaction of groups or populations and the third being the aspects of development and operation of regional interaction system, if any.

In India several scholars have significantly contributed their part in studying the archaeological record, through scientific enquiry belonging to different periods of cultural components and mention may be made of such work of Subbarao (1958), Zuener (1950, 1963), Joshi (1955,1970), Joshi et al. (1974), Richards (1933), Thomas (1989), Rajaguru and Ravikorisettar (1987), Dhavalikar (1984, 1989), Rajaguru et al. (1993), Pappu (1974, 1985), Pappu and Deo (1994), Paddayya (1992a, 1992b), Sharma et al. (1983), Misra (1987a, 1989), Murty (1981, 1989), Makkhan Lal (1984), Rajendran (1989), Shinde (1990), Arun Kumar (1985), Baddam (1979), Thomas (1977), Kajale (1979), Korisettar (1980), Deo (1991), Varaprasada Rao (1992), Raju (1981, 1988), and Venkatasubbaiah (1992, 2007), etc. More recently archaeologists are trying to visualise the man-land relationship (for a general concept of man-land relationship see Paddayya 1944: 1-28; Ravi Korisettar and Rajaguru 2002: 243-293). The present paper is one such attempt to study the Neolithic culture in the Upper and Central Pennar Basins of Andhra Pradesh for which the available material culture has been used to glean the relationship of the environment and culture during the 2nd-1st millennium BC. And also to highlight the environmental potential of the region in order to establish man's dependence on them in his quest of suitable habitats and adaptive strategies.

The Area

The physiographic and orographic features of the **Upper Pennar Basin**, the present Anantpur district, is largely similar to that of neighbouring Bellary and Raichur districts of Karnataka and western half of Kurnool district, which is an open plain country with a number of granite hills and hillocks, mostly castellated. The open stretch of land between hills is devoid of a tree, which is to a large extent covered with black cotton soils, and its elevation gradually falls into Pennar valley in the north and north-eastern region but steadily rises afterwards. The southern region has an average elevation of 600 mts, which is the coolest part of the region. Compared to this, the central part is about 330 mts, and the easternmost part is 270 mts. The whole area can be divided into four geographical units, the northern comprising Uravakonda and Gooty taluks and a portion of Tadpartri taluk extensively covered with black cotton soils. Except Muchchukota the range of hills covering the western part, is the main hill rage which is the flat-topped Erramalais binding the north and eastern portions Tadpatri taluk, there are only a few isolated hills (120 mts in height) and the plains of Tadpatri taluk are lower in elevation than any other part of the region. The central unit consisting of Anantpur, Dharmavaram, Kalyanadurgam and Rayadurgam taluks is almost an arid, treeless zone covered largely by poor, stony red soils with isolated patches of black patches of black soils. The general appearance is a level plain but broken to some extent by hills. There are many isolated granite hills and hillocks. The southern unit including Hindupur, Madakasira, Penukonda and Kadiri taluks cover a better variety of red soils and high proportion of reserved forest, which also forms part of the Mysore Plateau sharing a higher elevation, cooler climate, and hence support thick vegetation due to high rainfall. The physiographic character of the Upper Pennar region is an arid, treeless with general poverty of the soil zone which is also covered with isolated peaks and rocky clusters, the main characteristic feature of the region.

Geologically, the whole area is traversed by Archaeans and Dharwars except Tadpatri, Gooty and Anantpur, which are equipped with Kadapa and Kurnool system of rocks. The Archaean group of rocks consists of granites; graniticgneiss containing hornblende epidotemica pegmatite veins supposed to contain diamonds. They also contain hornblende schists composed of gold, schistose and quartz, mica, ferruginous quartzite, hematite, metadiorite, trap dyke of dolerite, diorite and basalt (exploited by the Neolithic population for their edge tools). Compared to this, the Kadapa and Kurnool system consists of lower Kadapa group of rocks comprising quartzite grits, shales, grits with pebble beds and sandy shales which uncomfortably overlay the Archaeans. The dolerite, quartzite and limestone formations consist of chert, quartzite grits, conglomerates, shales containing trap sills, sandstones, limestone, and calcareous tufa and shales. The minerals that occur in the upper Pennar Basin consist of gold, diamond, barites, asbestos, steatite, limestone, abrasives, clay, iron ore and soap stone.

Six distinct varieties of soils, which occur in the upper Pennar Basin, are black clay, black sand, red clay, red loam and red clay, among which red sand soils are most inferior. Black soil is mostly confined to the northern most and northern pockets of the region. However, the red and black mixed soils are fertile. The central part of the north-eastern unit is completely covered with black cotton soil leaving a little part of red soils, particularly, near the hills and along the margins of rivers. The south, south-central portion is covered by fertile red soils and the red soil of inferior variety occurs in the rest of the region. The principal river system is Pennar with important tributaries like the Chitravati, Hagari and China. Tributaries such as the Jyamangali and Kusavati directly fall into Pennar. The other subsidiary rivers are Swarnamukhi, Tadakaleru, Pandamery, Maddalery and Papaghni, which flow into the southern part of the region. Due to its geographical location in the central part of the peninsula, this region is extremely dry due to heated plains and hence experiences scanty rainfall neither benefited by the south-eastern monsoon nor south-western monsoon because of impediments of the high western ghats that make the region agriculturally precarious and hence often passes through draughts. The average annual rainfall is 586 mm. except the southern portion; the region is mostly treeless tamarind, mango, banyan, margosa, babul, ber, wild date but tangedu, kanuga, kusum, maddi, neredu, tortollis, pear, aloes and shrub vegetation. The fauna that occurs in the region consists of species belonging to four classes of mammals, birds, fishes, and reptiles which are also sporadically found.

The Central Pennar Basin, which represents the present Kadapa district can be divided into three geographical units, the north-western plains covering Jammalamadugu, Proddatur, Kamalapuram, Pulivendla and Kadapa taluks which is contiguous to the black cotton plains of Kurnool and Anantapur districts with an elevation of between 500-600 mts. The chain of Erramala hills bound the northern and southern parts. The eastern valley lies between the Velikonda hills and Seshachalam. This region is geologically equipped with the Archean system of rocks comprising crystallines (ranite-gneisses, traps, etc.) and Dharwars (Schists, Quartzites) and the Kadapa-Kurnool system of rocks.

Neolithic Culture of the Upper and Central Pennar Basins: A Regional Analysis

The upper Pennar Basin has been widely occupied by the Neolithic pastoral groups from the adjacent nuclear zone of Southern Neolithic Culture Raichur (Deavaraj and others 1995: 57-74; Allchin 1960: 129; Utnur 2170+-150: Allchin 1961) and Bellary districts of Karnataka, a cultural dispersal in search of pastures and their economic pursuits, areas congenial for occupation in the people's way of life and their domestic livestock. As a result, there are 75 sites (ash mound-cum-habitation) distributed in the northern half of the upper Pennar Basin mostly at the foothill zones where there is surety of spring activity for the supply of water.

The absolute chronology from the excavation of an ash mound and habitational debris at Palavoy, the principal site of the region where four ash mounds are found and one ash mound which has been subjected to excavation gave a carbon date of C.1965+-105 BC. (Rami Reddy 1976:122).

Even though the area has been described as one of the arid and semi-arid dry climate zones of Andhra Pradesh, with scanty rainfall characterised by thorn and scrub forest interspersed with sparse scrub grassland due to the accumulation of water in the form of pools and ponds. There is a possibility of water seepage from the granite hillocks in the form of spring activity especially at the foothill regions with flow of water available throughout the year. Such climatic conditions might have prevailed during the Neolithic period in the region and hence it was a congenial atmosphere for their economic activities, essentially a pastoral one covered with pastures.

The analysis carried out on the fossil soils obtained from excavations at Kupgal, a Neolithic ash mound site in the Bellary district of Karnataka (Majumdar and Rajguru 1966: 54-55) which has a similar settlement location to that of the present area, revealed similar environmental conditions of the present day. On the basis of the evidence of carbonised wood samples from other Neolithic sites, e.g. Kodekal (Zizyphus sp.:Paddayya 1973: 77), Maski (Acacia sp.:Thapar 1957: 140-141) and Hallur (Tectona grandis: Vishnu Mittre 1971:129-130) indicate the prevalence of similar climatic conditions during the 2nd millennium BC. Potholes, which are roughly circular with a diameter of 8 to 20 cms. and depth of 8 to 48 cms., found in the excavations at Palavoy (Floor 8, Fig. 5: Rami Reddy 1976: 115) indicate circular or rectangular plan of houses with mud walls or wattle-and-daub(like that of split bamboo matting plastered with mid cow dung found at Tekkalakota: Nagaraga Rao et al. 1965, Piklihal, Brahmagiri: Wheeler 1948) and bamboo net smeared with cow dung or mud, being kept as a wall, served the purpose of protection from wind, cold and heat. Material obtained through gathering activity such as chaff, grass, etc. might have served as thatch for roofs supported by the posts of Acacia or Dalbergia SP.

The floors were made of soil mixed with sand, plastered with cow dung and the uneven surfaces of floors were filled with materials like reddish murum, silt, rubble, etc. obtained from surroundings. This indicates that the Neolithic populations had a good knowledge of the availability of such resources in the area. Cultivated grains are not obtained from the Palavoy excavations. However, the presence of a large quantity of domestic equipment such as querns, rubbers, grinding stones which helped in the process of grinding, pounding, etc suggests the production of food grains. The seeds of Zizyphus horida (available seasonally in the area even today) recovered from the Palavoy excavations. Its ripe fruits are eaten directly or used in the sauce preparation. Stock rising, an important component of their economy, can be assessed through the animal remains. Animals like buffalo, sheep and goat formed their diet, as there is evidence of charring, cutting, splitting and chopping of the bones. Splitting of long bones was done for the purpose of extraction of marrow and bone tools.

Another specific character of the Neolithic culture flourishing in the

Upper Pennar Basin was the prevalence of massive structure of ash mounds and their occurrence indicate the intensive and periodic cow dung burning places. It has been viewed differently by several authors (for details see Paddayya 1991: 573-626, 2000-2001: 189-225 and 2002: 81-111; Rami Reddy 1977: 193-209 and 1990: 85-99; Sundara 1971c: 308-314). Paddayya's recent investigations show

a. The concentration of ash mounds in the hilly tracts occupied by the Achean granite-gneiss formations, which support plentiful pasture but are ill suited for agricultural purposes on account of poor, sandy soils.
b. Location of sites close to perennial water sources (large and small rivers, ephemeral nullah with year round water pools and natural springs).
c. Availability of large open spaces around ash mounds ideally suited for purposes of human occupations.
d. And the presence of thick and extensive occupation deposit in the open areas.

Paddayya (2006-07: 1-6) rightly points out that the presence of ash mounds represents the very character of the pastoral way of life adapted to granetic terrain. He further treats the ash mound structures as symbolic representations of Neolithic settlements where several daily activities took place. On the basis of field observations he exemplifies that the ash mounds surely constitute an excellent example of adaptation of cattle-dominated pastoral community to a rugged landscape of semi-arid climate and hence stand as the best view in interpreting the process of pastoralism.

There are 45 Neolithic settlements in the central Pennar Basin located mainly on the small streams and local nullahs, confined to an area geographically designated as the north-west plains stretched with black cotton soils. The material culture consists of pottery like coarse red ware, burnished red ware, black-and-red ware, unburnished red ware, grey ware, brown ware, buff ware, all black ware and black and red ware. The last one is Megalithic probably reaching the terminal stage or overlapping phase of the Neolithic-Megalithic period, as the case may be due to its presence mostly in the cist-burials from the present region and perhaps reached these settlements due to cultural contacts or by the adoption of method of manufacture. The pecked and ground tools comprising both edge tools and non-edge tools made on sandstone, quartzite, dolerite and granite useful for domestic and agricultural purposes and blade tool industry belong to short blade industry made of chert, agate, limestone, quartzite and chalcedony. The animal remains (Venkatasubbaiah and others 1992: 55-59) consist of Bos, indicus, Bubalus bubalis, Capra/Ovis, Gallus indicating the process of domestication of cattle, a dominant economic activity along with small numbers of buffalos, sheep and goats in which fowls also formed a part. The plant remains of cereals barley (Hordeum vulgare) and wheat (Triticum spp.), pulses (Horsegram: Macrotyloma unflorum), green gram (Vigna purpureus) and pigeon pea (Cajanus cajan), brown top millet (Brachiaria ramosa), foxtail millet (Setaria verticillata), brachiaria/setaria millet and sawa millet (Echinochloa cf.colona) and other tubers, fruit/nut, (for details see Venkatasubbaiah 2007: 160) formed the subsidiary diet along with the animal diet of both domestic and wild fauna, especially deer.

The evidence of parenchyma cells of plants of tuber and other vegetable variety suggests the collection of naturally available food along with seasonally available fruits and nuts. This activity was supplemented by seasonally engaged fishing activity of aquatic animal foods. The presence of both plants and animal remains suggests the combination of pastoral and agricultural activity of these first settlers of Central Pennar Basin. But the variety of plants indicates mixed farming depending on monsoon rainfall in which cattle not only played a role in agricultural activity but also in transporting people and things in a network of settlements. This view is supported by the absence of ash mounds when compared to the adjacent granite terrain area of the Upper Pennar Basin. As such, cow dung might have been put into use in manuring fields and for several domestic purposes. Hence, the tradition of burning cow-dung on the intensively made platforms as noticed at Palavoy (author's personal observation in the general survey along with Paddyya in 1994) practically ceased.

The raw material, necessary for the manufacture of pecked and ground stone tools (both edge and non-edge) and blade tools, were available at the out crops of dolerite formations and Neolithic populations exploited the same for making tools thereof and brought the ungrounded and polished ones to their settlements as there are no indications of grinding groves. Hence, in the granite terrains such workshops can be seen at these outcrops. However, if the raw material availability exceeded their exploitation territory, it was carried to the settlements, either by obtaining rough shapes after processing the first two stages of manufacturing such as flaking and pecking. The finished tools were obtained after processing them at the settlements through grinding and polishing methods or kept in reserve and were processed whenever the tools were required. As such, large amounts of dolerite flakes are noticed at the sites of the central Pennar Basin. It is clear from this assumption that the Neolithic groups not merely explored and exploited the life sustaining resources from the region surround their settlements.

The socio-cultural and economic groups of agro-pastoral and pastoral-cum-agriculturists inhabiting the Upper and central Pennar Basins can be visualised through an ecosystem concept of offering two different traditions such as the ash mound tradition and the non-ash mound tradition even though they differ in spatio-temporal features. As such, they were engaged in different economic activities such as pottery, stone tool and bone tool manufacturing. This suggests a strong social structure inter-linked with division of labour within a single settlement or between settlements. Their transhumance activity range would have been made possible in knowing their territories, better economic exploitation in connection with cattle, sheep/goat pastoralism as well as incipient agriculture. However, the necessary advancement in dry farming activities in which seasonality played a dominant role in the semi-arid climate had perhaps occurred due to cultural congregations prevailing in many parts of Southern Deccan. This had been possible only when a change occurred within a culture in pursuit of large-scale effects of secondary product revolution in creating new forms of subsistence economy and its effect on the texture of social relations. However, the black painting represented on the red ware was an outcome of a dominant feature identified as a regional variant and hence did not form a separate cultural entity in the whole complex of southern Neolithic culture.

REFERENCES

1. Allchin, F.R. 1960. *Piklihal Excavation.* Andhra Pradesh Government Publications Archaeological Series No.1: Hyderabad.
2. Allchin, F.R. 1961 *Utnur Excavations.* Andhra Pradesh Government Publications Archaeological Series No.5: Hyderabad.
3. Anderson, J.N. 1973. *Ecological Anthropology and Anthropological Ecology, in Handbook of Social and Cultural Anthroplogy* (J.J. Honigmann ed.), pp. 143-78. Chicago: Rand McNally.
4. Andrew Sherrat, Plough and Pastoralism: Aspects of the Secondary Products Revolution, in *Patterns of the Past: Studies in Honour of David Clark* (Ian Hodder. ed.), pp. 261-305. Cambridge University Press.
5. Arun Kumar, 1985. Quaternary Studies of the Upper Godavari Valley (A Study in Environmental Archaeology),Ph.D. Dissertation, Pune: University of Poona.
6. Badam, G.L. 1979. *Pleistocene Fauna of India.* Poona: Deccan College.
7. Binford, L.R. 1972. *An Archaeological Perspective.* New York: Seminar Press.
8. Blintliff, J.L. and C.F.Gaffeny (eds.), 1986. *Archaeology at the Interface: Studies in Archaeology's Relationships with History, Geography, Biology and Physical Sciences.* Oxford: B.A.R. International Series.
9. Blintliff, J.L., Donald A. Davidson and Eric G. Grant. (eds.) 1988. *Conceptual Issues in Environment Archaeology.* Edinburgh: Edinburgh University Press.
10. Boserup, Elster 1965. *The Conditions of Agricultural Growth: The Economics of Agrarian Change Under Population Pressure.* London: Allen and Unwin.
11. Brooks, B.K. 1987. *Landscape Archaeology, in Landscape and Culture: Geographical and Archaeological Perspectives* (J.M. Wagstaff ed.), pp. 77-95. Oxford: Basil Blackwell.

12. Butzer, K.W. 1964. *Environment and Archaeology: An Introduction to Pleistocene Geography*. Chicago: Aldine.
13. Butzer, K.W. 1975. 'The Ecological Approach to Prehistory: Are We Really Trying?' *American Antiquity* 40:106-111.
14. Butzer, K.W. 1982. *Archaeology as Human Ecology*. Cambridge: Cambridge University Press.
15. Clark, J.G.D. 1952. *Prehistoric Europe: The Economic Basis*. London: Methuen.
16. Clark, J.G.D. 1953. The Economic Approach to Prehistory. *Proceedings of the British Academy* 39:215-238.
17. Clark, J.G.D. 1989b. *Economic Prehistory: Papers on Archaeology*. Cambridge: Çambridge University Press.
18. Clark, Stuart. 1985. The Annales Historians in the Return of Grand Theory in the Human Sciences (Q. Skinner Ed.), pp. 177-98.Cambridge: Cambridge University Press.
19. Deo, S.G. 1991. Geomorphic Study of Palaeolithic Settlements in the Ghataprabha Basin, Karnataka. Ph.D.Dissertation. Pune: University of Poona.
20. Dhavalilkar, M.K. 1984. Towards an Ecological Model for Chalcolithic Cultures of Central and Western India, *Journal of Anthropological Archaeology* 3: 133-58.
21. Dhavalilkar, M.K. 1989. *Farming to Pastoralism: Effects of Climatic Change in the Deccan, in the Walking Larder: Patterns of Domestication, Pastoralism and Predation* (J.Clutton-Brock ed.), pp. 156-68. London: Unwin Hyman.
22. Dimbleby, G.W. 1978. *Plants and Archaeology*. London: John Baker.
23. Evans, J.G. 1978. *An Introduction to Environmental Archaeology*. Ithaca: Cornell University Press.
24. Higgs, E.S. (ed.) 1972. *Papers in Economic Prehistory*. Cambridge: Cambridge University Press.
25. Joshi, R.V. 1955. *Pleistocene Studies in the Malaprabha Basin*. Poona: Deccan College and Karnataka University.
26. Joshi, R.V. 1970. The Characteristics of Pleistocene Climatic Events in the Indian Subcontinent: A Land of Monsoon Climate, *Indian Antiquary* (Third Series) 4(1-4): 53-63.
27. Joshi, R.V., S.N. Rajaguru, R.S. Pappu and B.P. Bopardikar. 1974.Quartenary Glaciation and Palaeolithic Sites in the Liddar Valley (Jammu-Kashmir), *World Archaeology* 5(3): 369-379.
28. Kajale, M.D. 1979. Bioarchaeology of the Ghod Valley, Maharashtra. Ph.D. Dissertation. Pune: University of Poona.
29. Korisettar, R. 1980. Prehistory and Geomorphology of the Middle Krishna, Karnataka. Ph.D. Dissertation. Pune: University of Poona.
30. Makkhan Lal 1984. *Settlement History and Rise of Civilisation in the Gange-Yamuna Doab*. New Delhi: B.R. Publishing Corporation.
31. Misra, V.N. 1987. Evolution of the Lnasdscape and Human Adaptation in the Thar Desert, Presidential Address: Anthropology and Archaeology Section, 74th Session of the Indian Science Congress, Bangalore.
32. Misra, V.N. 1989. *Stone Age India: An Ecological Perspective* (Olga Soffer ed.), pp. 99-119. New York: Penum Press.
33. Murty, M.L.K. 1981. Hunter-Gatherer Ecosystems and Archaeological Patterns

of Subsistence Behaviour on the Southeast Coast of India: an Ethonographic Model, *World Archaeology* 13(1): 47-58.

34. Murty, M.L.K. 1989. Pre-Iron Age Settlements in South India, *Man and Environment* 14(1): 65-81.
35. Majumdar, G.G. and S.N. Rajaguru. 1966. *Ashmound Excavations at Kupgal.* Poona: Deccan College.
36. Nagaraja Rao, M.S. and K.C. Malhotra. 1965. *The Stone Age Hill-Dwellers, Tekalakota.* Poona: Deccan College.
37. Narasimhaiah, B. 1983. Excavations at Ramapuram, Kurnool District. *Indian Archaeology; A Review.* 1981-82: 3-7.
38. Paddayya, K. 1973. *Investigations into the Neolithic Culture of the Shorpur Doab, South India.* Leiden: E.J. Brill.
39. Paddayya, K. 1982a. *The Acheulian Cultures of the Hunsgi Valley (Pennisular India): A Settlement System Perspective*, Poona: Deccan College.
40. Paddayya, K. 1982b. Ecological Archaeology and the Ecology of Archaeology, *Bulletin of the Deccan College Research Institute* 41: 130-150.
41. Paddayya, K. 1994. Investigation of Man-Environment Relationships in Indian Archaeology: Some Theoretical Considerations. *Man and Environment* 19 (1-2): 1-28.
42. Paddayya, K., P.K. Thomas and P.P. Jogelekar. 1995. A Neolithic Animal Buthering Floor from Budihal, Gulbarga Distict, Karnataka. *Man and Environment* 20(2): 23-31.
43. Paddayya, K. 2000-2001. The Problem of Ash Mounds of Southern Deccan in the Light of Budihal Excavations, Karnataka. Deccan College Postgraduate and Research Institute, Vol. 60-61: 181-225.
44. Paddayya, K. 2006-207. Symbolic Approaches to the Study of Early Agropastoral Communities of Lower Deccan. *Puratattva* 35: 1-6.
45. Pappu, R.S. 1974. Pleistocene Studies in the Upper Krishna Basin. Poona: Deccan College.
46. Pappu, R.S. 1985. The Geomorphic Setting of Acheulian Sites, in Recent Advances in Indo-Pacific Prehistory (V.N. Misra and Peter Bellwood, eds.), pp. 9-12. New Delhi: Oxford and IBH Publishing Co.
47. Rajaguru, S.N. and R.K. Korisettar. 1987. Quarternary Geomorphic Environment and Cultural Succession in Western India, *Indian Journal of Earth Sciences* 14(3-4): 349-361.
48. Ravi Korisettar and S.N. Rajaguru. 2002. Understanding Man-Land Relationship in Pennisular Deccan: With Special Reference to Karnataka in Indian Archaeology in Retrospect (S. Settar and Ravi Korisettar, eds.), pp. 243-96. '*Archaeology and Historiography*', *History, Theory and Method.* Manohar and ICHR.
49. Ravi Korisettar, P.C. Venkatasubaiah and Dorian Q. Fuller. 2002. "Brahmagiri and Beyond: The Archaeology of the Southern Neolithic" in *Indian Archaeology in Retrospect: 'Prehistory' Archaeology of South Asia* (S. Settar and Ravi Korisettar, eds.), pp. 151-238. Manohar and ICHR.
50. Rajendran, P. 1989. *Preshistoric Culture and Environment: A Case Study of Kerala.* New Delhi: Classical Publishing House.
51. Raju, D.R. 1981. Early Settlement Pattern in Cuddapah District, Andhra Pradesh. Unpublished Ph.D. Dissertation. Poona: University of Poona.

52. Rami Reddy, V. 1968. *Pre and Protohistoric Cultures of Palavoy South India*. Hyderabad: The Government of Andhra Pradesh.
53. Rami Reddy, V. 1977. The Problem of Ash Mounds in South India: A Fresh Look, *The Eastern Anthropologist* 30(2): 193-209.
54. Rami Reddy, V. 1990. Ash Mounds in South India, in *Archaeology in Karnataka* (A. Sundra, ed.), pp. 85-99. Mysore: Directorate of Archaeology and Museums.
55. Richards, F.J. 1933. Geomorphic Factors in Indian Archaeology, *Indian Antiquary* 62: 235-43.
56. Roberts, B.K. 1987. Landscape Archaeology in *Landscape and Culture: Geographical and Archaeological Perspectives* (J.M. Wagstaff, ed.), pp. 77-95. Oxford: Basil Blackwell.
57. Sharma, G.R. and J. Desmond Clark (eds.)1983. *Palaeoenvironment and Prehistory in the Middle Son Valley (Madhya Pradesh, North Central India)*. Allahabad: Abinash Prakashan.
58. Subbarao, B. 1958. *The Personality of India* (2nd Revised Edition). Baroda: M.S. University. First Published in 1956.
59. Sundara, A. 1971. New Discoveries of Ash Mound of North Karnataka: Their Implication, in Professor K.A. Nilakanta Sastri Felicitation Volume (S. Ganesan, S. Rajan, N.S. Sastri Felicitation Committee.)
60. Thapar, B.K. 1957. Maski-1954: *A Chalcolithic Site of the Southern Deccan, Ancient India* 13:140-141.
61. Thomas, P.K. 1989. Utilisation of Domestic Animals in Pre-and Protohistoric India, In the *Walking Larder: Pattern of Domestication, Pastoralism and Predation* (J. Clutton-Brock and C. Grison, eds.), pp. 355-361. Oxford: B.A.R. International Series.
62. Ucko, and G.W. Dimbleby (eds.) 1972. *Man, Settlement and Urbanism.* London: Duckworth.
63. Varaprasada Rao, J.1992. Prehistoric Environment and Archaeology of the Krishna-Tungbhadra Doab, Andhra Pradesh. Ph.D. Dissertation. Pune: University of Poona.
64. Ventakatasubbaiah, P.C., S.J., Pawankar and P.P. Joglekar 1992. Neolithic Faunal Remains from the Central Pennar Basin, Cuddapah District, Andhra Pradesh. *Man and Environment* 17(1):55-59.
65. Venkatasubbaiah, P.C. 1992. Protohistoric Investigations in the Central Pennar Basin, Cuddapah District, Andhra Pradesh. Ph.D. Dissertation. Poona: University of Ponna.
66. Vincent M. LaMotta and Michael B. Schiffer. 201. Behavioural Archaeology: Towards a New Synthesis., In *Archaeological Theory Today.* (Ian Hodder, ed.), Cambridge: Polity Press.
67. Wheeler, R.E.M. 1948. Brahmagiri and Chancdravali 1947: Megalithic and other Cultures in the Chitaldurg District, Mysore State. *Ancient India*, IV, 180-310.
68. Zeuner, F.E. 1950. *Stone Age and Pleistocene Chronology of Gujarat.* Poona: Deccan College.
69. Zeuner, F.E. 1963. *Environment of Early Man with Special Reference to the Tropical Regions.* Baroda: M.S. University.

11

Gender, Class and Caste in Agricultural Production: A Review of Early North Indian Sources

Suvira Jaiswal

Reports on the contemporary agricultural scenario have revealed the crucial involvement of women in crop production both in tribal and non-tribal areas. But in historical studies, particularly those dealing with early Indian history, the role of women in agricultural production is generally seen as being confined to the role of being the 'producers of producers'. It is assumed that reproductive functions and domestic responsibilities forced women to withdraw from the public sphere, which factor ultimately resulted in their subordination and decline in status. But, as has been rightly pointed out[1], the low position of women in the social hierarchy was not because women's share of labour in agricultural production in relation to men became arduous, small or insignificant with the advent of plough-based agriculture but because of the overlapping of the zones of gender oppression and class exploitation. The issues of gender and class are inextricably linked, and it may be easily conceded that class has manifested itself as caste in early India.

Although agriculture was the mainstay of Harappa culture, we can hardly speculate on the structuring of gender and class relations in the production process of this civilisation, until its script is deciphered and more information is available. We have to begin with the *Ṛgveda* and examine carefully the mode or modes of production reflected in it, and analyse the hymns for traces of gender inequality and class formation.

Recently the generally accepted view that the tribes depicted in the *Ṛgveda* were mainly pastoral practising 'a little agriculture on the side' has been contested vehemently, but the textual evidence cited for the purpose mostly consists of late hymns and is often misinterpreted. I have examined this thesis in detail elsewhere.[2] The assertion[3] that the Rgvedic society was an agrarian society in which "the pastoral sector was important because of the requirements of agriculture" and large herds of cattle constituted a kind of 'capital' serving as a means to store "surplus extracted out of agriculture" in the hands of priests and rulers lacks conviction, as it is not explained how agricultural surplus was converted into animal 'capital' and what could have been the mechanism of surplus extraction. A stable surplus producing agricultural society would have a regular mechanism of surplus collection. But *bali* in the *Ṛgveda* is not a tax or even a regular customary tribute. It has to be collected by force from the *vis* (RV VII.6.5) and the defeated tribes (RV VII. 18019.) and therefore the chief is called *balihṛt*. If agriculture was the main basis of the Rgvedic economy, it is strange that the Rgvedic poets pray for gifts of cattle, horses, sheep, women, chariots, gold (VII.66.8), in one hymn (X.117) of the tenth *mandala* even grain but never land. The importance of land as the most precious item of property in an agrarian society can hardly be denied. The argument that land was plentiful and hence not a gift item is convincing, as winning and seizure of fertile lands presumably from the Dasas/Dasyus is mentioned in several hymns. At one place Indra is specifically said to have divided the field among his fair skinned friends killing the Dasyus and the Simyus (1.100.18). It is generally conceded that most of the terms related to agriculture found in the *Ṛgveda* are of non-Indo-European origin and derive from Munda and proto-Dravidian languages. This indicates that the Indo-Aryans learnt and adopted the agricultural practices of the local population with whom they came in contact upon their migration to regions of eastern Afghanistan, Punjab and its surroundings. The discovery of a furrowed field at Aligrama datable to the 11th century BCE[4] does not contradict the generally accepted view that the *Ṛgveda* depicts a pre-urban society evolving from pastoralism dependent on cattle to sedentary plough agriculture.

Changes are reflected not only in the economic but also social sphere. Like many other pastoralists[5] the Rgvedic tribes too had developed two specialist groups, the priests (*Brahmana*) and the warriors-rulers-protectors (*Ksatra*).[6] The priests specialised in rituals, which were supposed to increase the cattle-wealth of the tribe and ensure victory in cattle raids. The *Ksatra* warrior-chiefs carried out cattle-raids and provided protection to their own tribe. No doubt the *Brahma* and the *Ksatra* had superior rank and prestige but these categories were neither closed nor separated by a big gulf from the *vis* commoners who raised cattle and were engaged in producing food. The three functional groups of the Rgvedic tribes are first mentioned together in the eighth book of the *Ṛgveda* (VIII.35.16-18), and the hymn prays for the success of all three groups in their respective roles, but there is no indication of the way these were structured. There is no doubt that the units of social structure were comprised of family, class and tribe in the manner of concentric circles, and a typical patriarchal joint family system was still in a process of evolution. I have shown elsewhere[7] that despite its andocentric bias the *Ṛgveda* contains traces of the autonomy of women at an earlier stage and the embedding of the nuclear family in a wider clan organisation rather than a hierarchical patriarchal joint family. Similarly, the servile category of the Sudras appears only at the end of the Rgvedic phase and is mentioned for the first time in the late Puruṣa-sūkta hymn. The rise of social inequality among the Vedic peoples was simultaneous with the growth of patriarchy.

The important question is: What was the unit of production and of consumption? I have argued[8] that initially the *gṛhapati* or *vispati* among the Ṛgvedic tribes was a leader or head of an extended-kin-group or 'clan' and this was the main functional unit for social as well as economic purposes. The lineal patriarchal joint family emerges only towards the end of the Rgvedic period. The hymn addressed to Vastospati 'the tutelary deity of the site of the house or dwelling place' (*RV* VII.55) confirms this view. It gives a vivid description of the *vāstu* (site) or *harmya* (dwelling place) and tells us that within the *harmya* slept not only the father and mother of the girl but all the kinsmen (*jnatayah*) along with the *vispati*. The picture is that of a nomadic extended kin-group headed by *vispati* living together in the *harmya* and not that of a patrilineal vertically extended family[9]. The term *vis* denoted a 'kin-unit' or a 'settlement', apparently of a kin-unit in the *Ṛgveda,* but in the later Vedic texts it becomes a general designation of the peasantry, the surplus producing class sustaining the privileged elite of the Brāhmaṇas and the Rājanyas. A similar transition in the meaning of the term *gṛha* and *gṛhapati* may be seen with changes in the mode of production. The early nomadic *grhapati* could carry his entire household accoutrement (*garhapatyani*) on 'a cart driven by more than one horse' (*asthuri.* RV VI.15.19), and he headed a kin-unit which was also the unit of production. The term figures prominently in the early Buddhist sources, but in these texts the *gṛhapati* heads a production unit comprising a large patriarchal household, which includes both kin and non-kin members, such as slaves and hired labourers.

It will be useful to look at slavery as a contributory factor in the rise of class and gender inequalities. It has been argued that the notion of 'sale' and 'purchase' among the Indo-Europeans and even among the early Vedic peoples emerged in the context of 'sale' by auction of men, who were taken prisoner in battle or had lost their liberty in gambling and not in the context of merchandise.[10] For example, the 'Gambler's hymn' in the *Ṛgveda* (X.34.4) speaks of the binding and taking away of the gambler as a slave.

Several hymns club together the biped men and the quadruped animals, as if the two constitute a unity. A hymn of the first *mandala* (I.124.1) specifically speaks of god Savita as giving wealth (*artham*) in the form of bipeds (*dvipad*)and quadrupeds (*catuṣpad*). At another place (III.62.14) god Soma is requested to give salutary food to his devotees and their two-footed and four-footed 'tethered animals' ; the term *pasave* included both the two-footed and four-footed ones. Kosambi's thesis that the appropriation of the labour of the defeated Dasas by a particular family group of the tribe gave rise to private property (not yet of the individual, but of the privileged family), postulates a significant role of slavery in the rise of a class society, but his identification of Dasas as 'the descendants of the Indus settlers who had provided surplus for the Indus cities[11]' remains questionable.[12]

Slave labour must have been used not only for heavy domestic work but also for pastoral and agricultural requirements; although clear evidence of large-scale employment of slaves in agriculture in the Gangetic valley comes from the Pali Buddhist sources. Whether it was the land belonging to the *khattiyas* of *ganarajyas* or to the well-to-do *gahapatis* of the kingdoms, large farms worked by the slave and hired labour (*dasa-kammakara*) characterise the economy of the post-Vedic times in the northern regions. The term *gahapati* was applied not to an ordinary householder but to a wealthy entrepreneur, who had his farm cultivated by slaves and hired labour under his direct supervision and his slaves formed an intrinsic part of the patriarchal household. In the *ganarajyas* the *khattiya* landowners preferred the title *raja*, as they wielded political power as well. The *Digha Nikaya* definition of *Khattiya* as 'The lord of the fields' is significant in this context, as land was owned by the *khattiyas* in the *ganarajyas*.[13] Society was now deeply polarised. The ordinary peasant, the Vaisya of later Vedic times, who cultivated his land with his own labour was a simple *kassaka* (Skt. *kṛṣaka*) and was regularly clubbed with Sudra, the *vessa-sudda* compound being of frequent occurrences in the Pali texts. Many *gahapatis* with the surplus accumulated from agriculture turned towards trade and were known as *setthi-gahapatis*. The Buddhist texts speak of the *gahapati* as constituting one of the jewels of the universal king (*cakkavatti*) that shows the importance of this category. He is clearly distinguished from the *khattiyas* and the Brahmanas, although we have references to Brahmana-*gahapatis* too, as many Brahmanas owned large tracts of land and were engaged in the secular occupation of having their lands cultivated with slave and hired labour.[14] Apparently, Pali *gahapati* was a successor of Vedic *grhapati*, of the *vis*, who maintained the *srauta garha+patyagni (gahapatiaggi)*[15], which was the privilege of the srotriya Brahmanas and rich and influential people and is to be distinguished from *grhyagni,* the *smarta* fire, maintained by an individual householder upon getting married and entering *grhasthasrama*, the second stage of life.

Rich *gahapati/grhapati* landowners possessing hundreds of acres of land cultivated by slave and hired labour constituted an important source of revenue to the state in the early centuries preceding and succeeding the Common Era. Their decline and eventual disappearance is to be linked with the growth of intermediaries with a hierarchy of rights over the same piece of land in the late Gupta and post-Gupta times, which is regarded as the early phase of Indian feudalism. But a passage of the *Majjhima Nikkaya* suggests that in the early centuries preceding the Common Era *gahapati* was an important landed proprietor, something like a 'squire'. The text speaks of the *gahapati* Upali of the Balaka village sitting with the *gihiparisayu* (Skt. *Grhi-parisad*), which was the assembly of ordinary peasant householders.[16] A similar impression is given by Kautilya[17], who advises that the Administrator *samahartr* should station spies disguised as *grhapatis* in the villages, to find out the number of fields, houses and families in a village, information about the varna of the families, size of their holdings and total produce. Apparently, a *grhapati* acted like a village headman.[18] In the *Mrcchakatika* of Sudraka (II.14.15) and the *Dasakumaracarita* of Dandin (VIII.208), *grhapatis* figure as village headmen; and a verse of the *Gatha saptasati* of Hala describes the daughter-in-law of a *halika* (ploughman) descending into the waters of the river Godavari by a path 'difficult to traverse' in order to avoid the son of *gahavai* (Skt. *grhapati*) who was standing on the banks of the river.[19] This is perhaps an allusion to the vulnerability of the village women of poor classes before the young men of the elite. However, by the 10th century most of the *grhapatis* were reduced to the position of ordinary cultivators or subordinates with the new class of *ksetrapatis,* the landowning nobility, standing above them, as is shown in the *Mahapurana* of Puspadanta.[20] In the *Nitivakyamrtam* of Samedeva Suri (10th century) *grhapati* is equated with *gramakuta,* a village official.[21]

Side by side the growth of class inequities in which some groups engaged in religious and managerial activities while others were subjected to dependence and varying degrees of exploitation, we also come across evidence of gender discrimination. We have discussed elsewhere[22] the Rgvedic evidence of gradual displacement of women from privileged religious rituals. These tendencies are further accentuated in later Vedic texts. The *Taittiriya Samhita* says that women are not entitled to a share of the Soma drink, 'therefore women are without strength, take no *dāya* (portion) and speak more weakly than even a wretched man'.[23] However, this passage is used by the *Baudhayana Dharma Sutra* and the *Manusmrti* to prescribe the exclusion of women from any share in inheritance.[24]

Govindasvamin, the commentator of Baudhayana, explains that if women were to receive a share of the *dāya* they would become independent.[25] Even the *Satapatha Brahmana,* a text belonging to the latest stratum of Vedic literature, observes that the wives 'neither rule over themselves nor over *dāya* (share of property).[26] Deprivation of women and their dependent state is clearly pronounced in such passages.

Nevertheless, these theoretical formulations may not reflect contemporary social reality in absolute terms or may do so only partially. It is curious that while the mention of god Ksetrapati in three Rgvedic hymns (IV.57; VII.35; X.66) is cited to show the 'growing relevance of cultivable lad to the Rgvedic mode of production'[27], no attention is paid to the mention of ksetrapatni in the *Atharvaveda* (II.21). We may refer to another hymn of the *Atharvaveda* (III.24.6), which speaks of cultivators setting aside three measures of grain for the Gandharvas and four measures of grain for the *grhapatni,* supporting our thesis that the *grhapati* couple had a special position in their extended kin-group or clan, and hence the *grhapatni* was entitled to receive a portion of the produce. Moreover, these pieces of evidence, which relate to 'control' or 'possession' of cultivable fields and agricultural produce, do not seem to be in harmony with the pastoral-patriarchal traditions predominating the early Vedic compositions and may allude to a different cultural origin and growth of a composite society through assimilation of Aryan and non-Aryan elements. It is also possible that these reflect the custom of 'a community of goods between husband and wife; the two being joint owners. Although the Brahmanical law-books generally ignore the issue of 'joint control', a late passage attributed to the *Apastamba Dharma Sutra* and cited in the *Smrti tattva* states, that 'property is joint, or common between spouses' (*dampatayor madhyagam dhanam*)[28]. Nevertheless, mention of only ksetrapatni and *grhapatni* in the Atharvavedic hymns is pertinent.

However, women figure only rarely in Vedic hymns and that too mostly by way of a simile or metaphor. Absence of specific information on female personages could be one of the reasons why scholars of ancient India have mainly concentrated on the theoretical and formal dimensions of the position of women. But in actual practice it is plausible that the manner and extent of female participation in the production process of agriculture varied a good deal, and it had a direct relationship to the land rights of the family to which she belonged. Patriarchal framework characterises even the Pali Buddhisht sources, but as these are not always prescriptive but also narrative, we get occasional glimpses of women participating at various levels of agricultural production. Thus the *Vinaya Pitaka* speaks of a woman landowner returning home after having her field sowed (*khettam vapapetva*).[29] Although no woman is specifically called *gahapati* or *grhapatni* in these texts, we may note that in the list of *gahapatis* given in the *gahapati-vagga* section of the Nikayas, a Brahmana woman, Veracchani brahmani, is regularly mentioned.[30] Apparently she was a prominent woman, head of a large household owning and managing agricultural lands. Visakha Migaramata, the granddaughter of *gahapati* Mendaka was another prominent woman, a generous patron of the Buddhist monks. Although there is no mention of her direct involvement in agricultural operations, she is said to have received a dowry of '500 bullock-carts full of agricultural tools and hundreds of slaves[31],' and she was so influential that her advice was sought on disciplinary matters by the Buddhist Sangha.[32] In any case, neither women nor men of the elite classes would have done manual work on their farms. The seclusion of the women of the Ksatriya *varna* had already begun towards the close of the Vedic phase, as indicated by a passage of the *Satapatha Brahmana*.[33]

Kautilya's *Arthasastra* speaks of the employment of slaves and hired labourers on royal farms by Sitadhyaksa, the Superintendent of Agriculture (II.24.2). It is reasonable to suppose that the urban-rural elite, who are described in the *Arthasastra* variously as *paura-janapada* (II.1.16; IV.9.28; XIII.5.19), *pradhana*(I.13.26) and *mahajana* (IX.6.3) and differentiated clearly from the *ksudrakas* (I.13.13;26) and *prakrtis* (VII.5.36), the small, common people, also organised the cultivation of their lands in the same way and paid taxes to the king (*dandakara,* I.13.3).[34] It has been cogently argued[35] that the use of slavery and other forms of dependent labour coexisted along with free labour in the field of agricultural production till the early centuries of the Common Era. We may add that large farms cultivated through hired and slave labour existed in some parts of the country down to the 7th century CE, as according to Lama Taranath, Kumarila Bhaṭṭa owned many rice-fields, five hundred male slaves and five hundred women-slaves and many hundred men' (apparently, *Karmakaras,* hired workers).[36]

Irfan Habib has argued that improvement in agricultural technology, in the first thousand years after Christ made agrarian slave-labour superfluous and favoured peasant production.[37] R.S. Sharma suggests the likelihood of substantial *gahapatis* of the age of the Buddha turning into landlords under feudal conditions in Gupta and post-Gupta times.[38] However, apart from the big landowners, *gahapatis, khattiyas,* etc., the Pali sources also mention ordinary peasants cultivating land by using their own and their family's labour. The *Digha Nikaya* speaks of two *kassaka* "(Skt. *Krsaka,* i.e. farmer) brothers who were struck by lightning while ploughing their field. They died on the spot along with their four oxen[39]. The term *kassaka* seems to have been a neutral term applicable to both small peasants as well as big peasant-proprietors. In a Jataka tale a

Brahmana owning one thousand *Karisas* of land and going out to his fields along with his workmen to supervise ploughing is called a *kassaka-brahmana*.[40] But the Jatakas also describe poor Brahmana cultivators working in their fields assisted by their sons.[41] Not all the Brahmana donees would have received large estates in gift; and fragmentation of landholdings among them would have taken place due to demographic and other factors. However, it is significant that the Brahmana cultivators did not lose their varna identity and were known as *kassaka-brahmanas*.

Wagle cites a passage of the *Majjhima Nikaya*, which explains *kassaka* as 'one who lives by cattle-keeping' (*gorakkham upajivati*), and comments that as both agriculture and cattle-keeping were connected with food-producing activities, the passage has not differentiated between the two vocations.[42] In our opinion, the passage not only indicates close dependence of plough agriculture on cattle-keeping, but also the casual attitude of the elite class, which looked upon those who earned their living by their manual labour involved in cattle-keeping and agriculture as a lowly people belonging to the same class. Hence, the Pali texts regularly club the *vessa* (Skt. vaisya) with the *sudda* (sudra). It is a paradox that the Buddhist sources regard the occupation of agriculture as *ukkattha-karma*.

(Skt. *Utkrsta karma*)[43], i.e. a superior vocation giving it precedence over trade and cattle-herding, but the vaisya peasantry of later Vedic ties is pushed close to the level of sudra.[44] Young men of good families, the *kulaputtas* (Skt. *kulaputra*) had the option to pursue agriculture, trade or cattle-keeping[45] as their occupation without any stigma being attached to them, but the particular varna which was assigned these occupations in the Brahmanical scheme of things is considered low. It is pointed out[46] that the linear order of four varnas of the Brahmanical texts is reduced to a 'simple two-tier system of stratification' in the Buddhist texts with the *khattiya* and the Brahmana constituting the high and the *vessa* and the *sudda* the low strata. It was a deeply polarised society with flagrant social, economic and political disparities. Manual work had low status value[47] but was unavoidable for the majority of the peasantry. Apparently, this led to the splitting of the later Vedic *vis* with those who had greater resources emerging as *gahapatis*. They were differentiated from the mass of the *vessa* peasantry. They belonged to the upper strata and are mentioned together with *khattiyas* and the Brahmanas. In course of time such disparities led to a fundamental change in the perception of the Vaisya identity; and in early medieval times trade rather than agriculture was regarded as the characteristic calling of a Vaisya.[48]

We hardly come across any mention of the tenants or sharecroppers, who took land on lease in return for a certain amount of produce in the early Buddhist texts, such as the Nikayas. However, the Jatakas speak of traders or set this stationed in towns as owning rice-fields[49], and it is likely that these were given on lease to tenant-3rd century CE, although the practice may be traced back to a few centuries earlier. The *Vinaya Pitaka*[50] refers to a *setthi-gahapati* of Rajagrha who was obviously engaged in trade and lived in the city of Rajagrha but must have owned land in the countryside as well and may have given it on lease. Kosambi thinks that the *paura-janapadas* mentioned in the epics and the *Arthasastra* constituted the citizenry of the 'free cities' reported by the Greek writers. These cities were the headquarters of former or current tribal settlements, whose citizens, the *paura-janapada,* headed large patriarchal family groups into which the tribes had split up and which had claims over tribal land. They paid the *rastra* tax to the state and must have leased their lands to *ardhasitika* tenants on half share.[51] The interpretation of *paura-janapada* as upper class citizenry is disputed by Kangle[52], but there is no doubt that with the growth of urbanisation in the centuries just preceding the Common Era, tenancy-cultivation must have come into vogue.

The *Arthasastra* recommends that the countryside (*janapada*) should be settled with Sudra agriculturists (II. 1.2) or those who belong to lower varnas (*avara varna,* VI.1.8). The statement implies low status of those who were directly engaged in agricultural work, although we have no specific information on the varna/caste background of the various categories of persons involved in agricultural production of which this text has quite a hierarchy. Thus we have *ksetrika* or owner-cultivator (III.10.8), *upavasa* or the tenant cultivating land on lease (III.10.8; 16), *ardhasitika,* i.e. one who tilled the land for half the produce (II.24.16; III.11.23; III.13.9) and *dasa* and *karmakara,* slave and hired labourer, working on the crown land under the supervision of the Sitadhyaksa, the Superintendent of Agricultural (II.23.1-2). The *Parasara-smriti* (XI.22) regards *ardhasirin* as caste and enumerates it along with other Sudra castes such as Dasa, Napita (barber) and Gopala (cowherd) from whom a Brahmana could accept food.[53] A subsequent verse (No.25) of the same *smrti* names it as *ardhika,* a mixed caste originating from the union of a Vaisya female and a Brahmana male.

According to Kautilya, a wife was not responsible for the debts incurred by her husband, but he makes an exception to this rule with regard to the wives of the cowherds (*gopala*) and the sharecroppers (*ardhasitikas,* III.11.23). Apparently women of the cowherd and sharecropper families worked jointly along with their husbands in cattle-raising and cultivation processes and had to bear the burden of the indebtedness of their husbands.[54] Rural indebtedness is not exactly a modern phenomenon and Kautilya reflects on the attitude of the dominant classes of the countryside. Women of the *ardhasitika* class could be even pledged apparently to pay off debts. Hence Kauitlya lays down that if an *ardhasitika* female attendant, who is a pledge, is made to pick up a corpse, dung, urine or leavings of food, or she is made to give a bath to a naked person or is given corporal punishment and dishonoured, it will result in her freedom from the pledge (III.13.9). This rule is also applicable to a *dhatr,* the wet nurse, and a female attendant or maid, who must have been generally from the Sudra castes. The obligation of the women of cultivator families to do manual tasks in the households of the rich is also shown by a passage of the *Kamasutra* of Vatsyayana. It informs us that the peasant women had to render *visit-karma,* i.e. forced labour, and work in the fields (*ksetra-karma*) for the village headmen and other officials, such as *ayukta* and perform other unpaid jobs, such as, making yarn out of cotton and other fibrous material. All this made them accessible to sexual exploitation.[55]

A contextual analysis of the term *kutumbin* may also throw some light on the changing fortunes of the peasantry. The term is taken to be of Dravidian origin and is derived from *kuti* meaning 'cottage' or 'hut'.[56] It seems to have denoted a nuclear family in its early usages. Thus, in the *Vinaya Pitaka* a *gahapati* is said to have established the *kutumba* of his sister's son by fixing his marriage.[57] The Jataka tales refer to wealthy *kutumbins.* Some of them are located in villages and some others in towns being engaged in trade.[58] Sontheimer draws attention to a passage of the *Apastamba Dharma Sutra* (II.11.29.3), which suggests that the term described a family where the householder and the wife have joint interest in property.[59] It is perhaps for this reason that *kutumba* could also denote 'two' or 'a pair'.[60] In the Durganivesa-prakarana of the *Arthasastra* (II.4.24), the term *kutumbin* is applied to artisans, and it is said that the boundaries of their workshops are to be fixed as per requirements. This text uses the term *karsaka* for a peasant (II.1.2; III.9.11; III.14.19). However, the Sailarwadi inscription of the pre-Gupta times describes a ploughman (*halakiya*) as a *kutumbika* while his son is described as the *gahapati.*[60] Apparently, the father was an ordinary peasant cultivating his fields while his son had become a local dignitary, a leader of the peasant-cultivators or a landed proprietor. Whatever the case may be, in the Gupta inscription the terms *kutumbin* and *kutumbika* clearly denote farmers.[62] R.S. Sharma points[63] out that the names of several peasant castes, such as the Kurmis and Koeries in Bihar and the Kunbis in Gujarat and Maharashtra, are derivatives from the term *kutumbin.* The *Vedavyāsa Smṛti* enumerates[64] *kutumbins* along with the *vardhaki* (carpenter), *napita* (barber), *gopa* (cowherd), *kumbhakara* (potter), *vanik* (petty trader), *kirata, kayastha* and *malakara* (garland maker) castes and says that these and many other Sudra castes are differentiated according to their occupations. Apparently the peasant *kutumbins* had crystallised into a clean Sudra caste in post-

Gupta times. In the *Abhidhana-Cintamani* of Hemachandra *kutumbins* are defined as farmers and cultivators.[65]

R.S. Sharma is of the view that the word *kutumbin* derives from the Prakrit root *kud* and is connected etymologically with *kudi* meaning land measurement as well as a container for drawing water from the well or a reservoir and *kutumbins* were connected with land measurement and irrigation and hence were ostensibly cultivators[66]. Whatever may be the etymological in the sense of a nuclear family or household, later, even when it was used to denote peasants specifically and became a caste designation, it continued to be used in its primary sense as well.

In the *Katyayana Smrtisaroddhara*[67] it is laid down that the king should not ask for the personal appearance of a woman born in a *kula* (*kulajatam*, born in a high caste family) as a witness, but the text treats a *kutumbini* in a different fashion. Not only could she be summoned personally, but she was also grouped together with unchaste women, which shows the low esteem in which she was held. In fact *kutumbini* was at par with the wives of washermen, hunters, herdsmen and distillers, who could be summoned in the same way.[68] Clearly *kutumbini* here is not to be interpreted as any woman who by her earnings supports her family as is done by P.V. Kane[69], but as the wife of a *kutumbin*, which term by the time of Katyayana makes a clear distinction between a woman born in a *kula* and a *kutimbini*. This may be compared with the evidence of Jataka I.196 where a leading resident of a town described as *kulaputta*, i.e. of good aristocratic family, is shown seeking the hand of the daughter of a *kutumbika* living in a village for marriage with his son. Decline in the status of *kutumbins* is indicative of the depression of the peasantry in early medieval times and their reduction to Sudra status. It also implies that agriculture was a family activity; and, although there may have been division of labour within the family according to sex and age, it constituted a unit for economic and socio-cultural purposes.

As we have observed earlier, the mode of female participation in agricultural production varied depending upon the landowning status of a family based on agriculture, with greater participation of women of the lower strata working in the fields. The transplantation of rice seedlings is generally done by the women of the landless labour class in contemporary India[70], although attention is drawn to a nineteenth century line drawing from Kashmir which shows a woman transplanting paddy along with a man.[71] Buchanan's Purnea Report too informs us that both men and women were hired for weeding and transplanting rice in the Purnea district of Bihar.[72] In India the social status and caste ranking has had an inverse relationship with the participation of women in production processes, particularly in the agricultural farms and the *Kasyapiya-krsi-sukti*, a text of the early medieval period, recommends that the transplantation of paddy seedlings should be done by the *bhrtyas* of the peasant. The term *bhrtya* apparently included both men and women of the landless labour families.[73] This text also informs us that the *bhrtyas* in almost all villages belonged to the Sudra castes.[74]

The *Kasyapiya krsi-sukti* contains detailed instructions for rice cultivation and states that 'simultaneous sowing by the village people (*gramajanaih*) of one accord and by the use of a number of yokes is said to be fruitful'.[75] Ploughing the field by one, two, three, four, or five *kutumbins* at the same time with the help of ten yokes drawn by twenty oxen gives a great yield of rice (vv.436-7). Evidently *kutumbin* is used in this text for an independent farmer, who was advised to employ hired labourers (*bhrtya-varga*) to weed out wild grass row by row (v.450). However, generally it used the term *krsivala* for a peasant. The date of this text is uncertain and according to the editor it has many interpolations; nevertheless, as a whole it seems to reflect the social reality of early medieval times. It recommends that the king should appoint the Brahmanas for advice on policy matters (*nitisu*), Ksatriyas for defence (*raksana*) Vaisyas for accounting (*gananadkriya*), but for cultivation (*krsi karya*) only Sudras and not members of any other caste (v.211-3). However, earlier, we are told that people of all the four varnas and 'others' meaning the lowly 'mixed castes' (*samkirna jatis*) are engaged in agricultural activities (v.170) and it is added that in some places Sudras too (sudresu-api) are engaged in agriculture (v.208)!

The *Kasyapiya krsi-sukti* narrates an interesting myth regarding the origin of the science of agriculture. We are told that the creator-god Brahma created various types of seeds, which were held by the Earth-goddess with special care. In order to fulfil the wishes of Bhumi-devi, the goddess Earth, to have offspring (*praja*) it was granted that one seed would multiply manifold and give numerous fruits to the mankind. This science of agriculture (*krsi-sastram*) was first heard by the sages as uttered by Bhumi-devi, the wife of god Visnu. The sages brought it to the earth, and it was preserved by the kings, who were foremost in providing protection to their subjects. In course of time, it came to be studied by the Sudras in particular (vv.678-82). Here again it is the Sudra varna, which is specifically associated with the knowledge of agriculture and there is no mention of 'Vaisya' in this myth.

The text further informs us (vv.695-98) that there are people in villages, towns, provinces (*dese*) and other places, who are incapable of doing agricultural work (*krsikarmanyasaktanam*). For them, as well as for the sake of over populated towns and the capital cities, the kings should acquire fertile and both types of (i.e. wet and dry) lands and use them for agricultural purposes by employing their subjects, hired labourers (*bhrtyan*), those of mixed castes (*samkirnajatyan*) and unemployed Sudras. The work presents a well-developed complex picture of the varna-jati organisation in which the Sudra, although lower than the upper three varnas, nevertheless, does not seem to have suffered any disabilities.[77] He could even be nominated by the king to serve on the judicial council (*nyayasabha*) of the village if a suitable, Brahmana, Ksatriya or Vaisya was not available and the Sudra was endowed with good qualities, was devoted to Brahmanas, had faith in the sacred books, respected and served the saints, was intelligent, had the knowledge seasons (*kalapramanajnah*) and was keen on service (vv.205-10). At the bottom of the scale were persons born in mixed castes. It may be assumed who did not own or were dispossessed from their lands and had to earn their livings as field labourers. Most of them were regarded as 'untouchables' and the KKS advises that a wise man should carefully avoid water touched by an untouchable (v.802). The assimilation of backward tribal peoples as 'untouchable' mixed castes in the Brahmanical social ladder in early medieval times is well known.[78] Many Dalit communities today such as the Doms, Dusadhs and Mahars of Maharashtra had a tribal past. Only a fraction of these communities could have survived on the earnings from occupations traditionally ascribed to them. For example, the numerically large castes of Chamars of Uttar Pradesh and Bihar, the Madigas of Andhra Pradesh and Chakkiliyans of Tamil Nadu, whose traditional occupation is leatherwork, also constitute an important source of field labour. Their ranking as 'untouchables' in the traditional Indian society played an important role in agriculture production by making cheap labour available to the peasant in a labour intensive mode of production.

REFERENCES

1. Irfan Habib, *Exploring Medieval Gender History* (Symposium Papers, Indian History Congress, No. 23), p. 3.
2. Suvira Jaiswal, 'Reconstructing History from the *Ṛgveda*: A Paradigm Shift?', *Social Science Probings*, Vol.18, No.2, December 2006, pp. 1-7.
3. Irfan Habib and Vijay Kumar Thakur, *The Vedic Age: A People's History of India*, 3, Tulika Books, New Delhi, 2003, pp. 11-2.
4. Ibid.
5. See S. Jaiswal, *Caste: Origin, Function and Dimensions of Change*, Manohar, Delhi, 1998, p. 147.
6. The term Ksatriya derives from the same root as the term *ksaya* and *ksiti* meaning a 'dwelling place' or residence. In RV. IV.24.4 *ksitayah* means 'men'. The formation of *ksatra* by adding the suffix *tra* to the root *ksi* shows that the task of the *ksatra* was primarily to provide protection to the tribes and their dwelling place and this empowered them as rulers or chiefs.

7. Suvira Jaiswal, 'Process of Gendering in the Brahmanical Tradition: An Investigation into Her Story' in B.K. Choudhary (ed.,) *Prajna-Bharati*, Vol. XI, K.P. Jaiswal Research Insitute, Patna, 2005, pp. 17-61.
8. Suvira Jaiswal, 'The Changing Concept of Grhapati', in D.N. Jha (ed.), *Society and Ideology in India: Essays in Honour of Professor R.S. Sharma*, Munshiram Manoharlal, Delhi, 1996, pp. 29-37.
9. The hymn describes the women of the homestead sleeping on benches, inside the carriage and on the bed, which fact shows that this *vis* was nomadic.
10. Suvira Jaiswal, *Caste*, pp. 137-8; Emile Benveniste, *Indo-European Language and Society*, London, 1973, pp. 105-12.
11. D.D. Kosambi, *An Introduction to the Study of Indian History*, revised second edition, Popular Prakashan, Bombay, 1975, pp. 97-8.
12. For a critique of Kosambi's view and discussion on the role of slavery in ancient India, see Suvira Jaiswal, *Caste*, pp. 47-8; 154-8; 189-90.
13. *Digha Nikaya* (ed. T.W. Rhys Davids and J.E. Carpenter, 3 Vols, London, 1890-1911), Vol.III, p. 93, quoted R.S. Sharma, *Aspects of Political Ideas and Institutions in Ancient India* (Motilal Banarsidass, 3rd rev. edition, Delhi, 1991, p. 65). Mahanama, a Sakya *khattiya*, had inherited the family lands from his father and handed over the property to his brother Aniruddha when he decided to become a monk. He explained to Aniruddha in detail how the fields were tilled, irrigated and harvested and told him that agricultural operations are never-ending. "Even when our fathers and grandfathers passed away the operations were not stopped," *Vinaya Pitaka*, II, pp. 179-80 quoted in Narendra Wagle, *Society at the Time of Buddha*, Popular Prakashan, Bombay, 1966, p. 150.
14. A Brahmana of the Kosiya *gotta* owned one thousand *karisas* of land. He leased half his land to tenants and had the rest cultivated by his slaves and servants. Deveraj Chanana, *Slavery in Ancient India*, Reprint, People's Publishing House, Delhi, 1990, p. 42.
15. *Digha Nikaya*, Vol. I, p. 77 and *Anguttara Nikaya*, Vol. II, p. 419, quoted by Uma Chakravarti, *The Social Dimensions of Early Buddhism*, OUP, Delhi, 1987, p. 68.
16. Jaiswal, *Caste*, p. 213.
17. *The Kautiliya Arthasastra* (ed. and trans. R.P. Kangle), 2 parts, University of Bombay, 1970-73, II.35. Also see I.11..1; 9-10, V.3.22.
18. Commenting on this passage, Breloer remarks that '*grhapati* appears more and more like a jamindar' quoted in Kangle, Part II, p. 188, note 8. Kangle, however, finds Breloer's view unacceptable.
19. *Gatha Saptasati* (ed., and trans. Radhagovinda Basak, The Asiatic Society, Calcutta, 1971), II.7. In his translation Basak renders *gdhavai-suam*, i.e. *grhapati-sutam*, as the husband of daughter-in-law identifying *grhapati* with the *halika*. But there is nothing in the verse to suggest this interpretation. It is more likely that the daughter-in-law of a poor ploughman felt vulnerable facing the son of the village headman and hence tried to avoid him.
20. VIII.6, Cited in B.N.S. Yadava, 'Historical Investigation into Social Terminology in Literature: A Problem of the Study of Social Change (Mainly

in the context of Early Medieval Northern India), Presidential Address, *Indian History Congress,* 53rd Session, Warangal, 1993, p. 25.

21. *Nitivakyamrtam* of Somadeva Suri (with exhaustive Hindi commentary by Ramachandra Malaviya, Chaukhamba Vidyabhavan, Varanasi, 1972), XIV. 8; 11. The evidence supports my thesis, that the defining characteristic of *grhapati* was his 'headship' or leadership and hence not every peasant or 'householder could be described as *grhapati.*
22. Suvira Jaiswal, 'Process of Gendering....', pp. 31, 41-42.
23. *Tattiriya Sambita,* VI.5.8.2 P.V.Kane, *History of Dharmasastra,* Bhandarkar Oriental Research Institute, Poona, 1941, Vol. II, pt.1, p. 576.
24. *Baudhayana Dharma Sutra.* II.2.53; *Manu Smrti,* X.18. quoted Kane, Ibid.
25. Gunther-Dietz Sontheimer, *The Joint Hindu Family,* Munshiram Manoharlal, Delhi, 1977, pp. 44-5.
26. *Satapatha Brahmana,* IV.4.2.13, quoted Kane, op.cit.
27. R.N. Nandi, 'Archaeology and the *Ṛgveda*', *The Indian Historical Review,* Vol. XVI, No.1-2 (July 1889-90), p. 46. For references to ksetrapti and ksetraptni, A.A. Macdonell and A.B. Keith, *Vedic Index of Names and Subjects* (reprint, Motilal Banarsidass, Delhi, 1982) Ksetra, Vol. I, pp. 210-11. In order to overemphasise the importance of agriculture in the Rgvedic mode of production, Nandi, and following him V.K. Thakur in *A Discourse on Indo-European Languages and Culture* (Edited by D.N. Tripathi, ICHR, New Delhi, 2004, p. 142.) repeatedly state that ksetrapati is mentioned three times in Book IV of the *Ṛgveda.* What is left unsaid is the fact that all the three references to *ksetrasya pati* in the fourth book of the *Ṛgveda* occur in hymn 57, which is in praise of ksetrapati and is regarded as a very late interpolation. For further discussion, Suvira Jaiswal, *Caste,* p. 136; 171 note 28.
28. Sontheimer, *The Joint Hindu Family,* p.12.
29. *Vinaya Pitaka* (5 Vols. ed. H. Oldenberg, London, 1879-83, Vol. III, p. 131), Trans (I.B. Horner, 5pts. SBB. London 1938) Vol. I, p. 220; Jataka (ed. V. Fausboll, London 1877-96, Vol. II, p. 293) Devaraj Chanana, op.cit., p. 42.
30. *Samyutta Nikaya* (ed. L. Feer, 6 Vols., 1884-1904, Pali Text Society, London, Vol. IV, p. 109-24; *Anguttara Nikaya,* (Ed. R. Morris and E. Hardy, 5 Vols., London, PTS, 1885-1900), Vol. IV, pp. 209-35 quoted N. Wagle, *Society at the Time of the Buddha,* p. 152.
31. D. Chanana, op.cit.
32. Uma Chakravarti, op.cit., p. 137.
33. X.5.2.10. Sontheimer, op.cit., p. 10.
34. A.A. Vigasin and A.M. Somozvantsev, *Society, State and Law in Ancient India,* Sterling Publishers, New Delhi, 1985, p. 92f.
35. B.N.S. Yadav, 'The Kali Age and the Social Transition', *Indian Historical Review,* Vol. V, No. 1-2 (July 1978–January 1979), pp. 31-63.
36. Quoted in Chanana, op.cit., p. 149, note 40.
37. Irfan Habib, 'The Peasant in Indian History'. General President's Address, *Indian History Congress,* 43rd Session, Kurukshetra, 1982, p. 21.
38. R.S. Sharma, *Early Medieval Indian Society,* Orient Longman, Hyderabad, 2001, p. 105, et al.
39. *Digha Nikaya,* Vol. II, p. 131; N. Wagle, op.cit., p. 189, Note 140.

40. *Jataka* Vol. III, p. 293; Richard Fick, *The Social Organisation In North East India,* trans. by Shishirkumar Maitra, Calcutta, University of Calcutta, 1920, p. 243.
41. A Jataka speaks of a Brahmana going to the field with his on while he ploughed the field, his son collected the weeds and burnt them. *Fick,* ibid.
42. N. Wagle, op.cit., p. 151.
43. Ibid., p. 146.
44. Suvira Jaiswal, 'Caste in Socio-Economic Framework of Early India', Presidential Address to Ancient India Section, *Proceedings of the Indian History Congress,* 38th Session, Bhubaneswar, 1977, pp. 23-48.
45. U. Chakravarti, op.cit., p. 103.
46. Ibid., pp. 100-01.
47. For contemptuous attitude towards manual labour, D. Chanana. op.cit., pp. 59-60.
48. Suvira Jaiswal, *Caste,* p. 71. This is further supported by D.D. Kosambi's analysis of Megasthenes' account of the Indian caste/class system. Kosambi perceptively remarks that Megasthenes does not colour his report with ideas borrowed from the Brahmanical *dharmasastras* but describes what he saw. Kosambi equates the fourth class of Megasthenes, the 'artisans and retail merchants' with Vaisyas and the second class of 'husbandmen cultivators called *geogoi* with Sudras. (Kosambi, *An Introduction to the Study of Indian History,* pp. 193-4). The trend of he merchant-Vaisya groups forming a distinct class, which did not marry outside their own group and as such had acquired the characteristics of a separate caste, may go back to the 4th century BCE.
49. R. Fick, op.cit., p. 263.
50. *Vinaya Pitaka,* Vol. II, p. 155; N. Wagle, op.cit., p. 66.
51. D.D. Kosambi, op.cit., pp. 195, 223-27.
52. R. Kangle, *The Kautilya Arthasastra,* Vol. III, pp. 138-9.
53. *Bhojyanna, Parasara-smrti,* Chowkhamba, Varanasi, 1968, *Manu Smrti* (IV. 253) also describes the *ardhika* as a Sudra.
54. Suvira Jaiswal, 'Female Images in the Arthasastra of Kautilya', *Social Scientist,* Vol. 29, Nos. 3-4, 2001, pp. 5-9.
55. *Kamasutra of Vatsyayana,* V.5.5.6, Irfan Habib, op.cit., p. 23.
56. Mayrhofer, *A Concise Etymological Sanskrit Dictionary,* s.v. Quoted in Sontheimer, op.cit., pp. 5-6.
57. *Kutumbam ca santhapesi, Vinaya Pitaka,* Vol. III, pp. 66-7, quoted by Sontheimer, op.cit., p. 6, fin. 4.
58. R. Fick, op.cit., pp. 256-7.
59. Sontheimer, op.cit.
60. D.C. Sircar, *Indian Epigraphy,* Motilal Banarsidass, Delhi, 1965, pp. 230-1.
61. Jas Burgess and Bhagawanlal Indraji, *Cave Temples of Western India,* Motilal Banarsidass, Delhi, Reprint, 1976, p. 38; Suvira Jaiswal, *Caste,* p. 213.
62. Dhanaidaha Copper-plate Inscription, *Epigraphia Indica,* Vol. XVII, No. 23, L.6 and Supiya Pillar Inscription of Skanda-Gupta, ibid., Vol. XXXIII, No. 56(2), L.10.
63. R.S. Sharma, *Early Medieval Indian Society,* p. 30.

64. *Vedavyasa-Smrti* (in *Smrtinam Samuccayah, Anandasrama Sanskrit Series,* No. 48, Poona, 1929), L.10.
65. Cited in R.S. Sharma, *Early Medieval Indian Society,* p. 197.
66. Ibid., p. 30.
67. *Katyayana Smrtisaroddhara* ed., P.V. Kane, Bombay, 1934, Sloka Nos. 97-8; Sontheimer, op.cit., p. 8.
68. *Katyayana,* verses 569-70.
69. P.V. Kane, *History of Dharmasastra,* Vol. III, Bhandarkar Oriental Research Institute, Poona, 1946, p. 287.
70. Andre Beteille, *Man in India,* Vol. 52 (1972), p. 164.
71. Shireen Moosvi, *People, Taxation and Trade in Mughal India,* Oxford University Press, Delhi, 2008, p. 137.
72. Ibid.
73. Kasyapiya Krsi-Sukti ed. and trans by G. Wojtilla, *Acta Orientalia,* XXXIII (2) (1979), Budapest, pp. 209-52; Vol. XXXIIX (1), pp. 85-136, verses 431:450.
74. *Prayo gramesu sarvatra bhrtyah sudra prakiritah,* v.211.
75. v.438, Trans., p. 110.
76. This confirms our view that in early medieval times the term 'Vaisya' was applied to merchant communities only.
77. For a detailed discussion, Suvira Jaiswal, *Caste,* pp. 70-88.
78. Vivekananda Jha, 'Stages in the History of Untouchables', *Indian Historical Review,* Vol. II, pt. 1 (1975), p. 28f.

12

A Quest for the Ethno-Cultural Base of the People of Bihar and Bengal

Annapurna Chattopadhyaya

Eastern India in which Bengal (before 1947) and Bihar belonged was outside the pale of the Vedic culture. So, the inhabitants—the so-called non-Vedic or non-Aryans have not been given any prominence by the Aryan-speaking people. The Aryans of Aryavarta or Madhyadesa considered themselves as śiṣṭas, i.e. culturally superior and others living outside the śiṣṭa cultural horizon of Aryavarta or Madhyades as Aśiṣṭa, i.e. not of approved conduct. This does not imply that those Aśiṣṭa people were in reality culturally inferior to the people of Aryavarta or Madhyadesa. Eastern India, considered as unholy land was peopled by the non-Aryan tribal communities like the Māgadhas, the Kikatas, the Angas, the Nishadas, the Śavaras, the Pulindas, the Vangas, the Puṇḍras, the Suhmas, the Radhas, the Gaudas and others. It has been said that any person belonging to the śiṣṭa group who visited the land of the non-Aryans except for pilgrimage had to perform *prayaschita* or a purificatory rite. Undoubtedly there were ethnic, cultural and linguistic differences between the people of Aryavarta and the non-Aryan indigenes and ancient tribal and semi-tribal peoples of eastern India.

The people of eastern India have been mentioned in the literary texts like the *Atharvaveda-pariśiṣṭa,* the Brahmanas, the Aranyakas, the Epics, the Buddhist and the Jain texts, the Dharmasastras, the Puranas, the Chinese accounts, the *Ramacharita* of Sandhyakaranandi, the Charyyapada, etc., as well as in the inscriptions like the Mahasthangadh, the Hathigumpha, Mahakuta, the spurious Nalanda plate of Samudragupta, Nandanpur, Bhaturiya inscription, Belava copper plate, etc.

The *Ṛgveda* does not refer to Ang and Vanga (Bihar and Bengal). Both these names are mentioned in the Atharaveda pariśiṣṭa (5.22.14) as a compound word. In the Brahmana texts frequent mentions are made of the Vangas and the Pundras who are undoubtedly the original inhabitants of Bengal. From the *Aitareya Brahmana*, it is known that the Pundras, the Vangas, the Vagadhas (i.e. Magadhas), etc., belonged to the non-Aryan primitive tribal communities. Besides the Vedic texts, the Dharmasastras, the Buddhist and the Jain texts refer to the people of eastern India as barbarians or uncultured.

Present Bihar in ancient days was peopled by the non-Aryan tribes called the Magadhas, the Kikatas and the Angas, etc. The ancient tribe known as the Magadhas inhabiting the southern region of the modern state of Bihar played the most important role not only in the history and culture of Bihar and Bengal but of India as a whole continuously for centuries together.

The Sanskrit term Magadha is derived from Mong (go, move) + al na= mog: dha (hold/bear) +da ka = Magadha). Māgadha means a native of Magadha, i.e. he who hails from the Magadha country. Panini (IV.1.700) derives the word Māgadha from the Magadha country. There are also other meanings of the word such as the name of a flower, sugar, etc. The term Magadha was originally applied to mean the bard /minstrel. In other words, the wandering singers were actually called Māgadhas and their habitant came to be named after them as Magadha. The Māgadhas are not referred to in the *Ṛgveda* but instead Kikata is mentioned. In the *Aiterya Aranyaka* we find the expression Vanga-Vagadha.

According to this expression, it seems that Vanga refers to Bengal and Vagadha may be made identical with Magadha. The *Ramayaṇa*, the *Mahabharata* and the Puranas mention the Magadhas along with the Pundras, the Suhmas, the Kalingas, etc. In the *Gautama Dharmasastra* and *Manusamhita* the Magadha has been described as a mixed caste. Besides, in the Jain texts, in the itinerary of Fa-hien and Hiuen Tsang, the Magadhas and their country have been described. The inscriptions from the 3rd century BC onwards contain many references to Magadha.

However, the land of the Magadhas has been known throughout as Magadha named after them. Magadha actually refers to a territorial zone and as such it is difficult to identify it with any particular place. In fact, ancient Magadha included wide areas which may be roughly taken to denote at least the whole of South Bihar. Again, Magadha at the time of Buddha included the disctricts of Gaya, Patna and parts of Hazaribag. Subsequently, the territorial expansion of Magadha became so wide as to include the whole of Bihar including the neighbouring areas and parts of Bengal.

Even in early times, the Magadhas were not confined within the territorial limits of their own locate. They also spread over different regions of eastern India, more particularly over Bengal. In fact, the Magadhas were originally non-Aryan tribal people perhaps not very distinct from other tribal communities of Bihar. Gradually, the Magadhas rose from the slumber of their tribalism and succeeded in establishing a principality, which was transformed into a kingdom. It is to be noted that Magadha was the greatest political and cultural centre of India and this pre-eminent position was maintained throughout several centuries.

It is not, however, known for certain to what extent the Magadhas were responsible for making Magadha such a centre of pre-eminence. Undaubtedly Magadha became a veritable resort of all sorts of people coming from different directions and it turned out as a veritable centre of the mingling of diverse races and cultural groups. The Magadhan cultural accomplishments were the outcome of mixed culture, the base of which was however, formed by the Magadhas and other indigenes who once spread over the entire region. Aryanisation/Brahmanisation of the region gave a new spurt to the development of the Magadhan culture . This was followed by the inflow of many other cultures both from different parts of India and outside. Accordingly cultural elements called Magadha cannot be said to have been entirely the creations of the Magadhas.

Regarding the ethnic affiliations of Magadhas, it is to be noted that in the literary accounts, there is hardly any reference to their physical features. If the Magadhas are taken to have originally belonged to a non-Aryan tribal community the plausibility of their equation with other non-Aryan tribes of Bihar can not be denied. In that case, the Magadhas may be affiliated to the Australoid ethnic stock characterised by dark chocolate brown skin colour, wavy to curly hair, dolichocephalic head, platyrrhine nose, slightly prognothous and medium stature. It can not be however said that the Magadhas retained all these physical characters. In Bihar, they are mixed up with many people of different ethnic characteristics and became completely mixed. Since most of them formed low caste orders, their original ethnic characters underwent frat changes. Further, the mingling of the Magadhas with other people was so intense that they lost their separate identity completely and as such no trace of the original Magadhas is to be found now as a distinct ethnic and cultural group. Not only that, even the Aryans who migrated to Bihar described as mixed, and as such the people of Videha, Anga, Magadha, etc., have been described as of mixed origins. Some of the original Magadhas were Brahmanised and others again might have mingled with other non-Aryan tribal people who are to be found even today concentrated in Chhotanagpur and neighbouring regions. A few of the people originally were the primitive Magadhas as well. Like the Magadhas, the Kiktas were non-Aryan tribal people as described in the *Nirukta* (VI.32) the *Vayu Purāṇa, Bhagavata Purāṇa* (1.3.24), *Abhidhanachintamani*, etc.

Like the Magadhas and the Kikatas, the Angas were also non-Aryan people perhaps akin to the extant Munda group of people of Chhotanagpur. The Angas were not perhaps different from their other allied tribes like the Magadhas, the Suhmas, the Vangas, the Pundras, etc.

Yet, it is very difficult to establish the present identity of the ancient Angas. In the early literary texts the Angas have been branded as the non-Aryans belonging to different ethnic and cultural stocks. They have been associated with the Nishadas, the Magadhas, the Vangas, the Suhmas, the Pundras, the Kalingas, etc. This shows that in both ethnic and cultural spheres, the Angas and the other non-Aryan tribal communities mentioned above were alike. These people were also not distinct from the present tribal people of Chhotanagpur and its neighbouring regions. So, they mostly belonged to the Austro-Asiatic linguistic group and Australoid racial stock. If this hypothesis is accepted, the Angas may be included within the same ethnic group. Accordingly, the Angas were perhaps characterised by dark brown skin colour, wavy hair, dolichocephalic head and platyrrhine nose. But owing to intermingling with other people the physical characters of the Angas were changed to such an extent that their original ethnic characters were completely lost. These changes occurred more particularly when the Angas were brought within the fold of Brahmanism.

Like the Magadhas, the Kikatas, and the Angas, the Nishadas, the Savaras, the Punlindas, the Vanas, the Pundras, the Suhmas, the Radhas and the Gaudas are the tribal or semi-tribal communities of ancient Bengal. As to the ethnic characters of the Nishadas detailed descriptions are to be found in the Epics and the Puranas. From all these accounts it would appear that the Nishadas were characterised by black skin colour, short stature, copper-coloured or black hair, broad and depressed nose, long ears and projected chin. The Australoid racial stock is characterised by short stature, dark skin colour, broad or platyrrhine nose and short build.

Accordingly, the Nishadas may be affiliated to the Australoid racial stock. The Australoid people are supposed to have been the speakers of Austro-Asiatic languages like the Mundas, Santlas, Hos, Birhors, Kharias, Bhumihas, etc., distributed all over Chhotangpur and its neighbouring regions including Bengal. Prof Suniti Kumar Chatterji prefers to call these Austric languages of India by the generic name Munda. The Mundas are undoubtedly the Nishada people.

Like the Nishadas, the Savaras are found widespread in the forest areas of Chhotanagpur, Orissa, Bengal and other neighouring regions. The Savaras are also mentioned in the literary texts such as the *Aiterya Brahmana, Sankhyayana Srautasutra, Amarkosha, Brhastsamita, Chharyyapadas*, the oldest Bengali literature as well as the inscriptions like the Naihati copper plate of Vallasena, etc. As regards the identity of the ancient Savaras, it may be said that the aboriginal people called the Lodhas in Bengal are the surviving remnants of the Savaras. The Lodhas are found in large numbers in Angul, Orissa, Singhbum, Midnapur and Bankura. The Chiriamars of Midnapur are also said to be a branch of the Lodhas. The Lodhas are dolichocepalic and mesorrhine people with medium stature. The Savaras were characterised by dark complexion, flat nose, long eyes, projecting forehead, thick lips and red eyes. The present-day Savaras are also characterised by these physical features. Thus the Savaras and the Nishadas belong to he same ethnic stock as is evident from their physical features. Linguistically, the Savaras and the Nishadas belong to the Austro-Asiatic language group, i.e. akin to and affiliated with the Mongoloid ethnic stock. But the close association of the Pulindas with Savaras and the Nishadas perhaps speaks of their affiliation to the Australoid racial stock. Undoubtedly, these indigenes of Bengal were non-Aryan people.

Besides these real authochthons of Bengal there were many other tribal or semi-tribal people who were the ancient inhabitants of Bengal. These were the Vangas, the Pundras, the Suhmas, the Radhas, the Gaudas and others. The Vangas, the ancient people of Bengal may be affiliated and included within the Australoid racial stock. Subsequently, other people belonging to the Mediterranean ethnic stock and Dravidian linguistic family got inextricably mixed up with the primitive Vangas. Like the Vangas, another important non-Aryan tribal community of ancient Bengal is the Pundra. From the tribal and rural settings the Pundras like the Magadhas emerged as urbanised people. Gradually, they established a kingdom whose capital city was Pundranagara which has been mentioned in the Mahasthangadh inscription of the 3rd century BC. No positive information is obtainable regarding the ethnic characters of the Pundras. It has been presumed that they might have migrated from the Chhotanagpur region to North Bengal. If it be so, it is quite likely that they belonged to the same racial stock to which the tribal peoples of Chhotanagpur were affiliated, so, it may be said that the Pundras might have been Austro-Asiatic language speakers as well like other tribal people of Chhotanagpur. If this contention is accepted it may also be presumed that the Pundras perhaps belonged to the Australoid racial stock. This presumption would be considerably borne out by the physical characters of the surviving remnants of the ancient Pundras.

As regards the ethnicity of the Suhmas and the Radhas, it is difficult to specifically identify or affiliate these tribes to any particular ethnic group because of the non-availability of any materials regarding their physical characters. However, it may be presumed that those tribes of ancient time may be affiliated to the Australoid ethnic stock. The Bhumijas, the Lodhas, the Chuars, the surviving remnants of the Suhmas were/are the original inhabitants of Radhadesa. They may be affiliated to the Munda group of people. It is significant to note that the Bengali word chor might have been derived from Chuar or Choad, perhaps a word of Austro-Asiatic origin.

The Gaudas, another tribal community of ancient Bengal were mixed people. They may be affiliated with Australoid, Mediterranean, Mongoloid and Alpinoid racial stock. Having mixed with these people they lost their original ethnic features.

It is thus evident from the above mentioned discussion that linguistically speaking those people, tribal and semi-tribal of Bihar and Bengal might be affiliated to the Munda or Austro-Asiatic branch of the Austric family of languages. From the ethnic point of view they may be affiliated to the Australoid racial stock characterised by short stature, dark skin colour, broad or platyrrhine nose and short build.

This shows that the ancient people of Bengal and Bihar were closely related. Even in cultural and ethnic settings, all these people were allied. In fact, there was hardly any firm geographical boundaries between Bihar and Bengal in ancient times. On the other hand, the present state of Bihar and Bengal formed one historical, cultural and ethnic zone.

Thus, the ethno-culutral base of the people of Bihar and Bengal was primarily Austric in language and culture and Australoid in respect of ethnic affiliation. It is also significant to note that Australoid racial stock was not only the base of the people of Bihar and Bengal but this stock forms the substratum of the Indian people even today.

REFERENCES

1. Chakladar, H.C.: 'Problems of the Racial Composition of the Indian People' (Presidential address: Anthropology section), *Proceedings of the Indian Science Congress,* XXIII session, Indore, 1936, p. 371; Annapurna Chatopadhyaya, 'Presidential address, section-1', *Proceedings of Indian History Congress,* 65th session, Bareilly, 2004, pp. 44-61; *The Aryan Occupation of Eastern India* (rpt., Calcutta. 1962), pp. 9-10; Diverse Ethno-cultural Trends into Ancient Bengal: A Study of Processes of Acculturation, p. 17.
2. Haug, M. (ed & trans): *Aitareya Brahmana* (Vol. I & II, London, 1863, rpt., Allahabad, 1992), VII. 13-18, pp. 469-70. *Basudhayana Dharmasutra,* 1.2.15.
3. Bagchi, P.C. (trans): *Pre-Aryan and Pre-Dravidian in India of Sylvain Levi, Przyluski and others,* Calcutta, 1929, pp. 73-4; B.C. Sen: *Some Historical Aspects of the Inscriptions of Bengal,* Calcutta, 1942, p. 2; D.C. Sircar: *Studies in the Society and Administration of Ancient and Medieval India,* Vol. 1, Calcutta, 1967, pp. 2-3.
4. Haug. M. (trans): *Aitareya Brahmana,* VII. 13-18, pp. 469-70; A.B. Kieth:

Aitareya Aranyaka, (Oriental Series, Cambridge, 1920, Oxford, 1909), II, pp. 101, 200; *Satapatha Brahmana*, 1.4, 1.10, 14-17; B.C. Sen, op.cit.; S.K. Maity and R.R. Mukherjee: *Corpus of Bengal Insriptions Bearing on History and Civilisation of Bengal*, Calcutta, 1967, p. 39; D.C. Sircar: *Studies in the Geography of Ancient and Medieval India*, Calcutta, 1971, pp. 195-9. (for spurious Nalanda plate of Samudragupta); *Epigraphia Indica*, vol. XXIII, p. 54 (Nandanpur copper plate); N.G. Majumdar: *Inscriptions of Bengal, Rajshahi*, Vol. III, 1929, p. 14 (Bhaturia ins); *Epigraphia Indica*, Vol. XII, p. 37 (Belava copper plate of Bhojvarman).

5. Majumdar, R.C., (ed.): *History of Bengal*, Vol. 1, Dacca University, Dhaka, 1943, pp. 7-8; D.C. Sircar: *Studies in the Society and Administration of Ancient and Medieval India*, p. 23.
6. Keith, A.B. (trans): *Aitareya Aranyaka*, Oxford, 1909, 11.1.1, pp. 100-200; R.C. Majumdar: *History of Bengal*, Vol. 2, pp. 7-8.
7. Jacobi, H. (trans): *Acarangasutra, Sacred Books of the East*, XXII, *Jaina Sutras*, Pt. I, 1884, 1.8.3. pp. 84-5.
8. Kane, P.V.: *History of Dharmasastra*, Vol. II, Poona, p. 91
9. *Taittiriya Brahamana*, III.5.1.1: *Vajasaneyi Sambita*, XXX.5.22.
10. Keith, A.B. (trans): *Aitareya Araynyaka*, 11.1.1, pp. 101, 200.
11. Wilson, H.H.: *Mahabharata*, VI, 1.9; *The Vishnu Purana*, Calcutta, 1961, p. 143.
12. Kane, P.V.: *History of Dharmasastra*, Vol. II, pt. 1, p. 91; Shyamakanta Vidyabushan: *Manusambita* (in Bengali, Calcutta); X.11.17, 24-25, pp. 292-94; *Gautam Dharmasastra*, IV.17; B.C. Law: *Tribes in Ancient India* (Poona, 1943), pp. 93.112 ff.; J.A Legge: *Fahien's Record of the Buddhist Kingdom*, Oxford, 1886, p. 87; T. Watters (Trans.): *On Yuan Chawang's Travels in India* (rpt., Delhi, 1961), Vol. II, pp. 87-97.
13. Haddon, A.C.: *The Races of Man*, Cambridge, 1929, pp. 20-21.
14. Sen, B.C.: op.cit., pp. 128-30; Annapurna Chattopadyaya: *The People and Culture of Bengal: A Study in Origins*, Vol. I, Part 1, Kolkata, 2002, p. 415 ff; also, 'A Brief Note on the Ethno-Historical Approach to the Cities of Ancient Bengal', *Proceedings of Indian History Congress*, 62nd Session, 2001, pp. 64-70.; Panchanan Tarkaratna (ed. & trans into Bengali): *Mahabharata* (Vangavasi edn., Kalikata, 1830 Sakabda), Vol. II, p. 1002; Vol. 1, Chap. 30, p. 41; Chap. IX, p. 822.
15. Chaudhari, S.B: *Ethnic Settlement in Ancient India*, Calcutta, 1955, p. 45. Panchanan Tarkaratna (ed. & trans): *Mahabharata*, Vol. I, Adiparva, Chap. 109, 25, p. 117; Chap. 114, 12, p. 120; *Vayu-Purana*, 2.1.62, 137-48; 120-21; *Brahmanda-Purana*, II, 36, 144-46,158-73; V.R.R. Dikshitar: *The Puranic Index*, Vol. II, Madras, 1955, p. 253; B.C. Law: *Ancient Indian Tribes*, Vol.II, London, 1934, p. 63; R.P. Chanda: *The Indo-Aryan Races*, rpt., Calcutta, 1959, p. 4.
16. Tarkaratna, Panchanan: *Mahabharata*, Vol. II, *Santiparvan*, Chap. 59, 96-7, p. 1434; R.P. Chanda: *The Indo-Aryan Races*, pp. 4-5; A.Chattopadhaya: op.cit., Vol. I, pt. 1, pp. 323-4.
17. Haddon, A.C.: op.cit., pp. 20-21.
18. *Aitareya Brahmana*, VII, 8.2: *Sankhyayana Srautasutra*, XV, 6.; A.A.

Macdonell and A.B. Keith: *Vedic Index of Names and Subjects,* Vol. II, rpt. Delhi, 1958, p. 594; G. Oppert: *The Original Inhabitants of India,* rpt., Delhi, 1971, pp. 81-3; D.C. Sircar: *Studies in the Geography of Ancient and Medieval India,* p. 39. A. Chhattopadhyaya: op.cit., p. 329.

19. Hutton, J.H.: *Caste in India,* Cambridge, 1946, p. 285; P.K. Bhowmik: *The Lodhas, A Socio-economic Study of West Bengal,* Calcutta, 1963, pp. 10-13; A. Chaottopadhyaya: op.cit., pp. 346-7.
20. Risley, H.H.: *The People in India,* London, 1915, p. 400.
21. Muir, J.: *Original Sanskrit Text,* London, Vol. II, 1863, p. 411; E.B. Cowell and F.W. Thomas (trans): *The Harshacharita of Banabhatta,* Chap. VIII, rpt, Delhi, 1961, p. 70; G. Oppert: op.cit., p. 86.
22. Mitra, A.K.: *Tribes and Castes of West Bengal,* Census, 1951, (Calcutta, 1953), p. 24.
23. Maity, S.K. and R.R. Mukherjee: *Corpus of Bengal Inscription,* 39; D.C. Sircar: *Select Inscriptions Bearing on Indian History and Civilisation,* Calcutta, 1965, p. 82.
24. Sen, B.C.: *Some Historical Aspects of the Inscriptions of Bengal,* p. 130.
25. *Census Report of India, Bengal,* 1901, pp. 425-6.; *Census Report of India, Bengal and Sikkim,* 1931, pt. 1, p. 178; H.H. Risley: *The Tribes and Castes of Bengal,* rpt., Vol. II, Calcutta, 1981, p.178.
26. Risley, H.H. : *The Tribes and Castes of Bengal,* Vol. 1.
27. Chattopadhyaya, A.: op.cit., Vol. I, Pt. 1, p. 448.
28. Haddon, A.C.: op.cit., pp. 20-21.

13

Some Aspects of the Cult of *Stūpa* Architecture*

P. Gupta

In the Indian context, *Stūpa* architecture constitutes an early example of monumental art in stone. Chronologically speaking, it is generally accepted that *Stūpa*'s emergence in its lithic incarnation is contemporaneous with the Mauryan period. In this connection, one may refer to Ray's observation that the monolithic rail at Sarnatha in Chunar sandstone might have been erected under the patronage of Ashoka himself[1]. Its architecture forms had been literally transferred into stone from the wooden originals.

Generally the art historians are inclined to subscribe to the postulates of linking the *Stūpa* cult with funerary cult. We shall discuss this view at the appropriate moment. Recently John Irwin, a reputed art historian follows a different route of enquiry, which correlates cosmogenic myth with construction of sacred monuments including *Stūpa*. One should take this conceptual difference into consideration as an important component in the reappraisal of Mauryan art.

As mentioned above, Irwin's concept is concerned with the cosmogonic myth as the principal inspiration in the constructional sacred monuments. In this connection let us first define Cosmogony as a discipline that deals with the Genesis, i.e. the birth of Cosmos. This is in contrast with cosmology which is concerned with the structure of the dualistic universe after the creation.

Before Irwin, several scholars were seized with the idea of the cosmic correspondence between the universe and sacred architecture. For example, Prof. Mircea Eliade (1957) refers to ancient monuments as "architecture at microcosm" or "images of universe".

The cosmogonic route of enquiry was first opened by W.R. Lethby sometime in the eighth decade of the 19th century. He advanced the view that the concept of building as a sacred monument in the ancient world was primarily a ritual by which "man sought to identify himself with the source of cosmic order". This led Lethby to formulate the hypothesis of "Mythical Centre of Universe" which was subsequently equated with "navel of the earth": Omphatos in Greek/ *Pṛthvī-nābhi* is Sanskrit. Let us discuss these two terms briefly.

According to W.J. Woodhouse, Omphalus stands for navel stone of the temple of Delphi. Zeus, in search of the central point of the earth, once sent two eagles to fly simultaneously with some speed from east and west respectively. They ultimately met at Delphi where in Apollo's temple a navel stone, i.e. Omphalos made of white marble with a golden eagle on each side, was set up. This point was marked as the centre point of earth.[2]

In India's context, Gonda refers to Aditi's womb which is equivalent to navel of the earth.[3] But according to the connotation of Satvalekar *yajñsthāna,* i.e. *Uttaṛavedī* is the *Pṛthibinābhi* (navel chord). At this stage we propose to deal with different concepts of *Pṛithvī Nābhi* and their co-relation with Omphatos at some later date. What we do emphasise now is the conceptual need of a navel chord in a cosmic sense in describing cosmic obstetrics, i.e. cosmogony.

To proceed further, A.J. Wensinc (1916) develops further the hypothesis of navel of the earth. According to him, at this spot where heaven and earth were coalesced were separated leading to the birth of the world. In the Vedic context Kuiper indicates that the cosmogenic myth is the oldest one. The story of Indra's destruction of the demon Vṛtra is a creation myth. Irwin writes:-

"In the Vedic myth involving Indra, the demiurgic act of 'creation' was portrayed as Indra's destruction of the demon Vṛtra who held the waters of life within the primeval mound. At the same moment as Indra pegged the mound with his spear (which became the cosmic pillar) and released the waters, heaven and earth were separated, the sky was propped, the sun arose, the light was born simultaneously, for directions of space were created[4]."

Thus the cosmogonic act led to the creation of the dualistic structure of earth—a subject which is the concern of the postulate of cosmology as mentioned above.

Basing himself on the above hypothesis Irwin equates *Stūpa* with a microcosmic replica of the cosmic mound which was pegged by Indra at the time of releasing the waters of life. Besides, an axial pillar found within a *Stūpa* has been referred to Yūpa Yāsti in the *Divayāvadāna.* The wooden structure was replaced by stone as in *Amaravati* contemporaneous with Ashoka. Vedic Yūpa, i.e. sacrificial post is similar structurally to stone axial pillar of some *stūpas*. But the most surprising is the name of the axial pillar of *Stūpa* as Indra-Khila is Indrakila equivalent to Indra's stake. In this connection, one can refer to *puranavitan* for this alternative name of *Stūpa* axis. This leads Irwin to correlate the pillar with the cosmic event of the creation story as narrated in the *Ṛgveda*. Irwin thus argues that both terms *Stūpa* and Indira Kila symbolise the Indira's stake.

How can one explain the intrusion of the Brahmanical concept within Budhist architecture? Harvey explains it in the following way[6]:

The most ancient *Stūpas* lacked the sign of any axial pillar, probably because Buddhism was not sufficiently well established in the 5th and 4th centuries BC for the conversion of Brahmanical monuments. With the increasing popularity and power of Buddhism it was possible to accept the building of *Stūpas* around Vedic Yupas. These also marked sacred spots; building of *Stūpas* on these spots showed that they were now taken over by the new religion. In such early *Stūpas* the original wooden yupa was probably retained but later on a stone Yupa had been erected to mark the sacred spot, which would be in the centre of a new *Stūpa.*

This architectural syncretism thus emerges as a new component in the Maurya aesthetics. At the outset, we have referred to the linkage of the *Stūpa*-cult. One may refer to *Mah-parinibbna Sutta* (Dll, 141-3) where Lord Buddha commands that his mortal remains, after his death should be cremated and the relics should be placed in a *Stūpa* where four roads meet. Sanchi's four gate ways symbolise the cross roads as mentioned above. Harvey argues that this indicates the openness and universality of the Buddha's teaching which invites all to come and try its path and also to radiate loving kindness to all beings in all four directions.

Anthropologically speaking, the role of cross-ways is very important in the history of mankind. Maealooch classifies cross roads into the following four groups each dealing with the corresponding component of the cult:

1. Burial at crossroads
2. Ghost, spirits and demons at crossroads
3. Divinities at crossroads
4. Omen at crossroads.

For the moment we are concerned with the first group, i.e. burial. The custom of interring the remains of a person in a temulus or a barrow is located at the crossroad was widely polyvalent throughout the world. We have referred to Buddha's command in this connection. In fact, Coomaraswamy, Govind and Irwin consider it a pre-Buddhist cult. Buddha's command also suggests the erection of *Stūpa* of Srvkas (disciples of Tathgata).

Let us now narrate the examples of global dispersal of this cult:

1. In Slavic lands, one finds cairn or tumuli at crossroads. This is in connection with the cult of the dead.

2. A dead person who succumbed to the malice of a witch or demon was sometimes buried at the crossway as the custom was widely prevalent once in Hungary. This amounts to the riddance of evil at crossroads where the witch is supposed to be powerless.
3. Probably honourable burial at the crossroads is due to the desire for reincarnation. Among the Mongol, some North American tribes and also in West Africa, children are buried at the crossroad where more women are likely to pass and the chance of entering into one's womb is great and rebirth or incarnation can be relatively ensured.

Thus a global cult of pre-Buddhist era or possibly pre-Aryan was assimilated by Buddhism in course of time. Basham[8] pointed out that in becoming a religion, Buddhism borrowed and adopted the form and popular beliefs of the time. In fact, Kosambi elaborates the similarity of terms like *stūpa*, *chaitya*, sacred spot and marketplace. In this connection Mumford[9] refers to the Sumerian ideogram for market is Y- a crossroad.

The ritual of architectural location either at crossroad or navel of earth is further fused when one reads Woodhouse's following observation regarding Omphalos.

"It is thus not confined to Delphi nor associated with Apollo only. Its primary connection is with a primitive earth deity and the spirit of the dead.

Thus Ompholes is not only the navel of the earth but also the abode of the dead. Similarly the *Stūpa* is the abode of the dead where the mythology of cosmogenic stake of Indra was subsequently included. This bipolarity needs further investigation.

REFERENCES

1. Nihar Ranjan Roy, *Mauryan and Post Mauryan Art,* p. 44.
2. James Hastings, *Encyclopedia of Religion and Ethics,* VIX, p. 492 (Hereafter ERE).
3. Karel Warner (ed.), *Symbols in Art and Religion,* p. 35.
4. *Ṛgveda,* Mandal 10, p. 3 (Satavalen) A.J. Wensinc cited in.
5. Karel Warner, op.cit. p. 151, p. 10.
6. Ibid., p. 91.
7. *Encylopedia of Religion and Ethics,* V. IV, pp. 330-36.
8. A.L. Basham, *The Wonder that was India,* 1954.
9. Mumford, *The City in History,* pp. 14-5.
10. ERE, p. 493.

- This study contains a few incomplete citations. Readers will do well to ignore these and focus on the ideas it communicates.—Ed.

14

Study of Punchmarked Coins: A Case for a New Methodology

Shailendra Mohan Jha

There are several issues connected with the study of punchmarked coins (hereafter, PMC) in India. P.L. Gupta has tried to determine the chronology of PMC on the basis of classification of the symbol[1]; D.D. Kosambi shows a pattern in the relationship between the number of reverse marks and period of circulation and weight of the PMC[2]. An attempt has been made here to probe the validity of both these methods in the study of the PMC. We have recorded weights of more than six thousand PMC, lying in different museums of Bihar. This has given us an entry point to analyse the validity of the assumptions of earlier scholars.[3]

The exercise undertaken here is not based on sheer weight of coins. We have also made a note of other internal variants of the PMC such as their shapes, sizes, nature and number of symbols, etc. Further, an attempt has also been made to situate this numismatic data in the larger context of the material settings. After all, PMC represent not only the earliest but perhaps the only series of pre-modern coins that had a truly pan-Indian character.

It is generally noted that the rule of the Mauryas marks the beginning of an effort to implement uniform script, language, code of conduct as well as a broad-based concept of kingship; of course, minor local and regional considerations were not overlooked. For example, one may notice the use of Kharosthi and Aramic inscriptions in north-western India and certain dialect variations in the use of Prakrit. Similarly one can delineate features of daily life of common people on the basis of dispersal of culture associated with the Northern Black Polished Ware. A substantial part of the Indian subcontinent from north-western India to the Deccan Plateau came under its parameters (between c. 400 and c. 200 BC). Asokan pillar, bricks and seals used during the Mauryan centuries also show traces of some universalisation[4]. Here through the study of silver PMC from the Magadhan regions, it is shown that a systematic policy of monetary economy, specially a meticulous control over manufacturing of coins, was undertaken by the political authority of the time (c. 400- 200 BC).

Out of 6018 silver PMC, weights of as many as 5862 coins come under the weight group of 2.8 gms to 3.5 gms. There are only 123 coins with weight less than 2.8 gms. And only 33 coins have weight more than 3.5 gms each. This gives us an average weight of these coins, which can be pegged at 3.2 gms.

We can work out a pattern of uniformity in the size and shape of PMC. Out of 6018 PMC studied by us, the length of 3695 coins comes under the length group of 1.2 cm to 1.5 cm. There are 872 coins having a length less than 1.2 cm each and 1222 coins have length more than 1.5 cm each. The measurement of width and thickness of these coins show that as many as 4377 coins fall within the width group of 1.00 cm to 1.5 cm and 4098 coins come under the thickness group of 1.2 mm to 3.1 mm. (See Table 1 and Graph 1).

As a next step of our investigation, we have tried to show the linkages between the physical dimensions of coins under study and their weight pattern. Thus coins with an average length of 1.2 cm weigh 3.2 gms. Similarly, the majority of our coins falling in the width ranging from 1.00 to 1.5 cm also weigh 3.2 gms and their average weight remains steady vis-á-vis average thickness of these coins mentioned. (See Graph 1).

Numismatists have different opinions on the prevalence of round and square-shaped PMC. D.D. Kosambi is of the opinion that manufacturing of round coins was preferred because of the lower rate of reduction of their weight. He thought that square coins have linear regression, so their weight is reduced faster than round coins[5]. This is not borne out by our study of 6018 PMC. When the shapes of these coins were examined, as many as 4374 coins could be identified as square and 1626 as round-shaped. Significantly, no variation could be noticed in their average weight, which stands at 3.2 gms in both categories. About 2431 square coins come under the weight group of 3.2 gms, and 938 round coins also have an average weight of 3.2 gms. (see Graph 2).

Following P.L. Gupta's methodology, we have also catalogued and analysed symbols occurring on coins studied by us. It is found that most of our coins fall under what Gupta has called series V and VI and issued between c. 320 and c.150 BC[6]. However, we would also like to underline that the three important hoards of PMC studied by us (Machuatoli, Bhalua and Patraha) included many such coins which remained in circulation for a much longer period. In fact, the simultaneous occurrence of coins comparable with series I and VII of Gupta's classification (chronologically, these series span between c.500 and c.150 BC.) has a bearing on the methodology adopted by us, as delineated below.

How far can we reconcile the views of P.L. Gupta and D.D. Kosambi, the two most outstanding scholars of PMC studies? The former, it needs to be recalled, classified PMC into seven series on the basis of group of symbols.[7] In what relationship do they stand vis-á-vis Kosambi's theory of symbol-weight-age linkage?[8]

In all fairness to methodologies of both Gupta and Kosambi, it may be pointed out that while the former based his chronology of the PMC essentially on the grouping or clustering of symbols on the observe, the latter made the sequence of symbols on the observe and number of symbols on the reverse as his defining criteria. The weight system does not figure in Gupta's reckoning. Kosambi, on the other hand, makes it a cornerstone of his chronological inferences. For him, simply put the larger the number of reverse marks on a coin, the greater the period of its circulation, and lesser its weight.

We made a selection of 35 coins from hoards studied by us. Of these, five each could be compared with the seven identified by P.L.Gupta. Further, these coins were also chosen so as to meet Kosambi's criterion of the number of symbols on the reverse. Since the coins of Gupta's series, I, II, III, etc. continued up to the time of his series VII, the application of Kosambi's theory would imply (a) decreasing weight of the coins of series I, (b) possibly more reverse symbols on coins of pre-VII series. Regrettably, this does not seem to be the case. Table II shows that there was hardly any variation in the weights of coins of series VII and I.

Similarly, our Graphs 3 and 4 demonstrate that the number of reverse symbols also does not lead to any substantive loss of weight. Coins with only one reverse mark as well as those with two or three such marks peak at the same weight point, viz. between 3.2 and 3.4 gms. Such data dents not only Gupta's symbol based chronological deductions but monetary economy during the phase of the PMC.

Our methodology has tried to focus on the need to reconcile various internal and external variables of coin data. Our preliminary inquiry into Bihar's micro region has brought out certain elements of standardisation that could be tentatively placed in the Mauryan period. However, a more definite picture could perhaps emerge only if such an analysis is extended to other regions of the Indian subcontinent, which have yielded the punchmarked coins.

REFERENCES

1. P.L. Gupta and T.R. Hardekar, *Ancient Indian Silver Punchmarked Coins of the Magadha Maurya Karshapan Series,* Indian Institute of Research in

Numismatic Studies, Nasik, 1985, p. 10.

2. D.D. Kosambi, *Indian Numismatics*, collection of his essays with an Introduction by B.D. Chattopadhyay; Orient Longman, New Delhi, 1981, Chapters 1,2,4 and 6.
3. Shailendra Mohan Jha, *The Punchmarked Coins of Bihar (Machuatoli, Bhalua and Patraha Hoards)* unpublished Ph.D Thesis (1997) submitted to the University of Delhi under the supervision of Professor K.M. Shrimali. The present paper is largely based on this thesis.
4. For further details of this argument, cf. Ibid., pp. 60-64.
5. D.D. Kosambi, op.cit., pp. 7-9.
6. P.L. Gupta, op.cit., Table 1, p. 10.
7. Ibid., Catalogue of Coins, pp. 37-101.
8. D.D. Kosambi, op.cit., Chapters 1, 2, 4, and 6.
9. There is considerable merit in Oliviere Guillaume's methodology of similar nature in the context of Indo-Greek coins. Cf. his "An Analysis of the Modes of Reconstruction of the *Graeco-Bactrian* and Indo-Greek History," *Studies in History* (NS), Vol. II, No, 1, January-June 1986, pp. 1-6.

Table 1: Symbols-Weight Relationship

P.L. Gupta's Classification		*Our Classification*	
Series	*S.No.*	*Coin Number**	*Weight in gms.*
I	103	17	3.28
	165	20	3.09
II	274	15	3.09
III	291	11	2.91
	305	21	3.01
IV (a)	344	478	2.94
IV (b)	363	16	3.22
V (a)	480	639	3.26
	482	491	3.26
VI (a)	534	1265	3.46
VI (b)	542	2864	3.26
VII	586	4117	2.99
	589	1925	3.24

* For specific identification of coin number given in the column, see S.M. Jha, fn. 3

Graph 1: Variations in Physical Dimension of PMC and Total Number of Coins in each Category

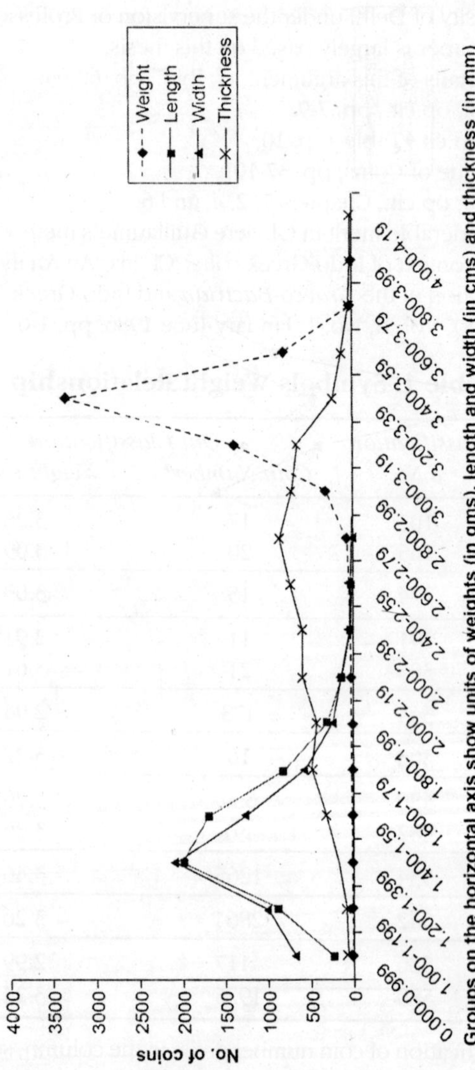

Graph 2: Weight-Shape Relationship

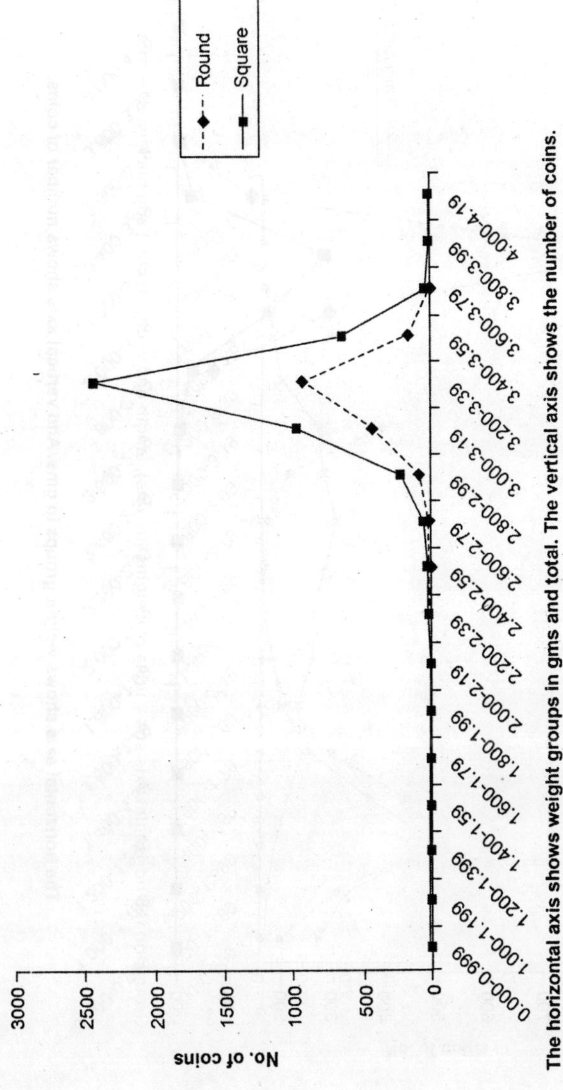

The horizontal axis shows weight groups in gms and total. The vertical axis shows the number of coins.

Graph 3: Weight Variations in Coins with Two or Three Reverse Marks

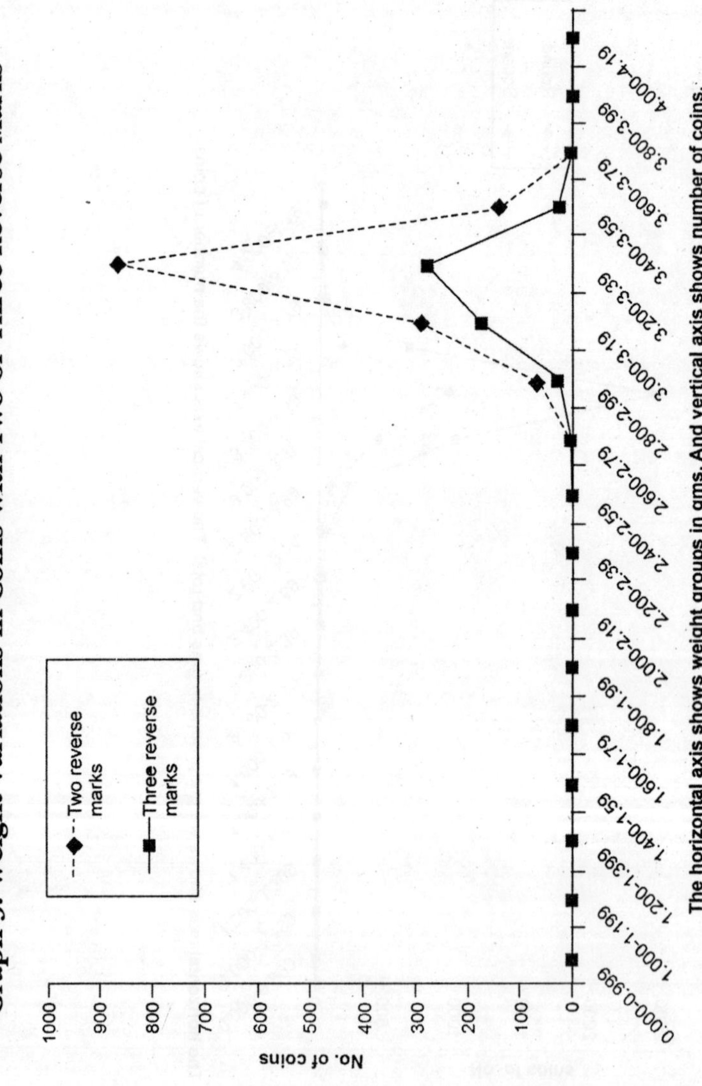

15

Aśoka's *Dhaṃma*: An Enterprise of Extraordinary Vision*

Vivekanand Jha

An attempt is being made in this paper to throw light on Aśoka's *dhaṃma* (Sanskrit *dharma*) on the basis of a close reading of the text of his edicts,[1] which are the most authentic source of information for his reign (*c.*270 BC—*c.*234 BC). That *dhaṃma*, which appears as *dhama*[2] and *dhāṃ*[3] as well, as conceived by this remarkable Maurya ruler, is the dominant theme of these edicts, written in Prākrit. Greek and Aramaic languages and in Brāhmī, Kharoṣṭhī, Greek and Aramaic scripts, and found inscribed on rocks, pillars and stone slabs at more than forty places from central Afghanistan to Karnataka, is indicated by the frequent application to them of such terms as *dhaṃmalipi*,[4] *dhaṃmalipī*,[5] *dhamalipi*,[6] *dhraṃmadipi*,[7] and *dhramadipi*[8] (*dhraṃma* and *dhramạ* are the Gāndhārī Prākrit variations of the Māgadhī Prākrit *dhaṃma* and *dhama* respectively; and *dipi* is the Old Iranian word for written decree). *Lipi*,[9] and *lipī*,[10] too, occur in the sense of an edict, and *lipikara*[11] and *lipikala*[12] in the sense of a scribe or stone engraver, though less frequently. Besides, *dhaṃmasāvanāni*[13] is employed in the sense of 'proclamations on *dhaṃma*', hearing which the people are expected to abide by it, progress considerably in it and be ethically elevated. Being the second most used term in the edicts (after Devānaṃpiya Piyadasi, spelt in many different ways throughout the edicts, meaning 'Beloved of the gods' and 'of pleasing appearance', and generally used in place of his name 'Aśoka'),[14] *dhaṃma* appears as the overarching ideal at the back of everything that Aśoka did, once he worked it out in his mind and decided to make it the guiding light of all his activities.

Dhaṃma in Aśoka's edicts, substantively alike in content and usually available in multiple copies, has an identity distinct and separate from Buddhism, his personal faith, to which also the term is occasionally applied.

For example, in the undated Bhabru or Bhabra or Bairat Rock Edict (Bhabru/Bhabra is a village 10 km north of Bairat, ancient Virāṭanagara, in Jaipur district of Rajasthan) or the Calcutta-Bairat Rock Edict (on the basis of its present location in the Asiatic Society of Bengal) addressed to the Buddhist *Saṃgha* (a Minor Rock Edict is also located at Bairat), Aśoka expresses his reverence to and faith in the Buddha, the *dhaṃma* and the *Saṃgha* (*hamā Budhasi dhaṃmasi Saṃghasī ti gālave caṃ prasāde ca*);[15] voices his conviction regarding the truth of the doctrine preached by the Buddha: 'Whatever has been spoken by the blessed Buddha (*bhagavatā Budhena*), is well-spoken (*e keci bhaṃte...sarve se subhāsite vā*)' and as regards the true *dhaṃma* (Buddhism) being long-enduring (*sadhaṃme cilaṭhitike hosati*); and recommends for repeated listening to and meditation by the monks and nuns as well as by the Buddhist laity seven expositions of *dhaṃma* (*dhaṃmapaliyāyāni*) with their titles selected by himself out of the numerous discourses of the Buddha in the Pāli Canon. Aśoka's adherence to Buddhism, to which he was probably attracted because of its stress on self-improvement, non-violence and ethical life, is also borne out by his pilgrimage to Lummini (Lumbini) village (*Lummminigāme*), the place of the Buddha's birth, in regnal year 20, his exempting it from *bali* (*ubalike*), a tax, and reducing *bhāga* to one-eighth share of the produce (*aṭhabhāgiye*), commemorated by the Rummindei Pillar Edict in the Nepalese Terai; his enlarging the *stūpa* of Konākamana, the mythical Buddha, to double its original size in regnal year 14, and pilgrimage to and worship at the site in regnal year 20, commemorated by the Nigali Sagar Pillar Edict, also in the Nepalese Terai; his claim to have maintained the unity of the *Saṃgha* through his order that no one should create a schism in it, and threat to expel those monks and nuns who cause a split in it (*Saṃghaṃ bhākhati*) (they were to be made to put on white robes and reside in a place not inhabited by the monks and nuns, *odātāni dusāni saṃnaṃdhāpayiyā ānāvāsasi āvāsayiye*), recorded in three versions of the Schism Edict on the pillars at Sarnath (near Varanasi, the most detailed), Allahabad and Sanchi (near Bhopal) and issued after regnal year 26 (the edict is addressed to the *mahāmātās*, who are asked to communicate it to the *Saṃghas* of the Buddhist monks and nuns as well as to the lay followers, to keep one copy at their office and another at a place of public assembly for study on the Buddhist day of fasting [*posatha,* Sanskrit *uposatha*], and to make it known even to the people in remote areas); his prohibition of the killing and sale of fish on each *posatha (anuposathaṃ)* in Pillar Edict V; inscription of *sveto hasti,* 'the white elephant', on the right side below Rock Edict XIII at Girnar (Gujarat), *seto,* 'the white (elephant)', at the top of the Dhauli rock (Odisha), and incision of the figure of an elephant with the label 'the best' (*gajatame*) on the north face of the Kalsi rock (near

Dehra Dun, Uttarakhand) (the Buddha is believed to have entered his mother's womb in the form of a white elephant).

In the entire series of Seven Pillar Edicts, the last among the edicts and found in Delhi, Uttar Pradesh and Bihar (Pillar Edicts I–VI were issued in regnal year 26 and Pillar Edict VII was issued in regnal year 27), there is a solitary reference in Pillar Edict VII to a few *dhaṃmamahāmātās* (Sanskrit *dharmamahāmātras*) having been ordered by Aśoka to busy themselves with the affairs of the *Saṃgha* (*Saṃghaṭhasi pi me kaṭe ime viyāpaṭā hohaṃṭi*), just as he asked other *dhaṃmamahāmātās* to take care of the interests of the Brāhmaṇas, Ājīvikas, Nigaṃṭhas (meaning 'without bonds, liberated', Sanskrit Nirgranthas or Jains) and other sects. (Except at three places, once each in Separate Rock Edict I at Dhauli and Jaugada and once in Kauśāmbī Pillar Edict, the edicts use *mahāmātā* in plural, because they mostly functioned as a collective body.) While *dhaṃma* is comprehensively treated in the relatively more voluminous Fourteen Rock Edicts, issued after the two Minor Rock Edicts (according to Pillar Edict VI, the earliest of these Rock Edicts, I–IV, were caused to be written for the happiness and welfare of the people when Aśoka had been consecrated for twelve years, *duvāḍasavasābhisitena*. Rock Edicts V–XIV, on the other hand, were issued in regnal year 13 or thereafter) and located in NWFP (Pakistan), Uttarakhand, Gujarat, Maharashtra, Andhra Pradesh, Odisha and Karnataka, the only time *dhaṃma* also conveys the sense of Buddhism therein is in the term *dhaṃmayātā* (Sanskrit *dharmayātrā*) in Rock Edict VIII. Here it refers to Aśoka's pilgrimage to Saṃbodhi (*ayāya Saṃbodhiṃ*), the place of the Buddha's enlightenment under the *pīpal* or Bodhi tree at Bodhgaya in Bihar in regnal year 10 (expired).[16] It marked the beginning of his tours of *dhaṃma* (*dhaṃmayātā*) in place of the tours of pleasure (*vihārayātā*) undertaken by kings in the past, and henceforth became a regular feature of his reign. 256, occurring in most of the Minor Rock Edicts I and II in figures, in Minor Rock Edict I at Ahraura in words, and at Sahasram in both words and figures, has been mostly interpreted as 256 nights/days spent by Aśoka on such a *dhaṃmayātā*.[17] In course of a *dhaṃmayātā*, instead of disseminating only Buddhism, Aśoka used to engage in activities which were an integral part of his more inclusive notion of *dhaṃma*. These included: 1) visiting and giving gifts to the Brāhmaṇas and Samaṇas (Sanskrit Śramaṇas; the Samaṇa connoted a non-Brāhmaṇa monk or ascetic; according to Rock Edict XIII, Aśoka found the Brāhmaṇas and Samaṇas everywhere except in the territory of the Yonas or Greeks), visiting the elderly (*thairānaṃ*) and distributing gold or money (*hiraṃna*) to them, visiting the people in the countryside (*janapada*), — this is regarded as the foremost duty (*mokhyamate*) in Pillar Edict VI, —instructing them in *dhamma* (*dhaṃmānusasṭi*), and making enquiries from them about *dhaṃma* (*dhaṃmaparipuchā*). As is obvious, the beneficiaries included not only the Buddhist monks, but also the monks and ascetics of other sects, Brāhmaṇas and old people leading mundane lives. Since *dhaṃma* signifies virtue, morality, duty, justice, custom, law and religion, anyone of these topics might have been hypothetically discussed in the course of interaction between the king and the people.[18] Aśoka admits that he derives more pleasure from his tour of *dhaṃma* (*esā bhuya rati bhavati*) than he did from his pleasure trips when he hunted animals and indulged himself.

An attempt is, however, made in Aśoka's edicts to elucidate the meaning of *dhaṃma* more precisely. *Dhaṃma* is presented here as a code of conduct—a set of rules or norms of interpersonal behaviour—for the ordinary worldly people, which seeks to promote mutual affection, courtesy, goodwill, large-heartedness, fellow-feeling and harmony within the family and society, and lays substantial stress on kind and humane treatment of the lowly and the meek as well as of the animals, birds and other creatures, and which could be followed without prejudice or harm to the various older *dhaṃmas.* There is nothing metaphysical, ritualistic or speculative about Aśoka's *dhaṃma.* Its essence is being right and doing right – doing to others what one would like to be done to oneself and sincerely endeavouring to lead a pure, ethical and useful life in the interest of all. Aśoka's concern, in his own words, is: 'How can I raise the (moral) level of the people through the promotion of *dhaṃma* (*kinasu kāni abhyuṃnāmayehaṃ dhaṃmavaḍhiyā ti*) (Pillar Edict VII, Delhi – Topra)? So much emphasis is laid on ethics, because it is considered vital for enriching the quality of human life.

The rules or norms of action constituting *dhaṃma* are laid down in the form of specific duties, which are held to be valid for all classes and sections of the people irrespective of the caste, sect or religion they belonged to.[19] In fact, Aśoka finds these suitable even for posterity and exhorts his descendants to observe and enforce them. Time and again he also affirms that he has got the edicts on *dhaṃma* inscribed for the welfare and happiness of mankind in order that these may endure long and the people of the future generations may live in conformity with them. The duties enjoined in these edicts usually appear in groups and are widely dispersed, though stray references to a particular duty, too, occur. Repetitions, far from being regarded as a demerit, are valued for driving home to the readers and listeners of these edicts the intrinsic worth of these duties and the necessity of performing them as daily routine. The accent is on performance. As Aśoka himself clarifies in Rock Edict XIV: 'Some of this (an edict on *dhaṃma* laying down a duty or a set of duties) has been stated again and again because of the charm or sweetness (*mādhūratāya*) of certain topics and in order that the people may act accordingly (*jano tathā paṭipajetha*). In Rock Edict IV he maintains that preaching *dhaṃma* is the best work (*seṣṭe kaṃme ya dhaṃmānusāsanaṃ*), and this edict has been caused to be written (*lekhāpitaṃ*) with a view to inducing his successors to aid the practice of *dhaṃma* till the end of the world, and to see that there is progress in this regard and no relapse is allowed (*imasa athasa vadhi yujaṃtu hīni ca no locetavyā*).

The chronology pertaining to Aśoka's *dhaṃma* is invaluable and of crucial importance for the history of the Maurya empire as well as for the Indian history. We are provided with the precise dates of Rock Edicts I-IV, Pillar Edict I-VI and VII, and the Kandahar Bilingual Edict as well as of such important events as the conquest of Kalinga appointment of the *dhammahamāmātās*, visits to Saṃbodhi, Luṃmini and the Konākamana Buddha *stūpa* at Nigali Sagar, gifts of three caves in the Barabar hills to the Ājīvikas, and the annual release of prisoners till regnal year 26. Even so, we do not know the exact date of such an important event as Aśoka's conversion to Buddhism – beyond the fact that it should have taken place before his pilgrimage to Saṃbodhi in regnal year 10, giving rise to several hypotheses, for example, a little less than 9½ years after his consecration,[20] regnal year 9,[21] and regnal year 8 or 7.[22] There is a consensus among the historians regarding the two undated Minor Rock Edicts found at seven places (five in Karnataka at Brahmagiri, Siddapur, Jatinga-Rameshvara, Nittur and Udegolam and two in Andhra Pradesh at Erragudi and Rajula-Mandagiri) (ten other inscriptions located at Maski, Gavimath and Palkigundu in Karnataka, Rupnath, Gujarra and Panguraria in Madhya Pradesh, Bairat in Rajasthan, Bahapur in Delhi, Ahraura in Uttar Pradesh and Sahasram in Bihar carry copies of Minor Rock Edict I only) being the earliest, regnal year 10 being their most likely date. (Minor Rock Edict II, never occurring alone and engraved soon after Minor Rock Edict I, is a kind of a supplement.) This is fully corroborated by the Shar-i Kuna (near Kandahar in Afghanistan) Bilingual Edict, its Greek version holding that ten years (since Aśoka's consecration) having been completed, he made his Eu'sebeia (*dhaṃma*) known to men, making them more pious from this moment, and everything thrives throughout the world; and its Aramaic text stating that ten years (since his anointment) having elapsed, he promoted Qšyṭ' (*dhaṃma*); evil has since then diminished among all men, adversity has disappeared, and there is peace and joy upon the whole earth.[23]

Harry Falk shows that though incised in the vicinity of the major settlements, the Minor Rock Edicts are found in or near the hill caves or pools of water away from the habitation sites and the people used to visit them in large numbers mostly at the time of the local festivals (*yātrās*) and not everyday or frequently.[24] He also holds the view that while Minor Rock

Edict I is meant to be inscribed on rocks at clearly defined places (the word *likhita* 'written' is used) and is addressed to a group of people at a specific spot, *likhita* is never used in the context of Minor Rock Edict II, which is intended to be orally transmitted in the entire country, and for which only *ānapayati* or *nivesayati* is used.[25] The Rock Edicts and Pillar Edicts, located on the trade routes and near the administrative centres, however, use several Prākrit terms for 'writing', such as *likhapita, likhapitu, likhapite, likhāpita, likhāpitā, likhita, likhitaṃ, likhitā, likhite,* etc., in the context of preaching *dhaṃma* within and outside the imperial domain. The location of the multi-lingual and multi-script edicts over such a large area also indicates the possibility of the élite being well-read and literacy being at least so widespread that the edicts could be read aloud any time anywhere to those who were unable to read them. The two Separate Rock Edicts in fact contain instructions regarding the reading out of the edicts before an assembled audience on the days of the constellation Tiṣya (*iyaṃ ca lipi tisanakhatena sotaviyā*) and also frequently in the interval even if one person was interested or present (*aṃtalā pi ca tisena khanasi khanasi ekena pi sotaviya*); unlike at Jaugada, the occurrence of Tiṣya every four months (*anucātuṃmāsaṃ*) is mentioned at Dhauli. (These two Separate Rock Edicts take the place of Rock Edicts XI, XII and XIII; portions of Separate Rock Edicts I and II, and incomplete texts of Rock Edicts XII and XIV, have also been found on a fragmentary slab inscription at Sannathi in Karnataka. It is presumed that since Rock Edict XIII describes the suffering of the people of Kaliṅga owing to the Mauryan invasion, it was considered impolitic to inscribe it in Odisha, and since Rock Edicts XI and XII had been issued with it, these, too, were omitted there.) Prākrit inscriptions in the Dravidian-speaking peninsula, too, would have required to be read out and possibly translated before the audience. *Dhaṃma* was, on the other hand, orally transmitted by Aśoka himself (Rock Edict VIII) and by the officials such as the *dhaṃmamahāmātās* (Rock Edict V), *rajūkas/rājūas* (Rock Edict III and Pillar Edict VII) and *yutas* and *prādesikas* (Rock Edict III) within the empire, and by the envoys (*dutā,* Kalsi; *duta*, Shahbazgarhi and Mansehra; the *dhaṃmamahāmātās* served as the envoys in the neighbouring Hellenistic kingdoms of West Asia) outside the empire (Rock Edict XIII) (the edicts mostly begin with the statement, *Devānaṃpiya Piyadasi* speaks thus, *aha, ahā, āha, ahati, hahati, āhā, aa,* etc., being used for speaking).

Though copies of the Minor Rock Edicts diverge much more than the Rock Edicts and the Pillar Edicts, a few qualities of *dhaṃma* (*dhaṃmaguṇā*), which are repeated or amplified in the Rock Edicts and the Pillar Edicts later on, are first enumerated in Minor Rock Edict II. These are: 1) obedience to mother and father, 2) obedience to elders, 3) reverence to the teacher (*ācariye*) by the pupil (*antevāsinā*), 4) courtesy to relatives (*nātikesu*), 5) compassion towards living beings (*prāṇesu drahyitavyaṃ*), and 6) speaking truth (*sacaṃ vataviyaṃ*). In order to motivate the people to practise them, these qualities are said to be conducive to longevity (*dīghāvuse*). While issuing the edict, Aśoka ordered that it be publicized through being engraved on rocks (*pavatisu,* Rupnath; *pavatesu,* Sahasram) and stone pillars (*silāṭhaṃbhasi,* Rupnath; *silāthaṃbha*, Sahasram); and the Brahmagiri version makes it clear that it was issued as a proclamation (*iyaṃ ca sāvane*) when Aśoka was on a tour.

Apart from Minor Rock Edict II and Rock Edict VIII, the qualities or features of *dhaṃma* are mentioned together in Rock Edicts III, IV, IX, XI and XIII and Pillar Edict VII. Thus Rock Edict III speaks of 1) obedience to mother and father, 2) liberality to Brāhmaṇas and Samaṇas, 3) liberality to friends, acquaintances and relatives, 4) abstention from killing living beings (*prāṇānaṃ... anāraṃbho*), and 5) moderation in spending (*apavyayatā*) and moderation in possessing (*apabhāḍatā*) as meritorious (*sādhu*). It also ordains that the *yutas* (*yuktas*) codify these precepts under the instructions of the *parisā* (Sanskrit *pariṣad,* Council), giving the reason and explanation (*hetuto ca vyaṃjanato ca*) as to why they are so esteemed. Rock Edict IV states that through the teaching of *dhaṃma* (*dhaṃmānusasṭiyā*) by Aśoka 1) obedience to mother and father, 2) obedience to the aged, 3) courtesy to Brāhmaṇas and Samaṇas, 4) courtesy to relatives, 5) abstention from killing living beings, and 6) non-injury to creatures (*avihīsā bhūtānaṃ*) have now increased as never before (*na bhūtapuve tārise*). Rock Edict IX describes the rite or ceremony of *dhaṃma* as immensely fruitful (*mahāphale... dhaṃmamaṃgale*), which must be performed (*katavyameva*); includes in it 1) courtesy to slaves and servants (*dāsabhatakamhi samyapratipatī*), 2) respect for elders (*gurūnaṃ apacitī*), 3) liberality to Brāhmaṇas and Samaṇas, and 4) restraint in respect of (not harming) living beings (*pāṇesu sayamo*); and exhorts the people to practise these to achieve their desired material object (*tasa athasa nisṭānāya*), in place of the many and various kinds of petty and useless rites or ceremonies of good omen (*bahukaṃ ca bahuvidhaṃ ca chudaṃ ca nirathaṃ ca maṃgalaṃ*), whose fruit is meagre (*apaphalaṃ*), and which men and women, especially women, observe during illness, at the birth of a son, marriage of a son or a daughter, and while going on a journey, to avert harm and induce luck. In a word, he wanted the people to imbibe the rational lesson that conduct and action in accordance with *dhaṃma* would bear fruit and should be preferred to the performance of ceremonies and rituals. Realizing that the people close to a person may be able to induce him/her to practise *dhaṃmamaṃgala*, Aśoka urges the father, son, husband/master, brother, friend, companion and well-wisher to do so.

Both Rock Edicts IX and XI refer to *dhaṃmadāna* (gift of *dhaṃma*) and hold it as superior to every other gift. This is a reiteration of verse 354 in the *Dhammapada.* In Rock Edict IX *dhaṃmadāna* is equated with *dhaṃmamaṃgala.* In Rock Edict XI *dhaṃmadāna* is said to consist of praise of *dhaṃma* (*dhaṃmasaṃstavo*), sharing in *dhaṃma* (*dhaṃmasaṃvibhāgo*) and kinship through *dhaṃma* (*dhaṃmasaṃbadho*); and *dhaṃma* is held to comprise 1) courtesy to slaves and servants, 2) obedience to mother and father, 3) liberality to Brāhmaṇas and Samaṇas, 4) liberality to friends, acquaintances and relatives, and 5) abstention from killing living beings. Here, too, Aśoka invokes help from the father, son, brother, friend, acquaintance, relatives and even neighbours in motivating the people to follow these precepts.

The characteristics of *dhaṃma* are also recounted in Rock Edict XIII and Pillar Edict VII without being designated as such. In Rock Edict XIII at Kalsi and Shahbazgarhi (the Girnar version has gaps), expressing his anguish and remorse at the large-scale slaughter, death and deportation of the people of Kaliṅga during the war, Aśoka avers that he is especially distressed because those who lost their dear ones included the Brāhmaṇas, the Samaṇas, the adherents of other sects and the householders, who showed 1) obedience to their superiors (*agabhuti* at Kalsi; *agrabhuṭi* at Shahbazgarhi), 2) obedience to mother and father, 3) obedience to elders (*guruna* at Shahbazgarhi), 4) courtesy to friends, acquaintances, companions and relatives, 5) courtesy to slaves and servants, and 6) firm devotion (*daḍhabhatitā* at Girnar; *diḍhabhatitā* at Kalsi; *dṛḍhabhatita* at Shahbazgarhi). The edict creates the impression that *dhaṃma* was already being vigorously practised in Kaliṅga before the war and that Aśoka was only trying to revive it after its disruption as a result of the bloody conflict. That Kaliṅga was a strategically and commercially important, powerful and populous state at the time of Aśoka's invasion hardly needs stressing. In Pillar Edict VII Aśoka claims that the world has consented to and followed the good deeds he has done, and in consequence 1) obedience to mother and father, 2) obedience to elders, 3) courtesy to the aged (*vayomahālakānaṃ,* Delhi-Topra), 4) courtesy to Brāhmaṇas and Samaṇas,5) courtesy to the poor and the destitute (*kapanavalākesu*), and 6) courtesy to slaves and servants[26] have increased and will increase (*vaḍhitā ca vaḍhisaṃti ca*).

We come across a lot of continuing emphasis on the acquisition of ethical qualities, including those mentioned earlier, in other edicts of Aśoka. Thus purity of conduct (*sīla)* is deemed to be essential in Rock Edict IV; self-control (*sayama*), purity of mind / motive (*bhāvasudhi),* gratitude (*kataṃnatā)* and firm devotion (*đaḍhabhatitā)* are extolled in Rock Edict VII; non-violence/harmlessness (*akṣati)*, self-control, impartiality/equability (*samacariyaṃ*) and cheerfulness (*rabhasiye*) (Hultzsch translates it differently) are commended in Rock Edict XIII; Aśoka also promises forgiveness (*kṣamanaye*) in this edict to all those who can be forgiven and to the unconquered border people (*aṃtānaṃ avijitānaṃ*) in Separate Rock Edict II; *dhaṃma* is defined as comprising compassion (*dayā*), liberality (*dāne*), truthfulness (*sace*) and purity (*socayelsocave*) in Pillar Edicts II and VII; the latter also includes gentleness (*madave*) and goodness (*sādhave*) in its list; self-control and distribution of gifts (*dānasavibhāga*) are praised in Pillar Edict IV; and strenuous effort (*pakama, parākrama*) and great zeal (*agena usāhena*) are esteemed in Minor Rock Edict I, Rock Edict X and Pillar Edict I. Undertaking fast (*upavāsaṃ*) is one of the options along with bestowing gift open to a prisoner condemned to death during three days' respite granted to him to prepare for the other world in Pillar Edict IV. Aśoka looks upon virtues as an intergrated whole and requires the people to cultivate as many of them as possible. Thus, he contends in Rock Edict VII that in the absence of self-control, purity of mind, gratitude and firm devotion, even a person who practises great liberality (*vipule dāne*) is very mean (*nicā bāḍhaṃ*).

The need to desist from sin (*pāpaṃ*) or demerit (*apuṃnaṃ*), accruing from evil deeds (*dukataṃ*), and to perform good deeds, which is difficult (*kalāṇaṃ dukaraṃ*), is underlined in Rock Edict V and Pillar Edicts II and III; the desirability of the absence of sin (*apāsinave*) and its great fear (*agena bhayenā*) are stressed in Pillar Edicts II and I; and introspection or careful self-examination (*agāya palīkhāyā*) is suggested as useful in this regard in Pillar Edict I. Ferocity (*caṃḍiye*), cruelty (*niṭhūliye*), anger (*kodhe*), pride (*māne*) and envy (*isyā*) are viewed as ruinous vile traits in Pillar Edict III; and the failure of the *mahāmātās* to provide justice to the prisoners impartially is attributed to such defects in their character as envy, cruelty, irritability (*āsulopa*), haste (*tūlanā*), heedlessness (*anāvuti*), sloth (ālasa) and weariness (*kilamatha*) in Separate Rock Edict I. That Aśoka earnestly tried to impart spiritual insight into right and wrong, doable and not doable, good and bad, through his edicts on *dhaṃma* (he himself calls it the 'gift of the eye', *cakhudāne*, in Pillar Edict II) is indisputable.

Of all the ethical qualities mentioned in these edicts, non-violence, the primary article of his faith as a Buddhist, is prized the most, and Aśoka did not hesitate to adopt even some unpalatable measures to promote it within the empire. Thus, while the *Arthaśāstra* of Kauṭilya (V.3.3) prescribed a salary of forty-eight thousand *paṇas* for the sacrificial priest (*ṛtvik*), Aśoka imposed a ban on the slaughter of animals at a sacrifice in Rock Edict I, which reads: *idha na kiṃci jīvaṃ ārabhitpā prajūhitavyaṃ*. '*Idha* (here)' apparently refers to the capital city of Pāṭaliputra. This is the only reference to the interdiction of sacrifice in the edicts, which, apart from being a major source of livelihood for the priests, was believed in by a large number of the adherents of Brahmanism.

Aśoka also prohibited festive gatherings (*na ca samājo katavyo*) in Rock Edict I, because he perceived many faults in them (*bahukaṃ hi dosaṃ samājambi pasati*). Although these faults are not specified, since this ban follows immediately after the ban on the sacrifice and precedes Aśoka's explicit reference to the drastic reduction in the slaughter of animals for curry in the royal kitchen from 'several hundred thousands' to just three, and his intention to stop killing even these in future (*pachā na ārabhisare*), and since there is no general ban on animal slaughter, one may reasonably infer that these festive gatherings were associated with the ritual slaughter or sacrifice of animals. Sharing intoxicating drinks and merry-making with drum-beating may have been other faults of these festive gatherings, for Aśoka claims in Rock Edict IV that owing to his efforts to boost *dhaṃma*, the sound of drum has become the sound of *dhaṃma* (*dhaṃmacaraṇena bherīghoso aho dhaṃmaghoso*). He, however, identifies one type of festive gatherings as meritorious in Rock Edict I (*ekacā samājā sādhumatā*). This was evidently the assembly of people in Rock Edict IV which was shown the divine spectacles to disseminate *dhaṃma*.

Aśoka had discontinued the practice of hunting (*magavyā*) as part of the pleasure-trip (*vihārayātā*) in Rock Edict VIII. In Pillar Edict II he professes to have conferred many benefits on the bipeds and the quadrupeds, on the birds and the aquatic animals, including the boon of life (*pānadākhinaye*). Pillar Edict V contains elaborate regulations in this regard, similar to the *Arthaśāstra* (II. 26.2–3, 5–6) proscription of the slaughter of and injury to a variety of fish, birds and animals. The sanctity attached to the animal life in Pillar Edict V is indicated by the inclusion of the animals 'neither useful nor edible' in the list of those which were not to be killed at all. But while the *Arthaśāstra* (II. 26.10–11) forbade the killing of the milch cow (*dhenu*), the calf and the bull, and imposed a fine of fifty *paṇas* on the offender, only the *saṃḍaka* (bull set at liberty and used for breeding) finds place in Pillar Edict V, not other cattle. A few female species of other animals were spared their lives along with their young ones till the latter were six months old. The fish could neither be killed nor sold, and some animals were not to be castrated or branded, on a few days during Tiṣya, Punarvasu and Cāturmāsa or on the Buddhist fast-day (*posatha*). The forest was not to be set ablaze uselessly or to kill animals, nor could chaff containing life be burnt. Living animals were also not to be fed living animals.

In Rock Edict II and Pillar Edict VII Aśoka underscores the fact that with a view to conforming to the practice of *dhaṃma*, in his philanthropic work such as arranging for medical treatment, importing and planting beneficial herbs, roots and fruits, planting banyan trees and mango-groves along the roads, digging wells and setting up drinking places, he had taken due care of the interest of both the human beings and the animals, including those living in the border areas and the neighbouring kingdoms.

What, however, gave a completely new dimension to non-violence was Aśoka's devastating war against Kaliṅga in regnal years 8, which proved to be a turning-point in his reign and in the history of the Maurya dynasty. Though first recorded after a gap of at least five years in Rock Edict XIII, his well-publicized momentous decision not to engage in aggressive warfare in future in spite of his incomparable military strength in the contemporary world, which he scrupulously honoured without a single break, meant a complete halt to the long process of continuous Magadhan expansion from the sixth century BC onwards, and inaugurated for nearly three decades (Aśoka died in *c.*234 BC) the first and only known and recorded period of peace in the Indian subcontinent and the adjoining regions. Aśoka certainly deserves to be duly remembered for this singular achievement. Henceforth the conquest by *dhaṃma* (*dhaṃmavijaya*), in place of the armed territorial conquest, became the settled policy of the Mauryan state, and he claims to have achieved this conquest repeatedly within his own domain and that of his neighbours, far and near, including the Greek kingdoms. This implied assuming virtually the moral leadership of the civilized world. Aśoka not only describes the conquest by *dhaṃma* as the foremost (*mukhamuta*) and the only true conquest, he even asked his descendants to abjure territorial conquest in future, and, if it takes place at all, show forbearance (*kṣaṃti*) and mete out mild punishment (*lahudaṃḍata*).

Aśoka had inherited from his grandfather Candragupta Maurya (*c.*322 BC—*c.* 298 BC) and father Bindusāra (*c.* 298 BC — *c.* 270 BC) a vast dominion extending deep into Afghanistan up to the borders of the Greek ruler Antiochus II of Syria in the north-west and the base of the Himalayas in the north, southern Andhra and Karnataka in the south, Gujarat and Konkan in the west, and much of Bengal in the east. Though the Colas and the Pāṇḍyas, the Keralaputas and the Satiyaputas (Tamilnadu and Kerala) and Taṃbapaṃnī (Sri Lanka) in the extreme south, and the Greek kingdoms of Syria and West Asia in the north-west remained independent, the former were friendly and sought Aśoka's goodwill, and the latter received his envoys and allowed *dhaṃma* to be preached among them. With the conquest and annexation of Kaliṅga, Aśoka became the ruler of the largest empire in ancient India. Owing to its lengthy duration, diversity of population, languages, religions and cultures, and the extraordinary personalities of its first three rulers, the Maurya empire may be hailed as the symbol of India's unity. In Minor Rock Edict I at Rupnath, Bairat and

Sahasram and in Minor Rock Edicts I and II at Brahmagiri Aśoka designated it as Jaṃbudīpa (Jaṃbudvīpa, 'the Rose – apple Island'), one of the earliest names of India. Gerard Fussman[27] rightly points out that ancient Indian literature, Brahmanical, Buddhist and Jain, has always considered India as a unit, even if it has not defined its borders precisely.

Aśoka also deserves to be remembered by posterity for the vision displayed and the approach adopted by him in his edicts on *dhaṃma*, especially in Rock Edicts V, VII and XII, to address the problem and prospect of the aggravating religious tension and acrimony caused by the heated theological debates and strident propaganda of the many rival sects, competing for a larger share of alms, gifts and patronage of the king, the affluent classes and the common people in his own time (according to Rock Edict XIII, there was no place where the people were not attached to one sect or another, *nāsti mānusānaṃ ekatarambhi pāsaṃḍambhi na nāma prasādo*), and to ensure their peaceful and harmonious coexistence. (The application of such pejorative terms as *pāṣaṇḍa*, I. 18.9, 12; I. 19.29; II, 4.23; II.36.14; III. 16.32, 33, 39 , and *vṛṣala*, I. 12.5; III. 20.16, in the sense of a heretic, to the Buddhists, Jain and Ājīvakas, so spelt, in the *Arthaśāstra* of Kauṭilya, and of *pāsaṃḍa* to the Brāhmaṇas and other non-Buddhists in the Buddhist Pāli texts, underscores the intensity of the sectarian rivalry.) Rock Edict V informs us that Aśoka created the office of the *dhaṃmamahāmātās* with a fairly large jurisdiction for the first time to establish and promote *dhaṃma* among all the sects (*savapāsaṃḍesu*) when he had been anointed for thirteen years. (*Pāsaṃḍa* ceased to be a term expressing contempt and came to denote a religious sect or denomination under Aśoka.) It is striking that in Rock Edict VII Aśoka distinguishes between the sects and their followers: while the latter were imputed many desires and several passions (*ucāvacachaṃdo ucāvacarāgo*), the sects themselves were exonerated of all faults and held to be yearning for self-control and purity of thought (*sayamaṃ ca bhāvasudhiṃ ca ichati*). As such, he expressed his will to let all the sects reside everywhere (*sarvata ... save pāsaṃḍā vaseyu*). Since the *Arthaśāstra* of Kauṭilya (II.1.32) did not permit an ascetic sect other than the Brahmanical forest hermit to settle in the Crown villages (*vānaprasthādanyaḥ pravrajitabhāvaḥ ... nāsya janapadamupaniviśeta*), which covered the greater part of the countryside, the significance of this grant of uninhibited freedom to settle and preach everywhere within the empire cannot be overstated. Kosambi rightly describes this as 'the most far-reaching concession'[28] granted to the heretical sects, making all the sects effectively equal in his domain. The *Arthaśāstra* prescription (II.1.7) regarding the land grants being conferred only on the Brāhmaṇa priests, preceptors, chaplains and Vedic scholars also became inoperative now. Aśoka was, however, alive to the danger of the misuse of this freedom by the sects and anxious to ensure that it did not degenerate into a licence to abuse each other and vitiate the communal atmosphere. With no intention to supplant or subvert them, he used *dhaṃma* as a binding force to weld them into a cohesive network. Hence, while the growth and development of the individual sects was to be facilitated, there was to be no compromise on the goal of inter-faith concord (*samavāya*), which Aśoka described as commendable (*sādhu*) in Rock Edict XII. The solution he found to this difficult issue on the basis of a masterly, detailed and cogent analysis of the contemporary situation in this edict[29] is astonishingly modern, possibly without a parallel in history, and Aśoka's another significant contribution and legacy to India and the world in the twenty-first century.

In promoting the essence of *dhaṃma* preached by the different sects (*sāravaḍhī*), Aśoka declares with all the emphasis at his command, lies the key to more knowledge about each other, empathy, friendliness, mutual accommodation and peace among them. He affirms that he bestows gifts and honours on both the ascetics and the householders (*pavajitāni ca gharastāni ca*) of all the sects (*savapāsaṃḍāni*) (conferring on all the sects honours of various kinds, *savapāsaṃḍā pi me pūjitā vividhāyā pūjāyā*, is also mentioned in Pillar Edict VI), but that he does not value either gifts or honours so highly as that the essence of the teaching of these sects be promoted (*na tu tathā dānaṃ va pūjā va Devānaṃpiyo maṃnate yathā kiti sāravaḍhī asa savapāsaṃḍānaṃ*). To underline the point he is making, the sentence is repeated with minor changes within the space of a few lines: *Devānaṃpiyo no tathā dānaṃ va pūjāṃ va maṃnate yathā kiṃti sāravaḍhī asa sarvapasaḍānaṃ*). Going into the many ways (*bahuvidhā*) in which this essence can be promoted, he pinpoints its root (*mūlaṃ*) to be guarding one's speech (*vacigutī*), not praising one's own sect (*ātpapāsaṃḍapūjā*), nor denigrating other sects (*parapāsaṃḍagarahā*) on improper occasion (*aprakaraṇambhi*), remaining moderate (*Iahukā*) even on those occasions, and duly honouring other sects (*pūjetayā tu eva parapāsaṃḍā*) on every occasion. The result of acting thus is the advancement (*vaḍhayati*) of one's own sect and benefit (*upakaroti*) to other sects, he perceptively observes; and warns that acting otherwise, one undermines (*chaṇati*) one's own sect and harms (*apakaroti*) other sects as well. Elaborating further, he points out that if a person out of devotion to one's own sect (*ātpapāsaṃḍabhatiyā*) and with a view to glorifying (*dīpayema*) it, eulogizes it and vilifies other sects, he injures his own sect very severely (*bāḍhataraṃ upahanāti*). The term *bhati*, Sanskrit *bhakti*, devotion, occurs here earlier than in the *Bhagavadgītā*, and is associated with someone's sect or religion, not with the king. Aśoka also considers it beneficial (*kalāṇāgamā*) for the people to be well-informed and knowledgeable (*bahusrutā*) about each other's sect (ignorance breeds fear and phobia), and asks them to both listen to and obey (*sruṇāru ca susuṃsera ca*) each other's *dhaṃma*. What is being advocated is not just tolerance, or even accommodation, but readiness to understand [30] each other through mutual dialogue, and accept and follow the best in all religions. And Aśoka does not seem to entertain even the slightest doubt that the adoption of the course suggested by him will unfailingly achieve the objective he has in view – progress of all the sects in the overall context of inter-religious accord and harmony. To enable even women and the most humble segments of the population to gain from his measures, he asked the *mahāmātās* in charge of women (*ithījhakhamahāmātās*: Sanskrit *strī-adhyakṣamahāmātras*) and the superintendents of pasture (*vacabhūmīkās*), along with the *dhaṃmamahāmātās*, to see to it that the royal guidelines are scrupulously observed by both the sects and their followers. The last four words of Rock Edict XII sum up Aśoka's joy and exultation at the prospect of the people being acquainted with the essence of different religions, and of concord and peace among them; to him it is nothing short of *dhaṃma* shining in all its splendour (*hoti dhaṃmasa ca dīpanā*).

Aśoka's even-handed treatment of the Brāhmaṇas and the Samaṇas (also spelt as Śamaṇas, Śramaṇas and Ṣamaṇas in the edicts) proves the earnestness and sincerity of his passionate advocacy of the policy of religious toleration. The Samaṇas represented a sizeable category of non-producing, casteless and classless ascetics, who rejected the authority of the Vedas and pre-eminence of the Brāhmaṇas, and played a leading role in the religious and intellectual movement of the sixth century BC. Castelesssness was in fact so deeply ingrained in them that even the Brāhmaṇas joining their ranks (their number was substantial; both Pūrana Kassapa and Sañjaya Belaṭṭhaputta, for example, were Brāhmaṇas, cf. Kosambi, *Introduction*, p. 157) lost their caste identity; and the Samaṇas were generally distinguished from the Brāhamṇa ascetics. 'Śramaṇa' in the sense of a Brāhmaṇa ascetic is mentioned only once in the Upaniṣads, in the *Bṛhadāraṇyaka Upaniṣad*, which states that the distinction between a Śramaṇa and a non-Śramaṇa vanishes in the world of spirit (*atra śramaṇo'śramaṇo bhavati*, V.3.22). 'Muṇḍaka', too, in the sense of a shaven-headed forest-dwelling Brāhmaṇa ascetic, occurs in the *Muṇḍaka Upaniṣad* (I.2.11); and the *muṇḍakas* are described as calm and wise (*śāntā vidvāṃso*), endowed with faith and practising penance (*tapaḥśraddhe*), and begging their food (*bhaikṣacaryāṃ carantaḥ*), who go where the immortal Person, the immutable Self, is (*te prayānti yatrāmṛtaḥ sa puruṣo hyavyayātmā*). The Samaṇas of the Buddhist texts and Aśokan edicts also sought knowledge and salvation, but never God or soul, preached, debated and spread their diverse doctrines, and competed with the Brāhmaṇa ascetics and among themselves as the followers of different non-Brāhmaṇa sects for more patronage and influence. The Buddha defines the Brāhmaṇa as someone endowed with wisdom and virtue (*vuddha-sīlī, Dīgha Nikāya,* Vol. I, p. 121) and speaks of the Samaṇas and the Brāhmaṇas as the objects of reverence; and Megasthenes refers to the 'Brachmanes' and 'Sarmanes' as the two classes of 'philosophers', ranking them as the first among his seven 'castes', The Brāhmaṇa is an idealized category, an epitome of saintliness, in the *Dhammapada*, which devotes one full chapter (XXVI) to him. Apart from possessing other qualities, he is a person who does no evil in thought, word or deed (verse 391), in whom there is truth and righteousness (verse 393), who is virtuous, free from anger and self-controlled (verse 400), who has profound knowledge, is wise, and discerns the right and wrong paths (verse 403), who is unattached, calm and friendly (verse 406), and whose lust and hatred, pride and hypocrisy have fallen off (verse 407). Aśoka's disallowing the sacrifice and festive gatherings,censure of the Brahmanical rituals, and measures to end discriminiation against the non-Brāhmaṇa sects are unlikely to have gone down well with the Brāhmaṇas, who had so far enjoyed a dominant position, and Patañjali compares the persisting mutual antagonism between the Brāhmaṇas and the Samaṇas with eternal opposition (*virodhaḥ śāśvatikaḥ*) between the snake and the mongoose (*Mahābhāṣya* on *Aṣṭādhyāyī*, II 4.9). The edicts, however, almost invariably dovetail the Brāhmaṇas and the Samaṇas, and portray them as the religious leaders of the community, receiving courtesy, alms, gifts and honours. The king even waited upon them in course of his arduous long tours and discussed *dhaṃma* with them. That Aśoka's adherence to Buddhism did not stand in the way of his fair treatment of the non-Buddhist and even anti-Buddhist sects is sharply brought out by his liberality to the Nirgranthas and donation of two caves in the Barabar hills near Gaya in south Bihar to the Ājīvikas, who were among the chief rivals of the Buddhists, in regnal year 12 and the third cave there in regnal year 19.

Like-non-violence and religious toleration, liberality (*dāne*) (Rock Edicts III, VII, VIII, IX, XI, XII, Pillar Edicts II and VII and the 'Queen's Edict'), too, is a salient feature of Aśoka's *dhaṃma*, because the number of people depending on it was quite large, and charity was not only a natural way to show compassion, but also a potent means to gain heaven (charity makes the giver happy in the next world, *sukhī parattha*, states the *Dhammapada*, verse 177). The beneficiaries included not only the Brāhmaṇas and the Samaṇas, and the relatives, friends and acquaintances of the donor, but also the aged, orphans, destitutes, and, according to Pillar Edict VII, the deserving recipients in Pāṭaliputra and the provinces (*tuṭhāyatanāni paṭi hida ceva disāsu ca*). The contribution for charity, in-cash and kind, was received principally from the king and the members of the royal family. Due attention was, however, also paid to collecting the subscription from all those who were inclined to charity (*dānasayute*, Rock Edict V, Shahbazgarhi). The distribution of charity on a huge scale was meticulously organized chiefly through the *dhaṃmamahāmātās,* who also played a key role in accumulating money and material for the purpose, and their effort was supplemented by other officials of the state. Special importance attaches to the undated 'Queen's Edict' found on the Allahabad pillar, because it not only takes note of Aśoka's order that the gift of his second queen Kāluvāki (Kāruvāki) be duly recorded in her name, but also because it mentions her actual gift—the mango-groves, retreats, alms-houses, etc.

The government machinery under Aśoka was fully geared to inculcate *dhaṃma* among the people, with most of the officials being seriously involved in it. The primary responsibility in this regard lay with the *dhaṃmamahāmātās*, who had unfettered direct access to the king, his female establishments and those of his brothers, sisters and other relatives. Working in Pāṭaliputra and the outlying towns, among the neighbouring peoples and the distant regions, they promoted mutual understanding and goodwill among the various sects as well as the essence of *dhaṃma*, and distributed charity among them. In Rock Edict III Aśoka is seen enjoining the *yutas, rājūkas* and *prādesikas* to instruct the people in *dhaṃma* along with discharging their other duties (*anāya pi kaṃmāya*) in course of their quinquennial tours. In Separate Rock Edict II the *mahāmātās* at Tosali and Samapa are exhorted to induce the unconquered border people to practise *dhaṃma* (*dhaṃmaṃ caleyū*, Dhauli; *calevū* at Jaugada). In Pillar Edict I Aśoka attests that his officials (*pulisā*) of various ranks, high, low and middle, are able to firm up the wavering in the practice of *dhaṃma.* That the officials were closely associated with issuing, engraving and setting up the edicts in every nook and corner of the empire is certain. In fact, the edicts create the impression that his officials were much more intimately connected with propagating *dhaṃma* than with safeguarding the interests of Buddhism, the Schism Edict providing the evidence of their closest association with the latter. Aśoka was, of course, himself the originator and ultimate source of the idea of *dhaṃma*, its content and form; he was also its inspiration and guide, and undertook extensive trips to make it a vibrant and dynamic reality in his own lifetime. Recounting his own experience in Pillar Edict VII, he states that of the two methods he had adopted for the progress of *dhaṃma, nijhati*, instruction, or, in the words of B.M. Barua, 'appeal to reason and understanding' or 'moral persuasion',[31] and *dhaṃmaniyama*, regulations pertaining to *dhaṃma*, he had found the former much more effective.

Aśoka's *dhaṃma* embraces the whole life, including its secular aspect, and promoting the well-being and happiness (*hitasukha*) of the people was the most cherished objective of his reign, repeated several times in the edicts. In Rock Edict VI he proclaims his most important duty (*katavyaṃ; nāsti kaṃmataraṃ*) to be to further the well-being of all men (*sarvalokahitaṃ, sarvalokahitatpā*). Recognizing that it is not possible to accomplish this without great exertion (*agena parākramena*), zeal and dispatch of business, he instructs his reporters (*paṭivedakā*), posted everywhere, to keep him informed of the affairs of the people all the time wherever he was, while eating, in the harem, in the bed chamber (*gabhāgārambhi*), at the cowpen (public place), in the conveyance (on a journey), or in the garden. He also asserts that all his effort is aimed at discharging the debt (*ānaṇaṃ gacheyaṃ*) he owes to living beings by making them happy in this world and by enabling them to attain heaven in the other. The notion of debt first appears in the sense of moral obligation in the *Taittirīya Saṃhitā*, a later Vedic text, which states that a Brāhmaṇa is born with a triple debt (*tribhirṛṇavā jāyate*), of studentship to the seer (*brahmacaryeṇa ṛṣibhyo)*, of sacrifice to the gods (*yajñena devebhyaḥ*) and of the offspring to the ancestors (*prajayā pitṛbhya...*) (VI. 3.10.5). This is quoted verbatim in the post-Vedic *Baudhāyana Dharmasūtra* (II. 11.33) and repeated in the *Vasiṣṭha Dharmasūtra* (XI. 48) with minor change of order (*yajñena devebhyaḥ prajayā pitṛbhyaḥ brahmacaryeṇa ṛṣibhyaḥ*). The notion of debt is, however, not extended to the Kṣatriya king, nor is there even a remote hint in Aśoka's edicts that he was aware of or derived it from any Brahmanical source. Under Buddhism the debtor does not find any relief in the temporal world and his entry into the *Saṃgha* is forbidden. Aśoka, however, seems to be using debt in a contractual or legal sense, in return for the tax or revenue received from his subjects.[32] The idea of the king's debt is repeated in Separate Rock Edict II; and in Separate Rock Edicts I and II the *mahāmātās* of Tosali and Samapa are reminded of their debt to the king, because they are well provided for (*suvihitā*) (by means of salary and perks obtained from him), and they must discharge the debt to him (*mama ca āṇaniyaṃ ehatha*, Dhauli; *mama ca ānaneyaṃ esatha,* Jaugada) by obeying his instructions to his satisfaction. As in Rock Edict VI, these instructions related to the welfare and happiness (*savena hitasukhena*) of all his subjects; that is his will (*dhiti*) and unshakable resolve (*paṭimnā ca acala*), he stresses in Separate Rock Edicts I and II. As if this is not enough, he also introduces the paternal principle in Separate Rock Edicts I and II: 'All men are my children (*savamunisā me pajā*)', and declares that just as he desires complete welfare and happiness of his children in this world and the next, so he desires for all men. In Pillar Edict IV he confides that after entrusting the welfare and happiness of the people in the countryside to the *lajūkas* (*rajūkas*) he feels relaxed like someone who has placed his child under the care of an intelligent nurse (*viyātāye dhātiye*). In Pillar Edict VI he professes to pay attention not only to his relatives (*nātisu*), but also to the welfare and happiness of the people, near and far. Clearly, the edicts leave nothing unstated or understated regarding his total commitment to the well-being of his subjects and his earnest endeavour to motivate and involve the officials in this noble enterprise.

That Aśoka was in theory an absolute ruler, the fountain-head of all authority in his empire, is definite. 'Whatever I recognize to be right, that I strive to carry out by deeds, and to accomplish by various means', he insists in Separate Rock Edicts I and II. In practice, however, he seems to have both shared and delegated his authority, and endeavoured to check its misuse. Thus, according to Rock Edict VI, the king's verbal order to the *mahāmātās* in connection with a donation or proclamation could be discussed in the Council (*parisā*) and an amendment moved there, though this was to be immediately brought to his notice by the reporters, probably for clarification or final decision. In Pillar Edict IV rewards and punishments in the countryside are left to the discretion of the *lajūkas* (*rajūkas*), who are asked to obey him and his officials (*pulisāni*) and be impartial in judicial proceedings (*viyohālasamatā*) and in punishment (*daṃḍasamatā*). Aśoka was fully aware that the officials in remote areas sometimes took their own decision. Thus he states in Rock Edict XIV that one of the reasons why the edicts were not uniform in size everywhere was that his motive was not liked. He was, however, not ready to allow this beyond a point. Thus to ensure that the *mahāmātās* at Tosali and Samapa observed his pro-people instructions, Separate Rock Edicts I and II were to be read before the latter on certain specified days to acquaint them with what these officials were expected by the king to do in the interest of the people. Trips by the supervisory officials and the king himself, too, served to keep them in track.

Coercive authority (*daṃḍa*) is at the root of the government; and this had been both the theory and practice before Aśoka. Telling the unconquered border people not to fear him and expect only love and goodwill from him, as Aśoka did in Separate Rock Edict II, meant opening a new chapter in the history of Indian kingship. Even in the case of the forest people, his policy involved a significant departure from that of his predecessors. Thus though they are told of the king's power to punish them in spite of his repentance so that they do not disturb peace and get killed, they are conciliated and made to practise *dhaṃma* (*anuneti anunijapeti*) (Rock Edict XIII; Hultzsch's translation of *anunijapeti* as 'converts', op.cit., p. 69, is somewhat inappropriate). The *dhammamahāmātās* are also asked to take care of the material well-being of all sections, and these included not only the Brāhmaṇas, the rich and the masters, but also the servants, the poor and the suffering prisoners. Aśoka himself used to declare amnesty for the latter once every year.

There is evidence in the edicts to suggest that the precepts of *dhamma* preached by Aśoka were being practised. For instance, progress in respect of obedience to mother and father as well as to elders, and with regard to abstaining from killing and hurting animals is attested in the Greek and Aramaic versions of the Kandahar Bilingual Edict; and in respect of non-injury to creatures is underlined in the Taxila (Sirkap) Pillar Edict. That Aśoka is relatively more favourably inclined to the lower segments of society is also indicated in a few edicts. For example, in Rock Edict X he maintains that progress in *dhaṃma* through zeal and concentrated effort would be more difficult for the great (*usaṭa*) than for an humble person (*khudaka*). Precedence given to the slaves and servants in Rock Edicts IX and X, while enumerating the constituent elements of *dhaṃma*, would have been avoided in most Brahmanical texts. The complete absence of the caste perspective is equally conspicuous. Neither the word *varṇa* nor *jāti* occurs even once in any of the edicts; and obedience to *varṇa* or *jāti* does not even implicitly form a part of Aśoka's *dhaṃma*. That in a period when caste was an important social reality, Aśoka should cherish a vision bypassing caste is remarkable indeed! The salutary influence of Buddhism in all this cannot be missed. Kosambi attributes the prescription regarding moderate possessions and moderate spending in Rock Edict III to the 'greatest economic strain' 'manifested in the heavily debased and hastily minted coinage'.[33] In the context of Aśoka's *dhaṃma*, however, it has an ethical dimension as well, for Aśoka certainly viewed crazy pursuit and accumulation of wealth and its enjoyment solely for selfish ends as unethical. That explains so much stress laid on sharing wealth with the indigent and the deprived through the practice of liberality with no discrimination against the householders and the people outside the realm of religion.

As regards 'firm devotion' occurring in Rock Edict XIII, the context does not suggest its connection with the king, as has been occasionally maintained,[34] for, as Kosambi notes, Kaliṅga had always been outside the Maurya empire and at the time of Aśoka's military conquest it did not have a king worth naming.[35] In Rock Edict XII devotion (*bhati:* Sanskrit *bhakti*) relates specifically to one's sect (*ātpapāsaṃḍabhatiyā*). Evidently devotion is used in Aśoka's edicts as a positive human trait indicating love, affinity and allegiance in interpersonal and social relationships, and is neither explicitly nor intrinsically linked to the king. Two extenuating factors in favour of Aśoka, however, do not let him be even implicitly excluded from it. First, Aśoka himself was so completely devoted to the interest of his subjects and did so much for their well-being throughout his reign that he amply deserved their devotion. Secondly, for a king who unequivocally asked his officers in Separate Rock Edict I at Dhauli and Jaugada to cherish the affection of the people (*panayaṃ gachema su munisānaṃ*), expecting devotion to oneself without categorically demanding it may not be improbable. B.N. Mukherjee points out that the Greek version of the Shar-i-Kuna inscription refers to 'keeping in mind the king's interest' in place of the expression 'firm devotion' of Rock Edict XIII, implying devotion to the king as a feature of Aśoka's *dhaṃma.*[36] In any case, though devotion (*bhakti*) to the ruler proved to be a useful ideology in the feudal age, there is nothing feudal about *bhakti* either in Aśoka's edicts or in the *Bhagavadgītā.* Kosambi is right in holding that Aśoka's *dhaṃma* paved the way for the 'conciliation of classes'.[37] Equating the regulation of the social order by Aśoka's *dhaṃma* with that by the Dharmaśāstra texts[38] is, however, valid only up to a point, for there were basic differences between the two, especially in respect of the attitude to caste and the lower segments of society. Bongard-Levin rightly thinks that Aśoka's *dhaṃma* contributed to the consolidation of the state.[39]

There is no doubt that the characteristics of *dhaṃma* occurring in Aśoka's edicts are in consonance with the Buddhist idea of good and purposeful life, as also with the specific advice given to the Buddhist lay followers in discourses such as the Sigālovāda Sutta of the *Dīgha Nikāya.* Scholars such as Hultzsch,[40] Bhandarkar[41] and T.W. Rhys Davids[42] have in fact traced many features of Aśoka's *dhaṃma* to statements in the Buddhist texts. A large number of phrases used in these edicts, too, have their counterparts in the Pāli Canon. Even so, the precepts of *dhaṃma* are too broad-based to be identified with a single religion; and there is nothing particularly or exclusively Buddhist about the qualities of Aśoka's *dhaṃma.*[43] To take, for example, just two references from one well-known pre-Buddhist Brahmanical text, truth, knowledge and deathlessness (deliverance from the succession of births and deaths) are the most cherished ideals in the *Bṛhadāraṇyaka Upaniṣad,* which prays:

> *Asato mā sadgamaya*
> *Tamaso mā jyotirgamaya*
> *Mṛtyormāmṛtaṃ gamaya*[44]
> (Lead me from untruth to truth!
> Lead me from darkness to light!
> Lead me from death to deathlessness!);

and Prajāpati (the Lord of beings, creator of the universe, generally identified with Brahmā) inculcates the values of self-control (*damyata*), charity (*datta*) and compassion (*dayadhvam*) to his three children – gods, human beings and demons – by teaching each of them just one syllable, DA.[45] The idea of the universal Self as the common identity of all, transcending individual differences, was presumed to generate unselfishness and benevolence, expressed later in the famous Brahmanical maxim, *sarve bhavantu sukhinaḥ; lokāḥ samastāḥ sukhino bhavantu*. The notions of good and bad deeds, unblemished conduct, sin and merit, and heaven and the other world are also pre-Buddhist (Upaniṣadic and pre-Upaniṣadic) in their origin. (The hell is not mentioned even once in Aśoka's edicts.) Furthermore, there has been a long pre-Buddhist phase of reverence to the parents, teachers and elders, and respect for the family values in the country. Candidly recognizing all this, Aśoka looks upon the attributes of his *dhaṃma* as merely a legacy from the past and describes them as *porānā pakitī* in the Brahmagiri, Siddapura and Jatinga-Rameshvara versions of his edicts. *Porānā pakitī* has been rendered variously by scholars as 'ancient rule',[46] 'ancient custom',[47] 'old usage or practice'[48] and 'traditional code of conduct'.[49]

In fact a careful look at Minor Rock Edict I, which portrays Aśoka as a Buddhist – he is spoken of as a Śākya (*Sake*) at Rupnath, as a Buddhaśākya (*Budhasake*) at Maski, and as an *upāsaka* (*upāsake*) at Sahasram, Bairat, Brahmagiri and Siddapura – manifests a conscious effort on his part to underplay the Buddhist element in his *dhaṃma*. (Aśoka's reluctance to tell the full story of his contribution to Buddhism is also amply borne out by the silence of the edicts regarding the Third Buddhist Council held at Pāṭaliputra during his reign under the guidance of Moggaliputta Tissa, at which the Tipiṭaka in its present form took shape, and about his own role and involvement in the Buddhist missionary activities within and outside India in the wake of the Council, for which we have to depend on other sources. That the edicts do not aim at providing a complete picture of his reign is evident from the fact that these do not dwell on the first eight years, and not a single measure to keep the state financially strong nor anything pertaining to the size of the army or the elegant stone sculpure or the rock-cut caves finds place in them.) We are told that Aśoka had been a lay follower of the Buddha for two and a half years, that he was not zealous for one year, but that for a year or more since he visited the *Saṃgha*[50] (*Sagha upete*, Rupnath; *Saṃghaṃ upagate*, Maski; and *Saṃghe upayīte*, Brahmagiri and Siddapura), he had strenuously exerted himself (*bāḍhaṃ ca me pakaṃte*). Aśoka's faith in Buddhism evidently grew with time and he gradually came to exercise effective authority in the affairs of the *Saṃgha*, but Vincent Smith's view in regard to his having also become a monk as well as the head of the *Saṃgha*[51] while remaining the monarch is generally not accepted; nor is Bhandarkar's claim that Aśoka began to live with the *Saṃgha*[52] borne out by the evidence.

And what is the upshot of this exertion? In Aśoka's own words it is this: men in Jaṃbudvīpa (India) who had till then remained unmixed with the gods mingled with them (*amisā ... munisā Jaṃbudīpasi misā devehi*). The Buddha's struggle before his enlightenment with Māra, who embodies worldly temptations and has the traits of Kāmadeva, the Brahmanical god of sensuality, lust and sex (the *Dhammapada*, verse 46, even refers to the flower-tipped arrows of Māra, *Mārassa papupphakāni*), and his being persuaded by Brahmā after enlightenment to preach *dhaṃma* are well-known. The Pāli Canon also represents the gods as coming down to the earth and interacting with the Buddha, the monks and men.[53] That this is a well-known Brahmanical concept may be seen from the *Āpastamba Dharmasūtra* statement: 'In ancient times gods and men used to live together in this world (*asmin loke*). Then the gods went to the heaven by performing rites (*karmabhiḥ*), while men were left behind. Men who perform the rites dwell in that world (*amusmin loke*) together with the gods and Brahmā (*saha devairBrahmaṇā*)' (II.16.1). We also see gods participating in human affairs in the Vedas, which set the tone for the future by making the gods the chief objects of worship and sacrifice, in the *Rāmāyāṇa* of Vālmīki and the *Mahābhārata*; in the Āraṇyaka Parva and the Ādi Parva we see them even producing sons on women. Thus, under a boon received from sage Durvāsā (Āraṇyaka Parva, 289.16-18) we see Kuntī giving birth to Karṇa through Sūrya before her marriage to Pāṇḍu (291.28;292.4). The Ādi Parva, too, refers to Kuntī's receiving the boon from Durvāsā (113.34-35) and then giving birth to Yudhiṣṭhira, Bhīma and Arjuna through Dharma, Pavana (Vāyu) and Indra respectively after her marriage at the behest of her husband according to the prevailing *niyoga* practice (114.1-5,9,27); Nakula and Sahadeva are similarly born to Pāṇḍu's other queen, Mādrī, through the two Aśvinī Kumāras (115.16-17).

But even if we take the statement in the edict as a rhetoric, the gods mixing with men only figuratively, the result has hardly anything to do with the basic tenets of Buddhism. Aśoka is, however, not satisfied merely with this. He goes on to maintain that such mixing with the gods is possible not only for a person of high rank (*mahātpeneva*); the 'great' heaven (*vipule svage*), too, can be attained by a lowly person (*khudakena*) through earnest exertion. Buddhism no doubt departed from the Vedic religion in many respects, but unlike God or the Supreme Being, gods and the heaven are not a taboo in Buddhism, and many Buddhist texts depict them quite favourably. The *Dhammapada*, for example, shows detailed knowledge of the Brahmanical religious ideas and devotes about a dozen verses each to gods including Indra, Yama and Brahmā; to Māra, the lord of evil forces and symbol of bondage to earthly existence in Buddhist mythology; and to heaven and the other world. Thus, manifesting a lot of respect for the gods, it states that only the virtuous, self-controlled, thoughtful, wise and enlightened people, and those devoted to meditation, delighting in peace, speaking truth and giving to the needy, and without anger, pride and taints reach the presence of the gods (verses 56, 94, 181, 224); Indra, designated Maghavā, became the overlord of the gods because of his vigilance and exertion (*appamādena*) (verse 30); a disciple treading the well-taught path of virtue conquers the world of Yama with its gods (*Yamalokaṃ... sadevakaṃ*) (verse 45), and a person looking upon the world as a bubble or a mirage escapes Maccurājā, the lord of death (Yama) (verse 170); and even Brahmā praises a person who is like a gold coin from the Jaṃbu river, that is, pure and flawless (verse 230).Looking upon the conquest of Māra and his hosts as imperative for liberation (verse 175), the *Dhammapada* prescribes detachment, not seeking pleasures, controlling the mind and the senses, eating moderately, being heedful and striving earnestly, along with rooting out craving, acquiring knowledge and wisdom, and pursuing the eightfold path as the means to achieve this (verses 8, 37, 40, 57, 274, 276, 337). Describing the heaven (*sagga, paraloka, dibba*) as the abode of noble persons (*ariyabūmi*), where someone goes only after his impurities are purged and he is rid of sin (verse 236), the *Dhammapada* maintains that only a few good people have access to it and the misers and sinners are barred (verses 126, 174, 177); good deeds receive a person when he goes to the next world (*paraṃ gataṃ*) (verse 220); taints (*malā*) are an evil even there (verse 242); and while the sinner grieves and suffers in the next world, the righteous man rejoices there (verse 15-18). There is substantial unassailable evidence in the edicts to show that Aśoka also shared this widespread belief in gods and the heaven or the next world, and used these well-established and long-cherished Brahmanical concepts to promote *dhaṃma.*

Aśoka's respect for the gods. for example, is quite evident from his assuming the meaningful title 'Devānaṃpiya' in his edicts. After a careful appraisal of the evidence in his article, 'Interpreting the Aśokan Epithet *devānaṃpiya*', Madhav M. Deshpande concludes: Aśoka 'seems to look up to them [the gods] respectfully'.[54] It is also significant that in Rock Edicts I and IV he deemed only those kinds of festive gathering (*samāja*) as meritorious and worth being continued in which such divine forms (*divyāni rūpāni*) as the aerial chariots, elephants and balls of fire were exhibited before the assembled people to attract them to his message of *dhaṃma.*

As regards the heaven and the other world, Aśoka projects them in his edicts as no less real than the earthly existence; and seeks them earnestly for his people, for those living on the borders, for officers assiduously discharging their duties according to the royal instructions, for his progeny and for even himself. Owing to the importance attached to the heaven and the other world, Prākrit terms such as *svaga, parata, paratra, paratrā, paratrika, pāratrika, paraloka, paralokika, pāralokika, palata, palaloka, palalokika, palaloga*, etc., abound in the edicts. As regards the actual statements therein, Aśoka proclaims in Rock Edict VI that enabling the people in his realm to attain happiness in this world and heaven in the other (*idha ca nāni sukhāpayāmi paratrā ca svagaṃ ārādhayaṃtu ta*) is the goal of all his endeavour. In Rock Edict IX at Girnar he asserts that heaven can be obtained by this (practice of *dhaṃma*) (*iminā saka svagaṃ ārādhetu iti*) and that there is nothing more worth doing (*katavyataraṃ*) than this; at Kalsi and Shahbazgarhi it is stressed that while the ceremony or rite of good omen (*maṃgala*) bears fruit only in this world, the ceremony or rite of *dhaṃma* is not bound by time (*dhaṃmamagale akālikye*, Kalsi; *dhramamagalaṃ akalikaṃ*, Shahbazgarhi) and yields endless merit in the other. The other world for all (*savaṃ pāratrikāya*) is held to be Aśoka's aim in Rock Edict X (here he also expresses his desire for glory [in this life, *yaso*] and fame [after death, *kiti*] for promoting *dhaṃma*); and in Rock edict XI happiness in this world and endless merit in the other are expected to result from the gift of *dhaṃma* (*ilokacasa āradho hoti parata ca aṃnaṃtaṃ puinaṃ bhavati ... dhaṃmadānena*), embodied in fulfilling a number of specified ethical obligations.

Happiness in the other world through the practice of *dhaṃma* is also cherished in Pillar Edicts I, III and VII; and in Pillar Edict IV the *lajūkas* (*rajūkas*) are exhorted to admonish the people in the countryside (*janaṃ jānapadaṃ*) to strive for happiness in this world and in the next (*hidataṃ ca pālataṃ ca ālādhayevū ti*). In Separate Rock Edict II at Dhauli and Jaugada (Odisha) the *mahāmātās* are asked to communicate to the unconquered border people (*aṃtānaṃ avijitānaṃ*) the king's sincere wish that they should follow *dhaṃma* (*dhaṃmaṃ calevū*, Dhauli; *caleyū* at Jaugada) and achieve happiness in this world and in the next (*hidaloka palalokaṃ ca ālādhayevū*, Dhauli; *hidalogaṃ ca palalogaṃ ca ālādhayevū*, Jaugada). Heaven is also assured (*svagaṃ ālādhayisatha*) to the officers securing the welfare and happiness of these border people. In Separate Rock Edict I at Dhauli and Jaugada, the *mahāmātās* at Tosali and Samapa respectively, who are also the judicial officers, are told that they will achieve heaven (*svagaṃ ālādhayisatha*, Dhauli; *ālādhayisathā* at Jaugada) if they stop the unfair and discriminatory treatment of the prisoners still being tortured, and render justice impartially (*majhaṃ paṭipādayemā*, Dhauli; *paṭipātayema* at Jaugada). Incidentally, the reference to the ongoing use of torture under Aśoka, which has no sanction in Buddhism, suggests that he did not change the basic administrative structure of the state, though he introduced many humane elements into it. It also shows that Buddhism did not encompass all the temporal and worldly aspects of life, many of which continued to be dealt with in the more comprehensive and practical Brahmanical way. Aśoka's own children (*pajā*) are the model on which he desires for all men (*savamunisesu*) complete welfare and happiness in this world and in the next (*savena hitasukhena yujeyū ti hidalogikapālalokikeṇa*) in Separate Rock Edict II at Jaugada. In Rock Edict XIII at Kalsi and Shahbazagarhi he tells his sucessors that the conquest by *dhaṃma* bears fruit in this world and in the next (*ṣe hidalokikya palalokiye*, Kalsi; *so hidalokiko paralokiko*, Shahbazgarhi). For himself, too he frankly admits that satisfaction at the conquest of *dhaṃma* is of little worth, and that he regards only the other world as of great merit (*lahukā vu kho sā piti, pālaṃtikyameve mahaphalā maṃnati Devenaṃpiye*, Kalsi; *lahuka tu kho sa priti, paratrikameva mahaphala menati Devaṇaṃpriyo*, Shahbazgarhi). The absence of any reference to heaven in the Greek version of the Kandahar Bilingual Edict shows that he used the notion of heaven only in areas where the people believed in it.

Belief in rebirth and *kaṃma* (Sanskrit *karma*) as the power which determines it is another important idea that Aśoka found Buddhism sharing with and adopted from Brahmanism. In Pillar Edict IV Aśoka refers to his order that prisoners sentenced to death be given respite for three days so that they may make donation and undertake fast for heaven or a better birth in the next life. The doctrine of rebirth or transmigration first appeared in the *Bṛhadāraṇyaka Upaniṣad* (IV.4.5-6) and the *Chāndogya Upaniṣad* (V.10.7); and it gained ground rapidly in the seventh and sixth centuries BC. In Kosambi's opinion, the doctrine of rebirth or transmigration (no matter what part of the personality was reborn) seemed natural in contemporary society.[55] Rhys Davids explains that since Buddhism rejected the concept of the soul or an eternal entity, maintained that the five *skandhas* (Prākrit *khandhas*) (the material elements or substrata of sensory existence) – *rūpa* (form), *vedanā* (feeling), *saññā* (sensation), *saṅkhāra* (motion or elements of consciousness) and *viññāna* (cognition) – when united in a body, form a living being, held everything to be impermanent, subject to the law of cause and effect, and in a state of continuous flux, the human being not remaining the same even for two consecutive moments, it pinpointed *kaṃma* of the previous set of *skandhas* as determining the locality, nature and future of the new set of *skandhas* or sentient being.[56] The acceptance of transmigration, in Warder's opinion, perhaps reflects the refusal to accept the apparently arbitrary experiences of happiness and unhappiness of men within a single life; a belief in some kind of natural law of compensation at work in the universe ensuring eventual justice.[57] The *Dhammapada* speaks of many births in the world (*anekajātisaṃsāraṃ*) and repeated births being painful (*dukkhā jāti punappunaṃ*) (verse 153). It also states that when your mind is completely freed, you will not return to births and old age (*sabbattha vimuttamānaso na punaṃ jātijaraṃ upehisi*) (verse 348). The *Therīgāthā* recounts seven former births of Isidāsī, a Buddhist nun (verse 400-47); and the Jātakas are an irrefutable proof of the widespread belief in the Buddha's many previous births as a Bodhisatta.

It is also significant that there is no mention in the edicts of the Buddhist doctrines of the Four Noble Truths (*cattāri ariyasaccāni*), the Eightfold Path (*aṭṭhaṅgiko maggo*), the Middle Way (*majjhimā paṭipadā*) or the chain of causal existence or dependent origination (*paṭiccasamuppāda*) (a series of twelve terms showing the causal chain leading from ignorance to suffering through imagination, self-consciousness or ego, name and form or corporeal existence, six senses including the mind, contact, feeling or emotion, craving, attachment, becoming and rebirth, a doctrine which Basham regards 'pedantic' , *Wonder*, pp. 271-72); nor is the practice of *dhaṃma* envisaged to result in enlightenment (*saṃbodhi*) or liberation from the cycle of births and deaths (*nibbāna*) (Sanskrit *nirvāṇa*). *Nibbāna* in the sense of the 'realization of the true nature of things in terms of their transience and subtancelessnes' is not even remotely hinted at, because such an abstruse idea would have made no sense to the ordinary people, for whom the edicts are intended. Furthermore, we do not come across any reference to false or evil doctrine (*michādiṭṭhi, diṭṭhiṃ ... pāpikaṃ*), which is attributed to the dissenting sects even in such a liberal early Buddhist text as the *Dhammapada* (verses 167, 316-18; verse 164), in Aśoka's edicts. Aśoka's interest in *dhaṃma*, too, is not ascribed to Buddhism, unlike the bloody Kaliṅga war, which is said to have led to his zealous practice of *dhaṃma* (*tive dhaṃmavāye*), love of *dhaṃma* (*dhaṃmakāmatā*), and the inculcation of *dhaṃma* (*dhaṃmānuṣathi*, Rock Edict XIII, Kalsi). Besides, the Buddhist monks are never used in the propagation of *dhaṃma*. Even so, the earliest references to both Buddhism and *dhaṃma* in the Minor Rock Edicts leave no room for any doubt about the fact that the process of issuing the edicts began only after Aśoka became a Buddhist and set his mind on expounding *dhaṃma*.

All this points to the incontrovertible historical reality that in its origin and development Buddhism was not without important links with historical Brahmanism,[58] and that Aśoka saw no good reason to try to disrupt them. In a sense as the ruler of a vast empire he himself acted as a bridge between Buddhism and Brahmanism, and aided the process of give-and-take between the two. One may see in this historical Brahmanism, which underwent considerable changes in course of its interaction with different religions and peoples, the precursor of later, yet pre-modern, pre-Islamic, ancient Hinduism – reality is far more important than the nomenclature – with caste and gender inequality as well as untouchability as part of its mixed baggage. Rhys Davids' observation that 'Buddhism grew and flourished side by side with the orthodox belief ...far from showing how depraved and oppressive Hinduism was, it shows precisely the contrary;... and Buddhism was the child, the product, of those phases of Indian belief out of which Hinduism afterwards arose'[59] still remains valid. History does not permit a vacuum, and Brahamanism contributed significantly to the developed class and caste structure of a large part of north India in the early half of the first millennium AD. (This is by no means a plea in support of the hypothesis of an ancient Hindu period, because the Vedic tradition coexisted with a parallel non-Vedic tradition which retained its separate identity and influence throughout the ancient period). Moreover, Brahmanism has not been a homogeneous phenomenon in the long course of Indian history; and celebrating the plurality of thought and ideas has been among its most notable features. As Rhys Davids notes: 'There was absolute freedom of thought in ancient India. The Brahmans themselves were often the leaders in enunciating new views, which would elsewhere have been condemned as heterodox; and men of other castes were allowed to set up as teachers of systems really incompatible with the inherited beliefs'.[60] Hultzsch, too, maintains: 'In reality Hindus have been at all times extremely tolerant to other creeds, and have allowed everybody to try to attain salvation in his own fashion. Among the six orthodox schools of philosophy they count the pantheist Vedānta and the atheistic Sāṃkhya, ... The same tolerance was practised by Aśoka'.[61]

The immense historical significance of Aśoka's *dhaṃma* and its substantial relevance to our own time can hardly be missed by anyone. It was certainly an enterprise of extraordinary vision.

REFERENCES

* The paper has been written in the wake of the decision of the ICHR-sponsored International Seminar on 'Reason and Tolerance in Indian History' held in New Delhi from 26 to 28 October 2006 at its valedictory session that I should contribute a paper on Aśoka to its thematic volume. Its earlier version has been printed in *Vikramshila Journal of Social Sciences*, Bhagalpur, January–June 2011.

1. Apart from the texts found in Alfred C. Woolner, *Aśoka: Text and Glossary*, reprint, Low Price Publications, Delhi. 1993 (1st published in 1923), and Radhagovinda Basak, *Aśokan Inscriptions*, Progressive Publishers, Calcutta, 1959, I have mainly used the text occurring in E. Hultzsch's monumental work, *Corpus Inscriptionum Indicarum*, Vol. I, *Inscriptions of Aśoka*, Indological Book House, Delhi, 1969 (1st published in 1925). That the latter needs updating may be seen from the fact that of the seventeen Minor Rock Edicts less than half are included in it. Such a need was indeed emphasized way back in a small but exceptionally useful article, 'Guide to Aśokan

Inscriptions' by F.R. Allchin and K.R. Norman, published in *South Asian Studies*, Vol. I, London 1985, pp.43-50. It contains a classified list of all the inscriptions published till then, their original findspots and present locations, two maps showing these, and select bibliography of the most important books and articles on the subject. A significant recent study is Harry Falk's *Aśokan Sites and Artefacts*. Verlag Philipp von Zabern, Mainz am Rhein, 2006. A product of hard work for over a decade, it furnishes the historical background, minute details and up to-date information about every Aśokan edict site. It has also an extensive bibliography.

2. Minor Rock Edict I at Maski, Rock Edicts VIII, IX and XIII at Girnar, Rock Edicts VIII and XI at Kalsi and Rock Edict IV at Mansehra.
3. Rock Edict V at Girnar.
4. Rock Edicts I, V and XIII at Kalsi, Pillar Edicts I, II, IV and VI at Delhi-Topra and Rampurva, Pillar Edicts I, IV and VI at Lauriya-Araraj and Lauriya-Nandangarh, Pillar Edicts II and VI at Delhi-Meerut and Pillar Edicts I and II at Allahabad-Kosam.

   Pillar Edict VII at Delhi-Topra (found only here) uses *dhaṃmalibi* once in place of *dhaṃmalipi*. The pillar was brought from Topra in Ambala district of Haryana to Delhi by Firoz Shah Tughluq (1351-88) and now stands at the Firoz Shah Kotla.

   The Delhi-Meerut pillar, too, was brought from Meerut in UP to Delhi by Firoz Shah Tughluq and now stands on the ridge north of Old Delhi.

   The Allahabad-Kosam pillar was probably located originally at Kauśāmbī (now Kosam) because its Schism Edict mentions the 'high officers of Kosaṃbī' (*Kosaṃbiyaṃ mahāmātānaṃ*), and brought from there to its present location inside the Allahabad Fort built by Akbar. J.C. Irwin has, however, voiced his doubt about this hypothesis, "The Ancient Pillar Cult at Prayāga (Allahabad): Its pre-Aśokan Origins', *Journal of the Royal Asiatic Society*, London, 1983, pp. 253 – 80.
5. Rock Edicts I, V,VI and XIV at Girnar and Dhauli, Rock Edicts I and VI at Jaugada and Pillar Edict VI at Allahabad-Kosam.
6. Rock Edicts VI and XIV at Kalsi and Pillar Edict II at Lauriya-Araraj.
7. Kharoṣṭhī version of Rock Edict XIII at Mansehra.
8. Kharoṣṭhī versions of Rock Edicts I, V, XIII and XIV at Shahbazgarhi and of Rock Edicts I, V, VI and XIV at Mansehra. Since both Shahbazgarhi (Peshawar district) and Mansehra (Hazara district) in NWFP, Pakistan, are in a zone where the Iranian language was well-known in the days of Aśoka, the presence of such Iranian words as *dipi* in the edicts is natural.
9. Twice each in Separate Rock Edicts I and II at Dhauli and once in the Minor Pillar Edict at Sarnath.
10. Twice each in Separate Rock Edicts I and II at Jaugada and once in the Minor Pillar Edict at Sarnath. Both *lipi* and *libi* occur in Pāṇini's *Aṣṭādhyāyī* (III.2.21), a work of the fifth century BC, though he does not identity the script he has in view. A.L. Basham regards writing in India pre-Mauryan, *The Wonder that was India* (hereafter *Wonder*), 3rd revised edn, Sidgwick & Jackson, London, 1967; 1982 reprint (1st published in 1954), p. 44.

Knowledge of writing in Aramic, Kharoṣṭhī and Greek in pre-Aśokan northern-eastern India is not in doubt.

11. Once each in Rock Edict XIV at Girnar and Minor Rock Edict I at Brahmagiri and Jatinga-Rameshvara.
12. Once in Rock Edict XIV at Kalsi.
13. Twice in Pillar Edict VII at Delhi-Topra.
14. 'Aśoka' as the name of the Maurya emperor occurs only in Minor Rock Edict I at Maski (Karnataka) and Gujarra (Madhya Pradesh) and in Minor Rock Edict II at Nittur and Udegolam (both in Karnataka).
15. It is the first epigraphic evidence of the Buddhist formula of faith in its three treasures (*triratna*),on whom enlightenment depends, the Buddha showing the way and preaching the doctrine (*dhaṃma*) and the *Saṃgha* elaborating, spreading and perpetuating it.

    Though the edicts were composed in Māgadhī Prākrit, the official language of the Mauryan court, in course of inscribing them in different parts of the country, they were seriously affected, *inter alia,* by the local Prākrit dialects spoken at the grass roots, which differed from one locality to another; words are, therefore, often not uniformly spelt even within a single sentence, for example, *ca* and *caṃ; Budhasi, dhaṃmasi* and *Saṃghasī*, Moreover, although Prākrit grammar is distinct and separate from Sanskrit grammar, Prākrit used in the edicts shares its vocabulary with Sanskrit, the spoken language (*bhāsā*) of the élite, especially of the Brāhmaṇas, up to 5 per cent according to Meena Talim, *Edicts of King Aśoka: A New Vision*, Aryan Books International, New Delhi, 2010, p. xii.
16. Aśoka's edicts are not only the oldest Indian inscriptions hitherto deciphered, they also provide the first historical evidence of writing in Brāhmī characters. Moreover, they furnish the first textual proof of the use of numbered years, numbers not being in the current years, but being invariably counted with reference to the years that had been completed since the expiry of Aśoka's consecration (*abhiseka*). See note 1.1 on 'Mauryan Chronology' in Irfan Habib and Vivekanand Jha, *Mauryan India,* 4th edn (paperback), Aligarh Historians Society and Tulika Books, New Delhi, 2009 (1st published in 2004), pp. 44-46.
17. Cf. B.N. Mukherjee, *Studies in the Aramaic Edicts of Aśoka* (hereafter *Studies*), Indian Museum, Calcutta, 1984, p. 54.
18. Basham finds his own translation of *dhaṃma* as righteousness 'inadequate', *Wonder,* p. 54.
19. The Erragudi version of the Minor Rock Edict, for example, wishes *dhaṃma* to permeate through all the social ranks, from the Brāhmaṇas down to the elephant drivers, Romila Thapar, *Aśoka and the Decline of the Mauryas,* New revised edn with Afterword, OUP, Delhi 1987 (1st published in 1961), p. 172. As she underlines, the principles of *dhaṃma* were such that they would have been acceptable to people belonging to any religious sect, *Early India: From the Origins to AD 1300* (hereafter *Early India*), University of California Press, Berkeley, 2002, p. 202.
20. Hemchandra Raychaudhuri, *Political History of Ancient India,* revised edn with Commentary by B.N. Mukherjee, OUP, Delhi, 1996 (1st published by University of Calcutta in 1923), p. 289.

21. D.R. Bhandarkar, *Aśoka,* reprint of revised edn with Foreword by D.C. Sircar, University of Calcutta, 1969 (1st published in 1925), pp. 72, 77, 122.
22. Irfan Habib and Vivekanand Jha, op.cit., p. 72.
23. B.N. Mukherjee, op.cit., pp. 33, 53; Romila Thapar, op.cit., p. 260; Irfan Habib and Vivekanand Jha, op.cit., pp. 63, 68.
24. Harry Falk, op.cit., pp. 55-6.
25. Ibid., pp. 57-8.
26. Just how integral the slaves and servants were to the household may be seen from a parable in which the Buddha asked Kisāgotamī, the mother of a dead child, to bring the mustard-seed from a house where no son or husband or parent or slave or servant had died, and she found none, *Therīgāthā*, verses 213-23; T.W. Rhys Davids, *Buddhism*, reprint of 1910 revised edn, Indological Book House, Delhi (1st published in 1877), pp. 133-4. The distraught mother in the story soon came to realize the painful truth about the inevitability of death and became a nun.

    The first lesson that Kṛṣṇa imparts to Arjuna in the *Bhagavadgītā*, a work of the third-second century BC (Vivekanand Jha, 'Social Content of the *Bhagavadgītā', The Indian Historical Review* [hereafter *IHR*], Vol. XI, Nos 1-2, July 1984 and January 1985, p. 3), meant, like Aśoka's *dhamma*, especially for the householders, is that death in unavoidable (*aparihārya*, II. 27). This is because to be at peace and not be overwhelmed with grief, even a householder has to accept death as a normal and inescapable end of life. Clearly, the bedrock of spirituality in both Buddhism and Brahmanism/ Hinduism is often identical.
27. Gerard Fussman, 'Central and Provincial Administration in Ancient India: The Problem of the Maurya Empire', *IHR*, Vol. XIV, Nos 1-2, July 1987 and January 1988, p. 49.
28. D.D. Kosambi, *An Introduction to the Study of Indian History* (hereafter *Introduction*), Popular Book Depot, Bombay, 1956, p. 193.
29. While Hultzsch refers to Rock Edict XII as the 'most remarkable', 'which does him [Aśoka] the greatest credit', op.cit., p. xlix, Irfan Habib aptly dubs it as the 'toleration edict', 'with some dose from the storehouse of reason', in his keynote paper presented at the ICHR- sponsored International Seminar on 'Reason and Tolerance in Indian History', op.cit., p. 4.
30. Upinder Singh, *A History of Ancient and Early Medieval India: From the Stone Age to the Twelfth Century*, Pearson/Longman, New Delhi, 2008, p. 352.
31. B.M. Barua, *Aśoka and His Inscriptions,* Vol. I, New Age Publishers, Calcutta, 1946, p. 251.
32. Hultzsch, op.cit., p. xlviii; Irfan Habib and Vivekanand Jha, op.cit., p. 66.
33. Kosambi, *Introduction,* p. 192; idem, *The Culture and Civilisation of Ancient India in Historical Outline* (hereafter *Culture*), Routledge and Kegan Paul, London, 1965, p. 164.
34. B.N. Mukherjee, *Studies,* pp. 55-58; R.S. Sharma, op.cit., p. 176.
35. Kosambi, 'The Line of *Arthaśāstra* Teachers', *IHR,* Vol. V, Nos 1-2, July 1978 and January 1979, p. 6.
36. B.N. Mukherjee, Commentary in Raychaudhuri, op.cit., pp. 606, 612, 621, 633.

37. Kosambi, *Culture*, p. 165. It was calculated to lead to peace and fellowship in the world, maintains Basham, *Wonder*, p. 56. Romila Thapar, too, observes that by making the ethical behaviour of one person towards another the prime basis and core of his *dhaṃma*, Aśoka sought to reduce social conflict, *Early India*, p. 201.
38. R.S. Sharma,op.cit., p. 176.
39. B.M. Bongard-Levin, *Mauryan India*, Sterling Publishers, Delhi, 1985, p. 368.
40. Hultzsch, op.cit., pp. xlix-liv.
41. Bhandarkar, op.cit., pp. 95-6, 107-16, 125-27, 131.
42. Rhys Davids, op.cit., ch. V. 'The General Moral Precepts of Buddhism', pp. 124-49, shows this, even though the author does not have the Aśokan edicts in view.
43. Cf. Kosambi, *Introduction*, p. 151; Basham, op.cit., p. 55; R.S. Sharma, op.cit., p. 176; H. Raychaudhuri, op.cit., p. 301; B.N. Mukherjee's Commentary in Raychaudhuri, op.cit., p. 632; Bongard-Levin, op.cit., pp. 343, 367, 368.
44. I.3.28. Constituting the concluding section of the *Śatapatha Brāhmaṇa* of the *Śukla* (White) *Yajurveda*, the *Bṛhadāraṇyaka Upaniṣad* is the oldest Upaniṣad, dated in the seventh-sixth centuries BC, Patrick Olivelle, *The Early Upaniṣads* (Annotated Text and Translation), Munshiram Manoharlal, New Delhi, 1998, pp. 12, 29-30; cf. Basham, *Wonder*, p. 235.
45. V.2. 1-3. According to G.C. Pande, the Upaniṣads regarded ethical discipline – the practice of virtue and restraint of passion – as the indispensable first step in spiritual life; and Buddhism further reinforced this, *Studies in the Origins of Buddhism*, 2nd revised edn, Motilal Banarsidass, Delhi. 1974 (1st published from Allahabad in 1957), p. 513. Contemplation of the true nature of the universe and one's own being, leading to the gradual abstraction and detachment of consciousness, was, in A.K. Warder's view, the next step in acquiring knowledge and salvation, *Indian Buddhism*, Motilal Banarsidass, Delhi, 1970, p. 37.
46. Hultzsch, op.cit., p. 178; Raychaudhuri, op.cit., 301; Bongard-Levin, pp. 347, 367.
47. Romila Thapar, op.cit., p. 260; idem, 'Aśoka and Buddhism as Reflected in the Aśoken Edicts' in *Cultural Pasts: Essays in Early Indian History*, OUP, New Delhi, 2000, p. 427.
48. Basak, op.cit., p. 143.
49. R.K. Mookerji, *Aśoka*, 3rd revised and enlarged edn, Motilal Banarsidass, Delhi, 1962 (1st published from London in 1928), p. 116.
50. Bongard-Levin finds this interpretation quite apt, op.cit., p. 341.
51. Vincent A. Simth, *Aśoka: The Buddhist Emperor of India*, reprint of 3rd revised edn, S. Chand & Co., Delhi 1970 (1st published by OUP in 1920), pp. 26, 35, 39; idem, *The Early History of India*, reprint of 4th edn revised by S.M. Edwardes, OUP, 1967 (1st published in 1924), pp. 166, 168.
52. Bhandarkar, op.cit., p. 122.
53. Narendra Wagle, *Society at the Time of the Buddha*, 2nd revised edn, Popular Prakashan, Bombay, 1995 (1st published in 1966), p. 83.
54. Patrick Olivelle, *Aśoka in History and Historical Memory*, Motilal Banarsidass, Delhi, 2009, p. 39.

55. Kosambi, *Culture*, p. 107; cf. Basham, *Wonder*, p. 244; Romila Thapar, *Early India*, p. 169. That the Buddha, like Mahāvīra, should adopt and endorse the doctrine is quite in order because both of them had renounced the world to achieve liberation; and *nibbāna* and *kaivalya*, like *mokṣa*, meant cessation of the cycle of rebirths.
56. Rhys Davids, op.cit., pp. 87-94, 97-9, 101.
57. Warder, op.cit., p. 36.
58. Romila Thapar describes *dhaṃma* as Aśoka's 'own invention', 'a compromise' of old and new beliefs, 'borrowed from Buddhist and Hindu thought', *Aśoka and the Decline of the Mauryas,* pp. 144-9; cf. Bongard Levin, op.cit., pp. 329-30.
59. Rhys Davids, op.cit., p. 85.
60. Idem, *Lectures on Some Points in the History of Indian Buddhism* (The Hibbert Lectures), reprint, Indological Book House, Delhi, 1999 (1st published in 1981), p. 26.
61. Hultzsch, op.cit., p. xlviii.

16

History and Culture of North-West India as Described by the Greek and Assyrian Travellers of the First Century AD

G.P. Singh

Apollonius, the Greek traveller, accompanied by a learned Assyrian called Damis travelled in different parts of north-western India AD. 43-44 for acquiring first hand knowledge of its history and culture. The former recorded all that he saw and heard in the course of his visit to India in his diary or notebook and the latter in his journal. Their works along with other relevant sources were later used by one of the early Greek historians called Philostratus the Athenian (C.AD. 170-245) for writing the biography of Apollonius.

Philostratus, the biographer of Apollonius, was born at Lemnos and studied at Athens but flourished in the reign of the Roman emperor Severus (C.AD 193-230). The Emperor's wife, Julia Domna, who was famous for her patronage of men of learning and genius, handed over the memoirs of Damis (which was bequeathed to her by his descendants) to Philostratus with a request to write the life of Apollonius on the basis of its contents. But Philostratus not only used the memoirs of Damis but also epistles or letters of Apollonius which were then in circulation and an account of his career at Aegae by a Roman historian, Marius Maximus (C.AD 165-230), to accomplish his task. The Empress, however, did not live to see the book, which saw the light of the day in, or some time after AD. 217. It was written in Greek. It is divided into eight books of which the second and third deal with his Indian travels. According to this biographical work, Apollonius was born about the beginning of the Christian era at Tyana, a city in Cappadocia (Asia Minor). He was a philosopher of the school of Pythagoras. It was his cherished desire to extend the frontiers of his knowledge by travelling into foreign countries. He is said to have travelled extensively.

In the earlier part of his life he visited Egypt, Italy and Persia. Later he turned his attention to the East. He wanted to explore the wonders of India and acquaint himself with the learning and wisdom of the Brahmans, the fame of which had been spread in the West by the companion of Alexander. He along with his Assyrian companion from Nineveh reached Babylon where they halted for sometime. From there they along with a guide supplied by the Parthian king Bardanes (C.AD 42-45) set out to visit India. First they entered Afghanistan by crossing the Kaukasos (Hindukush) north of Kabul. Further, westward of the Indus they crossed the Kophen (the Kabul river) and visited Kabul and the adjoining regions. After crossing the Indus into the Punjab eastward they stayed for a while at Taxila (Takcasil). Having passed the Hydraotes (Rvi) they pursued their way through several "countries" to the Hyphasis (Beas) beyond which they could not travel. On the return journey they visited Sindh as their itinerary shows. From the narratives of their journey it appears that they were provided with different new guides and interpreters proficient in the Greek language at different places in India in the course of their journey. They are believed to have interacted with all classes of population during the journey. Philostratus has furnished an original and authoritative account of their travels in his biography of Apollonius which is based on the information supplied by them in their respective works. It is very useful for throwing light on the early history and culture of north-west India to about the middle of the first century AD.

The travellers' accounts of society, economy, polity, religion, philosophy, education, urban life and art and architecture of the people of the north-west and that of the foreign invasions are preserved in the work of Philostratus.[1]

The social structure of the people of the north-west was somewhat different from that of other parts of India. The frequent allusions to the Brahmans called "Sophoi" (Sophists) or "Teachers of wisdom" and philosophers in the accounts of the travellers[2] give us an impression that they occupied the highest position in the society. They were held in high esteem. Their supremacy was well established in the society. They followed a variety of pursuits. Some were engaged in public affairs and attended the king as counsellors. Some of them were advisers to the king in the management of his estates. The others practised religious austerities, performed religious rites and rituals, conducted sacrifices and imparted religious instructions to their respective disciples.[3] They had their own chiefs who were invested with some authority in religious and administrative matters, which speaks of their hierarchical system.[4] Except the Brahmans there is no references to any other upper or lower social class despite the fact that the Kshatriyas had been living in both the Punjab and Sindh and the Sodrai or Sudras in only Sindh since time immemorial along with them. The traditional social system might have possibly undergone some changes by the time of the travellers' visit. The four-fold division of the society was no longer acceptable to them. The classes and castes as such were conspicuous by their absence in their society at that time. There is no mention of either their social stratification or social distinctions or caste restrictions in the travellers' accounts of the subject.

The north-west Indian society was basically patriarchal. The joint family system was followed. The mode of life was simple. Music, singing and dancing were three principal means of the amusement of the people. The kinship system formed an important part of their social life. The marriage customs were based on the rules of both endogamy and exogamy. The mutual choice of bride and bridegroom played its own role in the arrangement and performance of the marriages. The dowry system was in vogue. We are told by the travellers that they were informed by the contemporary king (Parthian) at Taxila that his father had "married the daughter of the Hydaspian king (whose kingdom was on the river Jhelum) and received with her seven villages as pin-money."[5] The monogamy was the rule and polygamy the exception. The women did not occupy a high position in the society because of the Brahmanical orthodoxy. They did not enjoy freedom in any walk of life. The incidental notices of slavery are also there in the accounts concerned. In Taxila the travellers saw some male servants with the king. They were employed for domestic purposes.[6] We do not come across any evidence of women slaves in their accounts. However, slavery was not a recognised social institution.

The travellers have provided a detailed account of the economic activities or material life of the people of north-west India. The most extensive and the most fertile plain in the whole country, and irrigated in all directions and well-cultivated which the travellers speak[7] of is no other than the fertile territory of the Punjab (eastward of the Indus) watered by the Indus and its five tributaries, namely, the Ravi, the Jhelum, the Chenab, the Sutlej and the Beas. About the land and its produce they observe: "The land here is the best in India, black and very productive; its wheat stalks are like reeds, and its beans three times as large as the Egyptian; its sesame (sesamum) and millet are also extraordinarily fine. Here, too, grow those nuts, which for their rarity and size are, as a sort of curiosity often found in Greek temples. The grapes of the country however are small, like the Lydian and Maconian....".[8] Like other parts of India in the north-west too agriculture was the backbone of the economy. It was the means of subsistence for the bulk of the population. The agriculture production was very high because of the fertility of the land facility of irrigation. All kinds of crops were produced. The people had achieved self-sufficiency in food. On the heights they witnessed various kinds of aromatic plants and the cinnamon-tree, and in the hollows the pepper-plant and frankincense-bearing trees. The paper was highly valued by the Indians.[9]

The Indus region was also fertile. In the words of the travellers: "The Indus like the Nile overflows the country, and deposits a fertilising mud, which as in Egypt, prepares the land for the husbandman (cultivator)"[10]. In the Punjab and Sindh groups were some artisans and craftsmen and other occupational groups engaged in various avocations. Some indigenous industry also flourished along with arts and crafts. There was a class of metalworkers in Taxila. They made several objects of gold, silver, copper, bronze and iron. There were some weavers, leather workers and manufacturers of cotton fabric. The paper made from the papyrus plant was used for writing. Taxila continued to be the centre of trade and commerce. The people were engaged in different occupations and professions for the sole purpose of earning their livelihood. The travellers inform us, "The people at Taxila wore cotton, the produce of the country, and sandals made of the fibre or bark of the papyrus and a leather cap when it rained. The better classes were clad in byssus (having a silky appearance).... This byssus (a stuff looking like the silky bunch of filament or thread used for making textiles, etc.) grows on a tree, "it is exported into Egypt for sacred uses".[11] The travellers' statement that "....the Indian money was of orichalcum and bronze purely Indian and not stamped like the Roman and Median coins" throw some light on the coinage system.[12]

The prevailing form of government in some parts of north-western India at the time of the travellers' visit was monarchy. The city-state of Nysa at the foot of the mountain called Meros between the Kabul river and Indus or in the valleys of Kohimor in the Swat was "ruled by a king"[13]. That city or hill state was one of the famous seats of aristocratic oligarchy at the time of Alexander's invasion and for some time in the post-Alexandrian period but later it adopted the monarchical form of government, the reason and the exact period of which are still unknown to us.

There was hereditary monarchy in Taxila which can be attested to by what its king himself told the travellers. The relatives of the king sometimes, according to Indian custom, acted as regents. The king was assisted by nobles in running the government. The city was governed by good laws. The king used to transact the business of his kingdom (between the Indus and the Jhelum) and to decide the cases according to the law of the land.[14] The punishments were awarded according to the nature of crimes. Strabo (C. 64 BC-21 AD) also makes a mention of the most excellent laws of Taxila.[15] The king "told his visitors among other things that he paid blackmail to a tribe of barbarians on his borders for the protection of his dominions against the attacks of other barbarous tribes".[16]

Porus the elder also ruled his kingdom between the Jhelum and the Chenab according to the monarchical constitution. All the sovereigns in Kabul and the Punjab at that time were independent.

The Indus region was then under the rule of the Satrap.[17] From the accounts of the travellers it distinctly appears that the people in the north-west were by and large followers of the Brahmanical culture. Buddhists were few and far between. The travellers like the classical historians failed to notice the distinction between Brahmanism and Buddhism.[18] There were two sects of philosophers, viz. "Brahmans" and "Sarmanes" (Skt. Sramana and Pali samaṅa), which correspond to the "Brahman" sages or ascetics and the Buddhist monks respectively.

The sun worship was prevalent among the Brahmans.[19] The sacrifices formed an integral part of the religious beliefs of the people. Where the travellers crossed the Indus the natives told them that "when the season for the rise of the river is at hand, the king sacrifices on its banks black bulls and horses and after the sacrifices throws into the river a gold measure like a corn measure... for an abundant harvest or. ...Rise of the river... would benefit the land."[20]

The age-old tradition of receiving the education under the care guidance of the Brahmans continued to exist in the north-west till about the middle of the first century AD We are informed by the travellers that the "Brahmans" before admitting anyone for educational purposes used to "inquire into his character and parentage".[21] They, like the sophists of Greece, used to teach their pupils various subjects. The philosophy was given the highest importance as a subject of study. Besides "astrology and divination" the subject relating to "those sacrifices and invocations in which the gods delight" were also taught by them.[22]

Both the travellers during the three days of their sojourn at Taxila[23] learnt from its king who possessed knowledge of Greek language about its past history and got an opportunity to see with their own eyes the city as well as all the relics and monuments of historical and archaeological importance. Their accounts of the growth of urban culture, art and architecture at Taxila are of exceptional importance. While giving a vivid description of Taxila as a city they observe that it was laid out on a symmetrical plan. "It was about the size of Nineveh walled like a Greek city, and was the residence of a sovereign who ruled over what of old was the kingdom of pours".[24] "They found the city divided by narrow streets, well-arranged, and reminding them of Athens. From the streets, the houses seemed only one storey, but they all had an underground floor.[25] "There were underground rooms equal in length to the chambers above.... The archaeological finds have revealed that access to inner chambers was from the upper chamber. The reverse process misled the traveller who could not speculate whether it was a single storeyed or a double storeyed building till he (Apollonius) actually went inside to find out the real thing".[26] The travellers also saw the king's palace, which according to them was not distinguished by any superiour splendour or extraordinary magnificence from the residences of the citizens of the better class. There were no sentinels or bodyguards, and only a few attendants or servants. The same simplicity was observed in the courts, halls, waiting and inner rooms; and it pleased Apollonius more than all the pomp of Babylon. [27]According to Philostratus, "It was no less magnificent an architecture and the male chamber and the porticos and the whole of the vestitute was very chaste in style".[28] The city visited by the travellers in 43 AD can undoubtedly be identified with Sirkap and its king called "Phraotes" with the Parthian.[29]

The credibility of the information supplied by the travellers regarding Taxila city can be tested by archaeological discoveries at the site. Sir John Marshall, who carried on excavations at the site for over a period of twenty years at regular intervals between 1912 and 1934, has proved that the city visited by Apollonius of Tyana in "AD 40 or thereabouts" was no other than the ruler. His findings at this particular site include the structural remains like the royal palace "looking like a glorified private house.... but with more spacious courts and rooms", blocks of the private dwelling-houses of the citizens, large houses belonging to the rich, single-storey structure of one or two rooms, narrow side-streets, small shrines and many other monuments and antiquities.[30] The palace complex was modelled on the same lines as its Assyrian counter-part and had several entrances and outer fortifications. This can also be more or less corroborated by the evidence produced by R.E. Mortimer–Wheeler on the basis of his findings in the course of excavations carried out at the same site in 1944-45. The remains of the stone city wall was also discovered.[31]

There is a striking similarity between the observations of the travellers and the findings of the archaeologists.

The travellers inform us that just outside the walls of the city were beautiful temples of shell marble with a shrine and many columns. Round the shrine were hung pictures on copper tablets representing the feats of Alexander and Porus. The various figures including that of elephants, horses, soldiers, and armours were portrayed or carved in a mosaic of orichalcum, silver, gold, and oxydised copper, but the weapons, including the spears, javelins and swords in iron. The metals were so ingeniously worked into one another that the picture they formed was comparable to the productions of the most famous Greek artists from the points of view of drawing, vivacity of expression and truthfulness of perspective. We are further told that it was not till after the death of Alexander (C.BC. 323) that

Porus placed them (all the above mentioned pieces of art) in the temple including one which was wounded and received from Alexander the kingdom of India".[32] This artistic representation constitutes the monumental evidence of Alexander's victory over Porus the elder of Punjab and the kingdom which the latter got back from the former (after tendering his submission) in recognition of the valour he displayed and the talent and ability he proved during the war.

Phiostratus explicitly mentions, "They saw a temple in front of the wall about 100 ft in length and built of steel like stone.[33]" The temple lay north to the wall and it was inside the city proper. Some scholars have mistaken this temple for Jandial temple exhumed in the excavations at Sirkap.[34] The former was obviously built in the time of Porus and the latter in the Scythio-Parthian period.

The travellers saw the famous "Temple of the Sun" inside the city and in it statues of Alexander and Porus, one of gold and the other of bronze of exquisite beauty, which excited their admiration. Its walls were of red marble, but glittering with gold and the image of the god was of pearls.[35] The art of painting was also known to the people of Taxila as mentioned by them.

The travellers' description of Taxila city as a whole shows the perfection the people had attained in all the branches of art, architecture, sculpture, iconography and painting, in the past. The originality of Indian art is also reflected in their objects. It was unaffected by Hellenistic influences. The deities and objects contrived bear the stamp of Indian influences and exhibit the ingenuity of the Indian artists. "They were so garbed in Greek costumes that it was difficult for a visitor to discriminate whether it was a Greek object or an Indian one. The fact that they were found in Hindu temples was the only clue for discrimination. This shows the highest achievements of the Indians in the field of art.[36] The antiquity of all the specimens of art preserved inside the temple of the fourth century BC. All of them remained in an excellent state of preservation till the time of their visit. Taxila was no doubt a large well-planned, magnificent and fortified city. Strabo and Arrian have described it as "the greatest of all the Indian cities between the river Indus and the Hydaspes (Jhelum)" but without giving any details thereof. In fact, among all the classical writers Philostratus is the only one who has provided a picturesque description of the city with all accuracy and precision based on the eyewitness accounts of Apollonius and his fellow traveller and friend, Damis, which can also be confirmed by archaeological evidence.

There are also some fragmentary but very rare types of evidence of Alexander's invasion (c. 326-325 BC.) in the accounts of the travellers. After leaving Taxila they set out on the journey to the Hyphasis or the river

Beas and after two days reached the plain where Alexander had defeated Porus. There they saw the place adorned with a triumphal arch and a statue of the great conqueror in a four-horse chariot, as he appeared in the battle of Issus. A little farther on they came upon two other arches on one of which was Alexander and on the other Porus—the one saluting, and the other in an attitude of submission. As they approached Hyphasis, they saw the altars Alexander had built there and also a bronze pillar with this inscription: "Here Alexander halted."[37] Philostratus conjectures that this pillar was raised by the Indians in joy at Alexander's homeward return. It is a proven fact that he did not cross the Hyphasis to occupy the neighbouring lands. We learn that the land of the Brahmans between the Hypahsis and the Ganges was never invaded by Alexander not out of fear but because of being dissuaded by the appearance of the sacrificial victims.

About the Scythian invasion we have only this much information that "the Indian people drove back the Scythians who invaded their territories".[38] However, we can not pass over it in silence. It is also said that many cities were built in the Gangetic region by the people of India the details of which are wanting. There is also a passing reference to the city of Paṭala in the lower oligarchical constitution. We are told by Apollonius that " He saw too the mouth of the Indus, and Patala, a city built on an island formed by the Indus where Alexander collected his fleet."[39]

There is no difference of opinion among modern scholars about the historical authenticity of the diary of Apollonius of Tyana but about the value of the journal or memoirs of his learned friend, Damis, which also formed the basis of the work of Philostratus their views are contradictory.[40] According to A. Cunnigham, Philostratus professes to have used Damis' narrative of the journey. "His account is manifestly exaggerated in many particulars regarding the acts and sayings of the philosopher, but the descriptions of places seem to be generally moderate and truthful. If they were not found in the narrative of Damis, they must have been taken from the journals of some of Alexander's followers: and in either case they are valuable, as they supply many little points of information that are wanting in the regular histories."[41] Professor Bigg, on the other hand, doubts the very existence of the memoirs of Damis. But others admit its existence and hold that it also abounds in some valuable information about India. It is true that there are some errors and discrepancies in his account of the subject but it can not be dismissed as entirely fanciful. Actually, the facts and fictions are jumbled in it. From the style of his presentation one gets an impression that he is a story-teller. While forming an estimate of Damis as a traveller, McCrindle observes: "His description of the country between the Hyphasis and the Ganges is utterly at variance with all known facts regarding it. As Alexander had not carried his arms into that part of India it had remained quite unknown, and hence for his account of it Damis had to depend entirely on the resources of his own imagination. For the geography, however, of the country between the Indus and the Hyphasis he was not without guidance for it had been traversed by Alexander and described by his historians.... Damis, in fact, tells us nothing that is true about India except what had been told by writers before him...."[42] Priaulx (reviewer of the work of Philostratus) is of the view that Damis never accompanied Apollonius on his Indian journey. He rather fabricated the journal Philostratus speaks of, for it contains some facts, from books written on India which he collected at Alexandria, the great mart for Indian commodities and resort for Indian merchants.[43] His view is no longer tenable. The doubts of both McCrindle and Priaulx about the visit of Apollonius to India can be set at rest on the basis of what he himself says about this visit: "...the very journey undertaken it," as recorded in his biography by Philostratus. It is a well proven fact that he along with his Assyrian friend visited north-western India during the reign of the Parthian king, Bardanes (AD 42-45), and kept a record of it. He was a great traveller and many of his descriptions embody the results of his personal observations during the travels. There is no valid reason to doubt the visit of either Apollonius or Damis. Their narratives of the journey also do not leave room for any doubt about their visit to India. Some of their statements regarding India are consistent with each other.

As a matter of fact, the works of both the travellers have relative value. Their accounts of life and culture of the people of north-west India and that of Alexander's invasion go to supplement the classical accounts of the subject. The early history of north-west India can be reconstructed to a certain extent on the combined testimony of both the travellers.

REFERENCES

1. *The Life of Apollonius of Tyana,* ed and trans by F.C. Conybeare, 2 vols, London, 1912, reptd 1927, Books II and III; trans by E. Bewrick, London, 1811, pp. 11ff.
2. Berwick, op.cit., 16f; Conybeare, op.cit., II, XXVII; III, VI-VIII; Osmond De Beauvoir Priaulx, *The Indian Travels of Apollonius of Tyana*, Paris, 1873, cf. *The Classical Accounts of India* (here in after abbrev. As CAI), compiled by R.C. Majumdar, Calcutta, 1960, reptd 1981, pp. 392, 396-99, 405-7, 411.
3. Conybeare, op.cit., II, XXVII; CAI, pp. 391, 396-7; Berwick, op.cit., pp. 17-29.
4. Conybeare, op.cit., CAI, pp. 399, 405-7; J.W. McCrindle, *Ancient India as Described in Classical Literature* (abbrev. as AICL), Westminster, 1901, reptd Delhi, 1984, p. 193.
5. Conybeare, op.cit., II, XXVI; CAI, p. 391.
6. Conybeare, op.cit., II, XXVI; CAI, pp. 388, 391, 404.
7. CAI, pp. 395-96; AICL, p. 193.

8. Conybeare, op.cit., II, XXVII-XXVIII; CAI, p. 395; AICL, p. 193.
9. Conybeare, op.cit., CAI, pp. 394-5; AICL, p. 193.
10. Conybeare, op.cit., II, XVI-XVIII; CAI, p. 387.
11. Conybere, op.cit., II, XVIII-XX; CAI, p. 387.
12. Ibid., op.cit., II, XVI-XVII; Ibid., p. 385.
13. CAI, p. 385; AICL, p.192.
14. Cai, pp. 391, 393.
15. H.L. Jones, *The Geography of Strabo,* VII, London, 1949, BK XV, p. 47.
16. AICL, p.193; See also CAI, p. 389.
17. CAI, p. 387.
18. See CAI, p. 411.
19. Ibid.
20. Ibid., pp. 387, 391.
21. Ibid., p. 391.
22. CAI, pp. 391, 406.
23. At that time no foreign traveller was allowed to enter Taxila without a permit and to stay there for more than three days as per the law of the land.
24. Conybeare, op.cit., II, XX, XXV, XXV; Cai, pp. 387-8; AICL, p. 192; See also *The New Encylopaedia Britannica* (abbrev. As EB, New Series), XVIII, reptd Chicago, 1980, pp. 1083.
25. CAI, p. 388.
26. B.N. Puri, *India as Described by Early Greek Writers,* Varanasi, 1971, pp. 148-9.
27. CAI, pp. 388-9; AICL, pp. 192-3.
28. Cf. Conybeare, op.cit., II, XX.
29. The three important sites of urban settlements in Taxila have been archaeologically located at Bhir Mound, Sirkap and Sirsukh, which are often described as three different cities. But, in fact, they formed parts of Taxila city. They successively saw their rise and fall at three different periods of history. The first remained under the occupation of the Persians in the fifth century BC. And the Indo-Greeks from the third century BC. To the beginning of the second century BC; the second was under the rule of the Indo-Greeks from the early second century BC. To the early first century BC., the Scythians or Sakas in the first century BC. And the Parthians in the first half of the first century AD. And the third was occupied by the Kusanas in the latter half of the first century AD and remained in their possession till the early third century AD. The city remained in existence until it was destroyed by the Hunas in the fifth century AD. The extensive ruins of Taxila city are lying scattered within a radius of about 3 miles from north to south, and 2 miles from east to west in the vicinity of Shah-dheri at a distance west of Rawalpindi in Punjab.
30. *Taxila,* I, Cambridge, 1951, pp. 140-41.
31. *Ancient India,* no. 4, 1948.
32. Conybeare, op.cit., II, XX, XXV,; CAI, p. 388; AICL, p. 192.
33. Cf. Conybeare, op.cit., II, XXII.
34. Puri, op.cit., pp. 147-9; EB, new series XVII, p. 1083.
35. CAI, p. 388.

36. Puri, op.cit., p. 150.
37. AICl, p. 193; CAI, pp. 393-4.
38. Cai, p. 400.
39. Ibid., p. 408; See also AICL, p. 195.
40. Conybeare, op.cit., vii.
41. *The Ancient Geography of India*, Varanasi, 1979, p. 91.
42. AICL, p. 195.
43. Cf. CAI, p. 412.

17

Antiquity of the Term *Mandira* and its Synonyms

Samarendra Narayan Arya

Image-worship in temples started gaining popularity with the decline of Vedic sacrificial ritual during the post-Vedic period; the ground appears to have been prepared by the Upanishadic resistance to Vedic ritualistic practices and polytheistic beliefs. The decline of Vedic religion was further accelerated by the emergence of new religious sects in the form of Jainism and Buddhism. This may have been the background for the emergence of a new religious system in the form of image worship in temples. The gods were already there in the Vedic pantheon and regularly invoked at the sacrifices. Almost the same gods or at least the more important of them were now being singled out as the basis of separate cults and sects. As these tendencies grew stronger, each separate group began to worship a favoured deity in some form of temple structure.

There are stray references to image-worship in temples in literary records of the post-Vedic period. Perhaps the earliest of these references is in the *Aṣṭādhyāyī* of Pāṇiṇi, who lived during the fifth century BC. The two words used by Pāṇiṇi are *Pratikṛti*[1] and *arcā*[2], the latter probably signifying a cult image. The priest, who maintained the image was known as *arcāvān* or *arcicā* or possessed of the cult-image[3], Megasthenese, who lived in the Mauryan capital of Patliputra towards the close of the fourth century BC also refers to worship of Heracles (Kṛṣṇa) by Sourasones, the people of Śurasena, the country around Mathura. The chief cities of Sourasones were Mathora (Mathura) and Cleisobora (Kṛṣṇapura) and through this country flowed the river Jobares (Yamuna)[4]. Kauṭilya in his *Arthaśāstra*[5] describes the worship of icons of Śiva, Viṣṇu and Vaiśrāvana in their respective temples in the fort. In the *Sutra* literature belonging to the period fourth-first centuries BC there are references to worship of images in temples. The *Śāṃkhāyaṇagṛhyasūtra*, the *Gautama Dharmasūtra* and some others contain references to image-worship in temples.[6]

Patañjali[7], who lived in the second century BC and performed a few Aśvamedha sacrifices for the Śunga ruler Puṣyamitra mentions recitals of dance and music at the temples of Rāma and Keśava. Here, Rāma is identical with Balarama or Balabhadra and Keśava with Kṛṣṇa. The evidence of Patañjali shows that the two streams of Brahmanical religion, the Vedic sacrifices and image-worship were continuing side by side, while rulers and their subordinates patronised both these systems, the common man found the later practice more acceptable. Interestingly, from the second century BC onwards, inscriptional reference to ritual sanctification of different deities began to surface. For instance the construction of the temple of Viṣṇu (*Garuḍadhvaja*) by Heliodorus is referred to in the Besanagar pillar inscription of the second century BC. Further, the Ghoshundi inscription of the Satavhana queen Nāgamaṇikā, which is assigned to the first century BC, also contains a sanctimonious allusion to Vāsudeva and Saṃkarṣaṇa.[8]

The Terminology

In the *Sūtra* literature the term which denotes a divine sanctuary is *āyatanam.*[9] The *Gṛhyasūtras* like *Laugākṣī*[10] and *Śāṃkhāyana*[11] and *Dharmasūtras* like *Gautama*[12], *Āpastamba*[13], *Vasiṣṭha*[14] and *Viṣṇudharmottara*[15] refer to term *devāyatana* (the abode of god). The *Mahābhārata* also refers to the same term for temples.[16] The *Raghuvaṃśam*[17] of Kālidasa dated in about the fourth-fifth centuries AD mentions that icons of different gods were installed in lofty *āyatana* of Ayodhyā and they blessed the king Atithi of Raghu family through their abstract presence in their concerned icons. The *Nāgānanda*[18] of Śrīharṣa assigned to the early seventh century refers to a woman playing on a lute in the *āyatanam* (temple of god). The hero of the play also wishes to go to *āyatana* to offer his prayers. The Bhilsad rock pillar inscription[19] dated 415 AD states that a man named Dhruvasena offered endowments to *āyatana* of Mahāsena *(Mahāsenasyāyatane)*.

The term *niketana* also has been referred to in inscriptions in the sense of temple. The earliest references to this connection may be observed in the Tumain rock inscription[20] of 435 AD which informs us about the construction of *niketana* of god by five brothers of Tumain.

The term *gṛham* also denotes a temple in our early sources. The earliest evidence may be found in the *Harṣacaritam*[21] of Bāṇabhaṭṭa, a work of the early seventh century. According to the text, *Śivagṛham* was reverberating with recitations of *Rudrāṣṭādhyāyī.* Perhaps the earliest epigraphic evidence of the term *īśvaragṛham* for the temple of god is the inscription of Dharmarāja Maṇḍapaṃ of Māvalipuram, assigned to the early eighth century (*Atyantakāma Pallaveśvaragṛhaṃ*).[22] The cave inscriptions from the Trisirapalli rock[23] (Cola dynasty) belonging to the eighth-ninth centuries and Karahad plates of Kṛṣṇa III[24] dated in 958 AD refer to the construction of *gṛha* (temple) of Śiva.

In the *Mahābhāṣya*[25] of Patañjali there is one clear reference of image in the temple. The word used in this particular connection is *'prāsāda'* elsewhere it means a majestic house or palace. Moreover, the Airan Varāha Statue inscription of the Huṇa ruler Toramāna[26] dated 500 AD states that the construction of *Viṣṇu Prāsāda* provides merit to the performer. The same merit is said to have resulted from the construction of a massive stone temple (*Mahāśaila Prāsādam*) dedicated to god Trailokeśvara mentioned in the Paṭṭadakal pillar inscription[27] of the time of Kīrtivarmam II (754 AD).

Interestingly, the term *bhavana* also denotes a sanctuary. The Mandasor cave inscription[28] dated 436 AD mentions that Viśvavarmā, who was appointed governor of Daspura by the Gupta ruler Kumāragupta I, got a *bhavana* of the sun constructed. Likewise, the Aphsad inscription of Ādityasena (660-75) refers to the lofty temple of Viṣṇu as *Viṣṇoḥ bhavanoṭṭamam.*[29] Two more inscriptions[30] dated 733 and 973 inform us of a splendid Śiva temple.

The term *ālaya* is frequently used to mean temple in several literary and epigraphic sources. The *Harṣacaritam*[31] refers to the term *surālaya* for the abode of gods. Two inscriptions of Baijnath[32] both dated 882 AD refer to donation of land at Navagrāma for the construction of a Śiva temple (Śivālaya). The king Keta II, born in the family of Bhīma is said to have caused the construction of *devālaya* in an inscription[33] of 1026.

It is pertinent to note that terms like *āśramam, dhāmam, maṇḍapam* and *sthānam* also indicate temple. The *Nāgānanda*[34] of Śrīharṣa refers to *gaurī-āśrama* as the holy abode of Pārvatī. The *Meghadūtam*[35] of Kalīdāsa describes the Mahākāla temple as the abode (*dhāma)* of god Śiva, the consort of goddess Candī and the lord of the universe (*tribhuvana gurudhāma Caṇḍīśvarasya).* An inscription of King Bhīmdev II of the Cālukya dynasty mentions the erection of a *maṇḍapam* for the god Someśvara.[36] The term *sthāna* finds its earliest mention in the Nandasyūpa inscription of 226 AD (*Brahmendra Prajāpati maharṣi viṣṇu sthāneṣu).*[37]

In this respect we may also refer to one important *devakula* which also represents a divine sanctuary. The Baigram copper plate of 448 AD, found in Bogra district of East Bengal[38] (modern Bangladesh) mentions a gift of free hold land (*agrahāra)* for repair and renovation of the temple (*devakula*) of Govinda Svāmī (Kṛṣṇa). The Damodarpur copper plate inscription of king Buddhagupta (AD 482) records the donation of land for the maintenance of a Śiva temple (*devakula*). The Gunaidhar copper plate inscription 507 AD (Bengal) mentions a gift of land for the temple(*devakula*) of Pradyumneśvara. In the *Harṣacaritam*[43], the constructions of temple (*devakula*) engraved with ensigns and emblems is recommended.

Last but not the least, the term *mandiram* literally means a house or a building, for example, the *Raghuvaṃśam* manifests that Rāvaṇa, king of Lanka came out of his *mandiram* (house) and directly went to the battlefield.[44] But the meaning of *mandiram* as a temple like structure seems to be evident from the sixth-seventh centuries onwards. Donation of land and complete villages to the Brāhmaṇa priest, concept of earning merit through construction of temples and early medieval gift exchange system went a long way in developing this social system.[45] The *Harṣacaritam*[46] lays down that the region of Thaneśvara is possessed with a number of glorious things including *mandiram* of god Viśvakarmā (*Viśvakarmāmandiram*). Moreover, an inscription at the Ganesh temple at Mavallipuram[47] (733-47 AD) records that the king Atyantakāma constructed the lofty *mandira* of Dhurjati (Śiva) in order to fulfil the desires of his subjects. Further the Jodhpur inscription of the king Pratihāra Bauka[48] (834 AD) states that the king built the temple (*mandira)* of god Siddheśvara at the holy place called Tretā (*Siddheśvara Mahādevakāritastunga mandiram*).

The Samgamner copper plate[49] inscription of AD 1000 mentions the term *mandira* in relation to a temple of Śiva, the lord of mountains (*Girīśamandiram*). It is interesting that the poet sketches the features of the temple in a very poetic style. The term *mandira* for a temple is used in three separate inscriptions of 1155 AD (Bheraghat inscription of Alhandevi)[50], 1163 AD (Ratanpur stone inscription)[51] and 1192 AD (Swapneśvara).[52] The expressions used in these inscriptions are *Dhurjaṭeḥmandiram, Mandiramindumauleri* and *Megheśvaramandira* respectively, all refer to temples of Śiva. Noticeably, the temple of Viṣṇu is also referred to as *Viṣṇoḥmandiram* in an inscription of the Vallabhaṭṭa Swāmin Temple at Gwallior[53] 862 AD (*Vikārśūya manaṣa Viṣṇoridaṃ mandiram*). The Chittorgarh inscription of Caulukya Kumara Pāla[54] of 1092 contains information of a gift in favour of a temple (*mandira*).

In addition to the above epigraphic records, there are other inscriptions which mention several synonyms of temple. The Gaṇapeśvaram inscription of Ganapati[55] dated in 1231 AD frequently refers to the terms *devālayaḥ, Caṇḍīśvaradhāma, Bhīmeśvaramandiram, Bhairavasyaprāsāda and Śivabhavanam,* all the terms denoting temples of Śiva.

It is important to note that synonymns of the term *'mandira'* referred to in early texts before the Christian era do not indicate any construction of housing structure for the abode of deities. It simply stands for the sitting place for them. They are invocated in hymns to take their respectful seats at a particular place called *devagrha, devalaya* and so on. Kautilya refers to term *devatākaru,*[56] i.e. builder of icons, but nowhere does he describe a constructed building for *mandira* (temple). Obviously in the Mauryan period the priest moved from place to place with icons of deities and got them adorned by the devotees. The income derived from this practice went to the state as religious revenues. During the second century BC, Heliodorus is said to have constructed a Visnuite temple at Bhilsa in Malva, MP, but it is virtually a pillar, not a temple like structure, dedicated to Lord Vishnu, popularly called 'Khambha Baba' by localites there.

The construction of fully-fledged houses for residing of cult-gods known as Brahmanical cave temples was actually carried on from the fourth century AD onwards and the process continued up to tenth-eleventh centuries, the Udayagiri cave temple of Viṣṇu perhaps being the earliest example. Then came the age of the brick built temple bearing summit in the mid-sixth century. Temples of Bhitaragaon in Kanpur and Devagarh in Jhansi, both in UP belong to this category.

NOTES AND REFERENCES

1. Pāṇiṇi, *Astādhyāyī,* 5.3.96
2. Ibid., 5.2.101.
3. Vasudev Sharan Agrawal, *Paṇiṇi Kālīn Bharat,* Chaukhamba Vidya Bhawan, Varanasi, 1969, p. 354.
4. J.W.M. Crindle, *Ancient India as Described by Megasthenese and Arrian,* Calcutta, 1960, p.198.
5. *Arthaśāstra,* 2.4.
6. Supra.
7. Prabhu Dayal Agnihotri, *Patañjali Kalin Bharat,* Bihar Rashtra Bhasha Parishad, Patna, 1961, p. 554.
8. D.C. Sircar, *Select Inscriptions,* Vol. 1, p. 200.
9. Ibid., p. 130.
10. *Laugaksigrhya,* 18.3
11. *Śamkhāyaṇa,* 4.12.15.
12. *Gautam,* 9.13.14.
13. *Āpastamba,* 1.11.30.28.
14. *Vaśiṣtha,* 11.31.
15. *Viṣṇudharmottara,* 69.7.30.15.
16. Ādiparva, 70.49, Anuśāsana, 10.20.21; Aśvamedhikā, 70.16; Bhiṣma, 112.11.
17. Kalidasa, *Raghuvamsam,* 17.36, *Ayodhyādevatāscainam Prasatāyatanārcitāḥ Anudadhyuranudhyayeyam Samnidhyaiḥ pratimgataiḥ.*
18. Srīharṣa, *Nāgānanda,* tr. Baldev Upadyāya, Chaukhamba Sanskrit Sansthan, Varanasi, 1986, Ch. 2, p. 32.

19. Vasudev Upadhyay, *Gupta Abhilekha* (hereafter G.A.)., Bihar Hindi Grantha Academy, Patna, 1974, inscription no. 96.
20. Ibid., p. 139.
21. Bāṇabhaṭṭa, *Harṣacaritaṃ* (tr. Mohan Dev), Patna, Motilal Banarsidass, portion 5, p. 298.
22. *El.*, Vol. 10, no. 1.D. (21), line 12.
23. Ibid., Vol. 4, no. 9(A), ll. 9-10, *Haragṛhametajjyotis tadiyamiva śankar jyotiḥ*
24. Ibid., vol. 4, no. 40, v-10, *yatkārite śvaragṛhai Kailaśaśila niciteva*
25. Infra, see in detail.
26. *G.A.*, p. 227.
27. *El.*, Vol. 3, no.1, line 14.
28. *G.A.*, p. 151, v.16, *Śreṇibhutaibhavanamatulamikāritamdipta-raṣmeḥ*.
29. Ibid., p. 184, v.26 tenedam bhavanottamam kṣtibhujā viṣṇoḥ kṛtekāritam.
30. *El.* Vol. 23, no. 1F(23), v 3; ibid., Vol. 2 no. 8, v. 44.
31. Op.cit., portion 3, p. 173.
32. *El*, Vol. 1., No.16(1), v.35, Ṣivālayastavadastu Samam andhasāsanaḥ.
33. Ibid., Vol. 6, no.15(A), v.43.
34. Op.cit., ch, p.82.
35. *Meghadūtam*, (First part), v. 37.
36. *El*, vol. 2, no.35, v23.
37. Ibid., Vol. 27, no. 43 B, lines 8-9.
38. *G.A.*, Vaigrama copper plate, 448 AD, p. 194, line 7, *Bhagavato Govindaswāmino devakule khanda phuṭṭa pratisamkara karmaya gandhadhūpa dīpa sumansā*.
39. Ibid., p. 81, lines 5-8.
40. Ibid., p. 79, line 29.
41. Ibid., the Khoh copper plate, line 11.
42. *El*, vol. 9, no. 28, lines 39-40.
43. Op.cit., portion 1, v.15.
44. *Raghuvaṃsam*, canto 12, v.83, *niryayāvathapaulastyaḥ punaryuddhāya mandirāt*.
45. R.N. Nandi, *Social Roots of Religion in Ancient India*, K.P. Bagchi & Company, Calcutta, 1986, (See in detail ch. 13.)
46. Op.cit., portion 3, pp. 175-6.
47. *El*, Vol. 18, no. 12, v. 20.
48. Ibid., Vol. 18, no.12, v.20.
49. Ibid., Vol. 2, no.15, l. 47, *VijayābharaGanayabhidhama bhinava Giriśamandiram*.
50. Ibid., Vol. 2, v. 27.
51. Ibid., Vol. 26, no. 35, v.36, *nirmitam mandiram ramyam Kumarākoṭapañne*.
52. Ibid., Vol. 6, no. 17(A), v. 23, *Mandirolankendhreṇaśilā cchayam gṛham*.
53. Ibid., Vol. 1, no. 20(1), vv. 23-25.
54. Ibid., Vol. 2, no. 33, line 8, *bhrāntvājaganti yatkīrti aragahebharamandiram*.
55. Ibid., Vol. 3, no. 15, vv. 9, 23, 25.
56. *Arthaśāstra*, 2.4, See S.N. Arya, *History of Pilgrimage in Ancient India, AD 300-1200*, Munshiram Manoharlal, Delhi, 2004, pp. 6-7.

18

The Methods and Stages of the Preservation of Scriptures in Ancient India: Oral Tradition

Radha Madhav Bharadwaj

The ancient Indian scriptures are great treasure-houses of knowledge which have fostered intellectual growth in the Indian subcontinent and other parts of Asia since the Vedic ages. The uniqueness about this great source of knowledge is that it was preserved for a very long time through the oral tradition. A great part of the canonical literature particularly the Vedic, the Buddhist and the Jain, was orally composed, preserved and transmitted for a long time.[1]

Max Muller in his *History of Sanskrit Literature* states that writing for literary purposes was unknown to Panini.[2] But P.V. Kane refutes it by saying that Indians had a kind of writing on the Harappan seals.[3] However, consensually the Ashokan inscriptions written in the Brahmi script and Prakrit language represent the earliest system of writing in India. Sanskrit was adopted as an epigraphic medium in the second century AD.[4] Our oldest manuscripts are not older that the fourth century AD which have been found in Central Asia.[5] It is well known that the earliest Vedic literature began to be composed around 1500 BC and continued till the end of the later Vedic period and perhaps even later. Lord Buddha and Mahavir delivered their teachings orally in the sixth fifth centuries BC and many of their disciples also gave sermons in the same manner many centuries after them.

The first institution which helped preserve the Vedic scriptures was the *Kula Parampara,* i.e. family tradition, in which the Vedic seers used to inculcate the knowledge of the scriptures to their sons, daughters, nephews and grandsons in their families. Nachiketa, the famous character of the *Kathopanisada,* also learnt his lessons from his father.[6]

The whole of Vedic literature is replete with examples in which pupils lived with their teachers in their families till they acquired the knowledge of their choice and in the end gave dakṣiṇā or a tuition fee to them. In this system the father-teacher or the teacher (guru or àcàrya) used to make their pupils learn the scriptures by rote. They were made to memorise the scriptures again and again till the time it was assured that the scriptures would not slip out of their memory.[7]

The study of the Vedas did not merely consist in learning the mantras (incantations) by heart, but one also had to understand its meaning. The *Nirukta* (1.18) quotes two verses which condemn a person who merely memorised the scriptures without understanding it. The system appears to have continued till the early medieval time. For instance, Daksha (11.34 quoted by Mitākshara on Yājnavalkya, iii, 310) says that the study of the Vedas involves five things, viz., first committing the Vedas to memory, then reflection over its meaning, keeping it fresh by repeating it again and again, Japa (inaudibly muttering by way of prayer), and imparting it to pupils,[8] the *Chhandogya Upanisad* talks of *Naisthikabrahmacarin* (devoted student) who stayed all his life with the teacher and repeated the scripture and led a life of self-restraint.[9] To preserve the ancient heritage, the ancient sages prevailed upon qualified members of the population to make it its duty to devote as much time as they could do to the study and conservation of the Vedic literature. Not only was the study of the Veda made an absolute duty for all qualified persons belonging to the three higher varnas, but the study of the Vedas was also essential for the performance of Vedic sacrifices (Jaimini, II 8.18).[10]

Certain grammatical rules were urgently needed to regulate the correct recitation of the scripture. This led to the emergence of a kind of incipient grammar known as *Pratisakhyas.*[11] Then came a glossary of Vedic words called the *Nighantu* on which Yaska wrote his famous commentary called the *Nirukta.*[12] We also see the rise of the Vedanga literature which was six in number. *Śiksa* was the text of pronunciation. *Chhandas* expanded the metres of the hymns. *Nirukta,* the book of grammar explained the words of the Vedas. *Kalpa* was related to Vedic rituals and *Jyotis* to astronomy and mathematics.[13] The importance of *Vyakarana* can be seen from the fact that Aindra and Katandra, two grammatical treatises proceeded with the writing of *Ashtadhyayi* by Panini.

Panini's grammar was a great work by any standard which must have helped the students understand the formation of the words and pronounce them correctly. Then the *Varttika* was composed by the great Katyayana, which was a commentary on Panini. Then Patanjali wrote his *Mahabhasya* (the great commentary) on *Ashtadhyayi* and explained the rules of grammar which could not be accommodated by these grammarians.

The tradition tells us that immediately after the death of Buddha, his direct disciples called a council at Rajagriha for the compilation and preservation of *Buddhavacan* (teachings of the Buddha). The Vinay rules were recited by venerable Upali and Dhamma (which comprised both the *Sutta* and *Abhidhamma*) by Anand and a few others. Together these constituted the corpus of Buddhist teachings. This was indeed a great historical achievement of its time. This council took seven months to compile the corpus and after it was orally compiled and accepted by all the monks present there, it was recited by all the monks to retain it in their minds. But within a hundred years distortions began to appear in the conduct of the monks because nothing existed in writing. Hence, around 383 B.C. a second council was called at Vaishali where the Purist Theravadin expelled a number of deviant monks who caused a split in the order and held a parallel council at Kaushambi. They called themselves Mahasamghikas and compiled their own *Tripitaka* in Prakrit by breaking up the order and distorting the original *Tripitaka*. During the time of Emperor Ashoka, a third council was convened at Pataliputra under the chairmanship of monk Moggaliputta Tissa.

Ashoka and the purist theravadin monks were pained at the distortion that had set into the Buddhist order (*Samgha*). The *Samgha* had come to be divided into eighteen different sects and the monks behaved against the monastic rules. Ashoka had come to realise that it was only to get food and clothing that the fake monks had come to join the *Samgha,* Ashoka asked them certain questions to test their knowledge of the authentic teachings of the master and after finding that a great many of them had deviated from the original path in Dhamma and Vinay, not only expelled them from the *Samgha* but also snatched monkship from them and derobed them. He patronised the Sthaviravadins and recognised them as men of merit and character who could carry forward the teachings of the Buddha in the purest form. But even then, the canon was not put down in writing. Ashoka did one great thing at this council by deciding to send religious missions to different parts of India and the world to spread the message of the master for the welfare of mankind. As part of this mission Ashoka sent his son Mahendra and daughter Sanghamitra to Sri Lanka to preach Buddhism. Noticeably they taught there orally.[14]

We know from the *Mahavamsa,* the Pali chronicle of Sri Lanka, that during the reign of king Wattagamani Abhaya (101-77 BC) a council (2nd Council in Sri Lanka) was convened where the theras (theravadin monks) recited the *Theravada Tripitaka* which was then reduced to writings in the Pali language, after noticing a sharp decline in the memory of the contemporary people.[15] There is not much of a problem in accepting the theory of oral tradition and its being reduced to writing in the first century BC during the time of king Wattagamani except for the fact that writing did appear in India in the third century BC. Ashokan time and that he issued a guideline for Buddhist monks and nuns in his Bhabru inscription that they should listen to the teaching (Dhamma Paliyaya) contained in the *Vinayasamukase, Aliyavasani Anagatbhayani, Munigatha, Moneysutta, Upatisapasine and Lahulovade.* It is, however not clear whether Ashoka was referring to recitation of certain excreted Buddhist teachings. Scholars are of the view that the Theravada *Tripitaka*, that is available to us in the Pali literature was finalised under the patronage of king Wattangamani in the first century BC.

Intelligence was one very important element which greatly helped the preservation of the Buddhist scriptures. The Buddha has been quoted as having declared one of his most intelligent desciples, Kacchayana as his principal disciple.[17]

In those days, when the mind was the only preservatory, where the knowledge could be stored, men of intelligence were most revered. The Buddha had eighty chosen disciples who must have been selected because of their devotion, hard work, moral conduct and sharp intellect. When the first council was convened, only 500 monks were selected to recite and recommend the Buddhavacana. The rest of the monks, who were asked not to go towards the venue of the council, must have been ordinary monks not worthy of attending the council. In the second council, only 700 were called. Thus, it seems that intelligence was valued and relied upon in the days of oral transmission.

To memorise any scripture, it was very essential to have knowledge of the grammar. The Pali grammarian Kacchayana has explained the objective of writing his grammar with a view to understand the meaning of the teachings of the lord. The Buddha himself had indicated the importance of grammar in the better understanding of the language and declared that Mahakacchayana would write a text on grammar. Among the Buddhists, the council played a very important role in the preservation, rectification and transmission of the scripture.

In conclusion, we may say that the ancient Vedic seers and the Buddhists faced an uncounted number of odds in the absence of writing and they deserve all the praise for their strong memorising and retaining power for preserving their respective scriptures.

NOTES AND REFERENCES

1. P.V. Kane, *History of Dharmasastras,* V.II, Part I, Bhandarkar Oriental Research Institutes, Poona, 1941. Pp. 348-49 (here after *Dharmasastras*).
2. Ibid., p. 348.
3. Ibid.
4. R.S. Sharma, *Ancient India,* NCERT, New Delhi, 1990.

5. Ibid.
6. Harikrishan Goyandaka, *Isadi nine Upanisadas* (Hindi), Geeta Press, Gorakhpur, Samvat, 2059 (23nd ed.), p. 53 (*Kathopanisad*), first valli, v.5.
7. Kane, *Dharmasastra*, p. 348.
8. Ibid., p. 375.
9. Vaman Shivaram Apte, *Sanskrit Hindi Kosa*, p. 523, also see M. Monier Williams, *A Sanskrit English Dictionary*, MLBD, Delhi, 1997 (rpt) p. 546.
10. Ibid., p. 975, also see M. Monier Williams, 'Dictonary', pp. 1016-17.
11. Apte, *Kosa*, p. 689.
12. Ibid., p. 523.
13. Ibid., p. 975 aslo see Williams, '*Dictionary*' pp. 1016-17.
14. Satkari Mukhopadhyaya, 'Glimpses of Buddhist canons and their Divisions' in Ratna Basu (ed.), *Buddhist Literary Heritage in India: Text and Context*. National Mission for Manuscripts and Munshiram Manoharlal, New Delhi, 2007, p. 11.
15. Wilhelm Geiger (ed.), *Mahavamsa of Mahanama*, London, 1958, (reprint), 33.100-101.
16. Laxmi Narayana Tiwari and Birbal Sharma (eds), *Kacchayana Vyakarana*, Varanasi, 1989, Introduction, p. 20.
17. Bhikshu Satyapal (ed.), *Kacchayana-nyaso Buddha Triratna Mission*, Eastern Book Linkers, New Delhi, 1991, p. 6.

19

Monetary Exchange under the Imperial Pratihāras

Shanta Rani Sharma

This article brings forth a new analytical perspective, resolving the controversy in regard to prevalence of coins in the Pratihāra Empire by highlighting the contemporary epigraphic evidence of widespread monetary exchange within this region. It refutes the idea which seeks to explain the paucity of coin finds in terms of diminishing use of coined metallic money. This is supported by literary evidence as well.

Systematic compilation of Indo-Sassanian coins, a large number of which have been identified as Pratihāra coins suggests considerable circulation of metallic money in the Pratihāra empire[1]. However, scholars have questioned the identification of Indo-Sassanian coins as Pratihāra coins.

Silver coins of the Pratihāra ruler Vatsarāja, bearing the legend 'Raṇahastin' have been found in Rajasthan, Kannauj and Saurashtra[2]. Two gold coins bearing the boar incarnation on the obverse and the legend 'Śrīvatsadamanārāyaṇa[3] and the cow and calf motif on the reverse can also be identified as Pratihāra coins. The weight of one of these gold coins is said to be 116.5 gr. These coins appear to be prototypes of coins issued by Bhoja, the successor of Vatsarāja. An identical gold coin of Bhoja bears the boar incarnation on one side and the cow and calf motif on the other. This coin weighs 7.91gr. The *Dravya Parīkṣā* of Thakkur Pheru also mentions the boar cow (*gavikā*) and calf (*paḍiyā*) types of coins among Gurjara Mudras.[4] An inscription of Gallaka (795 AD), a subordinate of Vatsarāja describes Nāgabhaṭa I as one who like Viṣṇu in his Varāha incarnation had saved the earth from calamity.[5] This bears out the special significance of the Varāha incarnation for the early Pratihāras. The *Kuvalayamālā* (8th century AD) also mentions gift/payment of coined money to astrologers, gardeners and painters, suggesting the wide circulation of metallic money during the time of Vatsarāja. The work refers to investment and earnings made by the traders in coined money.[6]

The widespread use of *dramma coins* in the time of the Pratihāra ruler Bhoja is suggested by as many as four epigraphic records, namely the Ahar documents of AD 864 and AD 867[7], the Pehova inscription of AD 882-838[8] and the Kaman document of AD 905-6[9]. The Ahar document of AD 864 states that two merchants spent some amount of *dramma* coins to purchase an enclosure dedicated to goddess Kañchanadevī. Certain Sauvarṇika traders together with two merchants assigned the rent (*āvārī*) to the temple of Kañchanadevī to provide funds for perpetual cleaning and plastering, saffron, flowers, incense, lamps, flags, whitewashing and the repair of buildings. The Ahar inscription of AD 867[10] states that the Sauvarṇika Mahājana purchased a house with money (*dravya*) for being attached to the temple of Kañcanadevī. The house together with its entire elevation was purchased by a lease deed of ninety-nine years. The document further records that the house was bought from a perfume merchant.

Further evidence of monetary transactions is furnished by the Pehova inscription, which mentions that certain horse dealers, who met at the horse fair held at Pehova agreed to impose upon themselves and upon their customers certain tolls payable in *drammas*. These proceeds were to be distributed among temples and priests, in proportions duly specified. The tolls consisted of two *drammas;* to be deducted from the sum received by the dealer for each animal sold in Pṛthudaka (modern Pehovā).[11] It is evident that the people engaged in monetary exchange included not only the horse dealers and the ruler, but also thakkuras, common people, priests and temples. The horse-dealers, who were thirty-three or thirty-four in number are said to belong to different places, Chutvariska, Utpalika. Chikkriselvaṇpura, Valadevapura, Sīharaudukkaka or possibly Sīharuddhakkaka, Ṭghāṭaka, Ghamghaka, and Aśval-Uhovaka. It is stated that these places lay in different countries.[12] Therefore *dramma* was a currency used by the dealers hailing from diverse areas like Lahore, Ahmedabad and Kathiawad, if one is to accept the identifications proposed by Buhler.[13] Cash donations, which are specifically made over to different temples, of which three were situated near Kannauj and one at Pehovā[14], further indicate the *dramma* endowments served the purpose at Kannauj and Pehovā as well.

The inclusion of common people and ṭhākkurās in the list of those participating in the *dramma* exchange is particularly significant. The mention of the former indicates that the handling of cash was not restricted to the elite classes, whereas the latter indicates that the ṭhākkurās were also engaged in monetary exchange.

The evidence regarding the use of *dramma* recorded in the Kaman document of AD 905-06[15] is of equal significance. It records the gift of some *dramma* coins by king Bhoja to one Acharya Chāmuṇḍaka, who in his turn donated it to the trustees (goṣṭhikās) of the temple.

The facts revealed by the record are many faceted. First, the gift of cash by grant by Bhoja to the preceptor (ācārya) could be meaningful only if coined money held substantial value in everyday life. The same can be surmised from the rent collected from the shops, undoubtedly a monetary return, being assigned for the explicit purpose of the provision of article used in daily worship and temple maintenance. Secondly, it is significant that the temple trustees chose to invest in shop and opted for rent accruing from these rather than invest in land and receive rent in kind. Thirdly, the ādivarāha *drammas* retained value well beyond the time of Bhoja, whose known dates range from AD 836 to 865.

The *drammas* of the Kaman inscription have been identified with the distinctive currency classified as ādivarāha *drammas*.[16] On the obverse, these depict the boar or Varāha incarnation of Viṣṇu, wearing a garland (*vanamālā*), and standing astride to the left. The strength and vigour revealed by the representation corresponds to that of the same incarnation in the plastic art of the Gupta age. On the reverse there are the traces of the Sassanian altar with two attendants and the Brahmi legend Śrīmadādivarāha in two lines.

Three other Ahar documents belonging either to the reign of Bhoja or Mahendrapāla I, provide further evidence of the use of coined money. One of these dated AD 886 records that the southern half of a building site, containing a dwelling and two *āvārīs* together with all the inner apartments was bought from certain bhaṭṭas.[17] The document dated 902 records that the sauvarṇika mahājana acquired on āvārī, comprising three rooms, with the temple money from certain brāhmaṇas (bhaṭṭas).[18] The documents testify to the participation of the temple sauvarṇika mahajana and brāhmaṇas in monetary exchange. They also record the use of money for purchase of immovable property.

Evidence of the use of coins in the reign of Mahendrapāla I comes from the Siyadoni inscription which testifies to the use of the coin denomination *Pañciyakadramma*. The very object of the document, dated AD 907 is to record daily endowment of a quarter of a *Pañciyakadramma* made by a brāhmaṇa in favour of god Viṣṇu.

Of the two inscriptions ascribed to Mahendrapāla I and testifying to the prevalence of money economy in his times, one is the Ahar record of AD 904.[19] It records that formerly those had been given as surety for the monthly payment of ten *viṃśopakas* out of its rent refers to the grant record in the Ahar document no.4, dated AD 886[20] which belongs either to the reign of Bhoja or Mahendrapāla himself. This house, at the time, had been acquired by the grandfather of the four donees for a term of 99 years and their descendants were to enjoy the rent from the house after they had paid the ten *viṃśopakas* to the temple of the goddess Kanakaśrīdevī. The object of the later document, dated AD 904, records that the entire rent and not ten *viṃśopakas* only, was made over to a deed of 99 years to the temple in consideration of payment out of the temple funds.

The second inscription of Mahendrapala's regime is the Ahar record of AD 904.[21] It records the purchase of six *āvārīs* from certain brahmanas (*bhaṭṭas*) by the sauvarṇika *mahājanas* with money belonging to the temple. The rent which accrued from this immovable property was to be applied to the provision of saffron, incense, flowers, lamps, flags, and whitewashing and the repairs of the broken portions of the temple. The two Ahar inscriptions confirm the role of coined money in the purchase of immovable property to secure further return as rent.

The continued use of *drammas* in the time of his successor Mahipāla is attested to by the Asni inscription dated AD 917.[22] The purport of the epigraph, which refers itself to the reign of Mahipāla, is that whenever there should be a special occasion, 500 *drammas* should be given out of the hereditary tax belonging to the king's household, *Maulakarā rājakulasya*, to a certain temple. The grant of *dramma* for the purpose of providing for needs on special occasions is a clear index of their exchange value. Since the sum was provided out of the hereditary tax, his predecessors must have also realised equivalent *dramma* amount in taxes.

Epigraphic evidence of the use of the coined money also comes from the Rakhetra stone inscription dated in AD 942[23] and 943[24], discovered in the village of that name near Chanderi, belonging to Vināyakapāla, identified as a Pratihāra monarch. It records the construction of some hydraulic device at a cost of 95 crores connected with the Orr river.

The reference to payment of tax in cash (*hiraṇya*) to the ruler by the village of Kharparapadraka in the Partapgarh inscription of AD 946[25] testifies to payment of dues in money in the time of Mahendrapāla II. The payment of the tax (*hiraṇya*) to the ruler by yet another village Dhara-padraka under jurisdiction of Madhava, the governor of Ujjain under Mahendrapāla is also recorded.[26]

Epigraphic testimony regarding the use of *drammas* in the reign of Devapāla comes from the Siyadoni document dated AD 948-9.[27] It records the assignment of monthly payment of one-third of *dramma* in favour of a deity by the merchants at the Dosihaṭṭa or the textile market. It also records the assignment of one-third of a Vigrahapāla *dramma* on every *bharaṇa* in favour of another deity by stonecutters (Śilākūta). The record is significant as it indicates different denomination of coins, the *dramma* and the Vigrahapāla *dramma,* were current at Siyadoni in the time of Devapāla.

The payment in *dramma* made by the dealers in textiles and the stonecutters indicates that coined money was used not only by the merchants but also by artisans.

Evidence of the use of *dramma* in the region of Mahīpāla II comes from the AD 955 Bayana inscription of queen Citralekhā, a descendant of the Śūrasena family, who was a subordinate of Mahīpāla.[28] The various monetary grants that formed part of the donation made by her to a temple included (a) three *drammas* given every day by the customs house (*maṇḍapikā*) at Śrīpatha, (b) another three *drammas* by the customs house at Vusāvaṭa, (c) a gift of one *dramma* per horse, either collected on every horse sold or on every horse-load of merchandise. There is a clear indication of the regular collection of *dramma* first by two different customs houses, secondly from merchants dealing in horses or horse-loads of merchandise and thirdly, eventually by the temple.

The AD 960 Rajor inscription of Mathanadeva,[29] a subordinate of the imperial Pratihāra ruler Vijayapala, testifies to the religious donation or three viṃśopakas as customary in the market, on every sack brought for sale to the market and two vimśopakas per mensem for every shop. This forms an important testimony of the fact that dealers in agricultural goods, possibly agriculturists, were in possession of coined money.

Two other documents found at Siyadoni, dated AD 908 and 912,[30] do not bear the name of the reigning monarch. But they are Pratihāra records since the Pratihāra rule over the region remained undisturbed,[31] as evidenced by two other Pratihāra records, one from Siyadoni itself dated 948-49, of a later successor, Devapala.[32] The continued prevalence of monetary exchange is available in both these Siyodini documents. The Siyodini document (980 AD) which records the endowments in favour of the deity states that distillers of the area were to pay half a vigrahapāla *satkadrama* on every cask of liquor. The AD 912 Siyadoni document records that a merchant Nagaka gave a capital of 1350 *śrīmadavarāha drammas*, invested with distillers of spirituous liquor, who were to pay every month half a Vigrahatungiya *dramma* on every cask of liquor.

It is manifest that these inscriptions of the Pratihāra period, recording donations to different temples are of remarkable numismatic value when viewed from a historical perspective. These contain explicit references to the use of coined money in the kingdom of Pratihāra rulers. Substantial epigraphic evidence relating to the use of metallic money in different parts of northern and central India like Asni (UP), Ahar (UP), Siyadoni (UP), Kaman (Rajasthan), Bayana (Rajasthan), Rajor (Rajasthan), Pehova (Haryana) and Rakhetra (MP) could not have found a place in the administrative records without considerable exchange of minted money in the Pratihāra Empire. The evidence discussed above shows that money changed hands frequently and across the society including elites like kings, feudatories, priests, traders as well as lower stratum of the society including masons, distillers, stone cutters and artisans.

Considerable evidence presented by the inscriptions, regarding the regular use of currency, relates to individual Pratihāra rulers with whom no distinctive coin-finds have been associated so far. The currency of different denominations of *drammas* and vimśopakas in the domains of Bhoja, Mahendrapala I, Mahīpāla I, a subordinate ruler of Mahīpāla II, Devapāla and Vijayapāla, the use of coins by Vinayakapāla in addition to the records of the use of specific coin types such as the ādivarāha *dramma* and Vigrahapāla *dramma* provide ample proof that the monetary exchange prevailed throughout the Pratihāra rule. Rulers received monetary payments in the form of cash collections from maṇḍapikas, village, and on agricultural produce brought for sale besides hereditary taxes. This is a clear pointer that the non-attribution of coin-finds to specific rulers and lack of discovery of distinctive coin-finds is not to be correlated with paucity of coins. The literary evidence of the *Kuvalayamālā* regarding the use of coins in the time of Vatsarja and the numismatic evidence relating to the period reinforces such a conclusion.

Temples located in different parts of the Prathihāra Empire were endowed with considerable monetary resources. An idea of vast monetary resources in possession of the temple of Kañcandevī/Kaṇakaśrīdevī situated in the town of Tattanandurma, is evinced by the Ahar inscription. The repeated purchase of considerable landed property made with the temple money spread over a large number of years emphasises the continuous significance inflow of coined money into the temple of Ahar, which again was not allowed to remain dormant but was invested to produce further cash returns in the form of recurring rent. The explicit assignment of the rent of immovable property rather than the immovable property itself to temples record in the documents indicates the relevance of coined money in the contemporary economy.

Evidence of many other temples within the Pratihāra Empire receiving monetary grants comes from the Pehoa, Siyadoni, Asni, Bayana, and Partabgarh inscriptions. Epigraphic evidence reveals that people from varied sections of the society were participants in the prevalent economy. The documents recorded in the Ahar inscription testify to monetary payments received by several brāhmaṇas, viz. the Bhaṭṭa Īśvara son of Mahādeva and Mahādeva the son of Asaiv, the Bhaṭṭa Divākara, son of Bhaṭṭa Tarangana, Acyutaśiva and Damodaraśiva the son of Saiva-Bhaṭṭa-Diyaka, Ananda-Bhaṭṭa Siva the son of Achyutasiva and the Bhaṭṭa Īśānandatta, as well as Ksatriyas, viz. Kokāka and Padmanābha in lieu of houses and āvārīs. Other classes engaged in monetary exchange at Ahar include the Sauvaurnṇika-Mahājanas who affected six monetary purchases for the Kanakadevi temple, vaṇiks Bhadraprakāśa and Maumka who also affected a monetary purchase and the merchants, from whom similar landed property was acquired, viz. the merchant Madhav, who belonged to the Māthura caste and was a seller of perfumes and merchant Sāhāka.

To conclude, the epigraphic references to the regular income in cash derived by the Pratihāra rulers from levies on various market transactions including sale of horses, movement of agriculture produce and shops, the substantial money resources made available to the temples and their investments to procure further cash returns, the evidence pertaining to use of coined money as a medium of exchange in daily as well as long distance commercial transactions, the use of coined money by a vast cross section of society, viz. Brāhmaṇas, Kṣatriyas, merchants common people, artisans, labour class, subordinate rulers and agriculturists, the existence of different coin denominations and testimony to their use in an extensive geographical area and by successive Mathur rulers, the numismatic finds and literary evidence provide incontrovertible evidence of widespread monetary exchange within the Pratihāra Empire.

NOTES AND REFERENCES

1. J.S. Deyell, *Living without Silver: The History of Early Medieval Northern India,* Delhi, 1990.
2. D. Sharma, 'Identification of Rajasthan with Vatsaraja Pratihāra', *JNSI,* XVIII, ii, p. 223; H.V. Trivedi, 'A Silver Coin of Rajasthan', *JNSI.* XVI, Vol. II, pp. 228-3.
3. Shanta Rani Sharma, Money Economy in Rajasthan, c. AD 600-1000: The Substantial Epigraphic and Numismatic Testimony', *Numismatic Digest,* Vol. 25-26, pp.101-15.
4. D. Sharma, *Rajasthan through the Ages,* Bikaner, 1966, p. 499 (henceforth RTTA).
5. *Epigraphica Indica* (henceforth *EI*), XLI, pp. 49f.
6. Shanta Rani Sharma, *Society and Culture in Rajasthan, AD 700-900,* Delhi, 1996, p. 212.
7. *EI,* XIX, pp.52f. The editor of the inscription, D.R. Sahni, *AD 700-900,* Delhi, 1996, p. 212. included in the Pratihara Ahar inscription ruler-wise on the basis of the known dates of these rulers.
8. Ibid., Vol. I. p. 84f.
9. Ibid., XXIV. pp. 329-36.
10. Ibid., Vol. I, p. 84f.
11. Ibid.
12. Ibid.
13. Ibid.
14. Ibid.

15. Ibid., XXIV, pp. 329f.
16. V.V. Mirashi, *EI*, XXIV, p. 332.
17. *EI*, pp. 154f.
18. B.N. Mukharjee, 'Numismatic Art' in the *The Comprehensive History of India*, Vol. III. Pt. 1, pp. 1426-7.
19. J.S. Deyell, op.cit., pp. 23-29; see P. Bhatia, 'Note on the Physical Distribution of the Indo-Sassanians, Sri Vigra(ha), Sri Adivaraha Coins in the Ganga Valley, c.AD 700-1000, *Journal Numismatic Society of India*, Vol. I, pp. 99-105.
20. *EI*, XIX, pp. 52f., document no. 5.
21. Ibid., document no. 6.
22. Ibid., document no. 7.
23. Ibid., Vol. I, pp. 162f.
24. Ibid., XIX, pp. 52f. document no. 8.
25. Ibid., XIX, pp. 52f., document no. 4.
26. Ibid., XIX, pp. 52f., document no. 10.
27. Ibid., XVI, pp. 173f.
28. Bhandarkar's list, no. 2110, cited, D. Sharma, RTTA, p. 188.
29. Ibid.
30. *EI*, XIV, pp. 176f.
31. Ibid.
32. Ibid., Vol. I, pp. 162f.

20

Journey of a River to Divinity

Karabi Mitra

The Saraswatī was one of the greatest rivers of pre-historic India. It emerged from the Sirmur region in the Sivalik ranges of the Great Himalayas and emptied itself in the Arabian Sea. It flowed through vast areas of northern and north-western India and supported a large number of people. Due to geological changes the river became extinct.

The *Ṛgveda* describes the river as *ambitame, nadītame, devītame,*[1] i.e. the best of the mothers, rivers and goddesses. Her origin is not clearly indicated in the *Ṛgveda* yet the fact that she emptied herself in the Sea is referred to in a stanza.[2] The mightiness of her water is described in several stanzas. The poet of the *Ṛgveda* refers to her high-sounding, great speed and plenty of water. We note that prayer was made to her so that she would not cause devastation to the people residing on her banks.[3] Several stanzas refer to her noble role in agriculture. She is glorified as the heavenly mother who nourishes her children with breast-milk.[4] Her water is compared to cream of milk and honey.[5] The Vedic poet prayed to her for health, wealth and well-being of the family. He offered her the best offerings in the *yajña.*[6]

Saraswatī is also described as the goddess of warfare in the *Ṛgveda.*[7] She protected the Aryans from the attack of the enemies like the son of Vṛṣaya and Vṛtra, the demon.[8] She rode on a bright golden chariot like lightning and was armed with deadly weapons.[9]

She was compared to the iron-fortress[10] dedicated to the protection of the Aryans. She was invoked to accept the offerings of the *yajña* along with Bhāratī and Iḍā in some stanzas.[11] She was also identified with goddess Vāch[12] (speech), in the *Ṛgveda,* Brāhmaṇical texts and *Śukla Yajurveda.* In the *Ṛgveda* the gods are predominant. Yet it is to be noted that *Saraswatī* was one of those limited number of goddesses who earned a significant space[13] and even described as the helping hand of Indra, in the hours of crisis and described to have treated him with medicines.

The *Manusmṛti* describes the land between the *Saraswatī* and Dṛṣadwatī as *Brahmāvarta,* the sacred land where great *yajñas* were observed.[14] The chanting of the Vedic hymns and flowing sound of the water probably created a perfect spiritual ambience, which led to the perception of the river as a goddess. It was the land where the five tribes known as Anu, Druhyu, Puru, Turbas and Yadu inhabited. They were said to be favourites of the goddess. Probably they contributed to the development of *pañchakṛiṣhṭayah* or five trends of culture.[15]

At present there is a small rivulet, known as the Sarsuti flowing west of Thaneswar. The river however does not match the mighty *Saraswatī* of the *Ṛgveda.* There is a dry river bed of Ghaggar or Hakra passing from the eastern Punjab through Bikaner and Bahawalpur to Sind in Pakistan. Sir Aurel Stein, excavated the lost river bed around 1942. He referred to the fact that the traditional Indian belief recognises in this well-marked bed the course of the sacred *Saraswatī,* once carrying its abundant waters down to the ocean and since antiquity 'lost' in desert sands.[16]

The river Ghaggar and its tributaries rise from the Siwaliks and after Ambala the system becomes non-perennial. In his report of the excavation, Stein pointed out the contrast between the scanty volume of water brought down by the Ghaggar and the width of its dry bed around Bikaner. This bed is lined on both sides by dunes varying in height but gathered into continuous bands or ridges. Seen from a distance these might suggest riverbanks, but they show no marks of erosion. The bed shows a firm, loamy soil easily distinguished from the light sand on either side. Whenever it receives adequate moisture it proves very fertile. The striking appearance of its merging ridges helped by this difference of the soil, accounts for the popular belief that the bed of the Ghaggar was once the course of the mighty river filling it completely. Both on the Ghaggar and its continuation the Hakra, Aurel Stein found this notion in popular legends.[17]

According to Stein, the evidence shows that down to historical times the Ghaggar carried water for irrigation under existing climatic conditions much further than it does now. This makes it intelligible how the *Saraswatī* has come into hymns of the *Ṛgveda* to be praised as a great river. The width of the Ghaggar-Hakra bed is so great that, even now local folklore believe in its having once been completely filled by a large river.[18]

The changes in the course of the river can also be explained differently shifting of the river channels in the area under discussion is a common feature. At present the highest elevation of the area is about 900 ft. above the sea level and it is a watershed dividing the drainage of the east from that of the west. In older times the picture was different. The river carried enormous loads of silt from the mountains, deposited it on their beds. As a result of continuous deposition the riverbed was raised to the level of the surrounding flat plain through which the streams flowed in ever-shifting channels.

From the geographical angle the extinction of the *Saraswatī* was a case of 'river capture' by Yamuna through the process of 'head ward erosion'.[19] River capture is the action of a river acquiring the headstream of second river. The process is carried out by a more powerful river which erodes its valley faster than its neighbouring stream.[20]

Coming back to the mythological aspects of *Saraswatī*, we note certain changes relating to her. In the *Sukla Yajurveda* she is imagined as the goddess of fertility. In the epics and Puranas however she loses much of her importance probably because the river was no longer in existence and the people who once inhabited its banks and sang it praises had moved far away from the region. Nevertheless, her status as a great divinity remained unaffected.

Saraswatī may be described as an exclusive goddess in the Hindu pantheon who was accepted in Buddhism and Jainism as well. She was revered as the goddess of learning and music in both the religions. The earliest available images corroborate the view. The earliest image of *Saraswatī* in India dates back to the 2nd century BC. This was found at Bharhut. A major portion of the image is damaged but the special features are clearly noticeable. Standing on a lotus, the goddess is playing a seven-stringed lyre.

The earliest image of the goddess from South India was found at Ghantasal, Andhra Pradesh. It is also a standing figure. She is holding a lotus bud and book in her upper two hands. The lower right hand is kept on a goose and the lower left hand is empty. Her eyes are half closed in meditation. The image depicts some features of later iconographic style. Throughout India numerous images of the goddess are found. According to the postures the images may be divided into three categories.... *āsīna* (seated), *sthānaka* (standing) and *nṛitya* (dancing). We note variations in her *vāhana* (carrier), *Ayudh* (articles) held in hand, number of hands, etc. Swan, sheep, lion, peacock were selected as her carrier. *Ayudh* included book, lotus, rosarie (*akṣhmālā*), *vīṇā* (lyre), *lekhanī* (pen), *kamaṇḍalu* (container of holy water). In exceptional cases she was also adorned with armaments. The *ayudh* connected her with major gods namely Brahma, Visnu and Shiva. Generally she was perceived as a milk white complexioned goddess adorned with jewellery and seated on a white lotus. In certain images, she is projected either alone or as the *pārśvadevatā* of Viṣṇu or Brahamā. In Bengal both types of images are found. Some images show sheep as her carrier. This feature links her with Agni the god of fire. In some exceptional cases the sheep was sacrificed to her.[21] The image of the dancing goddess is available in South India. Her association with a peacock is also interesting.

The goddess underwent certain changes in the Jain and Buddhist tradition. According to the Jains, she offers true knowledge to the devotees. She is the essence of knowledge and sacredness. As a *Śrutadevatā* she helps the Tirthnkaras in the propagation of religion. There are allusions to her like in the Jain scriptures *Bhagavatīsūtra, Mahāniśītha* sutra, etc. One of her oldest Jain images with head missing was found near Mathura. Her perception as divinity changed under the influence of Buddhism and accordingly she was projected as Vajrasaraswatī, Vajravīṇā *Saraswatī*, Vajraśaradā and perceived as the titular deity of knowledge, intellect and genius.

King Bhoja of the Paramara dynasty (11th century AD) was a great devotee of *Saraswatī.* He constructed a great lake known as Bhojasāgara and established a university at Dhara. A beautiful image of *Saraswatī* was erected there. According to the experts, this image is among the marvellous creations of the sculptors of the Paramara dynasty.[22]

Another beautiful image (12th century AD) was found in Mt. Abu. The four-armed goddess is seen enthroned in *sukhāsana,* holding her body erect. "Her pendent arms show on the right the gesture of boon giving (*varadā*) and a water vessel in the left; book and lotus are in her upper left and the right. Celestials hover above the image, whereas the small figures kneel at the bottom of the throne."[23]

Throughout the ages goddess *Saraswatī* has been the divine inspiration to poets who compose beautiful verses in her praise. The celebrated poet Kālidāsa is said to have been blessed by *Saraswatī*, the goddess of learning. In late medieval Bengal, she was referred to with great respect in numerous poetical compositions including *Śradātilaka tantra* by Raghunandan Bhattacharyya (16th century).[24]

At present, most Hindus worship her on the Vasant Pañchami day (the 5th day of the lunar fortnight in the Spring). It is generally observed as an auspicious day. Usually the children ritually start learning on that day. The worship is observed in most of the educational institutions and households. Books, pens, musical instruments are also worshipped with image. Children wear traditional yellow coloured dresses. The young stars observe the day with great enthusiasm because apart from being the goddess of learning she is also the deity of the youth.

REFERENCES

1. Ralph F.H. Griffith, *The Hymns of Ṛgveda,* Book, II, Hymn, XLI, 16, Motilal Banarsidass, Delhi, 1973, p. 15.
2. *Ṛgveda,* Book VII, Hymn LXXXXV, 2, Grifith, op.cit.

3. Griffith, op.cit., Book, VI, Hymn LXI,2, p. 323.
4. Ibid. Book, Hymn CLXIV, 49, p. 113; Book VI, Hymn LXI, 6, p. 323; Book II, Hymn XLI, p. 17.
5. *Ṛgveda,* Book X, Hymn LXIV.
6. *Ṛgveda Samhita,* Manmathanath Duttashastri, Book, Hymn III, 10.
7. Griffith, op.cit., Book II, Hymn XXX.
8. Ibid., Book Vi, Hymn LXI, 3, p. 323; Book Vi, Hymn Lxi,2, p. 323
9. Ibid., Rg, 7, p. 323
10. *Ṛgveda,* Book VII, Hymn LXXXXV, 1
11. Griffith, op.cit., Book I, Hymn III, 11, p. 7.
12. Shastri, op.cit., Book I, Hymn III, 11.
13. Ibid., Hymn LXXXIX,3, p. 191.
14. *Manusmiti,* II, 17.
15. Pallab Sengupta, '*Saraswati*: Sanskrit bhavanar vichitra samachar' in *Ṛgveda 'urvaratar devi Sarswato'* ed. Sanat Kumar Mitra, Loksanskriti Gabeshana Parishad, Calcutta, 2006, p. 18.
16. Sir Aurel Stein, 'A Survey of Ancient Sites Along the "lost" *Saraswati* River', *Geographical Journal,* 1942, p. 99.
17. Ibid., p. 176.
18. Ibid., p. 178.
19. Savinder Singh, *Geomorphology,* Prayag Pustak Bhawan, Allahabad, 1998, p. 348.
20. K. Siddhartha, *The Earth's Dynamic Surface: A Textbook on Geomorphology,* Kisalaya Publishing Pvt. Ltd., 1999, p. 412.
21. Ibid., p. 412.
22. Amulayacharan Vidyabhusan, *Saraswat,* Sahityalok, Calcutta, 1980, pp. 62-3.
23. C. Sivaramamurti, *Indian Sculpture,* Allied Publishers Pvt. Ltd., New Delhi, 1961, p. 106.
24. Stella Kramrisch, *The Art of India: Tradition of Indian Sculpture, Painting and Architecture,* Phaidon Publishers, INC, London, 1954, p. 211.

21

The Chauhan Dynasty of South Kosala: A Study of Rajput Origin

Shishir Kumar Panda

The Chauhans of South Kosala, an important ruling dynasty, played a prominent role in the growth of history and culture of western Orissa. B.C. Mazumdar[1], R.C. Mallick[2], S.P. Dash[3], J.K. Sahu[4] and D. Chopdar[5] have described them as the descendants of the Rajput Chåuhan dynasty of Garh Sambhar in Rajasthan. Similarly, compilers of the British Gazetteers like T. Motte[6], H.B. Impey[7], Richard Temple[8], L.S.S. O'Malley[9] and L.E.B., Cobden Ransay[10] have traced their origin from the Rajput Chauhan dynasty of Northern India. The only scholar who has questioned the Rajput origin of the Chauhans was R.D. Banerjee[11]. But Banerjee's contention was never taken seriously by the subsequent scholars dealing with the history of the Chauhans of western Orissa. The main source of information for the study of the Chauhans of South Kosala is the Sanskrit work *Kosalānanda Kāvyam*[12] authored by poet Gangahdhar Mishra in AD 1663. It is the earliest historical work which deals with the history of South Kosala in general and the history of the Chauhans in particular. The poet describes the family history and ancestry of Ramadeva or Ramai Deva, the founder of the Chauhan dynasty of South Kosala and traces the origin of the family from the Somavaṃīs (lunar dynasty) to the Chauhan kings of Garh Sambhar, Manikya Chauhan to Prithviraj Chauhan. Further, the poet has given an interesting story regarding the foundation of Chauhan rule in Patnagarh. According to the poet, Prithviraj Chauhan the twenty-fourth ruler of the dynasty was killed by the Yavanas after which the family migrated to different parts of the country and established their separate kingdoms. Vishaladev, one of these fleeing members was also killed in an encounter, but his wife managed to escape and give birth to a brave child, christened Ramadev. Once, Ramadev killed a white tiger which gave much relief to the inhabitants of the locality. This brave act is said to be the reason for the elevation of the Chauhan dynasty of South Kosala.[13] This story has been taken as authentic by scholars to show the Rajput origin of the Chauhans of South Kosala.

It is an established fact that the process of Rajputisation operated in the vast territory of Central and Eastern India from medieval times.[14] The Rajput model was accepted by many ruling families because for centuries, the Rajputs were regarded as the defenders of the Hindu religion, the patrons of Hindu culture who had shown their bravery and military powers by defending India from repeated onslaughts of Muslim invaders. The court poets and bards have glorified the Rajputs by concocting stories identifying them as Kṣhatriyas of solar or lunar lineage.

To examine the historicity of these facts, mentioned by Gangadhar Mishra, we have to examine his antecedents and the historical tradition followed by him. Originally the poet hailed from a Sasana village near Purushottom Kshetra or Puri. His father Pandit Gopinath and grandfather Vidyakara were eminent *smṛti* writers of a noble Vajapayi Brahmin family.[15] Since Puri was a centre of Sanskrit learning, it seems that the Chauhan king of Sambalpur, Baliar Singh had invited Gangadhar Mishra, a reputed Sanskrit scholar to his court and donated to him a piece of land for settling down. As a Sanskrit scholar, Gangadhar must have known about the Madala-Panji tradition of Puri which deals with the traditional account of the dynastic history of Orissa. It seems that the scholar was also well acquainted with the *Prithviraj Raso*[16], the *Hemmira Mahakāvya*[17] and the *Prithvirajavijaya*[18] which glorify the valour and heroism of the Chauhan Rajputs of Northern India. About the time of Gangadhar Mishra, Puri appears to have developed as a famous centre of pilgrimage attracting several religious preachers, philosophers and scholars from all over India. Inscriptions bear out that pilgrims from northern India were visiting Puri from as early as the seventh century[19]. According to *Chhamu Citaus* (Royal letters), the members of the royal families from Jaipur (Rajputana) had also visited Jagannath temple.[20] The poet Gangadhar was influenced by the works of the bards of Rajasthan as well as the *Raja Charita* of *Madala Panji* traditions[21] of Puri for writing the *Kosalānanda Kāvyam* to glorify his patron king Baliar Singh of Sambalpur kingdom, the purpose of writing this *kāvya* as mentioned by the poet himself was to get a rent-free village from the king.

The original *kāvya* of Gangadhar Mishra has, however under- gone several interpolations during later years to suit the interests of succeeding dynasties.[22] In 1700, another poet added hundreds of slokas to the original *kavya*. Thereafter from 1870 to 1945 various copies of the *Kosalānanda kāvyam* were reproduced by the court poets of Patnagarh, Sonepur, Bolangir, Khariar and Sambalpur. In all these versions, the poets have retained the tradition relating to Rajput origin of the Chauhans of South Kosala. In addition to this, they also added different sensational stories regarding the foundation of the Chauhan Kingdom in South Kosala.

While working on the history of Chauhans, scholars and Gazetteer writers have used the *Kosalānanda kāvyam* as their source. From their works, we get two theories regarding their origin, i.e. i) Pilgrimage theory and ii) migration of the pregnant queen of Rajput Chauhan king. The story of a Rajput prince of Northern India travelling with his pregnant wife on a pilgrimage to Puri is a common myth regarding the origin of the ruling dynasties in Central India and Eastern India.[23] The mythical origin of the Barbhum Raj family is a good example in this context.[24] Such types of myths with different versions are also prevalent among many feudatory ruling families of Orissa such as Athmallik, Bonai, Keonjhar, Mayurbhanj, Khandpara, Nayagarh, Talchar and Tigiria.[25]

For the first time the *Kosalānanda kāvyam* was printed and published by the Sonepur durbar in 1929 under the editorship of Maharaja Biramitrodaya Singhdeo with many interpolations.[26] In 1994 Sri Jagannatha at the Sanskrit University of Puri published the *Kosalānanda Mahakāvyam* under the editorship of Nirajan Kar where in the full texts of the original manuscript and Sonepur published version are reproduced in Sanskrit.[27] Recently in 2000 the Department of History, Sambalpur University published an Oriya version of the *Kosalānanda kāvyam* under the editorship of J.K. Shahu and D. Chopdar.[28] In this volume, the editors with much painstaking work have given Sanskrit texts of all versions of the manuscript with Oriya translation and introductory notes. This is the most exhaustive and detailed reproduction of all the manuscripts so far available. In this work the joint editors J.K. Sahu and D. Chopdar have raised many interesting and relevant questions regarding its authenticity. Though earlier J.K. Sahu had taken *Kosalānanda Kāvyam* to be a genuine authentic work[29], in this edited volume the scholars have agreed that later on there were many interpolations in the original *Kavya* by the durbar pandits of Sonepur. However, they have accepted the Rajput origin of the Chauhans of western Orissa with certain dissents.[30]

So to conclude, we can say that the claim of Rajput origin was prevalent among many ruling families of Central India and Eastern India. The Rajput claim of the Chauhans of South Kosala was no exception to it. In all the versions of *Kosalānanda Kāvyam* and writings of the British Gazetteers, we find a common pilgrimage theory. There are also instances of immigrant adventures from Northern India gaining power in the tribal areas by manoeuvring the narrow range of clan bound tribal chieftaincies or even by conquest. So it seems that the Chauhans of South Kosala descended from pilgrims of unknown lineage who came from Sambhar to Jagannatha

Puri on a pilgrimage and later on founded a kingdom at Patna. Subsequently, they claimed a Chauhan Rajput origin through the writings of the court poet Gangadhar Mishra in his *Kosalānanda Kāvyam.*

NOTES AND REFERENCES

1. B.C. Mazumdar, *Sonepur in the Sambalpur Tract,* Calcutta, 1911, Chapter VI, pp. 44-45.
2. Ram Chandra Mallick, *Samkshipta Kosala* or *Sambalpur Itihasa* (in Oriya), Part I, Patna, Part II, Sambalpur, 1931.
3. Siba Prasad Dash, *Sambalpur Itihasa* (in Oriya), Sambalpur, 1962.
4. J.K. Sahu, "The Chauhan Rule in Orissa", unpublished Ph. D. thesis, Utkal University, 1968; *"Chauhan Rule in Western Orissa",* in N.K. Sahu (ed.) *New Aspects of the History of Orissa,* Sambalpur University, Sambalpur, 1971, pp. 31-9.
5. J.K. Sahu and D. Chopdar (eds.), *Kosalānanda Kāvyam,* Sambalpur University, Jyoti Vihar, 2000.
6. T. Motte, "A Narrative of a Journey of the Diamond Mines at Sambalpur", Reprinted in *Orissa Historical Research Journal,* Vol. I, No. 3, Appendix-II, 1955, pp. 1-48.
7. H.B. Impey, "Notes on Gurhjat Satate of Patna", reprinted in *Orissa Historical Research Journal,* Vol. III, No. 2, Appendix-II, 1953.
8. Sir Richard Temple, *Report on the Zamindaries and Other Chieftaincies in the Central Provinces,* Reprint, Nagpur, 1923.
9. L.S.S. O'Malley, *Bengal District Gazetteer,* Sambalpur, Calcutta, 1909, pp. 21-3.
10. L.E.B. Cobden Ramsay, *Feudatory States of Orissa,* Calcutta, 1910, Reprint, 1982.
11. R.D. Banerji, "Rajput Origins in Orissa" in *Modern Review,* Vol. 43, 1928, pp. 285-91.
12. In the present work we have used the recent Oriya edition of the *Kosalānanda Kāvyam,* J.K. Sahu and D. Chopdar (eds.), Department of History, Sambalpur University, Jyoti Vihar, 2000 (henceforth KNK).
13. Ibid., pp. 32-3.
14. For details see, Surjit Sinha, "State Formation and Rajput Myth in the Tribal Central India", *Man in India,* Vol. XLII, No. 1, 1962, pp. 35-80.
15. K.N. Mahapatra, *A Descriptive Catalogue of Sanskrit Manuscripts of Orissa,* Vol. II, Bhubaneswar, 1960, Introduction, pp. CXXIX, CXXXII.
16. *Pritiviraj Raso* of Chand Bardai, Nagari Pracharini Granthamala Series,, Banaras, n.d.
17. *Hammira Mahakvya* of Nyayachandra, N.J. Kirtane (ed.), Bombay, 1878.
18. *Prithiviraj Vijaya* of Jayanaka, G.H. Ojha and C. Guleri (eds.), Ajmer, 1941.
19. K.N. Mohapatra, "Antiquity of Jagannath Puri as a place of Pilgrimage", *The Orissa Historical Research Journal,* Vol. III, No. 1, 1954, p. 17; A.K. Rath, "Jagannath-Puri as a place of Pilgrimage in the Early Medieval Period (C.A.D. 700-1200), A Study Based on Epigraphical and Literary Source", in *Studies*

on Some Aspects of the History and Culture of Orissa, Calcutta, p. 92.

20. There are two *Chamu Citaus* (royal letters) collected from the temple archives of Puri relating to the visit of the ruling family members of Jaipur (Rajasthan) to the Jaganath temple assigned to 1740 A.D., No.60, MP, 2,8,13R and No. 61, JSV, p. 90, ORP, SAI, Heidelberg University.
21. For Madala Panji tradition see, H. Kulke, "The Chronicles and the Temple Records of Madala Panji of Puri—A Reassessment of Evidence", *The Indian Archives,* vol. XXXVI, No.1, 1987, pp.1-224.
22. For details see. K. Panda, *"Koslananda Kāvyam and Making of a Rajput Dynasty: A Study on the Chauhans of Western Orissa",* Paper presented at the International Conference on "Centres out There? Facets of Sub-regional Identities", held at Salzau, Germany, May 13-17, 2003.
23. S. Sinha, op.cit.
24. E.T. Dalton, *Descriptive Ethnology of Bengal,* Reprinted, Calcutta, 1960, p. 174.
25. For details see, L.E.B. Cobden Ramsay, op.cit., pp. 114-5, 143, 213, 139, 262-263, 329, 335.
26. *Kosalānandam,* Biramitrodaya Singhdeo (ed.) Sonepur, 1929.
27. *Kosalānanda Mahakvyam,* Niranjan Kar (ed.), Sri Jagannath Sanskrit University, Puri, 1994.
28. J.K. Sahu and D. Chopdar, op.cit.
29. J.K. Sahu, "Chauhan Rule in Western Orissa", op.cit., p. 31.
30. KNK, pp. 37-9.

22

Vertical Castes and Caste Conflicts in Madras in the 17th and 18th Centuries

Radhika Sheshan

Through much of the medieval period, South India had a unique vertical division of castes. The left hand (*idangai*)/right hand (*valangai*) division is one that no longer exists. However, between (probably) Chola times and the late 18th century, it was an extremely important aspect of South Indian society. Historians have argued about what the division meant, with many seeing it as an expression of the separation of the industrial/artisanal castes on the other. While a clear cut distinction between the two divisions is difficult to maintain, the lists of those included in either segment are also debated.[1] Brahmanas were usually excluded from all lists of the castes, but had their own division, of Iyer and Iyengar, with the former being Saivite and the latter Vaisnavite. However, what is clear is that these castes also represented aspects of social mobility, for clashes between the castes were frequent, and involved access not just to material benefits, but also symbolic power.

The basis for such a division, the nature of divisions and the need for such a division in medieval south Indian society are questions that have not been raised here. This paper begins with the fact that the division existed, whatever be the origin or nature of that division. Further, the clashes that arose between the two are sought to be examined in the light of contested terrain. The terrain could be, and often was, physical—i.e. space for houses processions, etc. It was also over symbols—for instance, who had the right to carry what flag, with what emblem(s), and when. But the contest was not limited to the physical terrain alone, for it seems to have been, in addition, an affirmation of identity, of legitimacy, and of control over, and/or access to, economic resources, and thus took the dimensions of the ideological and material terrians as well.

This paper focuses mainly on three caste conflicts that took place in

Madras in 1652, in 1680, and in 1707. The first, that of 1652, in many ways laid out all the areas of contestation.

The factors at Fort St. George reported in 1652-53 that a conflict had broken out in Madras. Writing to the Surat factory, they stated that, historically, there were two "General Castes, namely the Belgewars [Balija-vaju] and the Berrewars [Beri-Varu], who, for many hundred years together have ever had a quarrel one with the other who should be the more honourable caste..."[2] According to the factors, the entire conflict had been instigated by the Company's merchants who were "indebted to the Company many thousand pagodas more then ever they are able to pay."[3] The conflict was therefore seen as a way for them to evade payment of the debt.

It is significant that for a few years prior to this, two Chettis, Sesadri Nayak and Koneri Chetti, who had been brokers to the Company, had been replaced by two Brahman brothers, Venkata and Kanappa. The latter was also the *Adigar* (person in charge of native affairs) of Black Town. Thus, the two were extremely powerful, both by way of their links with English, and their control over the Indian population. Sesadri and Koneri were both members of the right hand caste.

In a petition submitted to the Council at Fort St. George, the members of the right hand claimed that the Brahmanas were undermining their position by promoting the interests of the left hand over the right. As the then President of the Council at Fort St. George Baker was influenced by the Brahmanas, who seem to have been helping him in his private trade, the right were deliberately being denied opportunities for advancement.

Two things are clear from this petition. One is that the English, as early as the 1650s, had begun to use their official positions to help their private trade, a tendency that was to increase in later years. The second is that for the Indians, the English were the source of authority. The latter is perhaps the more important of the two, for it clearly implies the acceptance of authority as authority, irrespective of who exercised it. In other words, it did not matter whether it was the English, or any of the local political power (like the Nayaks or the Sultans) that was to decide in any dispute. There does not seem to have been a feeling that the Indian political powers had greater authority. On the other hand, there was, nevertheless, an awareness that there were other figures of authority to whom recourse could be had. However, it seems to have been generally accepted that Madras was the English town, and therefore the English had the right to adjudicate.

This is not to say that the castes in Madras were isolated from the rest of the countryside. On the contrary, the English complained that they had called in all the country round about of both castes to fight one against the other, and, corrupting the Towne Watch, have brought in 4 or 5 hundred armed men by night. The English also suspected that the local representative of Golconda had a hand in the entire business, for, when they had imprisoned two of the ringleaders, ...the Nabob presently....commanded us to release them again.... Thus, while the authority of the English in Madras was accepted, there was also at the same time, the knowledge of an alternative power system.

The solution that the English found, at this time, was the division of Black Town. It seems to have been assumed that the conflict was not over economic resources, but over living space. An elaborate plan was drawn up, designating streets within which the members of the two castes were to live, and the streets through which processions could pass, for weddings and funerals. Anyone found acting contrary to the agreement was to be fined 1,000 Dollars.[4] The plan effectively divided Black Town into two, with the left hand the areas to the west. Sesadri Chetti, the chief merchant, who in another report was called the instigator of the problems, was in this division of the town, called "mediator to each caste."[5]

The details of the clashes of 1652 lay out the areas of contestation very clearly. The first area was space, expressed in terms of which caste lived in what areas, the streets that each could use, and, most importantly, those areas that were common to both. The last included the fort and the street in front of the fort, thus providing access to the source of economic gain. Such demarcations also defined that which was forbidden. So, Sesadri Nayak, "the Company's servants and Painters" were not permitted "to pass these streets".[6] The second area of contest, over symbols, was also linked to space, in that the streets for processions were also designated. As flags and banners were carried in such processions, the English hoped that through separation, one area of potential trouble would be nullified. Finally, there was the issue of economic resources. The clash was primarily because one group of merchants felt that they were being denied the opportunities to advance. To bring pressure on the English, they attempted to demonstrate the extent of control they had over the artisans, and the numbers they could muster from outside Madras. This last included access to the power system outside Madras, and perhaps all along the coast as well, for Sesadri Nayak was a member of a very powerful family, that of Malaya Chetti. Malaya Chetti and his son, Chinanna Chetti, had been brokers to the Dutch, and had also been powerful at the court of the last Vijayanagar king, Sri Ranga. Thus, the conflict, though actually located in Madras, and appealing to the East India Company as representing authority, at the same time subtly sent out signals that there were other pressures that could be brought to bear on the English.

It also appears that there could be a shift in castes, at least a relegation of the right-left divide to the background. The Chettis apparently competed for control over the artisans—for example, one section of weavers agreed to place themselves under Sesadri's "protection"[7]. Here, the weavers are identified only by occupation, and not as part of right or left, which may indicate that they moved from left to right (Sesadri was part of the right). The petition submitted by the right hand also gives a similar indication, for it says that the "Bramennes, by their faire promised, got us to receive employment under them,"[8] even though the Brahmanas were excluded from the right hand-left hand division, and even though they had come to Madras through the agency of Sesadri.

The first caste dispute involves primarily the merchants, who then drew in the artisans so as to have the advantage of numbers. The next dispute, in 1680, involved mainly the painters.[9] However, here again, the merchants were involved, though they were rather more in the background.

It was reported that the "Painters and other disaffected Persons" had left Madras and gone to San Thome, and were threatening the artisans left in town. The council at this time decided to hire some "Black Portuguez" and use them to guard the "Washers, who do as yet stick close to their business", as well as to "encourage the Painters of the Malabar Coast."[10] The painters responded by sending letters to "the several castes of Gentues in Towns.... and threatened several to murder them...."[11], and by stooping provisions from entering the town. The English now decided to imprison their wives, who were still in Madras, and further, published a list of those involved in the affair. It was proclaimed that, if those involved did not return within ten days, all their goods, would be left "to the King's Governors of the country to be punished according to their just merit for such their Mutiny and their outrages committed in the country upon the kings, subjects to the disturbances of the King's peace."[12] By the middle of December 1680, many had returned to Madras.

This conflict was apparently over payments to the painters. However, there was, once again, the issue of debts of the merchants. Two merchants, again former chief merchants, the brothers Pedda Venkatadri and Chinna Venkatadri, were reported to owe a great deal of money to other merchants in Madras. These other merchants complained that, because of the pending debts, they themselves were unable to pay the painters. Thus, the painters pulled out of Madras, and with the brothers, they tried to get the representative of Golconda involved in the affair. The brothers were apparently part of the right hand, for there is mention of Pedda Venkatadri receiving "a custome of the Gentues... for the maintenance of the right hand dancing wenches,"[13] but the caste is not mentioned for the painters. Here again, caste comes to the fore in the context of economic gain or loss, and the artisans, as before, provide the numbers, and in this particular case, the façade.

The other notable aspect of this conflict is the issue of authority. Appadurai[14] had lined the idea of caste conflicts to authority, and has noted that conflicts are often mentioned in the context of weak authority. In the first conflict, the English were themselves divided along factional lines, and so, were unable to solve the problem. In the second, while the English were not divided, and were stronger than before, they did therefore, a bifurcation of authority—the King's justice and the King's peace outside, and the East India Company's justice and peace in Fort St. George. So, threats or action could be taken only against those in town, or their possessions in town—a limited authority and a limited area of justice. When conflicts escalated, or involved a larger geographical region, then the English could be seen as basically helpless. Thus, pressure could be brought on the English by pulling out of town, and thus removing themselves from that area of authority. The problem, however, was that of economic gain, for such gain was to be had in the port towns. Therefore, there seems to have been a very clear understanding that these were merely pressure tactics, and were not intended to end all contact with the English East India Company. This last point is even more clearly visible in the conflict of 1707.

In that year, it was reported that caste conflicts had again broken out. This time, they were not limited to Fort St. George, but they had also taken place at Policat, Negapatam, Porto Novo and Trincombar,[15] and also at Fort St. David. The first two were the Dutch settlements, Porto Novo was an Indian port, Tranquebar was under the Danes, and Fort St. David was the second English fort on the coast. It is significant that the caste conflicts were reported from all those ports that had a flourishing trade, for this was a time of drought, famine and war in the rest of South India. Trade was, at this point, perhaps the only source of continuous income.

As in 1652, the merchants were the prime movers, and again, as earlier, the conflict arose from the fact that the left hand seemed to be preferred to the right. The English reported that the Dutch had "turned off the right hand caste and use the left in their Investment....; the right hand caste owns the Dutch 40,000 Pagodas...."[16] They further stated that the basic cause for the dispute was that the "Old method of advancing money on contract" had been changed. As a result, the right hand was unable to contract for the supply of cloth. They therefore saw the dispute as an attempt to "drive out the heads of the other castes" so as to regain their position. To some extent, the merchants appear to have been successful, for the factors at Fort St. David reported that the conflict had escalated to such an extent that, at Madras, "they were destitute of boatmen, washers, handicrafts etc. ...."[17]

At Fort St. George, the conflict was, again, most frequently expressed in terms of space-living and passing through. As in 1652, the English attempted to solve the problem by demarcating the living space. The 1652 settlement was studied, deviation from that settlement outlined, and then re-imposed. As earlier, the superficial solution was useless, for conflicts broke out again in 1715. In that year, too, conflicts were reported from other parts of the coast as well, and as in Madras, at Fort St. David, too, there was a demarcation of living areas and streets for processions in 1715.

As mentioned earlier, the conflicts exposed the areas and the levels of contestation. Space was, of course, of primary importance. Here, space was necessarily both physical and economic. Thus, conflict over access to resources was most clearly articulated in conflicts over living space, in the perception of encroachment-i.e., one caste encroaching on the living space of the other. The English, in the settlement, found that many of the right hands had built houses in the areas designated for the left, and vice-versa, so they ordered those people to move back to their specific areas in Black Town. They further put up stones as markers of that demarcation. Addressing the issue of living space provided a temporary solution, but as the main issue, that of access to resources was never addressed, such solutions were necessarily short-lived. Caste then was an expression of the terrain that was being contested. It provided, (i) the security of numbers; (ii) an area for expression power, in terms of control over numbers; and therefore, (iii) an expression of identity and legitimacy. The legitimate right to be involved in trade belonged to those who had had that right earlier, to those whose identity and power were expressed through negotiations with local rulers and/or the European traders, and so to those who controlled either the artisans, or the production areas. The Chettis who were being replaced belonged to the right hand-therefore, what affected them, affected the entire caste. If they were denied the right to contrast for cloth, all those artisans whom they controlled would also suffer. As caste was, as mentioned earlier, not immutable, the Chettis had to assert their control over the artisans, so as to pressurise the English. Identity, though primarily economic, was linked to caste and space. Therefore, the contested terrain was primarily economic, but was most clearly expressed through the medium of caste.

REFERENCES

1. See, for example, Buchanan's list which has weavers, oil-mongers and Chettis in both. F. Buchanan, A *Journey from Madras through the Countries of Mysore, Canara and Malabar,* 3 vols. London, 1807.
2. H.D. Love, *Vestiges of Old Madras,* 3 vols. London, 1911, Vol. 1, pp. 118-25.
3. Ibid.
4. Ibid.

5. Ibid.
6. Ibid.
7. W. Foster (ed.), *The English Factories in India, 1651-54*, p. 258.
8. Love, op.cit.
9. The term 'painters' was used to designate those who painted designs on the finished cloth.
10. *Records of Fort St. George* (henceforth RFSG)-*Diary and Consultation Books*, November 1, 1980.
11. Ibid., November 4, 1680.
12. Ibid., November 29, 1680.
13. *RFSG-Despatches from England*, November 25, 1678.
14. A. Appadurai, "Right and Left Hand Castes in South India", *Indian Economic and Social History Review*, Vol. XI, Nos. 2-3, June-September, 1974, pp. 575-602.
15. *RFSG- Despatches from England*, December 22, 1707.
16. Ibid., December 23, 1707.
17. *Records of Fort St. David-Diary and Consultation Books*, September 15, 1707.

23

Comparing the European and Indian Renaissance

Sumanta Niyogi

The Indian Renaissance of the nineteenth and early twentieth centuries has been glorified by its supporters to the point of calling the medieval period of Indian history a 'dark age'. There is no doubt that the reformation and new awakening in India during the nineteenth and early twentieth centuries, which received the nomenclature of the Indian Renaissance, add an exceptionally outstanding chapter to our history. But, at the same time, one must not undermine the medieval period of our history, which also saw a number of accomplishments in every sphere. In fact, the religious movements of medieval India held some similarities in preachings and principles with the socio-religious movements of the nineteenth century. What Kabir, Nanak, Dadu, Tukaram, Namdev, Eknath and some of the venerable saints and sages preached and practised in medieval times were accepted later by the great reformers and saints of the nineteenth century, a situation very similar to that of the age of Abelard, St. Francis, Roger Bacon and Joachim. Both the risings, though separated by a time gap of four hundred years, carried trends like opposition to Brahminical preponderance, upper-caste dominated socio-religious order, rigid caste distinction, deprivation of the vast lower caste order, and both vouched for a socio-religious order based on brotherhood, tolerance and equality.

1. URBAN AND ELITIST

As regards the opinion of Sushobhon Chandra Sarkar and some other historians on elitist character and limited dimension("cultured elite of the city") of the Bengal Renaissance, and for that matter of the Indian Renaissance, it needs to be pointed out that the European Renaissance too was urban and elitist in character. It was confined chiefly to the Italian cities and later spread across the Alps to cities of northern Europe. And even in cities it was limited to a small section of the society, the vast majority of the population remained outside its purview, being unable to associate with it as well as deliberately kept out of it. This small section contained liberal intellectual individuals, broad-minded priests and rich merchants. Indeed, the European Renaissance was neither a religious nor a political movement, but a state of mind. Only those who yearned for a broad based, humanist and rationalist scheme of things in life and society opted for the Renaissance.

Indeed, the nineteenth century Indian Renaissance was elitist and urban. It was confined to cities like Calcutta and Dacca, and in towns of Hooghly, Chandernagore, Burdwan and others so far as Bengal was concerned, and as regards the Deccan, it made an impact in cities like Bombay, Poona, Nagpur and Ahmedabad, and in towns like Baroda, Kokhapur, Nasik and others. In the cities of Lahore and Karachi of the erstwhile Punjab and Sind provinces respectively it was very active. So far as southern India is concerned, the impact of the new awakening and new learning was felt at cities like Madras, Hyderabad and Bangalore, and towns like Vijaywada, Visakhapatnam, Rajmundhry, Kakinada, Masulipatnam, and Mangalore. As regards its adherents, the liberal enlightened section of the landed aristocracy and the vibrant intellectual section of the educated middle class had been associated with the Indian Renaissance. Further, it is to be noted that its impact was most noticeable in Bengal and Maharashtra. In other parts of India its influence was marginal, though noticeable.

2. HUMANIST

Besides being urban and elitist, the European Renaissance was also humanist, rationalist (anti-scholastic), past-oriented, secular, intellectual and cultural in nature. It was humanist because it considered man at the centre of the scheme of things. Before the Renaissance, man's position was negligible in society. The Renaissance brought man into prominence. Man's life, his feelings and emotions, and his achievements became the theme of a writer's story, a painter's canvas, a musician's lyric and a sculptor's statue. Moreover, man's individuality has never been so exalted before. This humanist element finds expression in the classic work of Jorjo Vasari (1511-74), entitled, *Le Vite de piti eccelenti archietti pittori et scultori italiani da Cimabure insio a tempi nostri,* published in 1550 and the expanded version in 1568. It presents the great characters of Italy who excelled in the spheres of paintings, sculpture and architecture, with particular stress on Michelangelo, Leonardo da Vinci, Donatello, Bramante, Raphael and Titian. The ingenuity and genius of man, which came to be termed as 'virtu', began to be taken note of with esteem. The artistic excellence and superb creativity attained by men of talent through various art forms between the fourteenth to sixteenth centuries, gave Italy the pride of place in the Renaissance. Through art, man strove to express the various aspects of nature, to communicate with her and to derive inspiration from the artistic genius of ancient Greece. In other words, Vasari puts emphasis on the outstanding artistic accomplishments of the period to glorify the Renaissance. This aspect has been completely overlooked by the Indian historians in their interpretation of the European Renaissance. This artistic and literary efflorescence also marked the Indian Renaissance. Indeed, India of the 19th-20th century did not produce a Michelangelo or Donatello, but it too produced men of genius in the various fields of art and literature.

The Indian Renaissance too saw an unprecedented upsurge in literary and artistic spheres. In every field of human activity there had been an amazingly observable element of creativity.

But the more significant point is that the Indian Renaissance too was very concerned with man. The Renaissance scholars insist that not only man's talent and creativity be recognised to give him an honoured status in society, but more notably, man must be given the status of man. He must be given security and protection, and be provided the opportunity for developing his skill and personality. The oppressed, exploited and subjugated man must be freed from the shackles that bound them for centuries. The vast multitude of hated, neglected and deprived men who had kept aloof in the traditional society for long on the ground of being born in lower castes must be emancipated and brought to the mainstream. And the overwhelming majority of the vast womenfolk, which had been kept confined to homes, being subjected to all sorts of restrictions, discrimination and deprivation, and in many cases put under a torturous state, all in the name of chastity and religiosity, must be salvaged and uplifted through education and grant of rights.

The Brahmo Samaj led the path in the emancipation of the lower castes and women. The Prarthana Samaj and other reform movements followed it up with tremendous force and enthusiasm. Thus, a humanist element is clearly discernible in the Indian Renaissance, which may have differences in nature with its European predecessor, but one positive common factor among them is the liberation of the human soul from the age-old bondage.

3. RATIONALIST

Again, the European Renaissance was rationalist in nature. It emphasised reason, which meant reaching the truth by means of reasoning and argument. Everything has to be tested and nothing should be accepted without verifying. Though the Church schools had lost their exclusive control over education by the mid-fourteenth century, because many private schools were set up by laymen with professional teachers in Italian and other European cities.[1] Yet the Church still held considerable sway over man's thought and action, and this proved somewhat a stumbling block to the sprouting of reasoning and free flow of knowledge. It was the Renaissance which openly pleaded an attitude of reasoning and independent thinking. A very significant fact of educational and intellectual activities during the Renaissance was that schools, universities and study centres became more open, liberal and broad based. In other words, rationalism and intellectualism of the Renaissance contrast with the scholasticism of the medieval period. Scholasticism implied human thinking being confined to the framework of Christianity and the Church jurisdiction. No doubt, during the Middle Ages, Virgil, Cicero and Cesar were popular authors. Works of Plato and Aristotle were studied too. But they were interpreted only in terms of the Christian doctrine. With the coming of the Renaissance, people began to see them in the light of reason and reality. Prior to the Renaissance, the guideline was "Thus sayeth the Lord." During the Renaissance the guideline began to be "I feel so". So, the individual's free judgment began to assert itself to a large extent over the Church dictate. In that sense, the Renaissance was anti-scholastic.

A rationalist trend was very much in evidence in India too during the nineteenth century; though it lacked the depth and broadness of its European counterpart of the sixteenth century (and subsequently of the seventeenth and eighteenth centuries). The period witnessed the advent of rationalist and scientific spirit, the endless endeavour for the acquisition and dissemination of knowledge, and the tireless struggle against the time-honoured orthodoxy, backwardness and superstition. Revered men of the time like Rammohun Roy, Vidyasagar and Akshay Kumar Dutt believed that reason must be applied to verify all views and ideas of the past and the present. Nothing should be blindly accepted and knowledge must not be imposed by traditional or scriptural authorities. Of course, sometimes the rationalist approach had to take recourse to Shastric (the scriptural) interpretation to establish itself. When Rammohun, during his tirade against the Sati system, found that it was impossible to convince Brahmin-dominated orthodox society about the inefficacy of Sati through a rationalist approach, he resorted to the Sastras and epics to justify his stand. It was a compulsion. There was no other way to convince the people of an irrational custom and to inspire them to fight against it. Of course, Rammohun's approach was empirical. He thoroughly scanned the *Sastras* and epics to prove to the obscurantist Brahmin priests that there might have been some examples of deeply bereaved women burning themselves on the funeral pyres of their deceased husbands. But they were doing so absolutely on their own will, not being forced by family members, society leaders or priests to do the same. Tapan Raychaudhuri puts it thus:

> "Raja Rammohun Roy is by common consensus regarded as the pioneer of modernisation in India. Arguments based on reason were among the most powerful instruments he used in the furtherance of causes—social, religious and political—which he espoused. Like many intellectuals in all parts of the world in all ages, his rationality conceded a space to beliefs which reason could not sustain. His classic statements against the practice of Sati do cite scriptural authority, but the clinching arguments anticipate the idiom and stances of contemporary feminism. He rejected the prevailing view that women, being of limited intelligence and naturally fickle, were likely to go astray if allowed to survive as widows."[2]

Rammohun's rationalist approach was further confirmed by his Persian work, *Tuhfat-ul-Muwahiddin* (Calcutta, 1804), in which he attacked superstition, magic and miracle, and held to a rationalist approach to religion. His letter to Lord Amherst advocating introduction of Western education "embracing mathematics, natural philosophy, chemistry and anatomy with other useful sciences" in place of the traditional Sanskrit-based Tola education; his works and tracts on Christ and Christianity describing Jesus as a saintly and humane rather than a divine figure and questioning the doctrine of trinity; and his struggles for freedom of press in India, all point to his rationalist frame of mind.

Vidyasagar's tireless struggle for the cause of remarriage of widows showed a similar approach. He advocated widow remarriage on rationalist and practical grounds. But finding the dominant orthodox and Brahmin section as severely hostile to the idea of widow remarriage and grossly reluctant to accept reason and science, he resorted to ancient scriptures to prove that the Sastras were not opposed to it. He picked up a sloka from the *Parashar Samhita*:

Naste mrite provrajite kleebe cha patite patau
Panchanswapatau nareenam patiranyo vidhiyate.

It means that a woman has every right to marry a second time provided her husband is dead or traceless or staying away for a long time without any hope of returning or impotent or incorrigibly corrupt. His attacks on child marriage and polygamy were based on scientific and rationalist grounds. Interestingly enough, in this case he severely criticised the Smriti texts for supporting the practice of child marriage.

Akshay Kumar Dutt can be regarded as the most uncompromising rationalist of India in the nineteenth century. He was very close to Vidyasagar, and to the pioneering spirit of the Brahmo movement, Debendranath Tagore, who made him the editor of his Brahmo mouthpiece, the *Tattwabodhini Patrika*. It was Akshay Kumar who compelled Debendranath to reject the doctrine of Vedic infallibility (interestingly enough, Rammouhn, conformed to Vedic infallibility). He held that "pure rationalism is our teacher."[3] Without denying the existence of God, he like a French Enlightenment scholar of the eighteenth century, could believe that natural phenomena were not beyond human comprehension and the universe could be analysed and understood by purely mechanical processes without indulging in supernaturalism.[4] He was immensely influenced by the writings of the French Philosopher, Auguste Comte, particularly his work, *Course of Positive Philosophy (1830-38)*,which advocated a religion of humanity and a society based on the knowledge gained from positive sciences. Comte's positivist philosophy greatly influenced the Bengali intellectuals of the time for its emphasis on pure reason and love for mankind.

Rationalism in the early nineteenth century Bengal got a versatile champion in Henry Derozio, the Eurasian Professor of the Hindu College. Influenced by the Enlightenment philosophy, his lectures on Descartes, Hume, Kant and other rationalist philosophers became immensely popular and left an indelible impact on his large number of students, many of whom rose to eminence in various fields later, and some of whom combined to form a group of intellectuals, known as the Young Bengal. To the members of the Young Bengal, "He who will not reason is a bigot, he who cannot be a fool and he who does not is a slave."[5] Remarkably enough, Derozio inspired his students to think for themselves. Reason was definitely the guiding factor in the education system introduced through the Hindu College and late adopted by other institutions of higher education. Western education, as introduced in Bengal, helped the Bengali youth to develop a secular attitude and rationalist approach in their day-to-day life. The very fact that booksellers of Calcutta imported one thousand copies of Tom Paine's *Age of Reason* and they were sold out within a few days at five times the original price indicates the growing consciousness and intellect among the Bengali youth. The interesting point is that even the conservative Hindu section led by Rammohun's opponent, Radhakanta Deb, resorted to rationality in day-to-day discussion on several topics. Deb made donations for setting up a girl's school. He, along with several other leading men of the orthodox Hindu section, were responsible for the establishment of the Hindu College, the first institution of higher education on the Western model in Asia.[6] The rationalist spirit was the quintessence of the new learning and new awakening; and this spirit was reflected in the setting up of numerous schools and colleges for the spread of modern education, in the formation of debating clubs, learned societies and political associations, and in the publication of numerous journals, newspapers, books and encyclopedias.

Not only in Bengal, but in Maharashtra too this rationalist attitude was very noticeable. As early as 1840s Balshastri Jambhekar, who has been called "the pioneer of the Renaissance in Maharashtra", took a rationalist line in order to bring social reform to the province.[7] Through his journal, *Mumbai Darpan*, he advocated widow remarriage, female education and ending caste restrictions. In 1848 Dadoba Pandurang's *Dharma Vivechan* (Discourse on Religion) was published. Born in a well-to-do merchant family of Bombay in 1814, Dadoba received his education there, served as headmaster of Bombay Normal School, and set up the religious reform society, the Manav Dharma Sabha (Society for Religion of Man). His ideas appeared to be revolutionary in the conservative Maharashtrian society. His rationalist approach to religion angered the orthodox Chitpavan Brahmin section of the province. While strongly believing that God alone should be worshipped, he advocated the individual's freedom of thought, the building of a casteless universal human society, promoting true religion based on love and moral conduct, right kind of knowledge, and above all, man's deed and speech be based on reason.[8] The Sabha can be regarded as the precursor of the Prarthana Samaj and Satyasodhak Samaj.

Gopal Hari Deshmukh (respectfully called Lokahitawadi) a social reformer, was another staunch advocate of rationalism. An outstanding personality of nineteenth century Maharashtra, he waged a relentless battle against "the follies of the age-old tradition and time-honoured orthodoxy of the Indian society". In his work, *Shatapatre* (Hundred Epistles), published in 1849, he vehemently attacked dogmatism, superstition and fatalism. He looked at the social issues from a rationalist as well as utilitarian point of view. The 29th epistle held that whatever is not accepted by reason should be rejected.[9] His advocacy of widow-remarriage, abolition of the caste system, equal rights for women, and spread of modern education turned him into a figure much ahead of his time in Maharashtra.

Rationalism was further boosted in Maharashtra with the advent of Jyotibarao Phule, whose struggle for social reform and spread of education among the lower caste children under the aegis of his organisation, Satyashodhak Samaj (Society of Truth Seekers), earned him an immortal place in modern Indian history. Purely secular in his thought and attitude, he became absolutely disillusioned not only with the Brahmin-dominated traditional socio-religious order, but with the entire gamut of the Aryan Sanskritic culture. His rationalist spirit and reformist zeal inspired him to struggle for the abolition of the caste system, uplift of lower and backward castes, and emancipation of women.

The foundation of the Prarthana Samaj in 1867, and the establishment of the Poona Sarvajanik in 1879, Deccan Education Society in 1880, and the Fergusson College in 1885 were the important landmarks in the history of Maharashtra. These organisations, though varying in nature and objectives, were instrumental in promoting a rationalist attitude in scientific, educational and political spheres. The venerated personalities of the

Prarthana Samaj, like Atmaram Pandurang, M.G. Ranade, R.G. Bandarkar, N.G.Chandravarkar and K.T. Telang, put great emphasis on modern education, which meant teaching of science and liberal subjects in a bias-free rational environment. Outstanding men like G.K. Gokhale, and G.C. Agarkar also went hand-in-hand with the Prarthana Samaj members to bring change in a positive manner through reform, education and rationalism.

4. CLASSICAL-ANCIENT-ORIENTED

Another important feature of the European Renaissance, as already discussed, was its attraction towards the wisdom of ancient Greece and Rome. So, it can be termed as classical or antiquity-oriented in nature. As mentioned above, a large section of scholars and historians, from Petrarch to Burckhardt, viewed that the Renaissance men had held ancient Greece in highest esteem and regarded the philosophy, literature, science and art of ancient Greece as the greatest legacies bequeathed to mankind and as the most reliable source of truth and wisdom. There is no doubt in the fact that ancient Greece had been the greatest source of inspiration for the Renaissance.

The Indian Renaissance too was immensely influenced by the wisdom and learning of our ancient past. Not only the vast mass of scriptures and the two epics, but also a considerable quantum of non-religious writings left a perpetual impact on our nineteenth century reformers, philosophers and litterateurs. The *Vedas*, the *Upanishads* and the *Bhagavad Gita* had been the major source of inspiration and guidance, while the great epics the *Ramayana*, the *Mahabharata* and other writings (like *Hitopodesha, Kathasaritsagar, Panchatantra, Betal-Pachabinshati* and *Jatakas*) continued to infuence the thought process both at intellectual and popular levels. The reformers, philosophers and scholars turned repeatedly to the writings of our ancient past in search of truth and wisdom. The concept of monotheism, focusing on the omnipotent, omnipresent and omniscient Supreme One, of the mankind as a universalistic fraternity transcending all barriers of caste, creed, race or religion, of the supremacy of truth and knowledge, of the immeasurable power of *Karma*, of the wide scope of *Dharma* (duty and piety), of the force of nobility, morality and honesty, of peace and non-violence, and of Nirvana (salvation), wielded a great impact on them. On the basis of the knowledge gained from these texts and scriptures, they could challenge the rituals, customs and practices coming down through the ages in the name of religion, spirituality and salvation. Here we find a striking parallelism with European Renaissance.

But it must be noted that the response to our ancient heritage was not similar in all cases. The socio-religious reform movements, which emerged in the nineteenth century, can be divided into two major categories. In the first category fall the movements, which called for reform and changes in socio-cultural practices and values of Hinduism on the pattern of the primordial traditions of the *Vedas*. The followers of such movements were, in terms of social science, 'fundamentalists' as they believed in going into the texts of original scriptures in order to seek the truth and wisdom in their pristine purity as bequeathed by seers, saints and scholars a long time ago.[10] Only by going to the original religious texts, one can find the aberrations, distortions and misrepresentations that crept into our mainstream socio-religious tradition (the Great Tradition) in course of centuries. They pledged to cleanse Hinduism and the Hindu society of these aberrations. The Arya Samaj, the Ramakrishna-Vivekanand and Kabirpanthi movements fall within this category. However, in their quest for truth they clung too rigidly to the ancient wisdom. For example, the Arya Samaj is absolutely focused on the cultural values and norms of our ancient heritage. The Arya Samajis feel that our heritage is so rich as we do need to derive anything from alien cultures. They stand on the supremacy and infallibility of the Vedas as the ultimate source of knowledge. The followers of the Arya Samaj are so attached to the *Vedas* that "Back to the *Vedas*" and "the *Vedas* are infallible" have become their cardinal principles. These movements have been described as "transitional" by Prof. Kenneth Jones.[11]

In the second category fall the Brahmo Samaj and Prathana Samaj movements. They too derive their ideas basically from the values and norms of ancient Indian culture. The *Vedas*, the *Upanishads* and the *Gita* had been their primary source of inspiration and guidance. But, at the same time, they are not averse to taking from the great ideas and ideals set by the external cultures. As Prof. Yogendra Singh points out, the movements belonging to this category advocated a synthesis of new norms and cultural themes with the traditional themes and value system of the Hindu cultures.[12] These movements can be regarded as what Kenneth Jones calls 'acculturative',[13] which indicates a trend of cultural synthesis.

The point is one of uniformity in character, principle and purpose. The European Renaissance had a more or less uniform objective when it spread over Italy and later to other parts of Europe. It had been basically an intellectual-cultural movement, characterised by a humanist, rationalist and secular attitude. The change in man's thinking, his posers to traditional norms, his indulgence in literary and artistic activities to know himself, all reflected a uniform pattern so far as Europe was concerned. But this was not the case with regard to India. The so-called Indian Renaissance was basically a socio-religious movement. Undoubtedly, it contained considerably high intellectuals, rationalist and humanist trends, but it basically aimed at reforming the traditional socio-religious order. This indicates its fundamental similarity with the European Renaissance and Reformation taken together.

Moreover, the Indian Renaissance was not as widespread as its European counterpart. The questioning of the norms and values of the traditional society was done mainly in Bengal and Maharashtra. The protest and dissent from the Great Tradition was effected through the acculturative socio-religious reform movements like the Brahmo Samaj in Bengal and the Prarthana Samaj movement in Maharashtra. The term 'acculturative' means that these movements, though inspired chiefly by the ancient Indian scriptures, particularly the *Upanishads* and *Gita*, they were liberal enough to derive the ideals and values of other cultures. These movements threw a challenge to the dominant Brahminical socio-religious order and strove to inculcate a broad-based, liberal, rationalist and humanist spirit in man's thought and action.

This cannot be said about the movement in other parts of India. The reformist activities were carried on with genuine dedication in north Indian states like the Punjab and United Provinces, in eastern Indian regions of Bihar, Assam and Orissa, all of which formed parts of the Bengal Presidency, and in all the regions of southern India under the Madras Presidency. The religious organisations like the Arya Samaj, Theosophical Society, Ramakrishna Mission and Kabir Panthi Sangh were transitional in character. This meant that they were based entirely on the values and culture rooted to ancient Indian heritage and did not think it necessary to derive anything from other cultures. This rendered a limited dimension to the movement in these regions, lacking rationalist secular trend.

Yet, taking all the above-mentioned points into account, the arguments in favour of retaining the term 'Indian Renaissance' appears to be justified to a great extent. Firstly, as already shown, the Indian Renaissance, like its European counterpart, was urban and elitist. It was confined to towns and cities, and that too within a very small section of conscious educated men. The term 'Renaissance' basically points to the state of mind and this can be seen in terms of the expansion of man's intellectual horizon. If we go by this paradigm, our search for clarity can be fruitful. In other words, the Renaissance was not a revolution, but an awakening, a consciousness, and a realisation, which grew in intensity with every passing year.

Secondly, taking the foregone point further, neither the European Renaissance nor its Indian counterpart was a mass movement. As already noted, one of the grounds for which Marxist scholars rejected the claim of the Indian awakening of the nineteenth century to the nomenclature of 'Renaissance' was its failure to reach the mass. Indeed it is true. The Renaissance men themselves never clamoured for mass appeal or for mass linkage of their accomplishments. They were concerned with ideas and creativity. Their ideas, their writings or thoughts were of exceptionally high standard to appeal to the masses in general. The main point here is that everything cannot be judged with regard to mass appeal or mass involvement. Moreover, they were not anti-mass. What they did was for people in general, without any discrimination of class, caste or religion. The importance of an idea or a work is judged by what it conveys. And without any doubt what the great men and women associated with the Indian Renaissance contributed are considered as legacies of unparalleled significance for all time to come. Through their writings and activities they have opened to us the treasure house of truth, knowledge and wisdom.

Thirdly, the critics of the Renaissance concept put too much emphasis upon the economic factor. We have already seen that some historians have identified the advent of the Renaissance with the rise of the bourgeoisie and their growing control over the socio-economic forces. There is no doubt in the fact that the bourgeoisie wealth and patronage played a role in promoting artistic and literary activities. But there were other forces and factors that promoted these activities during the Renaissance. It has always been a debatable proposition to link the Renaissance with the growth of capitalism and rise of the bourgeoisie.

Several studies have revealed that the Renaissance had very little to do with economic forces. They have questioned the attempt to link the Renaissance with the rise of capitalism and the growing influence of the bourgeoisie. The early 20th century German historian, Konrad Budach, amassing a huge quantum of information, tried to show that the fast growth of capitalism and the steady rise of the bourgeoisie have absolutely nothing to do with the Renaissance. It would have come even without the phenomenal rise of the bourgeoisie. It is true that the bourgeois influence resulting from the unprecedented expansion of trade and commerce and exercised through patronage of art and literature helped the spread of the ideas and message of the Renaissance. But it amounts to oversimplification to state that the European Renaissance took place due to "an internal socio-economic convulsion in which the bourgeoisie played the role of a catalytic agent" and that it was "a cultural reflection of changes brought by the irresistible socio-economic forces". The great but imperceptible changes were completely neglected by these scholars.

Some historians, like Barbagalo, Lavande and Lopez, expressed doubts about situating the economic factor. They accept the view, that Europe was passing though a phase of economic prosperity during the twelfth century; but the period from the fourteenth to fifteenth century, regarded as the period of the Renaissance, saw a serious economic crisis marked by wars, famine, slump in trade and agriculture, decline of population and a severe jolt to road transportation. Moreover, nothing comparable to the rise of the bourgeoisie in 17th century England happened in Italy in the 15th or 17th century. The rise of the bourgeoisie was much more prominent in 16th century Tudor England and seventeenth century Stuart England. But a Renaissance on the scale of the Italian Renaissance of the fifteenth-sixteenth century did not happen in England in either of the centuries. Indeed, England produced a literary genius like Shakespeare, but he was patronised by the royalty rather than the bourgeoisie. All these led Lopez to conclude that there may be links between economic and cultural happenings, but this does not mean that the one has been the cause of the other.

Fourthly, the colonial content advanced by some scholars too is open to challenge. According to Barun De, colonial rule ("alien rule") and modernisation cannot go together.[14] Here renaissance has been synonymised with modernisation. But it is to be noted that most of the Italian states were under alien rule during the late fifteenth and early sixteenth centuries. In the wider intellectual sense, modernisation means the germination of the rationalist spirit, widening of intellect and inculcating a sense of questioning of the traditional order, accompanied by a zeal for accepting the thought and education that is modern, liberal and progressive.

Arabindo Poddar, in his widely acclaimed work *Renaissance in Bengal: Quests and Confrontations 1800-1860* (Simla, 1970), tackles the subject with subtlety. To highlight the Renaissance in Bengal he points to intellectual activities, as we understand today. Poddar views, what distinguishes an intellectual in the context of our modern life is his concern for the values of rationality and free thinking, his refusal to accept the conditions of life passively and conform to a set pattern of behaviour.[15] Poddar very rightly points out that non-conformism is an intellectual's principal asset, which with constant emphasis on critical evaluation of experience, seeks to establish new standards of taste and conduct.[16] Thus, while modernisation and intellectualism confront old values, they also have their eyes on new ones.

Rigid adherence to old values, imposed customs and conformist tradition have made our society and culture static and conservative. In fact, conformism was an enforced and cultivated virtue in Pre-British India. Centuries of conformism lent strength to the Brahmin-Kshatriya dominated social hierarchy to become despotic in administering justice and authoritative in setting values, as evident in the existing social stratification. The dynamic, self-conscious and analytical mind was not there to throw a challenge to the traditional order.

The old, obscurantist and irrational values contributing to immobility and obstructing all routes to development must be discarded, and a situation be created for the rise of new awakening and new learning. This is exactly what the great men and women of India, whom we associate with the Indian Renaissance, had done in the nineteenth and early twentieth century and certainly the British colonial regime could not in any way stand on the greatness of their accomplishments. Remarkably enough, quite a few of these Renaissance personalities earned the esteem of the colonial authorities in spite of their distinctly anti-colonial stance.

NOTES AND REFERENCES

1. Lauro Martines, "The Italian Renaissance", in R. DeMolen (ed.), *The Meaning of Renaissance and Reformation*, Boston, 1974, p. 38-9.
2. Tapan Roychaudhuri, *Perceptions, Emotions, Sensibilities: Essays on India's Colonial and Post-colonial Experiences*, Oxford, 1999, pp. 50-51.
3. *Tattwabodhini Patrika*, Saka 1773, Phalgun, quoted in K.N. Panikkar, Presidential Address, Modern Indian Section, Indian History Congress, 36th session, Aligarh, 1975, p. 18.
4. A.K. Bhattacharya, "Akshay Dutt: Pioneer of Indian Rationalism", *Rationalism Annual*, 1962.
5. Quoted in Susobhan Sarkar, op.cit., p. III and also in K.N. Panikkar, op.cit., p. 18.
6. Tapan Roychaudhuri, op.cit., p. 52.
7. B.R. Sunthankar, "Social Reform Movements in 19th Century Maharashtra" in V.D. Divekar (ed.), *Social Reform Movements in India: A Historical Perspective*, Bombay, 1991, pp. 45-6.
8. Ibid., pp. 46-7 and Keneth W. Jones, *Socio-religious Reform Movements in British India*, Cambridge, 1989, pp. 139-40.
9. V.D. Divekar, *Social Reform Movements in India: A Historical Perspective*, Cambridge, 1989, p. 47
10. See S. Niyogi, "The Indian Awakening and Reform of the Nineteenth Century: A Study of its Impact on Bihar" in R.S. Sharma (ed.), *Social Science Probings*, Vol. 18, no. 2, December 2006, p. 69.
11. K.W. Jones, op.cit., p. 3
12. Yogendra Singh, *Modernisation of Indian Tradition*, Thomson Press, 1977, p. 43.
13. K.W. Jones, op.cit., p. 31.
14. Barun De, "Susobhan Chandra Sarkar" in Asok Sen (ed.), *Essays in Honour of Prof. S.C. Sarkar*, P.P.H., New Delhi, 1976, p. xxix.
15. Arabindo Poddar, *Renaissance in Bengal: Quest and Confrontations*, pp. 7-8.
16. Ibid.

24

Elementary Aspects of the 1857 Insurgency in Colonial India

Susnata Das

The 150th anniversary of the 'Revolt of 1857', that was now often being marked as the 'insurgency', 'popular uprising' or 'War of Independence', has generated widespread interest of scholars, leading to fresh investigations and also questioning of established stereotypes about the event. About over fifty years, the historians and research scholars of the Indian subcontinent and abroad were impelled to face the questions regarding the character and nature of the 'War of 1857' in India. The quest began in searching for the social roots as well as the economic basis of the revolt. It also needs to find essential motives of the common people for the participation in the uprisings, which have been continuing to varied from region to region, of the 'great Revolt' of 1857. Nevertheless, so far as characteristics of 1857 were concerned, we can find some common elements in it. In this paper those elementary aspects with a comprehensive study and historigraphical review of the 'War of 1857' would have to be reinvestigated.

I

The 'Sepoy Mutiny'—as it was labelled initially by the colonial official writings, focused on the 'Mutiny' theme. To colonial officials and writers it was the handiwork of a set of discontented *sepoys* who were unhappy with the induction of the new Enfield rifle, with its distinct ammunition, which required the cartridge to be bitten off before loading. Rumours that the grease used on the cartridges was either made from the fat of cattle or pigs had symbolic implications. Thus, whereas the Hindus considered cows 'sacred', the Muslims considered pigs to be 'polluting'. This created strong animosities and was marked as an attack on Hindu and Muslim religious beliefs. The first spark of the war of 1857 began on March 29, 1857, in Barrackpore cantonment, only 30 kms away from Calcutta, through the gun down of army officers of the English East India Company by Mangal Pandey, a sepoy belonging to the 34th Regiment of the Bengal Army, who was supposed to come from a Hindustani and upper caste (*Brahmin*) origin peasant family of Oudh.

However, several historians like the late Prof. Basudev Chatterjee and others argued unhesitatingly that Mangal Pandy should not be labelled by any means, as a drug addicted (drinking *Vang* or country made liquor was a common practice among the native sepoys) 'accidental hero', as stated in a recent 'post-modern' study of 1857 by a Calcutta-based eminent historian,[1] but should be considered as the first martyr of India's struggle for freedom, who was ordered to be hanged to death on April 8, 1857 through a farcical trial in the name of so-called 'Great British Justice'. Iswari Pande, who was not directly involved in the Mangal Pande incident was also given the death sentence on April 22, 1857.

Just only after a month of the Barrackpore incident, on May 10, 1857, the massive mutiny in the Bengal Army followed by a popular upsurge broke out gradually in Meerut, Kanpur, Bareily and other places of military importance in upcountry India. The throne of Delhi for the last time was gleamed by weak Mughal successor *Badshah* Bahadur Shah Zafar with the full support of the armed rebel regiment and the princely states of the adjacent areas. The Scottish author William Dalrymple, in spite of his readable account of rebel Delhi, was not able to trace the real role and function of Bahadur Shah Zafar properly in his latest novel on 1857.[2] We have a more accurate account of the Delhi rebellion gathered from various sources of Indian writings which certainly did not consider the Mughal gesture as *Jihad.*

It is true that in the beginning, the Last *Mughal Badshah* Bahadur Shah at the age of eighty lived in a distressed and disgraceful condition and the circumstantial evidence proved that he was passing through a crucial time with great anxiety, suspicion and hesitations. But in course of action gradually he, along with his *Durbar,* could be able to gather confidence and reign (though for four months only) as far as feasible. An eminent Indian Marxist scholar and communist leader E.M.S. Namboodiripad analysed the role of the last Mughal Emperor more correctly and argued that Bahadur Shah was an old man and did not possess the traditions and fame established by his predecessors. Nothing more can be said of Bahadur Shah than that he was born into the family of the Mughal Emperors who had ruled the country for several decades, in grandeur and glory. In other words, he represented only the outer shell of the renowned Mughal Empire. But even this shell turned into a sharp weapon in the anti-

British struggle. Weak or old whatever might be, he was the last of the Mughal Emperors and the symbol of a social and administrative organism, of which the people of Delhi and the surrounding areas had witnessed for several generations. It was seen that in his name the soldiers and the civilian population of that area organised the anti-British war in 1857.[3]

As a matter of fact, to the common people of rebel-regions, the Emperor of Delhi was not a distant ruler. They had lived directly under his authority for generations. The elite class discharge various duties and responsibilities as part of that administered system and received as remuneration of such service in cash or in the form of land or other benefits and concessions, and acquired authority and position. The Muslims among them were contented that the administration under the Mughal emperors was their own, while the Hindus were convinced that, though they belonged to a different religion, they were being treated with affection and respect as even under the rule of Aurangzeb, who would often be labelled as so-called 'anti-Hindu' in our school textbooks. Thus the Delhi Emperor was the head of an administrative system and generally enjoyed loyalty and trust from the inhabitants of Delhi irrespective of their creed and socio-economic status.

From the account of Allamah Fazle Haq, who was closely associated with the Emperor and his court in Delhi, it is worth quoting at some length[4]:

"He (Bahadur Shah) had his own Wazir (Hakim Ashanullah) and staff. He was advanced in years but was inexperienced, he was very old and wise in reality, governed by his wife Zeenat Mahal and Wazir...He issued no orders according to his independent opinion and could not understand good and evil. He could not decide anything openly or in secret and did no good to anyone..."

"He appointed as officers of the army some of his sons and grandsons who were stupid, dishonest and cowards. They hated honest and wise persons. They had never witnessed a battle nor had they any experience of the blows of swords and lances. They selected men from the gutter for their society and consolation. These inexperienced fellows drowned themselves in the ocean of luxuries and extravagance and submerged themselves in the flood of debauchery."

Yet it could not be denied that both religion and feudal hierarchy were distinctly used in the war of 1857 as strategic weapons. The mutineers were acquainted with the weakness and limitations of Bahadur Shah Zafar and his family. In spite of that they preferred him as an icon of Hindustan's sovereignty or *'Hukumat-I-Hind'* to the Muslims and *'Watan ki Malik'* to the Hindus. On the contrary, Allamah Fazle Haq of Khayrabad's view, Syed Moinul Haq of 'Pakistan Historical Society' gives an account of the government of Emperor Bahadur Shah and the mutinous *sipahis* in Delhi.[5]

Syed A.A. Rizvi had attempted something like this in his Hindi book *Swatantra Dilli,*[6] but Haq's account was 'more definitive and set in a wider context'. According to Haq's account the administration was run by a Supreme Council in Delhi popularly spoken of as the 'Kot' (Court), and formally designed as the *Jasla-I-Intizam-I-Fauzi-Wa Mulki* and the 'Rebellion had surely a mind, a direction and a centre.'

Many years ago in a paper presented at the Royal Historical Society in 1932, a renowned missionary, named F.W. Buckler argued that to the common people in the rebel areas of northern India, it was not the Mughal Badshah but the unruly English Company who was the real offender and they revolted against the *Badshahi Hukumat* by violating the law.[7]

Besides such a feudal legacy, the religious factor also played a significant role in the insurgency of 1857. But some British authors however misinterpreted or exaggerated the role to substantiate their argument that the uprising of 1857 was reactionary and revivalist in character. Some Western educated Indians, especially Bengali intellectuals became more or less convinced by their arguments without judging their merit and made adverse observations in analysing the nature and significance of the Great Revolt. This English-educated middle class, mostly grown up in privilege being gifted enormous opportunities and social status in the rule of the East India Company and suffered somehow under the conservative religious influences, were prejudiced against the 1857 upsurge.[8]

Even after one hundred years of the Great Upsurge of 1857, the most eminent historian like Prof. R.C. Majumdar had no hesitation in calling it the "dying groans of an obsolete aristocracy and centrifugal feudalism of the medieval age." The official historian of the Revolt, Dr. S.N. Sen also held the view that the "mutiny leaders would have set the clock back—they wanted counter-revolution." But Dr. Sen added cautiously with the pertinent comment— "whether military success would have ensured it is another question."[9]

In the 1950s the noted communist leader of India P.C. Joshi argued, "In the then historical context, traditional religious cultural concepts could not but be a very important constituent of the Indian ideological struggle against the foreigner's rule."[10] Joshi, in support of his argument, quoted from the writings of Karl Marx. From his own study of history and people's age-old struggles to remake their destiny, Marx had come to the conclusion:

"Men make their own history, but they do not make it just as they please; they do not make it under circumstances chosen by themselves, given and transmitted from the past. The tradition of all the dead generations weighs like a nightmare on the brain of the living. And just when they seem engaged in revolutionising themselves and things in creating something that has never yet existed, precisely in such periods revolutionary crisis they anxiously conjure up the spirits of the past to their service and borrow from them names, battle cries and costumes in order to present the new scene of world history in this time honoured disguise and this borrowed language."[11]

Irrespective of the comments made by the British communist and eminent Marxist scholar Rajni Palm Dutt regarding the reactionary character of the War of 1857 in the 1930s, the Indian Marxists in the second half of the twentieth century rectified the previous error by standing strongly in favour of the 'Mutineers' by describing them as the freedom fighters. Professor Sushovan Sarkar, another reputed Marxist intellectual, like P.C. Joshi, made the following statement unhesistingly,

"In the revolt of 1857 feudal ideas are clear enough in instinctive turn to the restoration of the empire; in the loyalties to the local chiefs; in the characteristic disorganization: in the hatred towards western reforms. But they are not sufficient to brand the great upsurge as reactionary."[12]

II

Why did the waves of anti-British feelings, expressed by the feudal elements, sweep through the common people? The answer is the people had looked upon the feudal lords, including the Emperor of Delhi, as their traditional leader and hence joined the anti-British struggles organised by them. They were conscious about the fact that the destruction of the domination of feudal lords actually meant disruption of the life pattern of the people. It also meant that the common people were compelled to move towards a situation wherein they would be dislodged from their small holdings. It became more alarming to the landed gentry, who were already suffering and almost destroyed by the British land and land revenue policy. Prof. S.B.Chaudhuri, for this reason branded it as 'Civil Rebellion' in which high and low in rural society combined; according to him "it was no mere mutiny; it was a rising of the people."[13]

As can be expected, this understanding gave primacy to the religious factor and reinforced a line of thinking which saw the Revolt as a 'Muslim conspiracy', which gained acceptance among contemporary official. Sayed Ahmed Khan (1817-1898) wrote a tract (*Rissalah Asbab-e-Baghwat-e-Hind)* to counter this allegation, where he sought to examine the common features that determined the nature of 1857.[14] Taking together these seem to be the basis for formulations like the 'clash of civilisations', which is being now argued in contemporary fashion; though by no means was the Revolt of 1857 a war of religion.

If someone goes through the official and British records of 1857 one gathers the vague impression that Muslim revivalist groups and the *Wahabis* in particular had something to do with it. There are casual references to calls of *Jihad* in almost all places, to *Fatwas* of Maulavis in big cities, to the display of the green flag in important rebel centres all of which suggest a certain Muslim revivalist colouring to the events of 1857. According to K.M. Ashraf,

"However, all this gives no comprehensive or clear picture of their role in or of their contribution to this revolt. In fact, it is never fully appreciated that the revivalist trend was the decisive factor in the political orientation of the Muslims, and the Wahabis were the only people who came not only armed with a consistent anti-British ideology but also with the backing of a network of organised centres spread all over northern India, with contacts in the south and moral influence on the Muslim intelligentsia throughout the country."[15]

In her recent studies, Ayesha Jalal has opened the jihad aspect of the Revolt. She writes:

"The sense of hopelessness was to become a recurrent theme in much of the Urdu poetry and prose written by Muslims after the formal loss of sovereignty. There were Muslims(Muslim) voices other than Ghalib's who were given to perceiving the turn of events from a more communitarian point of view. Momin Khan Momin, for instance, responded to the 1857 revolt by urging Muslims to wage a jihad against the British as a religious duty."[16]

In 1857 the Hindus and the Muslims were fighting for a common cause and in their battle against the Raj; the siphais and the people (*Janta*), the soldiers and the civil population, both rose in a spontaneous movement to drive the aliens (*firangis*) out of their land. This was a national deluge, a watershed in the stream of national life, which did not wait for holy war to be declared by clerics.

Astonishingly, in some European accounts of 'the mutiny', the rebels were almost all Muslim. If we go through a non-official French view as seen in the writings of Jensigny, the Muslims wanted to seize power and banish the Europeans from India. One French official advances an interesting hypothesis of the rebellion occurring within the space of a triangle area of Indian upcountry, where it sometimes says so clearly, that the Muslims were the chief conspirators and they were connected with the atrocities on the Europeans. That this was also the view of the English officials is well known and needs no repetition here. Besides, the French officials relatively underestimated the Hindu participation in the '1857 Revolt' in their correspondence, except the citation of the 'Kanpur massacre' by Nana Sahib. Regarding the involvement in the '1857 Mutiny', only one French source from Rajmahal in Bihar, however, mentioned the cases of participation not only of the Hindus but also of the tribals—the Santhals and Munda.[17]

Since we know that the Barelvi *ulema* in Saharanpur district did not allow the Muslims there to support a holy war against the Raj of the Company,[18] how could we accept the communal version of analysis of the 1857 uprising? Actually the revolt of 1857 established unhesitatingly the combined power of communal harmony. Both the Hindus and Muslims had shown unprecedented unity from top to bottom. The unique feature and the most important characteristics of the 1857 revolt lie in it. If we go through the proclamations issued at different times by the leaders of the insurgency, like Bahadur Shah from Delhi, Firuz Shah or Khan Bahadur Khan from Bareilly, Nana Sahib from Kanpur and Rani of Jhansi, the appeal to the Hindu and Muslim subjects for ironing their unity against British aggressors became the chief priority. The people totally honoured it and not a single incident to breach communal harmony or violating the appeal made by proclamations had occurred.

III

The British once propagated that what took place during the years 1857 to 1859 in India was only a 'Sepoy mutiny' and that it did not have any support form the people of India. William Muir, a civil servant who worked in the intelligence department in Agra, contended that 'the character of the affair is that of a 'Military mutiny'—a struggle between the government and its soldiers, not between the government and the people.[19]

On the contrary, Col. G.B. Malleson and some other army officers reacted sharply to that fake observation. G.B. Malleson, however in his *Red Pamphlet,* strongly rebutted the claim of the civilians that the cultivators of the soil, the class from which the sepoys were drawn, were solidly on the side of the British. Malleson expressed the opinion that the majority of the people of Oudh (Ayodhya) Rohilkhand, Bundelkhand, Sagar and Narmada were against the British and Ö *at first apparently, it was a mere military mutiny, it speedily changed its character, and became a national insurrection.*[20]

As a result of extensive research conducted by them, it came to light that the British officials who had either directly participated in those incidents or had witnessed them, were themselves divided on the character of the so-called 'Sepoy Mutiny'. G.B. Malleson, John William Kaye,[21] Charles Ball,[22] Rev. Alexander Duff[23], and many others had cited several instances of mass support that the insurrectionists had. According to Kaye, there was no one among the Hindus and Muslims from Ganga to Yamuna who was not against the British. J.W. Kaye, as an authentic historian of the mutiny, came to the right conclusion, on the basis of the massive records he had collected, that the Revolt of 1857 was brought up from the heart of Indian society. Kaye successfully illustrated the mindset of the Indians, the priest, prince and peasants, who were getting together to oppose the alien rule of the Company. His unbiased research revealed how and why the various sections of the people were extremely alienated by the British policy in terms of land and religion.

The propagators of the 'mutiny theory', however, either had no basic sense about the origins of the soldiers or the sipahis, or they intentionally distorted facts to defend the atrocities of the Company rule in India. In the famous terminology of Lenin, sepoys (soldiers) are "Peasants in Uniform". Their discontent became clearly explicit during revolutionary stages in the form of quintessence of all contradictions in society. That was why Lenin gave the "Soviets" which were the revolutionary organisations of soldiers as well as of the workers and peasants, a very prominent place in the advance of the Russian revolution.

The British built a military organisation with a new kind of relationship between officers and rank based on pay and bureaucratic discipline; the officers however at all levels were British in origin. Consequently, unlike in the earlier set-up, there remained absolutely no relationship between the officers and ranks touching upon the social and cultural aspects of life. The sepoys came to realize that the British rulers were using them to destroy the existing socio-cultural institutions that their predecessors had fondly built and also those who were heading those institutions. This naturally fostered anger and indignation in their minds. Karl Marx, as a matter of fact, sitting several thousand miles away in London, in his articles on India, written between 1853-1858 for the *New York Daily Tribune,* correctly exposed the disastrous and fragmented socio-economic condition of the Hindustani peasants and artisans who were ruined by the colonial rule of the East India Company. Karl Marx, indeed, was the first author who openly acknowledged the upsurge of 1857 as the Indian war of independence. [24]

We have many past experiences in our history during the colonial rule so far as army discontent was concerned. The 'Vellor mutiny' in the south in 1806 was probably the first outburst of the Indian sepoys followed by several small revolts of a similar nature that had broken out in various parts of the country, relatively smaller in extent. In 1924, a regiment of Berhampore (Bengal) belonging to the Bengal Army also revolted against their alien officers' atrocities.[25] Although each one of those was suppressed, the forces behind these struggles were undoubtedly the forerunners of the Rebellions of 1857-59. The sepoys were forced to discharge as tools of foreign rulers and the reality that they belonged to that section of the people who are ruined day by day, being the victims of the exploitation by the very same foreign dominators. The 1857-59 revolt was the outbreak of these forces. In a recent article Ray and Chaudhuri correctly made a comment, "Between them, Kaye, Savarkar and Buckler established the popular, traditional and anti-colonial character of the uprising. The Mutiny, in other words, was not just a mutiny."[26]

However the credit goes to *Babu* Rajanikanta Gupta[27] for writing the first historical account of the 1857 upsurge in vernacular, from a nationalist point of view. Gupta was a prolific Bengali writer who took the painstaking effort to compose the five volume history of the 'War of 1857' in the 1890s. Nagendranath Gupta,another famous Bengali writer from Motihari, Bihar, also wrote a novel *Amar Singh Bengali*, which was later, translated into Hindi by a famous litterateur Pratap Narayan Mishra. Both books, written separately by two Guptas in the 1890s, gave us a comprehensive account of the background of the 'Mutiny' years:[28] But for many years, those works were not known outside Bengal and when Sarvarkar wrote his *The Indian War of Independence* in Marathi in 1907-08, he believed that his book was the first book by an Indian writer in any of the Indian languages.[29]

Although Rajanikanta Gupta's version was the first and more accurate account than anybody else in analysing the Revolt of 1857 from the nationalist and patriotic point of view, yet since the publication of Savarkar's book, 1857 began to be seen popularly as the war of independence for a number of radicals who had been trying to mobilise Indian nationalists in London and America. Copies of this book were smuggled into India. Sikandar Hayat Khan who later became a famous politician of Punjab brought one of the boxes carrying copies of Savarkar's book to India. These books were distributed among the revolutionaries of India. Few editions of this book, published from France, England and somewhere in Southeast Asia were also in circulation among the revolutionaries of India and abroad. This book set the trend of calling the 1857 revolt as the war of independence for Indians.

IV

After the independence in 1947, as with the case of many other matters, a new impetus was given to research into the Indian freedom struggle. The centenary of the "1857 Events" (not just "Sepoy Mutiny", called as a common practice by colonial legacy) was celebrated under the auspices of the government itself. As a part of the celebrations extensive research work was being organised. Committees had been constituted under the tutelage of Maulana Abul Kalam Azad, then Union Minister for Education. Eminent Professor Surendranath Sen ultimately took the responsibility on the request of the Indian Government to write a comprehensive history of the 1857

Revolt and his monograph *Eighteen Fifty-Seven* is still being treated as an authentic official account of that time. Professor Tara Chand's *History of the Freedom Movement in India* was also an important endeavour. That was prepared under the official auspices of the Indian government. Moreover, a series of monographs, books and research articles were also published at that time by the private enterprises and individual initiatives. Some works are very superficial except those by R.C. Majumdar and several others; but these were not beyond criticism for their ambiguities in judging the real merit of the 1857 insurgency and for ambivalence and dichotomy to make an unequivocal conclusion indeed.

Nevertheless, it should not be denied that in 1957 to commemorate the centenary anniversary of the risings, various multidimensional exposures came into being in the realm of new researches on the episode of 1857. We can mention an anthology by P.C. Joshi, which for the first time revealed the rich folk sources on the revolt of 1857. It focused on both the diversities and the specificities of the 1857 revolt. This included assessing 1857 against the colonial backdrops, examining aspects of participation and focusing in a major way on the internal contradictions.[30] In many ways this work inspired a serious spell of writings on the Revolt. Here mention must be made of Eric Stokes who examined issues ranging from the way the nature of 1857 was conditioned by the backdrop, the demographic and ecological features to the social composition and the role of the peasants especially the 'rich peasants'. Interestingly, his research guided Stokes to reassess his position. Whereas in his first work he had focused on the 'rich' peasant leadership and mobilisation, in *Peasant Armed,* Stokes enlarged the social basis of peasant participation in the revolt.[31]

However, it was left to historians like Rudrangshu Mukherjee and Tapti Roy to enrich our understanding of the Revolt by their focus on the popular level of the Revolt. Their effort was based on specifice area studies—viz. Awadh and Bundelkhand—that brought to light fascinating complexities of popular militancy that had remained ignored.[32]

More recently—since the 1990s—historians have focused on the popular dimensions of 1857. Here one can refer to scholars like K.S. Singh who have highlighted participation of adivasis;[33] Badri Narayan who has focused on low and outcastes and popular culture; and Rajat Ray who has studied the mentalities of 1857.[35]

Today, in the light of modern research, it was known that the Revolt of 1857 was not an accidental phenomenon. As we cannot forget the famous maxim, 'since peasants did not write their histories, they did not document their interaction with the 1857 Revolt'. But, is it possible to ignore the folklore and traditions of resistance associated with the 1857 Revolt?

Moreover, can one afford to ignore the connections between 1857 and the peasant revolts of the preceding phase, or those outside the northern region of India—in spite of being told repeatedly about the role of the Permanent Settlements and the *Bahadraloks* (the Bengali Gentry), which supposedly left Bengal as a 'zone of peace' in this phase?

The armed revolts and resistance against the British armed forces by the adivasis spanned over 128 years. No other part in the subcontinent has been such armed revolts, resistance and sacrifice of the masses against the might of the British government for such a long period. Chronicle of such revolts include Mal Paharia revolt (1772-80), Santhal revolt under the leadership of Tilka Manjhi (1780-85), Munda revolt in Tamar under the leadership of Bishnu Manki and Maiju Manki (1795-1800), Chuar revolt (1798), Bhumij revolt of Manbhoom (1798-99), Chero revolt under the leadership of Bhukhan Singh in Palamau-Surguja (1800-02), Khurda Paika-feudal military retainers rebellion (1817) in Khurda-Orissa, Munda revolt in Palamau under the leadership of Bhukhanmunda (1819-20), Ho uprising (1821), Oraon revolt under the leadership of Buddhu Bhagat (1830-32), Kol uprising (1831-32), Kherwar revolt under the leadership of Bhagirath, Dubai Gosai and Patel Singh (1832-33), Bhumji revolt under the leadership of Ganga Narain Singh (1832-33), Revolts of the Bhills (1852) in Khandesh, Dhar, and Malwa, the Santhals in (1855-56) Rajamahal, Bhagalpur, Birbhum, Mapillas (1836-54) in Malabar, the Kandhas in Ghumsar and Baudh (1855-60), the Savaras of Parliakhemedi (1856-57) in Parliakhemedi-Orissa. All these peasant or tribal revolts were the products of the colonial as well as British sponsored feudal exploitation in the Indian subcontinent.[36]

Adivasi armed revolts and resistance characteristically differed from other contemporary currents of struggle for independence. Adivasis revolts were mass uprisings of peasants. They used bows and arrows and other traditional arms against firearms. Their struggle was for freedom, natural justice, identity and traditional rights on land, forest and water. They adopted the tactics of guerrilla warfare. They fought against the British army and their sepoys, police, zamindars, moneylenders and government administrators.

The permanent zamindari settlement of 1793 added to the woes of the adivasis. According to a contemporary periodical, "Zamindars, the police, the revenue and court also have exercised a combined system of extortion, oppressive extraction, forcible dispossession of property, abuse and personal violence and a variety of petty tyrannies upon the Santhals." (*Calcutta Review*, 1856). Under the Indian Forest Act, wastelands of adivasi villages were converted into protected forest depriving the adivasis of their traditional rights on forest produce. Obviously, adivasis in general did not have faith in the sepoys and feudal lords, who led the 1857 war of independence. Though all those from every section did not participate in the rebellion, yet it was unforgettable that the rajas, nawabs, taluqdars, zamindars, landless peasants, unemployed artisans, rural proletariat, tribes, from jungle or hill more or less were getting together on their common cause, i.e. to be free from socio-economic oppression of the outsiders. Such consciousness gradually turned into a sense of patriotism. Was it not the beginning of the process of nation building? It is indeed heartening that the new historians of the generation, from Eric Stokes to Tapti Ray, Rudrangshu Mukherjee and Rajat Kanta Ray to Badrinarayan and Biswamay Pati ultimately started to portray that hidden history of the people's participation in their first war of independence, irrespective of their caste, creed, and region.

V

This is the 150th year of that great rebellion. Let us remember the martyrs who laid down their lives against imperialism. The entire area in northern India, from Bengal to Delhi, was in ferment. The people rose in revolt against the foreign yoke. The sipahis and leadership of the then feudal society joined hands but could not succeed. The role of the toiling mass and their ideological and political struggle would again come much later with the contradiction growing in the changing material conditions.

We have mentioned previously that the British philanthropist missionary F.W. Buckler, made a noteworthy contribution illuminating the ideas behind the mutiny.[36] In an important paper at the Royal Historical Society in 1932, he demonstrated that the Mutineers considered themselves *not as rebels but freedom fighters* and they were committing no sin but trying to restore the legitimate sovereignty of their kingdom, which had been grappled unjustly by the alien aggressor. In other words, the Company's government had no independent constitutional basis. Its authority derived from the various *farmans* issued by the Mughal Emperor.

So, we must not consider that the 'War merely a part of traditional resistance movement, was propagated by a few historians of recent times.[37] It was essentially a struggle for liberation or the first war of independence. If it had not been crushed by superior military power with the help of the native renegades or lack of unity among all the sections of the people, it might easily have generated new ideas and new strength. The conservatism and feudal reactionary elements could no longer retain their hegemony because to defeat British power and to prevent a reconquest, a new energy, modern military technique, effective organisation, general cooperation, and overall a non-comunal or secular attitude in the state administration, which was seen during the time of uprisings, would have become highly imperative. If any one keeps his attention slightly on the *Proclamation*[38] pronounced by the different rebel leaders in 1857-58 from various regions like Bareilly, Lucknow, Delhi, Jhansi, Azamgarh, etc., the common element which would be certainly noticed is the *Hindustani* national brotherhood and an unprecedented communal amity against the colonial hegemony.

To conclude, on the whole, it is indeed difficult to discover a uniform pattern as it differed considerably from region to region. Political and social motives, and class or group interests got mixed up in the process before the general cry for the extinction of the alien. However, the more positive aspect of the 1857 insurgency was that the people of various castes, tribes, nationality and religions who lived under different kingdoms rose up together to end British rule. By no means can supreme sacrifice of the patriots of the 1857 war of independence be underestimated.

NOTES AND REFERENCES

1. Rudrangshu Mukherjee, *Mangal Pandey: An Accidental Hero,* Calcutta, 2001.
2. William Dalrymple, *The Last Mughal: The Fall of a Dynasty,* Penguin Books, New Delhi, 2007.
3. E.M.S. Namboodiripad, *A History of India's Freedom Struggle,* Thiruvananthapuram, 1984.
4. Allamah Fazle Haq of Khayrabad, 'The Story of the War of Independence 1857-58', *Journal of the Pakistan Historical Society,* Vol. V, pt. 1, January 1957, pp. 30-2. The revealing account of the Allamah is borne out by the British historians, officials and spies as well.
5. Syed Moinul Haq, *The Great Revolution of 1857,* Pakistan Historical Society, Karachi, 1968.
6. Syed Athar Abbas Rizvi, *Swatantra Dilli,* Publication Bureau, UP, 1957.
7. F.W. Buckler, 'The Political Theory of the Indian Mutiny', *Royal Historical Society Transactions,* Series 4, Vol. V, 1932, London.
8. For example, a number of Autobiographies or Memoirs of Durgadas Bandyopadhyay (*Bidrohe Bangali o Aamar Jiban Charit, 1986;* 1st edn. 1924, Bengali), Debendranath Tagore (*Atmajibani*; Satish Chakraborty ed. Visva Bharati, 1962), Shibnath Sastri (*Ramtanu Lahiri o Tatkalin Bangasamaj,* 1968; 1st edn. 1903, Bengali), Syed Ahmed Khan (*Riddalah Asbah-e-Baghawat-e-Hind* (In English *Causes of the Indian Revolt,* Benaras, 1873) could be mentioned.
9. R.C. Majumdar, *The Sepoy Mutiny and the Revolt of 1857,* Calcutta, 1957 and S.N. Sen, *Eighteen Fifty Seven* (with a foreword by Maulana Abul Kalam Azad), New Delhi, 1957.
10. Joshi, '1857 in Our History' in P.C. Joshi (Ed.), *Rebellion 1857,* New Delhi, 1957, Rpt. 2007, NBT, p. 78.
11. Marx-Engels, *Selected Works,* Vol. I, p. 225: cited in P.C. Joshi, ibid., p. 165.
12. Sushovan Sarkar, 'Views on 1857' in *Bengal Renaissance and Other Essays,* PPH, New Delhi, 1981 (2nd print).
13. S.B. Chaudhuri, *Civil Rebellion in the Indian Mutinies,* Calcutta, 1957.
14. Saiyyad Ahmad Khan, *Rissalah Asbab-e-Baghawat-e-Hind,* viz. (The Causes of the Revolt in the Indian Army), Agra, 1903.

15. K.M. Ashraf, 'Muslim Revivalist and the Revolt of 1857', P.C. Joshi (ed.), *Rebellion 1857,* New Delhi, 1957, rpt in 2007, NBT, p. 78.
16. Ayesha Jalal, *Self and Sovereignty: Individual and Community in South Asian Islam Since 1850,* Oxford University Press, 2001, p. 33.
17. Jacigny, *Histoire de l'Inde,* Paris, 1858. See also Anirudha Ray, 'Contemporary French Reaction to the Indian Mutiny of 1857' in Surendra Gopal (Ed.), *Colonial India,* V.K.S.University, 2006, pp. 33-53.
18. "In 1857 the Brelvi Ulema, of *thana* Bhawan in Sharanpur district had decreed against a Muslim jihad. This drove a wedge between thana Bhawan and Deoband, though they had no serious disagreements on religion"- Ayesha Jalal, op.cit., p. 422.
19. William Muir, *Records of the Intelligence Department of the Government of the N.W. Provinces of India during the Mutiny of 1857,* Vol. I, London, 1902, p. 31.
20. G.B. Malleson, *The Mutiny of the Bengal Army,* London, 1858, p. 63 and see also Malleson, *History of the Indian Mutiny,* in 3 Volumes, London, 1878-80.
21. Sir William Kaye, *History of the Sepoys War in India,* in 3 Volumes, London, 1867.
22. Charles Ball, *History of the Indian Mutiny,* in 2 Volumes, London, n.d.
23. Reverend Alexander Duff, *The Indian Rebellion: Its Causes and Results,* London, 1858.
24. Karl Marx and F. Engels, *The First Indian War of Independence 1857-59,* London, 1959. See also K. Marx, *On India,* Tulika, New Delhi, 2005.
25. Premangshu Banerjee, *Tulsi Leaves and Ganges Water,* Calcutta, 2001.
26. Nupur Chaudhuri and Rajat Kanta Ray, *Mutiny Debates;* Paper presented in a Symposium on the Revolt of 1857 in the 67th annual session of Indian History Congress held in Faroke College, Calicut Univeristy, on March 9-11, 2007.
27. Rajanikanta Gupta (1849-1900) wrote a number of books on the History of India in the 1890s. His volumes on the Mutiny appeared in the 1880s and the second editions were published in 1886. After the publications of the third volume it was feared that he would be charged for seditious writings. According to S.D. Singh the earliest references to the Mutiny in Indian literature were made by Govind Chandra Ghosh (1874) and Girish Chandra Ghosh (1884). See S.D.Singh, op.cit., p. 243.
28. Hitendra Kumar Patel, 'Aspects of Nationalist Response to 1857 in the Early Twentieth Century', *Modern Historical Studies,* Vol. 4, 2007; *Journal of the History Department,* RBU, Kolkata.
29. Savarkar wrote '1857 Chein Bharatiya Swatantrya samar' (in Marathi) at the age of 24. It could not be published in Marathi owing to foot problems. In Germany Roman fonts were used for the publication of Sanskrit books and attempts were made to publish Savarkar's book in Germany. These attempts were unsuccessful and ultimately the book was translated into English by some Marathi intellectuals, Marathi students living in London for the preparation of the Indian Civil Service examination, under the supervision of V.V.S. Ayyar. The manuscript travelled to France and ultimately to Holland where it got published in 1909. See the introduction by G.M. Jsohi in Veer

Savarkar, *1857 Ka Swadhinta Sangram,* Delhi: Hind Pocket Books Pvt Ltd, 1996, p. 10.

30. P.C. Joshi (ed.), *Rebellion 1857,* op.cit.
31. Eric Stokes, *Peasant and the Raj: Studies in Peasant Society and Agrarian Revolt in Colonial India, 1978,* and *The Peasant Armed: The Indian Revolt of 1857,* 1986.
32. Rudrangshu Mukherjee, *Awadh in Revolt, 1857-58: A Study of Popular Resistance,* 1984 and Tapti Roy, *The Politics of a Popular Uprising: Bundelkhand in 1857,* New Delhi, 1994.
33. K.S. Singh, 'The 'Tribals' and the 1857 Uprising', *Social Scientist,* Vol. 26, January-April, 1998; No. 1-4, pp. 76-85.
34. Badri Narayan, 'Dalits and Memories of 1857', *ICHR Conference Proceedings,* December 2006, unpublished: and 'Popular Culture and 1857: Memory Against Forgetting', *Social Scientist,* Vol. 26. January-April 1998; No. 1-4, pp. 86-94.
35. Rajat Kanta Ray, *The Felt Community: Commonality and Mentality before the Emergence of Indian Nationalism,* 2003, Oxford University Press, pp. 353-4.
36. Suprakash Ray, *Bidrohi Bharat* (in Bengali), Calcutta, 1970 and Biswamoy Pati, 'The 1857 Rebellion in Orissa: Looking for the 'Echoes'?' *Pepole's Democracy,* (weekly organ of the Communist Party of India (Marixist), Vol. XXXI, No. 25, June 24, 2007.)
37. F.W. Buckler, 'The Political Theory of the Indian Mutiny', *Royal Historical Social Transactions,* Series 4, Vol. V, 1932.
38. Nupur Chaudhuri and Rajat Kanta Ray, *Mutiny Debates,* op.cit.
39. Iqbal Hussain (ed.), *Proclamation of the Rebels of 1857,* ICHR, New Delhi, 2007. [Draft Copy]. See also S.A. Rizvi and M.L. Bhargava (eds.), *Freedom Struggle in Uttar Pradesh,* in 6 Vols., Lucknow, 1957.

25

Fairs and Festivals of Tribes of Orissa: An Analytical Study

Binodini Das

The quest of the evolution of mankind shows that whatever man has taken for granted has a beginning in the evolutionary process. His experiments with Nature made him acquainted with its typical characteristics, which appeared to him sacred, serene, pleasant, cooperative and an aid to some extent and on the other, he found it ferocious, fearsome exhibiting the spirit of 'deluge'.[1] Led by the innocence and ignorance, he started to believe in the existence of a superpower lying embedded with the forces of nature, which manifested its spirit in different visual aspects like stars and moon, sky and earth, rain and thunder, hills and rivers, plants and herbs, animals and reptiles etc. This belief in the supernatural became stronger as groups of men settled down as herding or cultivating communities.[2] Accordingly, the cult of animism grew with the preconceived idea of the divine spirit ingrained in the forces of nature to which the primitive man made an imaginary contract to worship if following certain rites and rituals perfectly with an expectation that the gods were bound to carry out on their part. Such religious ideas were expressed in rituals songs, dances, and ceremonies.[3]

The Oriya culture flows from the tribes through the non-tribes towards infinite adapting and adopting, each other's spirit. The folk saying that, "Odissa is the land of twelve months and thirteen festivals" symbolises to a substantial number of festivals celebrated in a month. The diffused 62 tribes of Orissa staying in various parts make the land colourful and elegant through their cultural activities. The fairs and festivals observed by the tribes round the year should be considered as socio-religio-economic phenomena in which tribal life finds solace and comfort. With a hope to obtain an intimate relationship with gods and goddesses, ancestral spirits and other supernatural forces that would secure for them all kinds of material prosperity and render them immune from all fatal diseases, the tribes prefer to perform certain rites and rituals in a ceremonial way. Since tribal economy is mostly agro-centric and partly pastoral in character, all rituals centring round the said spirit has been operated at the early phase of the commencement in the middle and finally at the end of the year. The fairs and festivals keep their rhythm with the seasonal changes. Song, dance, merrymaking and organising community feasts are some of the colourful pictures from which the tribes enjoyed gaiety and pleasure. Animal sacrifice is a common feature practised by the tribes in most of the rituals.

There are some dimensional differences in the methods, practices and observances of worship although all have a common objective. *Chaita Parab* or *Chaitra Parab* (during March-April) of the tribes of undivided Koraput, Bolangir, and Kalahandi districts deserves special attention as it is celebrated in a period when the atmosphere is surcharged with a mild breeze flowing over hills and hillocks, rivers and riverines, plants and trees, field and orchard spreading the essence of the blossoms and dhak flowers. The Chaitra Parab in Koraput begins with dancing and singing by the *dhangaras* and *dhangiris,* which bear the happiness and pleasure of conjugal love. It is the festival of tribes like Kandha Gadaba, Bhatra, Sabara, Bhumia, Desia Paroja, Saura, Rana and Domb, etc. Interestingly enough, the Desia tribe of Koraput plateau follows a very strange tradition during the celebration of Chaitra Parab, i.e. to block the roads (*Pojer Chekha*) for the last week of the month of Chaitra. Previously, young girls holding each others hands and dancing in tandem used to block the road. But at present, the roads are blocked by placing logs of woods and boulders on the road. Expressing her inability to find out the logic behind this type of "Road Blocking" tradition, Tina Otten mentions that the "Chaitra Parab" is closely linked to the beginning of the agrarian cycle.[4] She further states that the ritual hunting and luck in chase are associated with fertility.[5]

The Parojas of Koraput welcome Chaitra Parab through their performance of *Desia Nata* (Desia play), annual ceremonial hunting and worship of Mother-Earth with perfect rituals for ensuring reproductive capacity of the whole village. The specialty of the *desia nata* is that the actors of the tribe use the multicoloured masks in order to impersonate different characters such as gods, goddesses, animals, birds, etc. The music and dance are unsophisticated and blended with traditional tribal touches.[6] The Chaitra Parab is usually associated with the worship of the Mother-Earth, who is popularly called by different names like *Dharati Mata, Dangara Devi* and *Budhi Thakurani,* etc. It is also famously known as *Sikara Parab* (hunting ceremony) or *Bada Benta Parab* (big hunting ceremony). It is the Disari (village priest) who after performing the worship declares the auspicious moment to leave the village for hunting.

Accordingly, all the male-folks of the tribe after getting themselves fully equipped with hunting implements like arrows and bow, spears, etc. proceed to the jungle where they spend several days in search of a suitable hunt. If they are successful in hunting and return to the village with a good hunt, their wives warmly welcome them, otherwise they have to tolerate insults with all sorts of humiliations like cow-dung-water throw by the latter.[7] The successful hunter is carried on the shoulders to the village with the procession and is served with wine and molasses.[8] The men and women spend the whole night dancing and singing near the dead body of the hunted animal and return to their homes. Widespread deforestations taking place in modern times have considerably reduced the number of game in the forest. So this hunting ceremony only exists in name, but the dance and song continues as before.[9]

The Chaitra Parab is the festival of love and livelihood. In Korapu, the *dhangaras* and *dangiris* in groups create obstructions to the vehicles demanding some coins. And a mere ten paisa coin makes them dance with joy.[10] The real essence of the festival is that being untrammelled by obstruction; the *dhangaras* and *dhagiris* express their love and try to win each other's hearts. Jokes, laughter, erotic gestures, vulgar speech and body expressions all tolerated with catholic mentality and in such surroundings and situation one would find oneself vacillating in the air of melodious songs coming from the sweet voices of the *dhangaras* and *dhagiris.* As there is no restriction in freely mixing with each other, the tribal youths during this period select their own life partners. The Bonds youths, who are kept under strict surveillance and control in relation to free mixing with the opposite sex, eagerly wait for the arrival of *Chaitra Parab,* which would give them an opportunity to unleash their heart-felt love and would freely mix with each other in an isolated place which is not considered objectionable by their seniors. The Kandhas of Koraput also observe Chaitra Parab by worshipping *Chaurasi Devi* and *Tanapenu* (Mother Earth). A few years ago they made human sacrifices, which is called *Mariah* (a ritual to sacrifice the daughter of the officiating preist) with an expectation of getting an abundant harvest of good quality turmeric and other crops. The Bhattoda, Paroja and Gond tribes of Kalahandi also celebrate *Chaitra Jatra* and *Chaitra Parab* with much pomp and gaiety. The village deity or *Gramadevata* roams round the village and this is known as *boel* after proper worship on a Tuesday falling between dark fortnight and full moon night of the month of Chaitra. Usually, the unmarried girls carrying earthen pots filled with turmeric water on their heads visit different houses of the village. At every house the earthen pot is worshipped by the households.[11] This is called *Chaitra Jatra.* But *Chaiti Parab* of eastern Kalahandi, especially of Thuamula Rampur, Jaypatna, Konasara, etc. is a festival of entertainment. One would be beholden to see the tribes in a state of ecstasy. This festival is celebrated for at least 21 or 15 days in the month of Chaitra.[12] The village *disari* (priest) declares the inauguration of Chaiti Parab on an auspicious moment of a day near a common place of the village called "Shemal Guda". All the village people irrespective of age and sex assemble here to celebrate the festival. Some fowls are sacrificed to the village deity after which starts dancing, acting, feasting, drinking, singing and playing on different musical instruments that continues the whole night and next morning the village women request their husbands to go hunting. The men go to the jungle after being fully equipped with hunting weapons.[13] In some of the regions, especially in plain plateau, where the forest is destroyed and no animals are available, the tribes resort to symbolic representation of hunting and food gathering from the jungle through acting, which is displayed in "Shemal Guda".[14] The Bhatras or Bhattodas like Kandhas were also used to human sacrifice on this occasion, which in the later period changed to *podha vali* (buffalo sacrifice) and subsequently it is confined to only fowl sacrifice. Chitrasen Pasayat observes that, "man would naturally react to any kind of social change as he is completely dependent on the social environment".[15] So the devolution of Chaiti Parab does not seem irrational as the tribal society is passing through twists and turns of the evolutionary process.

The *Chaiti Parab* or *Chaitra Parab* of Koraput, Kalahandi and malkangiri is the *Parab* of love and marriages. The dhangaras and dhangiris carry out dance and song competitions throughout the night. Boys and girls form separate groups facing each other on the common dancing place and start dancing.[16] The dance is called *Tapa Nritya,* which is unique in character and creates a feeling of joy and pleasure. The eager waiting of the young tribal boys and girls come to an end when the folk bards of both the sexes called *Geet kudia and Geet Kudiani* finish the prayer and innovation songs in favour of Mother Earth and after which the boys and girls begin singing enchanting love songs before the onlookers without any hesitation. Some of the love songs of Chaitra Parab are mentioned below:

Kindari Gita of Parenga Tribe of Koraput:

"God kandi kandi kanta bausa/ Babu kale kalikate
Chaitra masara kindari gita/Goutiba gote gote
Ga ga mor, ga Kertan/Tumari amari ekanta tile
Pade pade gai dekhu/ Gailere babu/Chhank thibu
Nohile Grabu jiba/Chaita Mangal bar//"

Jeypore:

Male: *Rana bela katha/ Duara bandha/Lagichhi jhumpilantara*
Ketedure thile e nina tora/Kebe na karibu dura
Daya rakhitibu kanipanate/Pasoribu nai mote//

Koraput:

"He nini, kede sundara gita tu gauchhu/
He sunanaki jhia, Aau padia gaantuni
Ethi aukebi nahin, ame duhen
Tu Gita gaaki, ame duhen sethire dubi jiba
Satare nini, e mautschaba sabuele asibani tor//

Translation:

Hey! Damsel, what a beautiful song you are singing?
Hey! Gold-nosed beauty, please sing once again the rhyme.
Nobody is here except us
You sing the song, we two will be deeply engrossed in it.
Really Nini (damsel), this festival will not always come

Chaita Parab or Chaitra Parab marks the beginning of the hot season, the time of mangoes, which is the prime fruit of the year. So on this occasion mangoes are eaten ritually. The Gadabas of Koraput after worshipping and sacrificing fowls near the village deity, goddess Hundi, start to eat mangoes.[17] The principal deity of the Jatapu tribe of Koraput and Ganjam is *Jakiri Devi,* who is consecrated by the priest in a stone pillar during *Jhagadi Parba* after which a new mango is offered to her during the month of Chaitra and the members of the year have it afterwards.[18] But some other tribes like Kol, Langa Saora, Omantya and Pentia perform Baparab, Uda-n-a-Adur, Amura Ambanua festivals respectively in the month of Chaitra. The Kol's Baparab is otherwise known as *Phulbhaguri,* which is observed for four days in the month of Chaitra before eating fruits like mango, sad flower, jackfruit, etc.[19] Nandita Misra[20] in her unpublished Ph.D. thesis mentions Mahua flowers or fruits of the season. The Bhuyans of Kandujhar also observe *Akhipardha Parab* in the month of Chaitra by offering worship to Mother-Earth. The village Dehury (priest) fixes a day for performing rituals of which one brought in after hunting. However, increasing awareness among the tribes that animals are real strength of the forest, there has been a gradual decline in the practice of hunting animal of sacrifice.

The moment the Chaita Parab bids farewell to the tribes of Orissa, the month *Baisakha* (April-May) welcomes the tribe with its scorching heat reminding them of the forthcoming calamities, distress and disasters waiting for agriculture. So with unblemished love and absolute devotion the tribes surrender themselves to the god or goddess with the hope that his cattle, wealth and land will be protected from the wrath of nature. The Kandhas of Koraput celebrate *Jhagadi Parab* or *Kedu Parab* in the month of Baisakha for three to five days for obtaining material prosperity in the form of getting good rain, a smooth growth of crops, a life without disease and above all, let the domestic animals be free from becoming a prey to wild beasts. The *Kedu* festival is also one of the important festivals of the

Kandhas of the Baliguda area of Kalahandi district. The festival meant for human sacrifice is called *Kedu* in the Kui language of the Kandhas. The place of sacrifice is called *Baredi.*[21] The sacrificed man is called *Mrimenjju*. As the human sacrifice has been stopped, the buffalo sacrifice is made, which is called *Podhavali* and the sacrificial animal is called *Mimicroru*. The meat of mimicroru is distributed among the Kandhas, who bury it in the cultivated field to secure the blessing of the Bhuyani Peru (Mother Earth) for a handsome turmeric harvest. A song dedicated in her favour is mentioned below:

"Sendebura Nedebura/ Soru benu Nedubura
Padapunenu Rubu punenu/ Bate Dindi Batigimu Kotigamu"

[Translation: Oh ! Lord of the Heaven, oh! Lord of the Earth, Oh! Lord of Hills, Oh! Lord of water, Oh! Lord of the Village! I do not know your name or your village; you give everything to us. You will share this sacrifice among yourselves].[22]

The *Pendarunima Jatra* begins with the worship of Pendarunima in the month of Chaitra/ Baisakh by the Gonds, Bhattodas and Paraja tribes of Umarkote. According to the folk tradition, the goddess Pendarunima is a deified form of a spirit of the village headman's daughter, who committed suicide in the tank for the construction of which her husband was sacrificed by her brothers and brothers-in-law. Once in a year the pendarunima Jatra is performed to worship the goddess. Holding sticks and flags as a symbol of the village deity, the tribes from different parts of Koraput gather in the place of the village deity. The jatra is finished amidst a joyful performance of all the rites and rituals, animal sacrifice, songs of love in question-answer form, frenzied dances and emergence of *Kalishi,* who happens to be one of the tribes and acts as if the goddess has to enter his body, who could also make prophecies.[23] *Mati Jatra* or *Bihanachhina Jatra* is also another important festival of the tribes living in Kalahandi district. *Bihanachhina* means to receive seeds for cultivation from the respective tribes. The festival is celebrated in the month of Chaitra near the Devigudi, the place meant for the village deity (goddess), where some mud made up of soil are kept after proper worship and sacrifice of fowl, the *Jhankara* (village priest) offers the seeds to the deity, which he has brought from the house with a prayer to make the seeds potent enough for the best production. Then a handful of seeds is distributed by the *Jhakara* to each tribe to whom *Nariha* applies a mud-mark on everyone's forehead. It is a symbolical wish for fertility of the land for the coming year. When the tribe returns home with this seed, his wife offers a grand welcome through a lamp showing and keeps it in store after worship. On the day of *Akshitrutiya,* they mix it with other seeds and sow it in their fields for cultivation.[24] The Baigas perform *shail* dance wearing wooden mask during Chaitra Navami.[25] *Bhiemasen*

Puja of Chuktia Bhunjia tribe is also celeberated in the month of Chaitra with pleasure and merrymaking. The village deity is worshipped with offerings of wine and fowl sacrifice for bumper Mahua crop.[26]

The month of Chaitra is followed by *Baisakha* bringing a number of fairs and festivals to its credit. The Koyas of Maikangiri observe *Bijapandu* festival in the month of *Semiti* (Baisakha/Jyestha) in order to secure the blessings of the Mother Earth for good harvest. The festival begins with the worship of offerings of cock, pig, eggs, mangoes, etc. to Mother Earth with a request to be kind enough in rendering an abundant harvest. Seeds of paddy are also kept before the goddess believing that those seeds would be potential enough through divine grace.[27] Prohibiting the work as a taboo during the observance of the festival, the tribes ceremoniously observe the mango eating ritual and hunting expedition (*Bijjaweta*).[28] Seed-sowing rituals, especially of rice, begin in the month of Baisakha (April-May), which is known by different festival names. *Akshay truitya* or *Akhiturtia* or *Akhimuthi* or *Bihanabuna* is the festival in which the first seed sowing ritual is ceremoniously observed by the tribes of Bhuyans(Keonjhar, Sambalpur and Sundargarh) Bhottoda, Omantya and Kisan, etc.[29] Another important festival of the Didayis of Koraput is *Ghia Panda,* which is celebrated in the month of Baisakha in which the first eating of new fruits like sal seeds, mango, mahua flowers, etc takes place.[30] Besides, Bhumija's *Dhulla Puja* festival of the month of Baisakha is meant for the well-being of the village.[31] Also Dongira Kandhas *Ghanta Parab* is a festival for harvest of ragi.[32] Oraon's *Bisu Sikar* (Summer Hunt) is an interesting festival.[33]

The acculturisation process made the tribes adaptable to non-tribal festivals like performance of *Raja Parab* in the month of Jyestha. Sabara, Juang, Bathudi, Bhumija, Saunti, etc. observe *Raja Parab* for good rain.[34] The other festivals observed in the month of Jyestha (May-June) are *Matijatra* of Dals,[35] *Jeth-Jatra* of Oraons (Sundargarh, Sambalpur),[36] *Ambataku Parab* and *Bihan Parab* of the Kandhas[37] and *Nuakhai Parab* of Khadia tribes.[38] The *Matijatra* is a synonym for the worship of the soil of earth, which signifies the worship of Mother Earth. *Bihan Parab* is a festival which is celebrated with strict adherence to devotion in which a symbolic field is made out of sands wetted with water near the Devigudi, a place of worship for the village deity. The varieties of seed crops, which are already collected from each house of the tribal village, are sown on the sand-field. The merrymaking and enjoyment continue with worship rituals for two to three days so long as the sprouts come out of the seeds. These sprouted seeds are distributed among the villagers after which they start sowing the seeds in their respective fields. The month of *Asadha* adds to its feather some important festivals like *Asarhi* of Bhumija,[39] *Bondafun* or *Kuree* of the Bondos,[40] *Asadha Khai* of Dal and Kolha,[41] *Bandana Parab* and *Jana Parab* of Gadaba[42] tribes, etc. The Bhumijas of Mayurbhanj celebrate *Asarhi Parab* before reploughing and transplanting of paddy seedlings. The Dal's *Asadha Khai Parab* is a community-oriented festival in which the worship is made first at the village and then in the forest. *Janaparaba* of Gadaba tribes of Korapupt is meant for offering of the newly produced pumpkins to the village deity after which it is eaten by the tribe. The *Bandpana Parab* is celebrated after the sacrifice of fowls before Thakurani (represented by a slab of stone) at a Hundi (a place of worship) by the Disari. The Bhyuyans of Keonjhar offer some honorarium to the village priest called Dehury for officiating at the sacrificial ceremony near the village deity with the hope of obtaining a rich harvest.[43] Some tribes such as the Bhottodas and Binjhals have got modernised and are found to practise *Ratha Jatra* (Car Festival) along with their Hindu neighbours. *Herah Parab* of Ho and Kolha tribes is a festival of reminiscence of the heroic deeds of Lita (the mythical ancestral figure of Hos) and it is also called an agro-centric festival as Lita buried the sprouts of *bhalia* and *sal* trees on the ground.[44]

Sravana (July-August) as a month descends down the earth fully equipped with entertainment programmes and leisure activities, which could be realised in the performance of celebration of the festivals. They are *Gamha Purnima* of the Bathudis and Kisans, *Srabana Amus* of Bhottoda, *Herali Parab* of Binjhals and Bhuyans, *Koua Jatra* of Dal, *Nuakhia* of Kotra, etc.[45] Bathudis, Bhuyans and Santals observe *Gamba Purnima* to worship the cattle-wealth, whereas the Kisans celebrate it for posting *Kendu* twigs in the agricultural field.[46] *Herali Parab* is meant for ancestor worship. The Binjhals and Bhuyans believe that their ancestors are once again reborn as their children. So they must be worshipped once. They keep unboiled rice and unboiled milk on the feet of their children(sons and daughters) and start to offer them *Khira* (a kind of delicious liquid food prepared out of rice, milk and spices) and *Pitha* (rice cake), which is previously prepared.[47] *Kodua Jatra* of Dals is a festival to be performed by individual family members in which home deities and ancestral spirits are worshipped.[48] *Nuakhia Parab* of Kotias is observed on any Monday of Sravana.[49] The tribes of western Orissa wait till the performance of *Kadu Jatra* to plant the little paddy crops in their fields. A day is selected for cultivating the field so long it would become muddy and after which the fowls would be sacrificed in honour of Mother Earth to obtain her blessing for plentiful rain and fine harvest.[50]

The month of *Bhadrab* (August-September) brings in its train a number of colourful festivals like *Nuakhia* of Bhottoda, Bhuyan, Pentia and Paroja tribes, *Balijatra* of Bhottoda and Bhumia tribes, *Navenna Puja* of Dals, *Dhannuakhia* and *Pidika* of Dongira Kandha, *Amus* of Holvas,

Kurumpandu of Koyas, *Makar* of Rajaur and Sauri, etc. Dals, Oraons, Juangs, Gadabas, Binjhals, Pentias and Holvas observe the new rice-eating ceremony. The Dals confine this festival to their kitchen, whereas the Bhuyans and Pentias make it a community festival in which some fowls are sacrificed by the village priest before the village deity called Grama Devati.[51] *Dhannuakhia,* a festival of Dongira Kandha, is performed for obtaining a bumper crop of castor seeds, whereas *Pidika* of the same tribe is followed with a ritual of first eating red gram, small millets and jawar.[52] *Kurum Pandu* of Koyas is meant for performing rituals for first eating small millets.[53] The Hos of Orissa observe *Karam Parab* on the full moon night of the month of Bhadarab. All the houses would have to observe fasting throughout the day. In the evening, the *Karam* branch is brought to the courtyard for installation and consecration by the householder amidst a hearty welcome of the lighting of the lamps and performance of dance with rhythm of the music and song. After consecration, they worship the branch offering un-boiled rice, five coins on *Sal* and *Stali* leaves and making a sacrifice of goat. When the *puja* (worship) is finished, one of the experts of the village describes the legends related to this *parab* to the villagers as the Hindus read the legend books, which is called *Bratakatha* or *Oshakatha* after worshipping their gods and goddesses. When all the rituals for worship are over, both males and females make themselves busy in frenzied dances with rhythm of songs and beating musical instruments like *madala* and flute.[54] *Balijatra* of the Bhottoda tribe of Koraput is observed when crops fail for lack of rain for several years continuously. The effigies of *Bhima* and *Kandhuni Debi* are ceremoniously kept and worshipped.[55]

The Bhumias of Koraput and Sambalpur also celebrate *Balijatra Parab. Bhadraba Sukla Ekadasi* (11th day of the bright fortnight of Bhadrab), the festival is celebrated for fertility of the land. The festival takes the name of planting of various grains in wet sand (bali) brought from nearby streams and is placed on a structure called "Balijatra" or sand house.[56] The festival is ceremoniously inaugurated on the specific day by the Jani/Disari (the priest) by putting an auspicious pillar on the ground over which a special house is constructed of split bamboo frame in the village. Usually, this work is carried out while beating and playing of musical drums such as *baida, baja, mahuri,* etc. This small hut is called *Sitagudi*. The huts are probably named after Mother Sita who was also the daughter of Mother Earth.[57] Collecting the sands from the river or streambeds and reciting the mantras, the Jani/Disari keeps the sands in a special bamboo basket on the heads of the *dhangiris* or *bajunis,* who carry it out to *Sitagudi.* Here Jani/Disari makes an image of the Mother Earth in human form from this sand looking almost like a sand house. Some sand baskets are also kept in front. Then the Jani/Disari performs rituals through sacrifices of a hen, a goat and mahua wine to satisfy Mother Earth for making the land fertile. Seeds of various kinds of cereals and paddy, such as rice, corn, Bengal gram, *Kandula, simba, alasi,* and *jhuranga,* etc., which are previously collected from all the houses of the village, are buried beneath the sands of the baskets with recitation of mantras after which some water is sprinkled on it. The festival is continued for at least nine days. The *dhangaras* and *dhangiris* involve themselves in frenzied dances exchanging their feelings and emotions through songs of love in the form of questions and answers in the presence of their seniors. Dancing rhythmically with the beating of musical instruments and holding a peacock train in one hand and the jingle bell on the other, the *dhangaras* (young boys) try to win over the heart of their beloved. Every day some water is sprinkled on the sand basket. Gradually the seeds are germinated. Disari predicts an ample harvest for the year if the seeds are well sprouted. Sometimes the *bajunis* play on swings, the seats of which are studded with sharp nails and also walk or dance on hot fire or live charcoal holding swords in their hands.[58] During this festival young girls dance in a trance and act as medium for the spirit called Debta.[59] Symbolic agricultural work is inaugurated by the Jani/Disari through cultivating the land using the plough and plough-share and sowing the sprouted seeds. The wooden pillar painted with human form representing God Bhima is buried in the ground during the end of the night and the Bali Goddess is bidden farewell with all rituals sincerely performed including the animal sacrifices like hen, pigeon, egg, goat, ram etc. All the village people including young and old, men and women, priests and sorcerers make a grand procession with all sorts of joviality dancing in tune to the beating of musical instruments towards the river immersing the sand basket. Balijatra ends with love-episodes, the results of which are seen after a few days with marriage alliances.[60]

The *Karma* festival or *Karamasani* festival of the tribes like Bhumija, Binjhal, Mundsa, Oraon, Sauri Bhuyan, etc. is a festival of ecstasy and frenzied dances. The Bhumijas make a grand procession to the jungle and cut a branch of the Karma tree, which is carried out by an unmarried male to the village and is planted near the house of Dehury. All the villagers, irrespective of sex and age, eat, drink, dance and sing together for the whole night.[61] The Dehury offers germinated grams, liquor and sacrifices a fowl in propitiation to the deity, who grants the prosperity of the village.[62] On the following day, the same branch of the Karma tree is taken out from the soil and immersed in the river by an unmarried male.[63] The Binjhals also observe Karma festival on the same day and follow almost same rituals like that of the Bhumijas. The difference is that while returning from the forest in a procession, the boys and girls sing amorous songs and dance to the tune of musical instruments, the Karam Devata is worshipped by the

Jhankar (village priest) through offerings of un-boiled rice, milk, sweets and liquor, etc.[64] They worship for good fortune. While the Jhankar narrates the story of Karamasani Katha to the villagers, the young boys and girls keep dancing and singing and beating the drums for two to three days till the immersion of the Karma deity in the river. The Binjhals also celebrate *Badakarma* (big Karma) festival once in every three years. On that day the *Karamasani puja* is observed in the usual manner. The specialty of the Badakarma festival lies in making a dancing trip to five neighbouring villages by the young boys and girls, and staying one night in each village and dancing there. The host villages organise arrangements for their board and lodge for that night.[65] They also remind us of Lokamanya Tilak's organisation of Ganapati festival and Chhatrapati festival of Maharashtra. Mundas and Oraons also observe *Karma* festival for the well-being of the people. Dancing and community feasting are the special attraction of this festival.[66]

The Dussehra festival, a symbolic recognition of 'women potency' is unanimously observed in the month of *Aswina* (September-October) by a number of tribes scattered in different tracts of Orissa. Each tribe offers worship to the female presiding deity of his/her village on this occasion with a specific motive. The Bhujia tribe prays to goddess Sunadei for obtaining ample rain, prosperity to the village and to be free from illness, Hill Kharias veneration for the plough and axe symbolises the recognition services rendered by the two in agricultural produces and on the other, to seek the blessings from the goddess to energize the two strongly so that the harvest would be more fertile. Dussehra for the Bagata tribe is a reminiscence of the early shifting economic activity from cultivation to fishing in which the tribe has once shown its mettle. They also worship a fishing basket and trident on the same day. E. Thurston observes that the trident is probably the fishing spear, which the Bagatas use for catching fish.[67] *Dalkhai* festival is a colourful festival, which is observed by the tribes, especially of Binjhal, Soura, Mirdha, Kisan and Kandha, etc. of Sambalpur, Baragarh, Bolangir etc. With a strong belief in goddess Dalkhai's power and energy, the tribal girls worship hens with firm devotion. The festival starts from the eighth day of the bright fortnight of the month of Aswina (September-October) and continues up to Dussehra. Bhagirathi Nepak believes that the unmarried tribal girls observe *Dalkhai Osha* (fasting) with a hope that their brothers and family members would be blesses with good luck and fortune by the deity.[68] Chitrasen pasayat highlights that *Dalkhi Osha* is meant for bringing happiness, pleasure, good fortune, prosperity and good harvest both to the family members and to the village.[69] The celebration of *Dhalkhai Osha* begins with a procession carried by the jhankar (the priest) and followed by the village people to a jungle where goddess Dalkhi resides on a branch of particular tree. The goddess is offered wine, a black hen or goat by the jhankar on behalf of the village people. On the early morning of the *sukla ashtami* (8th day of the bright fortnight or Mahastami) of Aswina, this ritual is performed after which the young girls sing in chorus and in praise of the goddess and dance gracefully around the sacred tree.[70] Then it is followed by amorous songs and frenzied dances of both young boys and girls representing erotic signs and gestures. The dance continues till late at night with songs and dances and playing of different musical instruments like *dhol, nishani, timki, teas, mahuri,* etc. Dalkhi is an erotic dance of western Orissa which takes its name from "*Dalkhaire*" or "*Dalkhaibo*". Besides, Matipuja of Chuktia Bhunjia, *Punapadi* festival of Dongria Kandha, *Phulbhaguni* of Kol, *Karama* of Kollohar, *Dhana Nuakhai* of Konda Dora, *Sikupandu* of Koya, *Ashtanipuja* of Lodha, *Sarhul* and *Saharai* of Munda, *Dasaen Parab* of Ho, etc. are the tribal festivals celebrated during the month of Aswina.[71] *Matipuja* (Mother Earth worship) is the festival observed for gaining bumper crops throughout the year. The priest of the Chuktia Bhunjia sacrifices ducks, fowls and pigs. *Punapadi* festival is meant for ritual sowing of seeds in the agricultural field, whereas eating new rice is the important function of *Phulbhaguri* festival. Kollohar tribes observe *Karma* festival for the well-being of the people amidst dancing, drinking and enjoying special foods. *Sarhul* and *Saharai* festivals of the Munda tribe are associated with the welfare of the agrarian-cum-pastoral economy. At the *Sarhul* festival, the first reaping of paddy is done by the magico-religious head, whereas *Saharai* is observed by worshipping the cattle and enjoying special foods. The significance of the *Dasaen* festival of the Hos is to perform worship for spiritual teachers. The *Dasaen* parab is celebrated from the first day of the bright fortnight of Aswina till Dussehra. The festival is confined between the spiritual instructor called Dawan, who especially imparts knowledge on mantra and tantra (sorcery and magic) and their disciples whom the teachers can test on this occasion. Usually, the students from around different villages sing the hymns in praise of their teachers and begging rice and vegetables from door to door. This is the right period when the students learn about sorcery from their respective teachers and are also given an opportunity by the latter to prove their mettle.[72]

From among the most important festivals of the month of *Kartika* (October-November), mention may be made on *Vadhna* parab of Bhumija, *Kalipuja* of Birhor, *Bandanapuja* of Lodha, *Saharai* of Mahali, Santal and Bhottoda tribes, and *Maram Banga* of Ho tribes. Both Mahali and Santala perform certain rituals on the day of *Saharai* festival for worshipping their cattle. On the day of *Saharai,* worship is performed with a fowl sacrifice by the Naya (priest) at the outskirt of the village. Before *puja* is performed, all the cattle-wealth is driven towards the very spot where the worship is likely to be held. A strict vigilance is to be kept on the cattle preventing them from eating the *puja* materials failing which the particular cow or bullock is to be caught for a year. In the next year, the owner of the cow or bullock supplies a pot-full of rice beer to the villagers at the time of the same festival.[73] The cows and bullocks are well decorated with flowers and vermilion and tied to the poles in front of the houses. Drunk with wine, singing songs and dancing to the beat of the musical instruments, the young boys visit from door to door and also make the bullocks dance.[74] *Diwali,* for the Bhottoda tribe is also a festival for worshipping cows and bullocks. They offer rice and salt to the cows and are then involved in arranging a grand community feast. 'Eating new rice ritual' is known as *Vadhna Parab* or *Bandana Puja* of the Bhumija and Lodhas respectively.[75] *Maram Banga* festival of Ho tribes is observed once in every 30 years interval. It is a festival to make reminiscence of one's own family history, i.e. their culture, settlement and other activities, which is described by the chief of the householder to other members of the house. The head of the house is to worship the primeval father Lukukula by offering un-boiled rice, incense sticks, raisins, vermilion, and fowls like hens, goats and rams, etc. as sacrifice.[76]

Mage parab of the Ho and Kolha tribes is observed in the month of *Margasira* (November-December) from the 9th day of the bright fortnight to the first day of the dark fortnight of the month of Pausha is considered as a 'festival of sex' and 'festival of wealth'. Songs of ribaldry, frenzied dances, beating of musical instruments like hurdy gurdy (*kendera*), drum, flute, etc. accompanied by the ribald scolding of the gods like *Dasabhali* and *Paunsha Banga,* who were responsible for straining the sacred relationship between brother and sister (Lukukula and Lukukuli, the synonym of Adam and Eve) and for initiating them into the art of love-making respectively are the general characteristics of the festival. It is said that they use colloquial or slang words while scolding so that henceforth the gods will never repeat this sort of activities in future.[77] The spirit of festival represents a linear growth process since the origin of human kind. The Santhal tribes of Mayurbhanj district also celebrate the *Mamane* festival. The specialty of the festival lies in the fact that the tribes sacrifice fowl and wine to the village deity (gramadevati) to obtain blessings from her and these offerings are not to be consumed by women folk.[78] Besides, *Bandhana* or *Kalipuja* is observed by them. Community feasting and merrymaking are the traditional features of the *Anakakera* or *Lau* festival of the Kandhas of Koraput, who also celebrate it with much pleasure in the month of *Margasira*. Following the tradition, they plaster their houses with cow dung after which they collect, rice, paisa/money from each house of the village on the same day. Then they purchase wine and hens and go to the Jhankiri Devi's place with the jani with wine, hens and the first newly produced gourd of the village for worshipping her. In the meantime, the villagers prepare containers out of dried gourd though scraping inside and throw away the old ones. This is the occasion on which day the new gourd container is first used as per the tradition, which is to be used for preserving the gruel is seen to be worshipped by the Kandhas with offering of incese sticks, lamps, etc and sacrifices of the fowls. They pray to goddess Jhankiri Devi to make their gourd-container filled to the brim throughout the year.[79] Then all the village people irrespective of sex and age eat together enjoying rice, wine and meat, etc.[80]

Kandul Parab or *Meria Parab* is one of the important festivals, which is observed by the Sabara, Kandha and other tribes of Koraput district according to the beliefs of the respective tribes. Sometimes it is told as new *Kandula* eating ceremony. *Kandula* is one type of cereals harvested during the month of Margasira. The *Kandula Parab* serves as a medium of uniting and integrating the entire Sabara tribes into an integral whole with the feeling of belongingness to each other. After reaping the *Kandula,* it is first offered to their deity Tangima. Usually, all the tribes including young and old, wear new clothes on this occasion and celebrate it for a long period without doing any work.[81] The Kandhas of Koraput are seen following a number of rites and rituals prior to seven or eight days of the observance of the *Kandula* festival. On the scheduled day, collecting new *Kandula* from all the houses of the village, the Jani comes to Jhankiri Devi's place where he ignites the fire to observe the auspicious moment and then starts to fry the *kandula* in another pot.[82] This fire is considered as sacred fire. After the end of the celebration, the Jani offers an earthen pot full with fired charcoal to all the village people for frying *kandula* in their respective houses.

The Kandhas believe that a number of untold miseries affecting the community's economy as a whole in the form of the loss of cattle and livestock wealth will be inflicted on them if the *kandula* is fried before the celebration of *Kandula Parab*. Several references are also obtained indicating imposition of 'money-fine' on a man who violates the tradition.[83] *Siku Pandu* is the festival of the Koyas, which they observe in the month of *Kartika/Margasira* for eating new beans.[84]

Pausa Punia or *Puspunei* or *Pusa Parab* or *Pus Purnima* is a grand festival observed in the month of *Pausa* (December-January) by Bhottoda, Binjhal, Bondo, Dal, Gadaba, Kisan, Kora, Omanatya, Parenga Paroja and Pentia tribes of Orissa. *Pus Punia* for the Bhottoda tribe is a festival of pleasure, merrymaking and enjoyment. Both males and females participate in performing the *Cherechera* dance in separate groups during this festival.

They move their bodies very briskly and in a lively manner.[85] Parenga's *Pusa Punei* is related to the growth of cattle-wealth for which they wash and anoint their cattle with turmeric paste and offer them appetising food. Besides, a grand feast is arranged for all the village people.[86]

Celebration of the harvest of paddy and other crops finds expression in observance of Paroja's *Pus Parab* with performance of *Dhemsa Nach, Dandunga Nach* and *Laga Gita* (dances and songs).[87] *Podha Parab* or *Jhankiri Puja* is one of the important festivals of the Kandhas of Orissa. It starts from the first Magha. Symbolically consecrating two of the wood-logs of a Mahula tree as goddess Jhankiri Devi, the Jani inaugurates the *Podua Parab* on the first Tuesday of the month of *Pausha,* which continues till the end of the month of Magha. On the last week of the month of Magha, the Jani selects one auspicious moment for *Podhabali* (buffalo-sacrifice) after which the Jani cooks rice and meat of the sacrificed *Podha* in two of the big earthen pots and then all the village people sit down to relish it in a group.[88] On the day of dark fortnight, the Ho and Kolhas observe the *Balabaji* festival by worshipping the goddess Badam for obtaining her blessing to get rid of the diseases and the natural calamities. All the torn winnowing fans, bamboo baskets and small palm leaf baskets are thrown in a place outside the village by the tribes on the day of observation.[89] The month of Magha welcomes *Magha Parab, Bimud Pandu, Makara, Magha Tiar, Magh Sim, Ma-Mane, Ba-a-Parab, Surya Jatra,* etc. *Surya Jatra* of Bhottoda is celebrated amidst dance and music. *Magha Parab* of the Binjhals is observed with the offerings of sweets, fruits and sacrifices of fowls like hens and goats to Dangar Devata.[90] *Magh Pudi* is a festival of the Kolhas which is celebrated in the month of Magha after the harvesting is over.[91] The cultural programme of high order celebrated by the Kolha tribes on the occasion of *Ba-a-Parab,* is observed on the full moon night of the month of Magha, which enriches the historicity of the Kolha tribes from generation to generation. The theme of the myth seems to be related to Fakir Mohan Senapati's short story 'Patent Medicine', which tells the wife's revolutionary step taken against her husband for negligence of duty due to addiction. The Ho myth describes how Lukukuli went berserk kicking Lukukula on the foot to make him come to his senses when the latter paid little heed to the appeal of the former against his irrational behaviour due to indulgence in drug and liquor. The youths of Kolha and Ho tribes even today welcome the kick on the feet of the young girls while singing and dancing together during the festival. The young boys sing :

Bale bale Te-e-Khanja/ Te-e-Ganja da dayaga dabire
Kulu sunja karu sanja da / Lipira Kuamre
Nalre Hiating Tanja/ Surajam Baa Mulikatare
Nalrem Chakating Tanja/ Sule sagen tule talare//

[Translation: If you want to keep your feet, please keep them on my back. If you want to kick, please kick on my chest without any hesitation. He! Baula flower, today is Ba-a-parab. Make it pleasurable by touching your feet.][92]

Ma-Mane is a festival of the Mahali tribes, which is observed from the month of Kartika to the last day of Magha. The festival is related to agricultural operations. Before the harvesting of paddy in the month of Kartika (October-November), the Nyaya (priest) performs the puja in *jahirstan* (place meant for worship), which is followed by communal dancing and singing.[93] On the last day of the month of Magha, a puja is performed by the Nyaya on the outskirts of the village before collecting jungle products such as fruits, leaves, wood and wild grass for their use in building houses.[94] Santal's *Magh-Sim* marks the end of the year. Koya's *Bimud Pandu* is a really interesting one. Probably, the Koyas observe this festival in the month of Magha to express their gratitude and honour to the Rain God, whose unflinching support makes them blessed with a plentiful harvest of all types of corns. Making two small models of the rain god and his wife, the Koyas place it under a Mahul tree over a stone-slab on the festival day. All the village people with priest and headman gather on the spot carrying crops of all kinds. Ritualistic worship is then followed in which the priest fills the empty basket with the crops. All other empty baskets lying there are also filled by the headman of the villagers. An unmarried girl is made to stand between the Nayak and the priest. The villagers throw water over them and laugh saying the marriage of the rain god is over today (*Gajje Bimud nend Terta*)[95]. Dance, music, song and beating of musical drums follow. The Bhumijs celebrate the *Makara* festival on the first day of Magha only to entertain themselves through performances of dances, songs, music and organising feasts without observing any worship.[96] The Kolis worship *Thakurani,* the village deity and the kitchen God, *Ishta Devata* or *Isana* on the day of *Makara Samkranti* without the aid of the priest.[97] *Samkrat or Makara Samkranti* for the Mahali tribe is a festival meant for the worship of ancestral spirits. It is officiated by the village priest to whom every household offers food and other sacrifices to spirits. [98] Music and dance is also an important performances of the celebration.

The *Patakhanda Jatra* of the Bondos of Mudulipada of Koraput is celebrated in the month of Magha. It is a festival of par excellence inviting the attention of many people of the nearby regions to enjoy it in the month of Magha. Following the age-long tradition, the Bondos worship every year the iron made sword, which is placed between the two branches of a banyan tree of a three-feet height long. With a traditional belief, the Bondos worship the sword, which was given to their ancestor for protection and to get rid of all kinds of evils. The village Disari (priest) is present, who can predict the auspicious moment for wielding the sword from the branches to the ground for worship. All the village people, the Bondo Raja (king) and the Disari gather here to celebrate the festival with pomp and pleasure. The worship is performed with rites and rituals followed by animal sacrifice, music, song and dance throughout the night.[99] Observing the huge gathering, in *Patakhanda Jatra,* Rama Chandra Sathpathy concludes with the opinion that the visit to *Sitakund* (the bath tub of goddess Sita) is another attraction of the people.[100]

Phaguna/ Phalguna (February-March) is welcomed to the earth with the sweet melody of the cuckoos, mild breeze, the pleasant cold, the blooming flowers and above all, the amazing conditions making the minds of the tribes dance with joy celebrating certain festivals. *Mahul Kuchi* is a festival of the Dal tribes, who worship the ancestral spirits appeasing them with Mahua liquor and a cock and performing dance and music in groups.[101] The *Baha* festival is also observed by the Mahali and Santala tribes by worshipping the village deities in the village *Pirha* for the general welfare of the zyoung boys and girls throughout the night, is the special attraction of this festival. The Oraons celebrate *Phagu Parab* in the month of Magha to mark the end of the year and the beginning of the new year. The *Pulda Parab/ Baa Parab* is another festival observed by the Mundas in the month of *Phalguna/Chaitra.* On the day of the celebration, the priest offers fruits and jungle products to the village deity and other associated gods and goddess (Bangas). Unless and until the offerings are made, no one can take the fruits and flowers for use. The Munda houses are decorated with flowers and sal leaves during this period. Besides, they draw the picture of the sal tree on their walls with flowers and fruits, which they believe is a symbol to happiness and prosperity. Mostly, black, red, white and yellow colours are used for drawing the pictures. To draw the pictures, one has to take a bath in the morning and to fast till the drawings are completed.

Free from complexities of the social forces, the simple tribes never bother to think whether "man eats to live or man lives to eat". Born with a pastoral-cum-agrocentric economy, the tribes celebrate festivals to perform worship starting from the early phase to all the growing and sub-growing phases till the maturity of the agricultural harvest in honour of Mother Earth and the Rain God.

The association of cattle wealth and agricultural tools with agricultural operation further leads the tribes to worship them with pomp and valour. As the prosperity of agricultural and pastoral economy completely depends on the population growth, so the tribes follow a cult of ancestral worship. Probably, the Rigvedic Aryans worship God for material prosperity that is *praja* (subjects), *pasu* (cattle), and *sampada* (wealth) was a synthetic cult of socio-religious rites.

REFERENCES

1. Henry Lucas, *A Short History of Civilisation,* McGraw Hill Book Company Inc., New York and London, 1st edition, 1943, p. 1.
2. Ibid., p. 88
3. Ibid.
4. Tina Otten, "Changing Annual Festival Chaitra Parab: An Outsider's Overview" *Adivasi,* Journal of Schedule Caste and Schedule Tribe Research and Training Insitute, 1992, pp. 82-91.
5. Ibid.
6. Bhagirathi Nepak, *Tribal Festivals of Orissa,* Bhagirathi Prakashan, Bhubaneswar, 1st Edition, 2004, pp. 27-8.
7. Ibid., p. 26; Braja Mohan Mohanty (Ed.), "Odissara Anchalika Parab Parbani Osha-Brata Jani Jatra (Uttarardha)" (or), Utkal Pathak Sansad, Orissa Book Store, Cuttack, 1995, 1st ed. p. 90.
8. B. Nepak, op.cit., p. 26.
9. B.M. Mohanty, op.cit., p. 90.
10. Ibid., p. 89.
11. Mahendra Kumar Misra, *Kalahandi Loka Samskriti* (KLS) (Oriya), Benod Behari, Cuttack, 1996, p. 84.
12. Ibid.
13. Ibid., p. 85.
14. Ibid, Nepak, op.cit., p. 23.
15. *Konark, A Quarterly Literary Journal,* Vol. 121, Orissa Sahitya Academy, Bhubaneswar, 2001, p. 24.
16. B. Nepak, op.cit., p. 24.
17. *Konark,* op.cit., p. 25.
18. Ibid.
19. *Tribes of Orissa,* Harijan and Tribal Welfare Department (HTWD), Government of Orissa, Bhubaneswar, 1990, p. 158.
20. Nandita Misra, Transformation of Habitat and Shelter-Enviroment of Tribal Village in Mayurbhanj District of Orissa, Unpublished Ph.D. Thesis in Geography, Utkal University, Bhubaneswar, 1982, pp. 237-8.
21. B.M. Mohanty, op.cit., p. 164.
22. Ibid., p. 165.
23. Ibid., pp. 92-3; *Konark,* op.cit., p. 27.
24. M.K. Misra, op.cit., pp. 58-88.
25. *The Tribes of Orissa,* Schedule Caste and Schedule Tribe Research Training Instiute (SC & ST), 2004, p. 8.
26. Ibid., p. 10.
27. *Adivasi,* HTWD, Bhubaneswar, 1994, p. 180.
28. Ibid.
29. *Tribes of Orissa,* SC & ST, Bhubaneswar, pp. 8-14. Nepak, op.cit. p. 62.
30. Ibid., HTWD, 1990, p. 102.
31. Ibid., p. 60.
32. Ibid., SC & ST, p. 11.
33. Ibid., p. 188

34. B.M. Mohanty, op.cit., p. 150.
35. *Tribes of Orissa,* HTWD, p. 60.
36. Ibid., p. 215.
37. *Konark,* op.cit., p. 28
38. Ibid.
39. *Tribes of Orissa,* HTWD, p. 60.
40. Ibid., p. 88.
41. Ibid.
42. *Konark,* op.cit., p. 28.
43. Ibid.
44. Lata Bol (ed.), *Ho Parampara O Jnana Kaushala* (Oriya), Adivasi Bhasa O Samskriti Academy, Anuschita Janajati O Jati Unnayan Bibhaga, Bhubaneswar, pp. 49-50.
45. *Tribes of Orissa,* HTWD, pp. 39, 43, 93, 151, 174.
46. Ibid., p. 151.
47. B.M. Mohanty (ed.), op.cit., p. 151; B. Nepak, op.cit., p. 21.
48. *Tribes of Orissa,* HTWD, p. 93.
49. Ibid., p. 174.
50. *Konark,* op.cit., p. 28.
51. Ibid., pp. 28-29; *Tribes of Orissa,* HTWD, pp. 93, 233; B.M. Mohanty, op.cit., p. 151.
52. *Tribes of Orissa,* SC & ST, p. 11.
53. Ibid., p. 13.
54. Lata Bol, op.cit., p. 54.
55. *Tribes of Orissa,* HTWD, p. 43.
56. B. Nepak, op.cit., p. 69.
57. "Krushi O Premara Parab", *The Samaja* (Oriya daily newspaper) dated June 6, 2006. p. gha.
58. Ibid.
59. *Tribes of Orissa,* HTWD, p. 54.
60. B. Nepak, op.cit., dated June 06, 2006.
61. *Tribes of Orissa,* HTWD, p. 60.
62. Ibid., B. Nepak, op.cit, pp. 15-6.
63. Ibid.,
64. Ibid., 73.
65. Ibid., B. Nepak, op.cit., p. 21.
66. Ibid., SC & ST, p. 14.
67. Ibid., HTWD, p. 34.
68. B. Nepak, op.cit.
69. *Konark,* op.cit., p. 11.
70. B. Nepak, op.cit., p. 29.
71. *Tribes of Orissa,* SC & ST, pp. 8-15.
72. Lata Bol, op.cit., p. 55.
73. *Tribes of Orissa,* HTWD, p. 200.
74. Ibid.,
75. Ibid., pp. 11-2, 43.
76. Lata Bol, op.cit., p. 55.

77. Ibid., p. 54.
78. *Konark*, op.cit., p. 32.
79. Ibid., p. 33.
80. Ibid.
81. Ibid.
82. Ibid.
83. Ibid., p. 34.
84. *Adivasi*, HTWD, p.180.
85. Ibid., p. 43.
86. Ibid., p. 220.
87. Ibid., p. 229.
88. *Konark*, op.cit., p. 34.
89. Lata Bol, op.cit., p. 56.
90. *Tribes of Orissa*, HTWD, p. 72.
91. Ibid., p. 158.
92. Lata Bol, op.cit., pp. 47-48.
93. *Tribes of Orissa*, HTWD, p. 200.
94. Ibid., p. 180.
95. Ibid.
96. Ibid., p. 60.
97. Ibid., p. 163.
98. Ibid., p. 200.
99. B.M. Mohanty, op.cit., p. 92.
100. Ibid., pp. 92-93.
101. *Tribes of Orissa*, HTWD, p. 93.
102. Ibid., p. 200.
103. Ibid., p. 225.
104. *Adivasi*, SC & ST, p. 46.
105. Ibid., p. 53.

26

Gandhi and Integral Nationalism: Ethics, Economy, Environment

Chittabrat Palit

Introduction

Integral nationalism is not merely a freedom struggle to end colonial rule. It also has a constructive side of 'nation building' efforts. The country has to be ready to take over the reins of government from the colonial masters after independence. This requires considerable homework and will to work for national reconstruction. Gandhi had both aspects happily blended in his unique style of freedom struggle. His *satyagraha* or doctrine of non-violence was the technique of agitation for an unarmed nation against military persecution. This he introduced and perfected in the struggle against apartheid in South Africa. He brought this experience to bear upon the Indian freedom struggle.

But this struggle did not end in achieving freedom. He also believed in constructive Swadeshi. His prescription of Charkha was a symbol to empower the poorest among Indians, particularly women. On the other hand, he advised the big bourgeoisie to act as trustees of the people to promote their welfare. This was a moral appeal to big business to solve all labour disputes peacefully.

Gandhi had a deep concern for the environment and its pollution. For him, it was plain living and high thinking in a serene eco-friendly ambience. He was inspired by the Indian maxim to give up in order to enjoy.

All these thoughts are enshrined in his day-to-day work. In the next sections his thoughts will be presented in his own sayings.

Ethics

In his autobiography Gandhiji says that he did not belong to any particular religion. He has an ethical God. Truth was for him the goal. All his life he made various experiments with truth. He sought truth in politics, in economics and in environment.

Gandhiji spent twenty-one years of his life in South Africa as a lawyer and political leader of the Indian immigrants who brought him from India and hired him to fight a legal battle for their right of citizenship. During this long tenure, he developed his concept and practice of Satyagraha. This has been understood by many as non-cooperation with the oppressive authorities. But to Gandhiji it was a positive concept of attainment of truth; non-cooperation was only a step to achieve that. In the course of his court cases to establish the right to citizenship of Indian immigrants, he found that the laws were such that this could never be established without a political struggle. But how could a disarmed people fight against the armed authorities who had deliberately designed the laws in an exclusive racist spirit? Obviously some other tangible method had to be adopted to vindicate human rights.

Gandhiji's *satyagraha* had for its goal the establishment of truth in the end. His method was to make a case study of the issue on the spot. He studied both sides of the case with reference to existing unequal laws. He was convinced that the authorities were guilty of the denial of justice. His next course of action was to petition the government for redress of the grievance and to ascertain government's attitude to the question. Truth could only be established by hearing both sides and weighing the evidence. When the government's attitude proved negative and stubborn, the only course left was to organise *satyagraha*, the non-violent march and demonstration before the authorities, thereby exposing injustice. Such demonstrations would invite repressive measures by the government. But repression could not continue for long. Torture on disarmed people on questionable grounds was of limited application. Even bullets are blunted before moral force. Gandhiji's satyagraha was built on his moral force. It was the weapon of the weak. In South Africa, Gandhiji used it successfully to achieve his aim. He was arrested and sent to jail but released again. The authorities finally consented to meet him and discuss the issue. The immigration laws were finally relaxed and Indian immigrants were admitted to citizenship. Gandhiji had a moral victory. Back in India, he would apply the same principle of Satyagraha to Indian politics.

He began his discovery of India by locating a few storm centres of protest to do his fieldwork. One such area was Champaran in North Bihar. Here a peasant agitation had been going on for a long time against the oppression of indigo planters who had reduced the peasants to bonded labour and forced them to cultivate indigo against their will. In his search for the truth in the matter, Gandhiji chose a Harijan village in which to do social work in order to gain their confidence. He came to know the nature of their grievance, and his sage-like appearance and beneficial activities made him their spokesman. Gandhiji's way of arriving at the truth was to explore the point of view of the adversary which could also contain the same grain of truth. In this case he sought appointments with government officials and planters to elicit their views. On weighing the evidence, he was convinced the planters were the unjustifiable oppressors. Once he found out this truth, he decided to take up the cause of the peasants and asked them not to sow indigo or any other crop dictated by the planter. This is known as the 'Champaran Satyagraha'. It was peaceful but full of moral force. The government had to relent before this non-violent struggle, and persuaded the planters to desist from such oppression. Gandhiji thereby proved that justice could be obtained by non-violent non-cooperation, without bloodshed and violence. The success of his South African experiment was repeated here. This would be followed by other movements such as the Ahmedabad Textile and the 'Kheda Movement'. These proved that moral force can overcome the brute force or the adversary, and truth triumphs in the end.

Economy

Gandhiji's experiments with truth were extended to economic issues as well. His propagation of the charkha (spinning wheel) came out of his experience in rural Champaran. He found village women here in shabby and dirty clothes and held their dirty habits responsible for it. He enquired through his wife why they wore such clothes. They were surprised that Gandhiji being a Mahatma did not know the cause. They were so poor that they could not afford a pair of saris, and they did not have any facility to wash their dirty clothes. Gandhiji shuddered at the thought and as he deeply pondered over the matter, the idea of the charkha came to his mind as the only solution. As they could not afford buying another mill made sari, they could weave one themselves by resorting to the charkha. This would make them self-reliant and if they could weave more, they could sell the extra produce in the market and earn a few rupees. This would lead to overall improvement of their living conditions.

He therefore decided to propagate the message of the charkha wherever he went in his later wanderings among the rural poor. He urged his followers and Congressmen, in particular, to buy homespun cotton from these poor folks so that they could become solvent; 'Buy Khadi' became the new slogan of the Gandhi-led Congress. Giving priority to the charkha over modern industries in search of the indigenous and the pure was not a backward looking idiosyncrasy. It was born out of his experiments with truth and concern for the poor. His contemporaries and posterity have grossly misunderstood him for his penchant for the charkha. Even

Tagore and Nehru did not spare him on this account. They came out with lengthy criticisms of his so-called 'backward economic ideas'. He was not basically against big industries. As is well known, he was very close to Indian business magnates such as Lalbhai Kasturbhai, Purushottamdas Thakurdas, Jamunalal Bajaj, G.D. Birla among others. He implored them to be trustees of the people and solve all labour disputes amicably. He urged them to work for the welfare of the nation as a whole.

Environment

He had a penchant for cleanliness. He befriended the untouchables and called them 'Harijans' (God's People). On one occasion during his tour in rural districts, he remarked that the 'Mehtar' (sweeper) was like a mother. The mother keeps the baby clean and beautiful, the Mehtar keeps the public clean and civilised.

All his life, he struggled for a better deal for this community. His whole idea of rural reconstruction was based on primary education, health care and economic self-reliance, which were most needed by the poor. To him, small was beautiful, and plain living was divine. After meeting the necessities, one should not strive to satisfy unnecessary desires; that breeds unhappiness.

Gandhiji like Tagore was against consumerism and overexploitation of nature. For an enduring civilisation, he thought, a serene environment was desirable. This could only be achieved by limiting wants and rendering service to mankind. In this age of global warming and environment pollution, Gandhiji is becoming increasingly relevant for his message of plain living and high thinking.

Gandhiji's concern with environment began in South Africa where he went to set up his legal practice among the Indian community at the turn of the 20th century. The house in which he lived in Durban was built after the Western model and the rooms had no outlets for dirty water. Each room had chamber pots. Young Mohandas and Kasturba did not engage any sweeper or servant but used to clean them themselves. This was the common practice with the clerks who lived there. Gandhi supervised the work, Mohandas insisted on doing his bedroom. Kasturba fell out but ultimately yielded to his cajoling. Gandhiji writes in his autobiography, "I regarded myself as her teacher and so harassed her out of my blind love for her." He calls it his sacred recollection and penance. This is how he practised cleanliness as godliness and moralised the issue.[1]

This environment pollution and Gandhiji's concern mounted when he became familiar with coolie locations or ghettoes in Johannesburg. The term 'coolie' ordinarily meant a porter in India, but in South Africa it meant a pariah or untouchable. The location was like a labour concentration camp and the coolies were sardine-packed in their hutments. The municipality did not provide for even the minimum sanitary facilities, much less good roads or lights. The bulk of the Indians who went to South Africa were ignorant poor peasants who needed care and protection. " The criminal negligence of the Municipality and ignorance of the Indian settlers made the location thoroughly insanitary," write Gandhiji. This unbearable condition was made the excuse to destroy the location without rehabilitation of the settlers when he arrived in Johannesburg. The location was soon visited by the dreaded black plague. As the location was to be destroyed, all semblance of municipal care was withdrawn. The settlers, as tenants had neglected their hygiene so much that as the number of tenants increased, the squalor and disorder spread accordingly. There was a sudden outbreak of the black plague, more terrible and fatal than the bubonic. It spread from the nearby gold-mine and twenty-one infected Indians returned to the location causing the epidemic. This was Gandhiji's first major experience of health care. With Dr. Godfery by his side, he began the nursing required. To give them their doses of medicine, to attend to their beds clean and tidy and to cheer them up was all that we had to do".[2]

The nightmare was over. The location was gone. Gandhiji moved to his Phoenix Farm to live in communion with nature and launch the journal, the *Indian Opinion.* He writes, "In order to enable everyone of us to make a living by manual labour, we parcelled out the land round the press in pieces of three acres each. One of these fell to my lot. On all these plots we, much against our wish, built houses with corrugated iron. Our desire had been to have mud huts thatched with straw or small brick houses such as would become ordinary peasants." To be closest to good earth, "the idea of having an engine to work the press had not appealed to me. I had thought that hand power would be more in keeping with an atmosphere where agricultural work was also to be done by hand. But as the idea had not appeared feasible, we had installed on oil engine."[3]

Life in the farm was guided by the teachings of Tolstoy and Ruskin. Ruskin's *Unto the Last* remained the gospel of his life ever since he read it on a railway journey from Durban to Johannesburg. He summed up it contents as follows: "1) That the good of the individual is contained in the good of all. 2) That a lawyer's work has the same value as the barber's in as much as all have the same right of earning their livelihood from their work. 3) That a life of labour, i.e. the life of the tiller of the soil and the handicraftsman is the life worth living." This was the substance of his later idea of *Sarvodaya* in harmony with nature.[4]

This brings us to the impact of another book on him, namely *Fend's Return to Nature* which contained much of what he called earth and water treatment. Gandhiji picked up his idea of prescribing fresh fruit and nuts as the natural diet of man from this work. He writes approvingly in his autobiography, " I did not at once take to the exclusive fruit diet but immediately began experiments in earth treatment and with wonderful results. The treatment consisted in applying to the abdomen a bandage of clean earth moistened with cold water and spread like a poultice on fine linen. This I applied at bedtime removing it during the night or in the morning whenever I happened to wake up. It provided a radical cure. Since then, I had tried the treatment on myself and my friends and never had reason to regret it." He remained a staunch advocate of naturopathy since then. He states his conviction in no uncertain terms: "Though I have had two serious illnesses in my life, I believe that man has little need to drug himself. Nine hundred and ninety-nine cases out of a thousand can be brought round by means of well-regulated diet, water and earth treatment and similar household remedies. He who runs to the doctor, *Vaidya* or *Hakim* for every little ailment and swallows all kinds of vegetable and mineral drugs not only curtails his life, but by becoming the slave of his body instead of remaining its master loses self-control and ceases to be a man."[5] Though this was written back in India, the idea had originated in the African surroundings. Dietetics became his agenda for natural health care in which fasting occupied a central place. This is how he narrates his experiment in naturopathy: "I began to take an exclusive fruit diet or to fast on the Ekadasi[eleventh day of the lunar fortnight] day and also to observe Janmashtami[birthday of Lord Krishna] and similar holidays. I began with a fruit diet but from the standpoint of restraint, I did not find much to choose between a fruit diet of food grains. I, therefore, came to attach greater importance to fasting or having only one meal a day on holidays. And if there was some occasion for penance or the like, I gladly utilised it too for the purpose of fasting. But I also saw that the body now being drained more effectively, the food yielded greater relish and the appetite grew keener. It dawned upon me that fasting could be made as powerful a weapon of indulgence as of restraint." Gandhiji made experiments with fasting as a means of physical fitness and moral fervour at the Tolstoy farm along with his friend Kallenbach from whom he learnt it first. He writes in his autobiography: "When I started on this experiment, the Hindu month of Sharvan and the Islamic month of Ramzan happened to coincide. During this month, therefore, I persuaded the Muslim youngsters to observe the Ramzan fast. I had of course decided to observe *Pradosa* myself but I now asked the Hindu, Parsi and Christian youngsters to join me. I explained to them that it was always a good thing to join with others in any matter of self-denial. The result of these experiments was that all were convinced of the value of fasting and a splendid *esprit de corps* grew up among them".

Here at the Tolstoy Farm, "We were all vegetarians", writes Gandhiji, "thanks, I most gratefully confess, to the readiness of all to respect my feelings. The Muslim youngsters must have missed their meat during Ramzan but none of them ever let me know that they did so. They delighted in and relished the vegetarian diet and the Hindu youngsters often prepared vegetarian delicacies for them in keeping with the simplicity of the Farm. Thus an atmosphere of self-restraint naturally sprang up on the Farm". All these experiments created the ambience for curbing animal passion, learning self-restraint and drawing sustenance from the joys of a simple community life close to nature. It also created what he later called the mental environment for service to humanity.

His experiments with life in South Africa gradually led him to theorise his convictions, and its best exposition is in *Hind Swaraj,* written in 1909. Gandhiji led the life of modern environmentalist in this work. "Formerly men worked in the open air only as much as they liked. Now thousands of workmen meet together and for the sake of maintenance work in factories or mines. Their condition is worse than that of the beasts. They are obliged to work at the risk of their lives at the most dangerous occupations for the sake of millionaires. There are now diseases of which people never dreamt before and an army of doctors is engaged in finding out their cures and so hospitals have increased". Condemning the materialistic civilisation of the West, Gandhiji further writes: "Civilisation seeks to increase bodily comforts and it fails miserably even in doing so. This civilisation is irreligious and it has taken such a hold on the people in Europe that those who are in it appear to be half-mad."[6]

Commenting on the destructive side of the railways, Gandhiji avers: "It must be manifest to you that but for the railways, the English would not have such a hold on India as they have. The railways too have spread the bubonic plague. Without them, the masses could not move from place to place. They are the carriers of plague germs. Formerly we had natural segregation. Railways have also increased the frequency of famines because owing to the facility of means of locomotion, people sell out their grain and it is sent to the dearest markets. The holy places have become unholy. Formerly people went to these places with very great difficulty. Generally, therefore, only the real devotees visited such places. Nowadays, rogues visit them in order to practise their roguery."

Gandhiji was votary of nature cure. He is unsparing in his criticism of practitioners of Western medicine: "Hospitals are institutions for propagating sin. Men take less care of their bodies and immorality increases. European doctors are the worst of all. For the sake of a mistaken case of the human body, they kill annually thousands of animals. They practise vivisection. No religion sanctions this. Most of their medical preparations contain either animal fat or spirituous liquors. To study European medicine is to deepen our slavery. Doctors make a show of their knowledge and charge exorbitant fees. Their preparations, which are intrinsically worth a few pence, cost shillings."

That is not Gandhiji's obscurantism. The noted demographer Mckeown in his work makes the same observations.[7] The passage above also reflects his concern for the cruelty to animals which would later form his anti-cow slaughter plank back in India.

Resuming the critique to Western civilisation, Gandhiji goes on: "We have had no system of life-corroding competition. Each followed his own occupation or trade and charged a regulation wage. It was not that we did not know how to invent machines but our forefathers knew that if we set our hearts after such things, we would become slaves and lose our moral fibre. They, therefore, after due deliberations decided that we should only do what we could with our hands and feet. They saw that our real happiness and health consisted in a proper use of our hands and feet. They further reasoned that large cities were a snare and a useless encumbrance and that people would not be happy in them, that there would be gangs of thieves and robbers, prostitution and vice flourishing in them and that poor men would be robbed by rich men. They were, therefore, satisfied with small villages."[8]

This environmentalist manifesto brings Indian handicrafts on its agendas: "When I read Mr. Dutt's *Economic History of India,* I wept; and as I think of it again, my heart sickens. It is machinery that has impoverished India. It is difficult to measure the harm that Manchester that Indian handicraft has all but disappeared. Machinery has begun to desolate Europe. Ruination is now knocking at the English gates. It represents a great sin." Turning to Indian mills and their owners, Gandhiji laments: "The workers in the mills of Bombay have become slaves. The condition of the women working in the mills is shocking. When there were no mills, these women were not starving. If the machinery craze grows in our country, it will become an unhappy land. We cannot condemn mill-owners. We can but pity them. If they are good, they would gradually contract their business. They can establish in thousands of households the ancient and sacred handlooms and they can buy out the cloth that may be thus woven. Machinery is like a snake hole which may contain from one to a hundred snakes."

This is the rudimentary stage of his thoughts on Khadi as a solution for Indian poverty and pollution together. The African exile was over while the world was gripped by the Great War (1914-18), and for Gandhiji, it was an uproarious return of the native aided by stalwarts like Gokhale. Gandhiji was accepted into the Congress as its messiah and he began his field discovery of India by identifying storm centres for newer experiments in political and social reconstruction.

His supreme concern was for *Khadi* even beyond *satyagraha* for freedom, which was a passing phase in his whole career of service to humanity. It all began at Champaran as he writes himself: "Sanitation was a difficult affair. The people were not prepared to do anything themselves. Even the field labourers were not ready to do their own scavenging. But Dr. Dev was not a man easily to lose heart. He and the volunteers concentrated their energies on making a village ideally clean. They swept the roads and the courtyards, cleaned out the wells, filled up the pools nearby and lovingly persuaded the villages, they shamed people into taking up the work, and in others the people were so enthusiastic that they even prepared roads to enable my car to go from place to place. It may be out of place here to narrate an experience that I have described before now at my meetings. Bhitiharva was a small village in which was one of our schools. I happened to visit a smaller village in its vicinity and found some of the women dressed very dirtily. So I told my wife to ask them why they did not wash their clothes. She spoke to them. One of the women took her into her hut and said. 'Look now; there is no box or cupboard here containing other clothes. The sari I am wearing is the only one I have. How am I to wash it? Tell Mahatmaji to get me another sari and I shall then promise to bathe and put on clean clothes every day.' Gandhiji observes: "This cottage was not an exception but a type to be found in many Indian villages. In countless cottages in India, people live without any furniture and without a change of clothes, merely with a rag to cover their same."[9]

In search of a cover for every cottage, Gandhiji turned to the cottage industry of *Khadi* which used to serve this purpose of self-employment and self-robing even when afflicted with poverty before the onset of mill made cloth and ruin of handicrafts. Gandhiji calls *Khadi* sacred from this ethical point of view, and not due to any obscurantist belief. His deepest concern was for women who were unemployed but were too poor to buy their own pair of saris. But the two hands once engaged in spinning could not only end their poverty and shame, but could also make the *Charkha* a pollution-free wheel of progress.

Gandhiji says that in *Hind Swaraj,* he described it as the panacea for the growing pauperism of India. In that book, he took it as understood that "anything that helped India to get rid of the grinding poverty of her masses would in the same process also establish *Swaraj.*"[10]

He had nothing against the mills. "Our mills will not be in want of customers for a long time to come. My work should be and therefore is to organise the production of homespun clothes and to find means of the disposal of the *Khadi* thus produced. I swear by this form of Swadeshi because through it I can provide work to the semi-starved, semi-employed women of India. My idea is to get these women to spin yarn and to clothe the people of India with *Khadi* woven out of it.

Gandhiji was not going a backward alternative to modern industries, as G.D. Birla wrongly understood him and Nehru shunned it in favour of heavy industries. The two programmes were on two different plans, and did not cut across each other. That Gandhiji was not totally opposed to textile mills is evident from his role of a mediator in the Ahmedabad Textile Mill Strike. He was on the best of terms with Ambala Sarabhai, Jamunalal Bajaj and G.D. Birla, and wanted them to be trustees of the people. He clarified: "Do I seek to destroy the mill industry? I have often been asked. If I did, I should not have pressed for the abolition of the excise duty. I want the mill industry to prosper- only I do not want it to prosper at the expense of the country."[11] But basically he was against gigantic industries and opened for cottage industries in his mission for *Sarvodaya.*

He never tired of highlighting *Khadi* as the sacred thread "because it removes poverty and we cannot put the teaching of the Vedas before a famished man. If you want to preserve your villages, you should accept Khadi." He went to Sonepur to collect ornaments for promotion of *Khadi* from rich women. This was his language of appeal: "Think of Sita. Do you imagine she went about with Rama in his 14 years' forest wanderings with heavy ornaments like yours? Do you think they add to your beauty? Sita cared for the beauty of her heart and covered her body with pure Khaddar. The heavy ornaments you wear are not only ugly but harmful in as much as they are the permanent receptacles of dirt. Free yourselves of these shackles and relieve the poverty of the people who have no clothes, much less ornaments to wear. Every yard of Khaddar you purchase means a few coppers in the hands of these women. A few coppers and not more. But it means a few coppers where none was earned before."[12]

The idea of *sarvodaya* including sanitation is also replete in the following exhortation: "You can never integrate the poor of India with yourselves without the spinning wheel. The common man in India is starving for want of an occupation. Our seven hundred thousand villages have no work on hand. That is why I maintain I am not going to give up the wheel even if you all do so. If you wear one yard of *Khadi,* put six annas since they fly to foreign lands. Ask yourselves why thousands of women flock to me. They crowed around me, as they know I am their humble servant. And think of the plight of the poor woman of your province. She has not even a spare sari to change after her bath."[13] It is *Sarvodaya,* it is women's cause, health and hygiene–all rolled into one. He was fighting against the collapse of the Indian village as the hub of our traditional culture, of the ashram without recompense.

On a visit to Abhay Ashram in Barisal, he aptly remarked: "The Ashram is rightly called so as you find there all signs of an Ashram life–simplicity, poverty, spinning and morning and evening prayers." This was his beautiful ideal pitted against the materialistic civilisation of the West towards which the world is getting oriented today in the context of global tension and pollution.[14]

Now we turn to his crusade for the untouchable, which was inspired by both his humanism, and concern for sanitation. During his visit to a Namasudra school in Bengal district, Gandhiji said: "I am very happy to be here. I am confident the blot of untouchability is being erased. All life is one. It is the Hindu Dharma to give up regarding the so-called 'untouchables' as untouchables. Indian villages suffer from horrible insanitation. We must keep our water supply pure. Not attending to sanitation makes our bodies impure. Mental sanitation too is necessary and in order to keep our minds pure, we must keep them engaged in some healthy activity."[15]

This was the norm in Sabarmati Ashram. Gandhiji writes: "In the very beginning, we proclaimed to the world that the Ashram would not countenance untouchability. Those who wanted to help the Ashram would not countenance untouchability. Those who wanted to help the Ashram were thus put on their guard and the work of the Ashram in this direction was considerably simplified. The fact that it is mostly the real orthodox Hindus who have met the daily growing expenses of the Ashram is perhaps a clear indication that untouchability is shaken of its foundation. There are needed many other proofs of this but the fact that good Hindus do not scruple to help an Ashram where we go to the length of dining with the untouchables is no small proof."[16] During his stay in Santiniketan, he taught the principle of self-help to the boys of the Ashram by organising teamwork. The paid cooks of the kitchen were dispensed with. Gandhiji approvingly writes: "A person began to wear away his body in making the experiment a success. A batch was formed to cut vegetables, another to clean the grains and so on. Nagenbabu and others undertook to see the sanitary cleaning of the kitchen and its surroundings. It was a delight to me to see them working spade in hand."[17] The Phoenix experiment was repeated in the Kumbha Mela. Gandhiji narrates it thus: "Our stay in Santiniketan had taught us that the scavenger's work would be our special function in India. Now for the volunteers in Hardwar, tents had been pitched in a dharamshala and Dr. Dev had dug some pits to be used as latrines. He had to depend on paid scavengers for looking after these. Here was work for the Phoenix party. We offered to cover up the excreta with earth and see to their disposal, and Dr. Dev gladly accepted our offer."[18]

As a sequel to this, he could say, "I am a non-Brahmin by birth and have become a sweeper by action. It is no calamity to be a sweeper. One can become a Bhangi in two ways: somebody may call me a Bhangi by way of an abuse as if a sweeper is a burden to society, though he does the very useful work of cleaning latrines and sweeping streets. Or one may call that man a bhangi whose service of the people reaches its acme. The Bhangi's service is like that of our mother's, but we never call them untouchables. Far from it, the mother is revered as a goddess worth remembering during our morning prayers. The Bhangi, therefore, is a true servant of society. Just as we cannot live without mothers, so we cannot live without sweepers. That means that by their work they do only their duty to society. But to untouchables themselves I say another thing. You eat putrid flesh, become drunkards, commit adultery and keep yourselves dirty. Do away with these serious defects."[19]

In another context, Gandhiji confirms: "They are not untouchables. Let them have every kindness. I saw two villages. Had I not been told that untouchables lived there, I would not have believed. I saw no difference between them and us. They live like us, have the same feelings as me. If the sum total of our virtues and vices and privileges were taken, I am sure in God's book we should find our debit side greater and credit side less than theirs."[20] This is what he meant by mental and physical sanitation working together. This last stance is more explicit in the following: "It (Gita) says that the Bhangi is entitled to as much service by you as the Brahmin. If a Brahmin and a Bhangi are both starving, I shall first feed the Bhangi and then the Brahmin. That is really what Hindu culture teaches. If we do not purify the untouchables, i.e. we do not purify ourselves, what else do we have to do?"[21] This was his rebuttal of the orthodox purity-pollution paradigm.

Gandhiji's penchant for cow protection can be related to his concern for flora and fauna. In *Hind Swaraj*, he had strongly censured the killing of thousands of animals in the name of guinea pig experiment for drugs. The rule of not killing venomous reptiles had been practised or the most part at phoenis, Tolstoy Farm and Sabarmati. Gandhiji writes: " At each of these places, we had to settle on waste lands. We have had, however, no loss of life occasioned by snakebite. I see with the eye of faith in this circumstance the hand of the God of Mercy. Even if it be a superstition to believe that complete immunity from harm for twenty-five years in spite of a fairly regular practice of non-killing is not a fortuitous accident but a grace of God, I shall still hug that superstition?"[22] The so-called funny story of his switching over to goat's milk has to be interpreted in this light. Gandhiji himself describes the incident: "While I was engaged on the recruiting campaign in Kheda, an error in diet laid me low and I was at death's door. I tried in vain to rebuild a shattered constitution without milk. I might not take cow's or buffalo's milk as I was bound by a vow. The vow, of course, meant giving up of all milk, but as I had mother cow's and mother buffalo's only in mind when I took the vow and I wanted to live, I somehow beguiled myself into emphasising the letter of the vow and decided to take goat's milk. I was fully conscious when I started taking mother goat's milk that the spirit of my vow was destroyed."[23]

This vow was, however, kept in another more lasting form, his crusade for cow protection. This had its origin during his tours in North Bihar. Gandhiji narrates: "I had seen in the course of my travels that cow protection and Hindi propaganda had become the exclusive concern of the Marwaris. A Marwari friend had sheltered me in his dharmashala while at Bettiah. Other Marwaris of the place had interested me in their *goshala* (dairy). My ideas about cow protection had been definitely formed then and my conception of the work was the same as it is today. Cow protection in my opinion included cattle-breeding, improvement of the stock, humane treatment of the bullocks, formation of model dairies, etc. The Marwari friends had promised full cooperation in this work but as I could not fix myself up in Champaran, the scheme could not be carried out. The goshala in Bettiah is still there but it has not gone beyond its capacity and the so-called Hindu still cruelly belabours the poor animal and disgraces his religion."[24] The cruelty to animals pained him more than ill management of animal husbandry. In another context, he bewailed: "Raw hides worth 90 million rupees are exported. There are 1500 *pinjrapoles* (houses for animals) in the country at present and still you are unable to have the slaughter house closed."[25]

In the same context he says, "All the activities—Khadi, removal of untouchability, cow protection—all of them are equal in my eyes. Don't mix up *Shuddhi* and *Sangthan* (activities of conversion to and organisation of Hinduism) with the khadi work of mine. I cannot understand the shuddhi and the tabligh (conversion to Islam) as they are carried on at present. This attempt to make people change their religion is beyond my ken."[26]

Indeed his whole range of activities centred round humanism and natural harmony. Last but not the least is a small incident reported by Louis Fischer. "He did the same with floral garlands thrown around his neck. 'Why kill flowers unnecessarily', he asked, 'when they could garland him with a ring of yarn'. Yarn garlands became an Indian custom."[27] It was an Indian custom of the poor. It was now the raging fashion of the rich and the poor alike.

In the context of global pollution, ecological imbalance and mounting lethal diseases, in other words, the crisis of civilisation, Gandhiji appears to be the prophet of environmentalism with his panacea of naturopathy, vegetarianism, a simple and austere life in fresh air away from sooty factories and concrete jungles in communion with nature with its flora and fauna. One has to breathe into this idyllic setting his deep concern for the dignity of man. This is the alternative he was posing to materialistic civilisation in his *Hind Swaraj* in his younger days. This again makes him the prophet of the 21st century.

NOTES AND REFERENCES

1. M.K. Gandhi, *Indian Home Rule or Hind Swaraj*, 1909 from the *Collected Works of Mahatma Gandhi*, Vol. X, Delhi, 1963, p. 20.
2. Ibid., p. 26.
3. Ibid., p. 36.
4. T. Mckeown, *The Modern Rise of Population*, London (Conclusion), 1976.
5. Gandhi, *Hind Swaraj*, p. 39.
6. Ibid., pp. 57-58.
7. Gandhi, *Autobiography*, pp. 351-5. op.cit.
8. Ibid., p. 407.
9. Ibid.
10. Mahadev Desai, *Day to Day with Gandhi: Secretary's Diary*, Vol. IX from December 21, 1926 to March 19, 1927, Varanasi, 1974. p. 171.
11. Ibid., p. 289.
12. Ibid., p. 106.
13. Ibid., pp. 110-11.
14. Ibid., p. 71.
15. Ibid., p. 72.
16. Gandhi, *Autobiography*, p. 333. op.cit.
17. Ibid., p. 317.
18. Ibid., p. 324.
19. Desai, *Day to Day*, p. 182. op.cit.
20. Ibid., p. 78.
21. Ibid., p. 218.
22. Gandhi, *Autobiography*, p. 358. op.cit.
23. Ibid., p. 226.
24. Ibid., p. 355.
25. Desai, *Day to Day*, p. 212. op.cit.
26. Ibid.
27. Louis Fischer, *The Life of Mahatma Gandhi*, Jonathan Cape, London, 1962, p. 252.

27

India's Relations with South East Asia: A Study of Indo-ASEAN Partnership in Post Cold War Days

Lipi Ghosh

Introduction

In the history of international relations for decades, South East Asia has been the storm centre of fierce contest among the big powers as well as of intra-regional rivalries. There is, perhaps, no country in the world that neglects the region in its foreign policy calculations. Consequently, the region often turns into the chessboard of power games of various powers. Not only the superpowers but also countries like Japan, China and India seek to influence the course of South East Asian international relations each in her own way. This makes it obvious that any study of India's relations with the South East Asian countries has to be made only under the overall context of the policies of different big powers. This article provides a close contextual analysis of India's strategic and foreign policy calculations in the region in the post Cold War days.

ASEAN: Its Formations and Relations with India

The year 1967 marked the beginning of a further change in India's foreign policy when she became friendlier towards the USSR. This was the year sowing the white seed of the Janata Coalition, which culminated in capturing the coveted seat of power in India after quite a long time in 1977. For the policy-makers in India it was, however, a period of realisation that internal threats to their stability in the seat of power were gaining more ground than the threat of foreign aggression.

The rulers of the island countries of South East Asia also realised that the real threat to their stability would come not from without but from within. They understood that neither the British presence nor even the US presence would be able to cope with armed struggles in their lands. It was this feeling of self-strengthening which gave birth to the formation of the Association of South East Asian Nations (ASEAN) in 1967. Still some of them urgently needed big power support to remain in power. Naturally, they preferred to establish friendly relations with the USSR with an eye to counterbalancing the Chinese ideological influence politically as well as militarily by way of suppressing the armed struggles of the Communists. Even Indonesia openly expressed her willingness to have close cooperation with the USSR.

However, India's policy towards the South East Asian countries in this phase to a great extent was still handicapped by the Indian misconception about the policy of the countries of the region towards China. A discussion about India's relations with ASEAN will perhaps better clarify the point.

Just after the formation of ASEAN, the Indian government expressed the view that India had a vital interest in promoting economic, technical and other ties with neighbouring South East Asian countries. It is expected that the creation of an organisation like the Council of Asia would help to promote such ties within the framework of regional economic cooperation. Such co-operation could help the countries in this region to achieve economic independence and freedom from economic domination[1].

India's interest in the ASEAN was quite obvious. The grouping, primarily anti-communist, would check communism's sway in South East Asia, while their political stability would indirectly help India to go on with her 'parliamentary democracy'. This reality made most of the ASEAN partners look upon India as their natural friend. As Lee Kuan Yew had said:

"We in South East Asia, as members of the countries of ASEAN, want to coexist peacefully with all the Communist states to our north, whatever their ideological idiosyncrasies. India's commitment to non-Communism and Non-alignment makes her a natural friend of the countries of ASEAN."[2]

Long before the formation of the ASEAN, Morarji Deasi, former Indian Deputy Prime Minister, made it clear that *India believed that the best answer to subversion and military threat was economic development of countries in the region and cooperation among themselves even in the matter of defence.* But at the time of formation of the ASEAN its members could not think of including India in the grouping. Their fear was that not only might the association be dominated by India, but also that it would evoke the Western reservation about the association.

Later on, however, in the wake of the Sino-American rapprochement, and the possible US disengagement in South East Asia, it was commonly felt all over the world that India would play an active role in the region. At that time the Soviet assurances regarding her non-intervention in the affairs of

South East Asia, particularly, in matters of Communist armed struggles in the region, was of utmost importance for the countries of the region.[3] They thought that India might play the role of a balancer, by virtue of her very close relations with the USSR, Indonesia hinted to India that she might get the chance of becoming a member of an extended ASEAN. Singapore's Foreign Minister, Rajaratnam also stated that it would not be difficult to open " a passage for India into the ASEAN" provided New Delhi entered into bilateral agreements with five nations concerned. But in spite of these good gestures to India, India's relations with the ASEAN did not grow better and remained almost static till 1976. We can identify two reasons responsible for this. Firstly, there were mixed reactions to the Indo-Soviet Treaty and the Indian role in Bangladesh affairs. Some of the ASEAN partners, particularly Thailand, the Philippines and Indonesia, read in them the possibility of bigger Soviet involvement in Asian affairs through India. Secondly, the ASEAN countries themselves were then bogged down in some disagreements about the real nature of the ASEAN. Malaysia and Singapore were eager to uphold the 'non-political' nature of the association. But Thailand, in particular, was eager to parade the grouping's political entity.

India did take part in the South East Asian Ministerial Conference held at Singapore in April 1968 as an observer where a decision was taken to establish a study group on basic problems of regional co-operation. As Mrs. Indira Gandhi stated that India had attended this conference as an observer and not as a participant, it was not involved in its decisions.

Mrs. Gandhi had earlier admitted that India had put forward the idea of broad based organisation of South East Asian states to promote economic cooperation and more fruitful relations among the countries of the region. But there was no substantial response to this suggestion from the countries in South East Asia.

After the formation of ASEAN was accomplished and the initial enthusiasm had decreased, the Government of India lost all interest in it. Whenever there was an occasion to comment on the efforts at regional cooperation in South East Asia, stock responses were considered sufficient. For instance, when the government's attention was drawn to a news item published in *The Statesman* (Calcutta) dated June 18, 1973, under the caption "Move for Organisation All South East Asian States", Minister of State in the Ministry of External Affairs, Surendra Pal Singh said:

The government attaches great importance to regional cooperation and welcomes ideas to promote it. But nothing concrete happened.

After the fall of Mrs. Gandhi it was hoped that the pro-Soviet tilt in the Indian foreign policy would go and that would help India to improve her relations with the ASEAN countries very fast. In its first major foreign policy review the Janata Government expressed its eagerness to cultivate closer and meaningful cooperation with the South East Asian countries.

Indian interest in regional integration in South East Asia was revived rather abruptly in January 1976 at the time of the Bali Summit of ASEAN nations. The Bali Summit, an important landmark in South East Asian Affairs, was held in the last week of January 1976. This Summit was criticised strongly by the North Vietnamese who accused the USA of mounting the Asian Summit in Bali as part of its schemes of intervention and aggression against the governments in South East Asia. The Hanoi army newspaper *Nhan Dan* said that some ASEAN members had sent troops to invade Vietnam, Cambodia and Laos during the Indo-China war. The paper charged that the US imperialists were trying to oppose revolutionary movements in South East Asia.

At the time of the Bali Summit there was also a lot of discussion whether the membership of ASEAN should be expanded. Dato Hussein Onn said on February 6, 1976 during a visit to Singapore that he did not think that Japan and Australia were in South East Asia to entitle them to join ASEAN or attend the Summit. Commenting on US involvement in the region, he said: *involvement per se was not harmful but would depend on the type of involvement, military, economic or diplomatic.* He emphasised that ASEAN countries wanted to be left alone.

The Bali Summit resulted in a declaration of Asian Concord and a Treaty of Amity and cooperation in South East Asia. Marcos made a clear statement that ASEAN was not directed against anyone, adding that "the legitimate interests of big powers—USA, USSR, Japan and China—converge in Asia". He said: *To these quadramirates we should perhaps add India which has acquired the capability of becoming a nuclear power.* It seems that India was included as an act of courtesy only. There is no evidence to suggest that there was any substantial discussion or consideration of Indian association with the ASEAN.

It is interesting at this point to look into the question of the Indian Ocean and relative relations between India and South East Asia. Security of India depends to a large extent on the security of the Indian Ocean. But India, unfortunately, is not in a position to defend the Indian Ocean on its own. Time and again there has been discussion about collaboration between India and South East Asian countries.

It has been declared repeatedly that the Government of India's view is that the India Ocean should remain an area of peace, free from domination by any power. It has realised, however, that it has no juridiction or capability beyond its territorial waters and the government could do little more than keep a close watch on the activities of foreign powers on the high seas.

Replying to a question seeking clarification on India-Indonesia cooperation in the Indian Ocean region, Surendra Pal Singh, Deputy

Minister for External Affairs made a detailed statement on May 1, 1969:

"It is India's policy that we do not want any kind of tension to be introduced in this area. We want this area to remain free of nuclear armaments, free of tension, and we do not like any foreign power from outside this area to come and dominate this area especially with its naval fleet. The policy has been made clear many number of times. We are also informed that as far as ours and the latest statement made by Mr. Adam Malik, Foreign Minister of Indonesia, was to the effect that some countries of the region should get together not with the idea of evolving a defence pact or defence arrangements but with the idea of working out some sort of arrangement and ways and means to prevent big powers to come into this area and establish their areas of influence."[5] He further stated that India had not received any specific proposals from the Indonesian side.

Speaking in the Lok Sabha on February 26, 1969 Dinesh Singh, Minister for External Affairs declared: "India is fully aware of her role and position in South East Asia". It is difficult to share the smug satisfaction, as the Indian contribution to the debate on the important political and strategic subjects in the region has been negligible. The declaration of the Indian Ocean as a zone of peace, freedom of navigation in the Malacca Staits, neutralisation of South East Asia and the formation of ASEAN were developments of significance. But Indians remained on the periphery. They were passive spectators rather than interested participants.[6]

When it was suggested that a conference of regional powers should be convened to study the question of filling the vacuum created by the withdrawal of western naval powers from the Indian Ocean, Surendra Pal Singh stated that the Government of India's policy in this matter was clear and that it did not believe that a vacuum would be created in the Indian Ocean region. He repeated that the government had not been approached by the Indonesian Government with any concrete proposal regarding joint naval action in the Indian Ocean area.

At the Lusaka Non-Aligned Nations Conference in 1970, India together with Indonesia, Malaysia, Singapore and Laos, besides others agreed to exert special efforts for the adoption by the UN of the declaration of the Indian Ocean as a zone of peace. India also co-sponsored the UN General Assembly Resolution No. 2832[XXVII], designating the Indian Ocean as a zone of peace for all time. From South East Asia, Indonesia, Khmer Republic, Laos and Malaysia supported this Resolution. India along with several countries from South East Asia (Indonesia, Khmer Republic, Laos, Malaysia, the Philippines, Singapore and Burma) also supported the United Nations General Assembly Resolution No. 2992 [XXVII] establishing an Ad Hoc Committee to study the implications of the proposal for the peace zone.

Ever since 1968 the New China News Agency has been accusing that the Soviet revisionist were acquiring naval bases in India through helping the Indian reactionaries expand their navy so as to gain a foothold in the Indian Ocean and South East Asia. The Asia collective security plan of Brezhnev and the Indo-Soviet Friendship Treaty only encouraged the Chinese to start a propaganda campaign in South East Asia to generate an anti-Soviet and anti-India atmosphere in the region. The Chinese propaganda was not taken seriously but the countries of South East Asia did not like the Soviet and Indian initiative either. Subsequently the Government of India took note of the South East Asia sensitivities in this matter. Addressing a news conference on April 29, 1973 Mrs. Indira Gandhi said that increased regional cooperation was the only way to strengthen the security of Asian nations since in the ultimate analysis security depended on internal political cohesion and economic strength.[7]

In August 1977, The External Affairs Minister, Atal Bihari Vajpayee was reported to have said, that a conference of the 'Indian' envoys of the region, in the past, priorities accorded to that area had not been adequate. He added that economic exchange would constitute a major part of Indian foreign policy formulations in respect of the region.[8] Vajpayee's remark revealed that the new government realised that India had failed to create a respectable image of her own in the countries of the region. India's failure to secure a ringside seat along with Japan, Australia and New Zealand at the Second Summit meeting of the ASEAN at Kuala Lumpur in August 1977, was regarded as a diplomatic one. It is true that there were differences among the ASEAN partners over inviting Japan, Australia and New Zealand at the Summit. But they were ultimately invited, while India was intentionally excluded. If India's image was really meaningful she would surely have been invited.

Under the changed political condition in India during 1977-78, the Janata Government had been to some extent successful in widening India-ASEAN relations. The remark made by the Indonesian Foreign Minster Kushumatmaja, during his visit to India in November 1978 revealed that the ASEAN also began to attach some importance on India-ASEAN cooperation.[9] He said that India's desire to have closer relations with the ASEAN had been favourably received by the countries of the region. He added that his country had played a major role in preparing the ground for a close relationship between India and Vajpayee, on his part, expressed the hope that the "ASEAN would assist in the creation of an Asian personality."[10]

The return of Mrs. Gandhi in 1980 was marked by some unresolved issues and challenges. During this phase of Mrs. Gandhi's administration, Indian interest in South East Asia underwent qualitative transformation, both for economic and strategic-political reasons. The glut in the international oil market, the bickering within OPEC over pricing policy and uncertainties connected with the Iran-Iraq war carried major implications for India's foreign economic policy since appreciably decreased attractiveness of the Gulf and Middle East as markets for India's surplus man power. Thus the economic imperative forced New Delhi to look elsewhere. From this perspective of Indian planners, South East Asia, particularly ASEAN appeared to be a major logical alternative for future development of India's technological and economic capabilities.

The Post 1990 Era: New Challenges and Emerging Complementary Relations between India and South East Asia

The new thrust of the Indian policy in the decade of 1990 emanates from three sets of factors- one, the end of the Cold War and the merging primacy of the economic issue on the global agenda, second, the emergence of South East Asia as the growth pole of the world economy. Thirdly, the shift in the Indian economic regime, calling for more extensive and intensive interaction with the world market. During the Cold War years, the South East Asian region was split between the two super powers. India in the region was seen as the Soviet ally.

The invasion of Afghanistan by the Soviet troops, and Indian attitude towards it further marginalised India from the strategic map of the region. But the end of the Cold War has made the old understanding redundant. India started pursuing a 'look east' policy with a view to mobilise finance from the region and become a partner in the Pacific community. The shift in South East Asian perception of India has emanated from two factors the new potentials of the Indian market and China's gaining eminence in the region.

A matter of great concern for New Delhi in the 1990s was the developments in Myanmar, a country with which India shares common land and maritime boundaries. It is unfortunate, but true, that India had yet to evolve a comprehensive policy towards Burma. What is more tragic according to Indian popular opinion, some of the recent initiatives taken by New Delhi to mend fences with Rangoon is likely to provide legitimacy to Myanmar's tyrannical regime. The latest position in Indo-Burmese relations is that the Government of India and Myanmar have signed a memorandum of understanding in recent times to legalise the illegal border trade and the MOU to decide not to extend support to Burmese refugees in India.

A crucial point for India was that with Indonesia finally normalised relations with China in the 1990s. Beijing in fact now enjoyed good-neighbourly relations with the entire ASEAN community. This latter has viewed the China factor in a differentiated rather than a uniform manner and has been uncertain about China's peacetime conduct. Territorial disputes between China and some of the South East Asian countries have yet to be resolved. By laying claims to the islands of the South China Sea (the Paracles, Pratas, Macclesfield and the Spratlys), China has disputed the claims not only of Vietnam but also of Malaysia, the Philippines and Brunei.

However, in spite of these loopholes in view of the past failures and missed opportunities, it is heartening to note the high priority that India has given to South East Asia in refurbishing her foreign and economic relations with the outside world. This is signified by the exchange of visits of high officials and dignitaries from both India and South East Asian countries. "There have been positive signs in the past two years of India's changing attitude," noted Suring Pitsuan, the deputy foreign minister of Thailand during his recent visit to India.[11] "Never before had an Indian Prime Minister visited the region at such short intervals. ASEAN countries have taken note of this," he added.[12] Prime Minister Narasimha Rao recently visited Singapore and Vietnam. Rao was the first Indian Prime Minister to visit Singapore in 26 years. Earlier, he stopped in Seoul on his way to China. Senior ministers, including finance minister Manmohan Singh, have been in and out of the region. "In the past we have not paid as much attention to Asia as we ought to have. It is important for us to know them," declared finance minister Singh.[13] The momentum of India's Singapore welcome for Rao, Lee Kuan Yew went as far as to compare Rao to Deng Xiaoping, China's paramount leader and the architect of its economic reforms.[14]

Among the initiatives India took to strengthen its relations with the region are naval exercises with Indonesia and Malaysia in 1991, with Singapore in 1993 and defence-related memorandum of understanding with Malaysia in the same year. Attempts at stepping up trade and investment ties with the region also lad some success, particularly with Thailand, Malaysia, Singapore and Indonesia. One important development of the decade is India's sectoral and later full-fledged dialogue partnership with ASEAN. India's newly acquired status of sectoral dialogue partner of ASEAN and the commencement of that dialogue is an important step towards greater economic interactions and an eventual integration with the ASEAN. While the major role in promoting economic relations in the changed environment rests with business and industry, both in public and private sectors, the governments of India and the various South East Asian countries will continue to have an important role to play. Naturally, the governments have to provide the appropriate framework of upgraded political relations based on well-conceived enmeshing of strategic interests, but they also have a direct continuing responsibility in the economic field.

It is within that framework the dialogue partnership assumes importance.

The first dialogue took place in Bali in early 1994, and emphasised the boosting of trade and investment cooperation, and stressed the need for scientific and technical cooperation in such fields as non-conventional energy, fibre optics and laser technology on a region-wide basis; as well as tourism. In the field of trade and investment it was agreed that the dialogue should tackle trade promotion, trade facilitation (customs, standards, etc.) and industrial cooperation. Two experts from both ASEAN countries and India were asked to produce recommendations on trade and investment within the next six months. The dialogue partnership will help India eventually to enter the newly formed Asia-Pacific Economic Cooperation group, which India is very keen on joining. According to official reports, Singapore is looking favourably on India's desire to join the APEC, which currently has 18 members extending from Indonesia to China. But with a three-year freeze on new memberships imposed at last November's APEC summit in Seattle, India faces at least a two-year wait. Even while India is staking its claim on the membership of the organisation, there is a debate among officials and scholars within APEC countries about whether India really belongs in the grouping.[15]

India's inability to develop closer multilateral Asian ties was apparent also when the ASEAN Representatives Forum (ARF), formed in the middle of 1994 in Bangkok. While the representatives of China, Russia, the USA, Japan and the European Community were all in attendance; India was the only major power without a seat at that particular table. The establishment of the ARF is, to quote Surin Pitsuan, the Thai deputy foreign minister, "an initiative of preventive diplomacy."[16] The new forum is built around the core of six ASEAN states, seven dialogue partners who are Australia, Canada, the European Union, Japan, New Zealand, South Korea and the USA; and the consultative partners, namely, China and Russia, while Laos, Papua New Guinea and Vietnam, the ASEAN observers, also are participants. It is the first effort in the Asia-Pacific region to address traditional sensitive security issues, and the aim is to discuss concrete measures to build trust and confidence, to prevent tensions from escalating into armed conflicts. The first meeting held in Bangkok on July 25, 1994 marked the effort of regional countries to enter into a multilateral dialogue and redefine post-Cold War regional security, economic cooperation, as well as other non-traditional issues, which affect the region.

Naturally, India's absence form such an important forum is a matter of great regret, yet India need not feel too diffident and should not be in a hurry to plead for its inclusion in the forum. Instead, it should move cautiously and slowly. India's primary objective should be to enter the region through ASEAN, i.e. a full dialogue partnership along with easier entry into the market. *The eventual evolution of India to a full-fledge member of the ASEAN group is only a matter of time,* declared Surin Pitsuan, the Thai deputy foreign minister during his visit to India, but added that, while South East Asia welcomed New Delhi's policy over the last two years to pay attention to the region, lingering doubts about India still remained.[17]

Prime Minister Narasima Rao's visit to Thailand, Vietnam and Singapore in 1993 had set the stage for a further part in economic collaboration between India and those two important countries of the region. With Vietnam, India already had strong ties of friendship, and Rao's visit was aimed at further cementing that bond by providing an economic content to that relationship, particularly in the light of vast changes taking place in both the countries—liberation in India and *doi moi* policy of Vietnam. India has assured Vietnam to help in building its infrastructure. Vietnam in turn has assured India of its support for a bigger role in the Asia-Pacific region. Agreements on closer consultation between foreign ministries of the two countries, avoidance of double taxation and defence cooperation were signed. An Indian business delegation has already signed six joint venture agreements with the Vietnamese worth US $158 million. Vietnam could expect a minimum investment of $500 million from this country in the next five years in such areas as agro-based industries, advanced technology and oil. A decision to set up a joint working group for identifying projects in key areas for India's assistance was also taken.[18]

Rao's Singapore visit and his lecture there on September 8, 1994, was significant in more than one way. For one, it was the first time that India had clearly enunciated a new policy of 'look east' by seeking closer relationship with countries of East and South East Asia and inviting them to participate in India's adventure of economic progress.[19] For another, in his speech, he tried to dispel apprehensions and suspicions left over from India's growing military prowess when New Delhi acquired a nuclear powered submarine from Moscow in the late 1980s. While appreciating that India could appear as " a large enigma" between the Asia-Pacific region and West Asia, Rao said alarmist views about Indian expansionism or its blue water navy had no basis. Citing United States and Australian studies, Rao said his country's defence spending was comparatively low and its force projection capability limited. While New Delhi maintained a keen analytical interest in South East Asian security issues like the South China Sea territorial disputes, Rao said India's official position on regional security is that New Delhi could contribute most to it by keeping herself stable.[20]

With the changing production structure induced by new technology and the pressure of opening up of markets, there is new rationale for promoting economic relations between India and South East Asia. During the last one decade, ASEAN countries have transformed themselves into a manufacturing base of global companies. The shift of labour-intensive units from NICs to ASEAN has created new complementarity.[21]

To take a solid example for Thailand in 1999 exports of goods and services rose by 8.9 per cent that year in value terms after falling by 6.8 per cent in 1998. Exports were helped in the same year by an improvement in the economies of many trading partners, especially those in the Asian region.[22] This is a very good sign. A symbiotic relationship between state-to-state and market-to-market is the new premise of India's economic relations with South East Asia.

The visit of Mr. Jaswant Singh, External Affairs Minister of India, to Bangkok in the 7th ASEAN Regional Forum in July, 2000 and the visit of Atal Behari Vajpayee, the Prime Minister to Malaysia in May, 2001 also mark two concrete steps forward. The Bangkok Forum reviewed the political and security situation steps forward. The Bangkok Forum reviewed the political and security situation in the Asia-Pacific region, the positive effects brought about by globalisation and emphasis was placed on the constructive and stable relations between the major powers.[23] The Post Ministerial Conference (PMC) identified several areas of development cooperation and hoped for further consolidation of ASEAN-India joint cooperation.

During Vajpayee's visit India has identified several key areas to focus her developmental cooperation with South East Asia. These are in human resource development, science and technology, people-to-people contacts, trade and investment and tourism. The focus of ASEAN-India activities is technology, space technology or information technology. Such collaboration is expected to address two major areas of mutual interest—food security and bio-diversity conservation and its utilisation. Two sides are also cooperating in two other important areas—Rare Earth Magnet and Surface Engineering. Such cooperation is significant due to its potential for use in various high technology and commercial applications. Both India and ASEAN have special strengths in information technology. India provides training and related scholarships to prospective candidates from ASEAN countries in this field. The ASEAN-India cooperation agenda has also identified Electronics and Information Technology as a sub-group under the working Group on Science and Technology. Currently proposals of ASEAN-India interactive portal to facilitate trade and investment exchanges and to promote e-commerce, etc. are under consideration. ASEAN and India have also already worked on a Digital Archives project (AIDA), which compiles multi-lingual and multi-cultural information. Above all, ASEAN is thinking ahead and pushed ahead to achieve greater economic liberalisation in the ASEAN Free Trade Area (AFTA) and the ASEAN investment AREA (AIA). India and ASEAN can find a new partnership in each other's markets. Trade and investment working groups are active in finding out practical measures to fuel energetic commercial exchanges between the ASEAN countries and India. The process to prepare the study of AFTA-India linkages of enhancement of trade and investment has already begun. Meantime the notable point is that ASEAN's total exports to India tripled from US $ 1.48 billion in 1993 to US $ 5.36 billion in 1998. This represents an annual growth of 52 per cent.[24]

India's cooperation with ASEAN in the area of space technology is also under consideration. Identified areas of common interest in this direction relate to capacity building including training, formal education, on the job attachment and exchange of scientists, access to IRS remote sensing data and subsequent applications for environmental management such as forest fires, marine and coastal management, mini-satellite developmental, optical and microwave sensors. There is also initiative for regional cooperation on space applications for sustainable development in the Asia-Pacific region which in turn recognises the essential role of space technologies and their applications in environment, agriculture, food security, disaster management, natural resources, education and poverty alleviation. Finally to note, India has made definite plans to join the Mekong Development project as well as to cooperate in the *Suwannaphumi* project. The former will identify India's definite roles in global developmental projects in the Mekong sub-region, while the latter will enhance her cooperation in tourism, culture and education with Thailand, Laos, Cambodia, Vietnam and Myanmar.

Conclusions

It is now crucial time to access the role of 'Emerging Asian Powers' in the region and to replace those with pro-super-power affinity. A Pan-Asian feeling of economic cooperation based on a solid infrastructure of political ties is needed to be developed. We need to forget the colonial hangovers in this new age of globalisation and we people are the force to undo the complications produced by our forerunners. So, the real future potentiality to develop healthy relations of India with South East Asia is to take into account people-to-people interaction parallel to government initiatives, and the basic issue of discourse in such dialogue is to develop more strong functional economic collaborations, setting aside narrow political issues. And here lies dynamism and the glittering future prospect of India vs. South East Asian countries relations.[25]

REFERENCE

1. Ramesh Dixit, *South East Asia in Indian Policy,* New Delhi, 1998, p. 60.
2. *Straits Times,* February 24, 1979 and *Indian and Foreign Review,* Vol. 16, no. 6, 1 January 1979.
3. *The Statesman,* New Delhi, July 11, 1969.
4. Ramesh Dixit, op.cit., pp. 61-2.
5. Lok Sabha Debate, May 1, 1969 as quoted in Ibid., pp. 63-4.
6. Ibid., p. 64.
7. Ibid., p. 65.
8. *The Times of India,* April 30, 1973.
9. *The Times of India,* September 2, 1977.
10. *The Tribune,* Novmember 15, 1978.
11. Ibid.
12. *Asian Age,* New Delhi, November 12, 1994.
13. Ibid.
14. *The Times of India,* November 20, 1994.
15. Baladas Ghosal, India South East Asia: Prospects and Problems in Baladas Ghosal (edited), *India and South East Asia: Challenge and Opportunities,* New Delhi, 1995. p. 101.
16. Ibid., pp. 106-7.
17. *Security Concern in Asia and the Pacific,* Speech by Surin Pitasun, Deputy Prime Minister of Foreign Affairs of Thailand at the India International Centre, New Delhi, November 10, 1994, p. 9 as quoted in Baladas Ghosal, op.cit., p. 109.
18. Ibid., p. 109.
19. Ibid., p. 111.
20. For details see P.V. Narasima Rao, *India and the Asia-Pacific: Forging a New Relationship,* Singapore Lecture, Institute of South East Asian Studies, Singapore, 1994.
21. Ibid.
22. Romesh Dixit, op.cit., p. 153.
23. *Country Profile,* The Economics Intelligence Unit, London, 2000, p. 30.
24. Statement by H.E. Jaswant Singh, Hon'ble External Affairs Minister, Government of India, The ASEAN PMC 10+1, Bangkok, July 29, 2000 [Courtesy, Indian Embassy, Bangkok]

28

Socio-Economic Survey of the Madras Provincial Cooperative Society, 1935-45

G.J. Sudhakar

One of the reasons for the failure of the early Weavers' Cooperative Societies during 1905-35 was due to lack of a central organization of weavers to look after their interests and plan properly the functioning of the primary societies. Moreover, it was felt that the society would help the weavers through much needed credit and marketing facilities for them. Further, the overall handloom industry itself was in sore straits during the depression as the price of cloth was affected and it could not face the stiff competition from the textile mills.

Thus, the topic was brought up prominently at the Industries Conference held in Simla in July 1933.[1] The Government of Madras made a proposal for levying tax on Indian mill yarn with a duty on the Indian and imported cloth, the proceeds of which were to be applied to the setting up of a proper organization for the handloom industry mainly on a cooperative basis. Though this suggestion did not receive general approval as provinces were represented by Directors of Industries and not Registrars of Cooperative Societies but it was recognized that the handloom industry had been hit hard on account of the import duty on yarn and along with the Tariff Protection (Amendment) Act 1934, a grant to the handloom industry equivalent to the proceeds of an import duty of 1/4 anna per pound on imported yarn up to the 50s was included in the budget for 1934-35. The Government of India distributed the grant to the various provinces.

Thus, a scheme was drawn up by the development department of Madras which had received the approval of the Government of India. In essence, the scheme provided for the setting up of a provincial Cooperative Society in Madras for developing cooperative buying and selling on behalf of the handloom weavers and for the introduction on a cooperative basis of small units of power machinery for preparing and distributing readymade warps for the looms. In general, its main objects were:

1. To arrange for the purchase of raw materials and appliances required by affiliated societies and for their sale on reasonable terms.
2. To arrange for the supervision of production by primaries so to ensure manufacture of goods according to specifications.
3. To arrange for the sale of finished products of the affiliated societies and
4. To give financial and other help to the societies.
5. To maintain demonstration centres for educating weavers in improved methods of weaving.
6. To generally direct and coordinate the activities of the primary societies.
7. To dye yarn for its primaries by running dye factories on modern lines and
8. To do propaganda and engage in such other activities as may be conducive to the improvement of the industry.

The Government of India had sanctioned grants-in-aid for a period of five years to develop cooperative buying and selling on behalf of the handloom industry using lower counts of yarn. At the request of the Government of India, the Government of Madras framed and sent a scheme. This scheme provided for the spending of the Government of India's subvention through the Provincial Handloom Weavers' Cooperative Society consisting of individual members as well as weaver societies members. The scheme was approved by the Government of India.

The grant allotted to this presidency was Rs 26,500 for 1934-35 and Rs 59,500 for 1935-36, Rs 68,800 for 1936-37, Rs 68,800 for 1937-38. The Government of India had decided that any unspent balance of the grant remaining at the end of a financial year would be again included in the budget for the ensuing year.

The grant was used to provide a subsidy to the Madras Handloom Weavers' Provincial Cooperative Society Limited, which had been registered on April 2, 1935 with an authorized capital of Rs 5 lakhs, divided into 10,000 shares of Rs 50 each. But it took some time for the Government to pass orders sanctioning the first instalment of the grant to the society and it was actually received in December 1935 and so the subsidies to societies and other help could not be sanctioned till January 1936. It started working regularly for October 1935 from the headquarters of the society in Madras, although officially it was supposed to have started its work on August 12, 1935.

At the end of 1935, there were on the rolls of the Provincial Society, 37 weavers' cooperative societies, 29 individual members and 8 firms. The supply of yarn was arranged to the primary societies on the guarantee of the Provincial Society. Guarantees to the extent of Rs 25,070 were given in respect of 16 societies and yarn to the value of Rs 5,000 was supplied by the mills during the year. On the recommendation of the Cooperative department, subsidies were granted to 25 production societies. With a view to popularize, an emporium was opened at Madras and the cloth produced was so good as to receive special recognition at an exhibition[2] at the Park Fair, Madras. Goods to the extent of Rs 900 were sold. The Presidency had been divided into seven circles and a supervisor of the production societies had been appointed for each circle.[3]

Though the authorized share capital of the Provincial Society was Rs 5 lakhs, the paid up share capital at the end of the year was only Rs 14,200 and an amount of 21,831,100 had been drawn by the Provincial Society up to March 31, 1936.[4] On June 30, 1936 there were on the rolls 55 individuals and firms (47 individuals and 8 firms) and 43 societies and the share capital contributed by them was Rs 13,700 and Rs 2,700 respectively, aggregating to Rs 16,450. There were only about 1,000 looms working under the primary societies. The Provincial Society had earned a net profit of Rs 596 in 1935-36.[5]

During 1936-37, the membership of the society increased from 98 to 128 and the share capital from Rs 16,400 to Rs 19,540. There were three classes of members, individuals, firms and societies. The first and third classes increased from 47 to 58 and 43 to 62 respectively, while the other class remained stationary at 8. The society was in need of more share capital and public support. On the advice of the Registrar, it had introduced a B class of shares of the value of Rs 5 each, the value of the A class share being Rs 50 each, and had thrown open the membership to central banks and other cooperative institutions.

During the year 1936-37 under study, it gave subsidies ranging from Rs 10 to Rs 50 per month to 52 member societies, the amount disbursed being nearly Rs 16,000 as against Rs 3,371 disbursed among 31 societies in the previous year. It extended its guarantee for the supply of yarn from 19 to 41 societies. The rate of interest on the latter was reduced from 6 to 4 per cent. A sizing machine was installed at Malapalayam in Tirunelveli district to supply ready-made yarns.[6]

The Madras Handloom Weavers' Provincial Cooperative Society had been able to infuse new life into several weavers societies during the year 1936-37. The number of such societies rose from 43 to 62 and there had been considerable expansion in their business. The provincial society had earned a net profit of Rs 1,747 during the same year.

The Madras Handloom Weavers' Provincial Cooperative Society continued to make steady progress during 1937-38. The share capital of the society increased from Rs 18,450 at the beginning of the year to Rs 33,165 at the end of the year. The value of goods sold in the Madras Emporium and the sales depots amounted to Rs 71,158. There were 93 weavers primary societies, 14 central banks, 8 firms and 88 individual members affiliated to the society.[7] On June 30, 1938, the Provincial Society had 97 affiliated primaries with 2,543 looms. The progress, now was obviously not rapid.[8]

At the end of the year 1938-39, the Provincial Society had on its rolls 276 members with a paid up share capital of Rs 40,070 as shown below:[9]

Type of Member	*Amount in Rs*
143 Weavers' Societies	16,100
87 Individuals	15,850
9 Firms	2,850
36 Cooperative Central Banks	4,270
1 Institution	1,000
Total	40,070

Further, goods to the value of Rs 1,04,635 were supplied to the depots by the productive Weavers' Societies and sales to the extent of Rs 86,623 were effected.[10] The society ran 7 sales depots in the mofussil. A calendaring plant was installed. The society made a net profit of Rs 6,385.[11]

By June 30, 1940, the Madras Handloom Weavers' Provincial Co-operative Society had 302 members including 165 Weavers' Societies, 40 cooperative central banks and societies and 97 individuals, firms, etc.[12]

At the end of the cooperative year 1940-41, there were 327 members on rolls, composed of 181 primary Weavers' Societies, 87 individuals, 49 cooperative institutions. Nine firms and one institution with a paid up share capital of Rs 63,423 as against Rs 41,930 on June 30, 1940.

The eight sales depots working on the last day of the cooperative year 1939-40 continued to work during the following year also. The ninth depot was opened at Salem on July 1, 1941. Goods to the value of Rs 1,59,161 were sold through the depots during 1940-41 as against Rs 1,38,800 during 1939-40. Three new designers had also been appointed making the total number of designers five.[13]

In January 1941, the Executive Committee of the Provincial Society had appointed a Sub-Committee, which made several radical recommendations, that were later adopted. Seventy-nine societies had appointed paid secretaries or managers as recommended by the Sub-Committee and the share capital of the Provincial Society had been raised during the year from Rs 41,930 to Rs 63,425. Since the close of that year the share capital had increased to Rs 80,000; 28 Central Banks and nine spinning mills had taken shares in the society. Central Banks sanctioned advances to weavers' societies to the extent of Rs 2.5 lakhs during that year. The Provincial Society had appointed a standardization assistant to regulate production in societies, as well as eight marketing officers who had guaranteed sales upto a fixed minimum of Rs 10,000 a month. To increase the sales, arrangements were also made to supply the requirement of depots under the local government as well as the army, as, far as possible. The government recognized the need for the appointment of a special officer for the development of Handloom Weavers' Societies in the province and sanctioned the appointment of a Deputy Registrar for period of two years.

While it was true that the Provincial Society had touched only the fringe of the problem and much remained to be done, but, considering the difficulties and handicaps under which the society had worked and comparing the progress made in other provinces, it could be stated without exaggeration that the Provincial Society and its affiliated primaries had passed through a year of steady progress in 1942.[14]

During 1942-43, the Madras Government had reorganized the Handloom Weavers' Provincial Cooperative Society and provided it with more capital, more borrowing capability and a trained designer. It negotiated an agreement with Harvey Mills, Madura and the few mills in Coimbatore to provide yarn of forward contract at discount rates and agreed to underwrite some of the losses that might be incurred in the attempt to make cooperative marketing work. But, the government also realized that any stimulus to the Central Cooperative organization was unlikely to prevent the cloth shortage that was imminent. So, the government also established collective weaving centres, where weavers manufactured goods for government requirements and also partly for the market, and in an attempt to prevent speculation and boarding, the government appointed a Yarn Commissioner to issue licenses to all dealers and to oversee the movement of yarn in the province.[15] All this time, the Handloom Weavers' Provincial Cooperative Society grew from strength to strength with expansion of its activities.

Actually from 1942, the government had used its monopoly of controls over the yarn trade to encourage the growth of handloom cooperative societies. Cooperatives were given a better chance of getting supplies of yarn than private entrepreneurs and also they received considerable inputs of government capital.

During the year 1943, the government initiated the production of handloom standard cloth through the Provincial Society and its affiliated societies and the government collective weaving centres under the Provincial Textile Commissioner, Madras, and guaranted repayment of loans taken by the Society for this purpose to the extent of Rs 50 lakhs on the whole. This sheme was started in April 1943 and owing to the efforts of the officers, practically all the societies took up the sheme in right earnest and not less than 20,190 looms in 192 societies were harnessed for this production by the end of June 1943.

The passing of the cotton cloth and yarn control by the Government of India early in July 1943 and the import of mill made standard cloth into the province in large quantities, however, resulted in a setback in the handloom standard cloth scheme, as the immediate effect of these measures was a collapse in the prices of yarn and cloth leading to a fall in demand for handloom cloth. The result was the accumulation of stocks with the Provincial Society. The production of handloom standard cloth was thereupon gradually curtailed and it was finally given up.[16]

By June 30, 1943, the Provincial Society had 462 members. Its share capital was Rs 1.25 lakhs and working capital was Rs 20.66 lakhs. It had also supplied yarn to the primary societies to the tune of Rs 57.41 lakhs during a period of acute distress for the handloom industry.

There were 264 weavers' societies on June 30, 1944 affiliated to the Madras Handloom Weavers' Provincial Cooperative Society with a total number of 15,292 working looms.[17] During 1944-45 the Madras Handloom Weavers' Provincial Society had a membership of 618 and a paid up share capital of Rs 1.40 lakhs. Its working capital was Rs 1.91 lakhs. The value of yarn supplied by it to primary societies was Rs 79.51 lakhs and its purchase of finished goods from them amounted to Rs 15.62 lakhs.[18] It sold yarn and cloth valued at Rs 121 lakhs.

The progress during the early years, though steady, could not be considered to be satisfactory. A sum of Rs 3.25 lakhs was spent from the Government of India grant up to January 1, 1941, but the number of looms benefited was only 5,257, an insignificant fraction of the looms in the Presidency, out of the total of 250,000. Judged by the sale of cloth manufactured and sold, the results could not also be said to be encouraging. The total value of cloth sold upto January 1, 1941, was Rs 33.61 lakhs, which was hardly 10 times the subsidy spent. During the war period, the Provincial Society played a commendable role. It entered into forward contracts with certain mills for yarn. In 1941-42, it procured and distributed yarn valued at Rs 5,66,393 to 198 societies having 11,604 looms. It undertook to dye some yarn at its own dye factories and supplied it to the societies at fair prices. It also endeavoured to dispose of the production of the societies by securing orders from the government for the supply of long cloth, etc., to the war supply department.

Marketing was also improved during the Second World War by the Provincial Society. For example, it had 26 Emporia and numerous deports by 1942-43. It had also enlisted many cooperative stores and merchants as agents. Further with a view to ensure a regular supply of cloth to the emporia and the agents and also with a view to enable the societies to find money for their goods, the Provincial Society had started in 1942-43, the system of outright purchase of goods by which the society paid cash against goods supplied by the primaries at the cost of production plus six per cent.

REFERENCES

1. A. Victor, *Cooperation in Madras State,* Palaniappa Brothers, Madras, 1964, Introduction.
2. *The Madras Journal of Cooperation,* Volume XXXVII, No. 9, Madras Co-operative Union, March 1946.
3. Madras Legislative Council Debate on March 11, 1936.
4. *Administration Report of the Industries,* Madras, March 31, 1936.
5. *Report of the Administration of the Madras Presidency for the Year 1935-36,* Superintendent, Government Press, Madras, 1937.
6. *The Madras Journal of Cooperation,* Volume XXXIX No. 8, Madras Co-operative Union, Madras, February 1938.
7. *Administration Report of the Department of Industries,* Government of Madras, Madras, March 31, 1938.
8. *The Madras Journal of Cooperation,* Volume XL, No. 9, The Madras Co-operative Union, Madras, March, 1949.
9. *Report of the Committee on Cooperation in Madras,* 1939-40, Superintendent, Government Press, Madras, 1940.
10. *The Madras Journal of Cooperation,* Volume XXXVII, No. 9, The Madras Cooperative Union, Madras, March 1946.
11. *Madras Administration Report, 1938-39,* Superintendent, Government Press, Madras, 1940.
12. *Report on the Working of Cooperative Societies in the Madras Province for the Cooperative year ended June 30, 1940,* Superintendent, Government Press, Madras, 1940.
13. *The Madras Journal of Cooperation,* Volume XXXIII, No. 4, The Madras Cooperative Union, Madras, October, 1941.
14. *Report on the Working of Cooperative Societies in the Madras Province for the Cooperative year June 30, 1942,* Superintendent, Government Press, Madras, 1943.
15. C.J. Baker: *An Indian Rural Economy, 1880-1955, The Tamil Nadu Countryside,* Oxford University Press, Madras, 1984.
16. *The Madras Journal of Cooperation,* No. 6, Volume XXXVI, The Madras Cooperative Union, Madras, December 1944.
17. W.R.S. Sathianathan: *Madras Cooperatives and the De-Mobilized Soldier,* The Director of Publicity, Victory House, Madras, 1946.
18. S.Y. Krishnaswami: *Rural Problems in Madras,* Monograph, Government Press, Madras, 1947.

A Brief Biographical Sketch

PROFESSOR BHAKAT PRASAD MAZUMDAR

❖ Born	March 1, 1924

Academic Record

❖ Matriculation	from Ram Mohan Roy Seminary, Patna, 1939, Patna University
❖ I.A.	1941, Patna University
❖ B.A., Hons	1943, Patna University
❖ M.A., History	1945, Patna University
❖ Ph.D.	1960, Patna University

Service Record

❖ March 21, 1946	Joined as Lecturer in History, B.N. College, Patna
❖ December 1, 1962	Appointed Reader in History, Patna University
❖ May 26, 1973	Appointed University Professor of History, Patna University
❖ April 01, 1980	Appointed Head of the Department of History, Patna University
❖ February 29, 1984	Superannuated

Positions Held in Professional Institutions

1. President, *Ancient India Section*, Indian History Congress, Calicut Session, 1976.
2. President, Silver Jubilee Session of the Annual Conference of the Institute of Historical Studies, Santiniketan, October 1986.
3. Member, Panel of History, University Grants Commission, 1980-81.
4. Research Fellow, Indian Council of Historical Research, 1985.
5. Member, Executive Committee of the Institute of Historical Studies, Calcutta, 1978.
6. Member, Executive Committee of the Bihar Research Society, Patna.
7. Vice-President, Bihar Itihas Parishad.

Invitation Lectures Delivered

1. Extension Lectures at the Department of Ancient Indian History Culture and Archaeology, Visvabharati, Santiniketan, March 15-16, 1980.
2. Nirlepananda Lectures, Calcutta University, September 1983.
3. P.C. Bagchi Memorial Lecture at Visvabharati, March 24, 1984.
4. S. Das Gupta Lectures at Ramakrishna Mission Institute of Culture, Calcutta, May 1985.

Books Published

1. *The Socio-Economic History of Northern India, 1030-1194,* Calcutta, 1960.
2. *Congress and Congressmen in Pre-Gandhian Era, 1885-1917* in collaboration with Dr. B.B. Majumdar, 1967.

Papers Published

1. Nagas in the Pre-Buddhistic Age, *Patna University Journal,* Vol. II, 1946.
2. Role of Damaras in Medieval Kashmir, *Proceedings of Indian History Congress,* Henceforth *PIHC,* 1946.
3. Common Man in the Political Philosophy and Gandhian Reorientation, *Modern Review,* 1948.
4. Basic Industries in Northern India on the Eve of Turkish Conquests, *PIHC,* 1949.
5. Iron Industry in Northern India on the Eve of Turko-Afghan Conquests, *Indian Culture,* 1949.
6. Somadevasuri on the Art of Administration, *Indian Journal of Political Science,* 1950.
7. Public Opinion and Social Reforms 1829-1929, *Indian Journal of Political Science,* 1950.
8. Lalkulisa Pasupatas and their Temples in Medieval India, *Journal of Bihar Research Society,* Vol. 39, 1953.
9. Panchayati Raj Administration in Bihar, *Problems of Public Administration in India.*
10. Rama Cult in Early Medieval India, *PIHC,* 1960.
11. A Re-evaluation of Buddhism in Bihar and UP, *Journal of Bihar Research Society,* Special Issue, 1960.
12. Measurement of Land in Northern India, *PIHC,* 1960.
13. Date and Concordance of the *Zukranīti Sra, Journal of Bihar Research Society,* 1961, Vol. 47.
14. Vaishnavism in Medieval Mithila, *Journal of Bihar Research Society,* 1962.
15. Amātya, *Bharat Kosa,* Vol. I, 1964.
16. Ayodhya, *Bharat Kosa,* Vol. II, 1966.
17. Rise and Decline of *Tīrthas* in the Mathura Region, *Patna University Journal,* Vol. 21, 1966.
18. Merchants and Landed Aristocracy in the Feudal Economy of Northern India in *Land System and Feudalism in Ancient India,* ed. D.C. Sircar, 1966.
19. The Perturbed Individual and Vedanta, *Vedanta for East and West,* 1966.
20. Madhya Yuger Yuddha O Bhratiya Samaj, *Itihasa,* New Series Vol. II, 1967.
21. Divine Love in Indian Sufism and Vaishnavism, *Journal of Bihar Research Society,* 1968.
22. Writers of Medieval Mithila on Gorakknath, *Sashibhushan Dasgupta Commemoration Volume, 1968.*
23. Significance of Collective Land Grants, *PIHC,* 1968.
24. Collective Land Grants in Early Medieval Inscriptions, *Journal of Asiatic Society,* 1968.
25. Polity of the Andhaka-Vṛṣṇi Sangha, *Dr. Satkari Mookerji Felicitation Volume,* 1969.

26. Political Theory and Practice in the Malava and Yaudheya Republics, *Journal of Indian History,* 1969 .
27. Manus in the Puranas, PIHC, 1970.
28. New Forms of Specialisations in Industries of Eastern India in the Turko-Afghan Period, *PIHC,* 1971.
29. A Comparative Study of the Sixty-four Kalās in Medieval Sanskrit Literature, *Journal of Bihar Research Society,* Vol. 56, 1970 .
30. Kara as a Fiscal Term in Northern India, *PIHC,* 1972.
31. Nibaran Chandra Das Gupta, *Dictionary of National Biography,* ed. S.P. Sen, 1972 .
32. Ram Manohar Lohia, *Dictionary of National Biography,* 1973.
33. A Note on Khala, Bhikṣā and Dānī, *Journal of Bihar Research Society,* Vol. 59, 1973 .
34. *Tīrthas* in Bihar, *Comprehensive History of Bihar,* Vol. I, part 1, Kasi Prasad Jaiswal Research Institute, Patna, 1974.
35. Religion and Philosophy in Bihar, *Comprehensive History of Bihar,* Vol. I, part II, 1974.
36. Sarat Chandra Roy, *Dictionary of National Biography,* Vol. III, 1974.
37. Guru Prasad Sen, *Dictionary of National Biography,* Vol. IV, 1974.
38. Jimut Bahan Sen, *Dictionary of National Biography,* Vol. IV, 1974.
39. Payment of Land Revenue in Cash in Early Medieval North India, *PIHC,* 1976.
40. Historical Writings on the Nationalist Movement in Bihar (*Historical Writings on the Nationalist Movement in India,* ed., S.P. Sen, 1977)
41. *Dāsīputra* in Ancient and Early Medieval India, *Quarterly Review of Historical Studies,* Vol. 18, 1977-78.
42. A Survey of Bengali Association, *Annual Souvenir,* 1981, pp. 94-113.
43. Epigraphic Records on Migrant Brahmanas in North India, C. AD 1030-1225, *Indian Historical Review,* Vol. V, Nos.1-2, July 1978-January 1979, pp. 64-86.
44. Political Geography of Bihar, *Bihar: Past and Present,* Ramakrishna Mission Ashram, Patna, April 14, 1981, pp. 1-7.
45. Guilds in Early Mediaeval North India, C.AD 606-1206, *Aspects of Indian Art and Culture,* eds. J. Chakrawarty and D.C. Bhattacharya, 1983, pp. 48-55.
46. A Survey of the Sources of History of Ancient Bihar, *Sources of the History of India,* Vol. IV, ed. N.R. Roy, 1982.
47. Endowments to Early Medieval Temples in Andhra Pradesh, C.AD 1000-1325, *Religion and Society in Ancient India,* ed. P. Jash, Published by Roy & Choudhury, Calcutta, 1984, pp. 420-430.
48. Observations on the Chief Priests of Early Medieval Temples in Andhra Pradesh, AD 1000-1325 in *Dinesh Chandrika, Studies in Indology,* ed. B.N. Mukherji, et al., New Delhi, 1983 pp. 125-30.
49. New Hindu *Tirthas* in Early Medieval North India, C.AD 606-1206, *Studies in Indian History and Culture,* Vol. I, 1985-86, ed. P.N. Ojha, K.P. Jaiswal Research Institute, Patna.
50. Some Aspects of the Historicity of the Nibandhas of North Bihar, C.AD 1097-1526, *Studies in Ancient Indian History,* (DC Sircar Commemoration

Volume), eds. K.K. Das Gupta, P.K. Bhattacharya and R.D. Choudhary, Sundeep Prakashan, New Delhi, pp. 82-91.

51. Some Aspects of the Social Milieu and the Puranas, *Studies in Orientology: Essays in Memory of Prof. A.L. Basham,* eds. S.K. Maity, Upendra Thakur, A.K. Narain, Y.K. Publishers, Agra, 1988, pp. 192-209 .
52. Changing Profile of Ancient Indian Economic History, *PIHC,* Calicut, 1976.
53. Non-Muslim Society in Medieval Bihar, *Comprehensive History of Bihar,* Vol. II, pt. I, eds. S.H. Askari and Q. Ahmed, K.P. Jaiswal Research Institute, Patna 1983.
54. Stages in the History of Religious Beliefs, *Bulletin of R.K. Mission Institute of Culture,* Calcutta, Vol. 37, No 4, April 1986, pp. 85-8 .
55. Society and Religious Belief, *Bulletin of R.K. Mission Institute of Culture,* Calcutta, Vol. 37, No.5, May 1986, No. 6, June 1986, No. 7, July 1986 .
56. Dimensions of National Integration, Presidential Address, Annual Session of Institute of Historical Studies, Calcutta, held at Visvabharti, October 25, 1986.

❖ Died : December 18, 1989

Contributors

Bhagaban Prasad Majumdar, Former Professor of English, Patna University, Patna.

C.P.N. Sinha, Former Professor of History, Bhagalpur University, Bhagalpur and Sectional President (Ancient India), Indian History Congress, 55th session, 1994.

Rajendra Ram, Former Professor of History, Patna University, Patna.

R.C. Thakran, Professor of History, Presidential Address, (Ancient Section), Punjabi University, Patiala, 2002, Delhi University, Delhi.

R.N. Nandi, Former Professor of History, Patna University, Patna and Sectional President (Ancient India), Indian History Congress, 45th session, 1984.

S.C. Mishra, Reader in History, Satyawati College, Delhi.

R.K. Sharma, Former Professor & Head, Department of Ancient Indian History, Culture & Archaeology, Jabalpur University, Jabalpur.

P.C. Venkatasubbaiah, Associate Professor, Department of History, Archaeology & Culture, Dravidian University, Kuppam (Andhra Pradesh).

Suvira Jaiswal, Former Professor of History, Jawaharlal Nehru University, New Delhi and General President, Indian History Congress, 68th session, Delhi, 2007.

Annapurna Chattopadhyaya, Former Professor & Head, Department of History, N.L.K Women's College, Midnapur, West Bengal and Sectional President (Ancient India), Indian History Congress, 65th session, 2004.

P. Gupta, Physician, Social Activist and Art Historian, Patna.

Shailendra Mohan Jha, Reader, Department of History, Delhi University, Delhi.

Vivekanand Jha, Former Director, *Indian Historical Review*, New Delhi and Sectional President (Ancient India), Indian History Congress, 51st session 1990.

G.P. Singh, Professor of History, Manipur University, Imphal.

S.N. Arya, Professor of History, Magadh University, Patna Campus and Sectional President (Socio-Economic History), The Loyola Forum of Historical Research, Chennai, 2013.

Radha Madhav Bharadwaj, Associate Professor, DDU College, Delhi University, Delhi.

Shanta Rani Sharma, Reader, Dyal Singh College, Delhi University, Delhi.

Karabi Mitra, Reader, Department of History, B.K.G. College, Howrah (West Bengal).

Shishir Kumar Panda, Professor of History, Berhampur University, Berhampur, Orissa and Sectional President (Ancient India), Indian History Congress, 70th session, Delhi, 2010.

Radhika Sheshan, Reader, Department of History, Pune University, Pune.

Sumanta Niyogi, Former Professor & Head, Department of History, Patna University, Patna

Susnata Das, Professor of History, Ravindra Bharti University, Kolkata.

Binodini Das, Reader & Head, Department of History, BJD College, Bhubaneswar, Orissa.

Chittabrat Palit, Former Professor of History, Jadavpur University, Kolkata, West Bengal and Director, Institute of Historical Studies, Kolkata.

Lipi Ghosh, Reader, Department of South and South East Asian Studies, Calcutta University, Kolkata.

G.J. Sudhakar, Associate Professor, Department of History, Loyola College, Chennai.